A History of Muslim Civilization

From Late Antiquity to the Fall of the Umayyads

Vol. I

Huseyin Abiva - Noura Durkee

IQRA' International Educational Founation

Part of a Comprehensive and Systematic Program of Islamic Studies

**A Textbook in the IQRA' Program
of Islamic Social Studies
Senior/General Level**

Chief Program Editors
Dr. Abidullah A. Ghazi
(Ph.D., Harvard)

Dr. Tasneema Ghazi
(Ph.D., Minnesota)

Copyright @ 2003, IQRA' International
Educational Foundation. All Rights Reserved.
ISBN 1563164558
Library of Congress Catalog #2003107918

Printed in Thailand by Imago

This books is part of IQRA's comprehensive
and systematic program of Islamic
Education.

**IQRA' International Educational Foundation
7450 Skokie Blvd.
Skokie, IL 60077 USA
Tel: 1-847-673-4072
Fax: 1-847-673-4095
E-mail: iqrapdc@aol.com**

Editing & Review
Prof. Ahsan Abdullah
Prof. Omid Safi
Prof. Khalid M. Shaikh
Susan Douglass
Fadel I. Abdullah
Sven DeBacker
Dilshad Ali

Graphics & Design
Huseyin Abiva
Aliuddin khaja
Samir Biscevic (map design)
Photo Grafix (images)
Robinson Design (layout)

Cover Design
Robinson Design

Illustration Credits
ARAMCO World and all the individuals who

Bir şaha kul olmak gerek hergiz ma'zul olmaz ola

– Yunus Emre

Acknowledgements

In the course of producing this work, I have contracted enormous debts of assistance which no simple confession of my gratitude could begin to repay; nevertheless I will attempt to do so. I would like to extend my thanks to Mr. Aamir Mahmood and family without who's generosity this work would never have come to print. In addition I wish to thank Susan Douglass, who's insights on the text of this volume were priceless; Professor Khalid Mahmood Shaikh and Mr. Fadel Abdullah, who pointed out many overlooked yet important aspects of early Muslim history; Professor Ahsan Abdullah, for his work on the first two lessons of this volume and his continued encouragement; Emin Lelic and Sead Puskar, who assisted in the tedious work of compiling the glossary and index; my wife Nilofer who put up with the long hours I spent completely absorbed in books and computers. Lastly my appreciation goes out to Drs. Abidullah and Tasneema Ghazi who never once gave up on this project. Regardless of the input of these fine individuals I alone, lamentably, must accept responsibility for any deficiencies in this work, its conculsions and its final production.

Huseyin Abiva
Chicago
July 3, 2003
Jumada al-Awwal 3, 1424

Chief Editor's Note

The history of any given people is not only a record of its past but also a mirror of its present and a window to its future. Every society must learn from its past and work out a plan for its future. Muslim history, in many ways, is like any other, with its own fair share of villains and champions, its moments of grandeur and tranquility and its moments of failure and disappointments. But in one way it is special to itself for it is the history of the continual opportunities, offered to every man, woman and child, of realizing themselves and of coming closer to their Creator. The record of Muslim civilization is in fact the history of many different cultures and civilizations that shared one central quality: they kept alive the faith of Islam, they allowed the possibility of being both Muslim socially and individually, they kept alive the vision of the perfect society, which existed only once but remained an ideal for all generations. These civilizations kept alive a model of a perfect life, the model of a most generous and spiritual people, a model for each life as it comes and goes.

A History of Muslim Civilization, written by Huseyin Abiva and Noura Durkee, is a unique textbook written specially for the younger generations of Western-born Muslims and all those interested in learning about the History of Muslims from a Muslim perspective. This volume is the first one in the series of three. It deals with a past which can easily be divided into three parts:

- The world before the mission of Prophet Muhammad.

- The life and teachings of Prophet Muhammad.

- Muslim civilization after the demise of Prophet Muhammad until the collapse of the Umayyad regime.

The Qur'an views human history not from the modern secular dimension but through a spiritual prism. Spiritual history starts with the creation of Adam and his spouse Eve who, after being removed from Paradise, are sent to earth as the *Ashraf al-Makhluqat* (The Best of Creation) with the well-defined mission of being God's vicegerent and establishing His Will on Earth. Allah is a Merciful Lord who created human in His own image and who gave man the power to choose between good and evil.

God, in His mercy, sent messengers, guides and counselors to every group of people to show them one straightforward and common concept: to believe in One God and follow a way of good behavior. For Muslims, both Judaism and Christianity stand out as clear examples of faiths that received earlier heavenly messages in the form of books and are hence, intimately interconnected with the Qur'an and Islam.

The life and mission of Prophet Muhammad brought to a final conclusion the cycle of Divine Revelation; the Prophet was the last and final prophet and his revelation, the Qur'an, the final and divinely secured message for all times to come. For Muslims success is defined in following the path of Islam via the message of the Qur'an and the life and teachings of the Prophet Muhammad.

Subsequently, most Muslim history is testimony of the veracity of Islam, which gave impetus to the creation of a unique global civilization. Muslim history introduced to the world the most modern of ideas such as globalization, individual rights, open society, rational thinking, social justice, and sectarian tolerance. Islam was the motivating force that created a global civilization in which various elements from classical Greece, India, Iran, Central Asia, Egypt and Far East were integrated and harmonized.

Muslims have, in general, looked at their progress and failures in terms of their ability to sincerely respond to the Divine call, whereas a secular historian sees it in light of various political, social and economic factors. The Fall of Baghdad in 1258 CE is viewed by many historians as the end of the Golden Age of Islam, or at best a major setback from which the Muslim World has never recovered. Yet clearly the Fall of Baghdad was simply another beginning in the Muslim historical experience and the message of Islam continued to play a momentous role in opening the mental horizon of its followers, showing them the harmony of our rich human existence and teaching them the value of working together. Islam as a religion and a social phenomenon represents the richest diversity of human race and human experiences.

Task of developing a modern, as well as comprehensive, Islamic History is daunting indeed, and the labor is made much harder by the fact that it has to be geared towards Muslims who know of no other homeland than these United States. Nevertheless we at IQRA' International Educational Foundation have embarked on this humble attempt to at least lay the groundwork for this immense project. We have scheduled a three-volume history of Muslim civilization to be ready for classroom-use no later than the end of 2005. We hope and pray that the project is completed on time as the work is overwhelming in many respects. The sheer amount of time spent on just research and initial drafting has taken years.

By the help of the Almighty, IQRA' was able to utilize the services of several outstanding scholars and researchers. The work that you now hold in your hands is the result of their efforts to convey the flow of Muslim civilization and its impact on the world in terms that young Muslims living in the West can understand and relate to.

No matter how insufficient our situation may be in terms of current scholarly Islamic research, we must all agree that we can no longer afford trivializing the importance of history in the formation of an identity for our future generations as Western Muslims. The time to act is now.

Chief Editors
July 3rd 2003
Jumada I 3rd, 1424 AH

Introduction

By Susan Douglass

Thinking About World History

World history is such a large subject – everything that ever happened, everywhere on earth – that its biggest problem is finding a way to break it down for study. Two divisions would make the most sense. Since world history happened over a long time, historians divide the study of the past in chronological order from past to present. Words for dividing time can be long or short. Words like "period," "age" and "era" refer to longer and shorter spans of historical time. These words are very flexible, and may refer to several thousand years, a few hundred or a few dozen years. What scales of time should we use? The Stone Age, which includes Paleolithic (old) and Neolithic (new), refers to the thousands of years when people used stone tools. The Atomic Age includes less than a century, since humans learned to harness the energy from nuclear fission. Using time scales is a gift of imagination, seeing relationships and differences among events of many types. Use of technologies like metalworking, the wheel, agriculture, gunpowder, steam engines, computers, and space flight mark stages of human development. Births, deaths, wars, the reigns of kings and dynasties, forms of government like empires, democracies and dictatorships were some of the first ways people recorded historical time. Cycles of trade and the flow of wealth among regions form economic periods that historians can recognize. Patterns of political, technological, economic, social and ecological change are some of the overlapping time scales people recognize to help them understand world history.

Some historians think of world history as including natural history, from the creation of the universe, the solar system, the planets and the earth. Certainly, those events were critical to human history. Natural cycles like ice ages, drifting continents, and periods of global warming dramatically affect human history as plants and animals people depend on are affected. Sciences like physics, chemistry, biology and geology are now tools we use for learning about the past. Without this knowledge, humans could not continue to develop their societies. To study history, we need to be able to move from the smallest scale of each human life's moments to the largest scales of cosmic time, and everything in between.

Another way of dividing world history for study is by place, or geographic region. We often hear terms like Far East, Near East, or Middle East, as well as the West. But we have to be careful to remember that such terms are connected to the location of those who use them. For example would Chinese people think of themselves as being in "the Far East," while China is west of Japan and the Pacific? People in western Europe first used the terms "Middle East" and "Near East" to talk about lands, people and cultures that are located to their southeast. These two terms, "Middle East" and "Near East", often refer to the same place, which many geographers now call Southwest Asia. Other regions such as sub-Saharan Africa, South-Central- and Southeast Asia are more neutral. Today, land masses are divided up into countries or nations. Climate zones like tropics, temperate and polar zones are useful regions, as are deserts, forests, grasslands and mountains. So dividing lines are not always easy to draw up. Regions, like time scales, are changing ideas about organizing space to help in our understanding of the past.

Dividing human history into different cultures or ways of life has been another common way that historians and teachers describe world history. They identify major civilizations as regions where societies developed distinct characteristics of government, cities, economy, language, religion, arts, sciences and complex social organization called civilizations. Mesopotamian, Egyptian, Chinese, Indian, Greek, Roman, Muslim and European, African and American civilizations determined the units of study in generations of textbooks and classes. Each one of these units has its specialists, its museums, its libraries and web sites. However there are a number of problems with studying world history in this way. First, the term "civilization" refers to a highly advanced way of life. Words like "culture" and "society" are used to compare levels of human development. But who belonged to a certain civilization, and who did not? When did a group of people "make the cut", so to speak, by deserving the title "civilization"? Where were the boundaries of civilizations in time and space? What marked their rise and fall? What influence did governments really have on people and their ways of life, especially those that were far from the cities? A history of the world that studies only the so-called major civilizations leaves out many geographic areas and important human activities and groups. Some educators have argued that there is not enough time in a school year to learn much about minor societies, and that those groups of people who achieved progress and contributed to advanced civilization are the most important. In a diverse world, however, people are not satisfied to see their history left out of the story.

Students may learn about one civilization after another, but what about relations between them? How did ideas, religions, trade goods, and inventions pass from one group to another? What made some societies become stronger, then weaken and finally collapse? In what ways did societies other than the "big civilizations" contribute to human history? Another major problem is whether historians can really talk about "civilizations," and identify their characteristics. It is easy to fall into thinking of civilizations as "things" that have qualities almost like "personalities." Human groups also need to be studied at different scales of size and shifting membership. An individual may be a citizen of a country, member of an ethnic group, a profession, a religion, a community, male or female, generation. Circles of belonging overlap. All of these factors affect people's way of life, or culture.

Finally, all of these methods of organizing study of the past are affected by what we know. Historians are limited by the record of the past that has survived, and constantly make efforts to fill the gaps left by lack of written records and found objects from the past. They look for clues in many disciplines, or branches of the arts and sciences. Even if we could somehow put together a complete picture of the past in all of its detail, historians would differ in the way they understand it. Our own perspective in time, place and culture affects what we see and how we organize and judge what happened in the past. What we call history is constructed out of evidence from the past, a never-ending puzzle or mural painted by many individuals.

What is "Islamic" or "Muslim" History?

Like any other large topic, the study of Islam and Muslims shares all of the problems of organizing world history. To begin, the Qur'an describes Adam, the first human, as the first Muslim, so Islamic history is the study of humankind's relationship with Allah, God the Creator. The messengers of God, as prophets who submitted to Allah, are also described as Muslims in the Qur'an, and the history of people to whom they preached is part of Islamic history. Most historians view the history of Judaism and Christianity as separate, but related to Islamic history. They consider Islam as the third of three major monotheistic faiths. Again, the Qur'an teaches that prophets were sent to many peoples over time, and we know that some other religions described and worshipped one God.

The words "Islamic" and "Muslim" are different adjectives. Islam is a word used in the Qur'an to describe faith in God, worship and other forms of practice based on belief, or Iman. In human affairs, Islam is a religion, a set of beliefs and ideals to live up to. People are described as belonging to the religion of Islam when they accept and practice its principles. They become Muslims. The terms Islam and Muslim are associated with the prophethood of Muhammad ibn Abdullah, who lived from 570CE to 632 CE, to whom the Qur'an was revealed in the 23 years before he died, at Makkah and Madinah, in Arabia. Historians speak of the spread of Islam from a few followers among the Arabs, to a world religion with thousands, then millions, and now over a billion people who belong to it. They are Muslims. We often read that these are "Islamic people," but Islam and Islamic should really be used to talk about the religion, its beliefs, practices and ideals. What Muslims have done in this world strives for (but does not meet) these ideals. Since the adherents of Islam are called Muslim, it is best to describe their history and human affairs as "Muslim." That is the practice in this book.

Muslim history can be viewed from many perspectives in the world history toolbox. Muslims have lived in many geographic regions, but they have been a majority mostly in parts of Asia, Africa, and Europe. World historians like to speak of these geographically and culturally linked continents as Afro-Eurasia, which includes the bodies of water that connect them. A region of deserts called the Great Arid Zone, from the Sahara to the Arabian and Central Asian deserts overlaps much of this area. Muslim history can be divided into periods of time by its spread, by the rulers who followed Prophet Muhammad, and by its relationship with periods of time used for describing many cultures or civilizations, such as ancient, medieval and modern.

World Eras and Muslim History

Many world historians over the past decades have written and taught about history by organizing it into large "eras," or periods of time across the globe. This is something like graphing human history. One axis, or line, of the graph is chronology, or time. The other axis is world geography, or space. The history of

---

The following section of the historical overview was adapted from the National Standards for World History, Eras 4 and 5, "Giving Shape to World History," National Center for History in the Schools at www.sscnet.ucla.edu/nchs/standards/

Muslims and Islam can be plotted in time and place, era by era, from the distant past to the present. We may include the history of all the prophets on this graph, as well as the history of religions before and alongside of Islam, and their followers. We may plot the spread of Islam through the eras, and the migration of Muslims, the formation, expansion and breakup of governments that ruled Muslims. We may trace the development of Muslim culture and civilization in the times and places where it has existed and changed. We may study the interactions, or relationships, of Muslims and Muslim institutions among each other and with people of other faiths wherever they lived. Their economy, politics, social order, arts, technology and military history can all be followed in the scheme of eras that links time, place and human events, individuals and communities.

What was the world like during the era in which Islam spread and Muslim civilization developed?

300-1500 CE, An Era of Growing Exchange Across Afroeurasia

To define a world era, historians look for patterns of events and change that affected not just one or two, but many regions. Until regular contact was established across the Atlantic and Pacific Oceans, there were really two main theaters of human activity. North and South America were one theater, and Africa, Europe and Asia, as well as the islands in the Indian Ocean and the Pacific, were another. Most of the world's population lived on the huge land mass called Afroeurasia.

Crises, New Empires and the Spread of Religions and Trade, 300-1000 CE

Beginning about 300 CE many regions of Afroeurasia experienced dramatic change, with the collapse of the large Han and Roman empires. By the 800s, however, new states and empires formed, and peoples of Afroeurasia interacted through trade, the development of culture and exchange of ideas and inventions. Transportation, migration and the spread of religion helped to bring regions of the eastern hemisphere together. The Grand Canal in China, camel caravans across the Great Arid Zone, and sailing ships on the Indian Ocean linked peoples across great distances. Afroeurasia was joined by a network of routes that formed a zone of communication from the Mediterranean to the China sea. In the Americas, trade among Mesoamerican groups also expanded.

World historians see broad patterns of change from around 300 CE to 1000 CE.

World Religions: The rise of Islam as a world religion, the rapid expansion of territory under Muslim rule, and the development of a diverse but unified Muslim civilization affected a large part of the Eastern Hemisphere. From the 7th-10th-centuries, the early khilafah, then the Umayyad and Abbasid dynasties, ruled over a huge part of Afroeurasian territory from the Atlantic coast to Central Asia. Muslim-ruled territory, with its rapidly expanding cities and economic growth was a major hinge for the exchange of goods, ideas, and technologies across the hemisphere.

Before Islam, world religions such as Buddhism, Christianity and Hinduism had begun to spread in Afroeurasia. These four faiths and other major traditions spread widely during this 700-year era. Judaism became established through Jewish communities living in urban and other centers from Europe, North

Africa and Southwest Asia to Central and South Asia, though it is not usually considered a universal religious tradition. Wherever people adopted these faiths, they developed cultural traditions, artistic and intellectual ideas, and ways of organizing society. Universal faiths included people of different classes, languages and cultures, joined by common elements of belief and practice. Buddhism declined in India but spread into East and Southeast Asia. Christianity spread into eastern and western Europe, where Christian institutions influenced political, economic, cultural and social life in important ways. Hinduism spread and influenced Indian culture under the Gupta Empire and influenced merchants and rulers in Southeast Asia.

New Patterns of Society: Growth of population and cities, and development of regional cultures was accompanied by the break-up and formation of states and empires. From the 4th to 6th centuries, the breakup of the Roman and Han empires, as well as migrations and invasions by pastoral (herding) peoples to the east, west, and south caused serious disturbance for peoples across Eurasia. By the 7th century, however, China had become unified under the T'ang dynasty and its economic prosperity rose. Japan developed during this time as a distinctive civilization. Europe, on the far west of Afroeurasia, experienced the spread of Christianity and the development of a new political and social order. In West Africa, the Niger River bend was a region where trading towns grew up and Ghana rose with the trans-Saharan gold and salt trade. In southern Africa and the Pacific islands, groups migrated and settled into new farming societies. Mayan civilization emerged in Mesoamerica, with the growth of cities in the rain forest.

Growing Hemispheric Networks of Exchange, 1000-1500 CE

During the last five hundred years of this era, many regions of Afroeurasia were drawn together into tighter networks of trade and exchange than ever before. Innovations in ship design and growing demand for trade goods increased the amount of trade across the chain of seas extending across the eastern hemisphere: China seas, Indian Ocean, Persian Gulf, and the Red, Black, Mediterranean, and Baltic Seas. River, sea and oceanic trade connected with and formed alternatives to overland caravan routes across Central Asia, Southwest Asia and the Sahara Desert. Travelers included merchants, diplomats, religious pilgrims, pastoral nomads and migrating farmers, as well as scholars, scientists and artists. These cultural ambassadors brought many new ideas, and the spread of paper-making technology, books and libraries encouraged new inventions, scientific knowledge and religious thought. Diffusion of important food and fiber crops like cotton, citrus, rice and vegetables expanded diets and economic growth through trade. By the time Europeans (first the Portuguese and Spanish, then others) began to carry out transoceanic voyages, the Eastern Hemisphere had already become woven into a single zone of intercommunication in which knowledge, technology and ways of life were shared across vast regions.

Several important trends can be identified during the last 500 years of the era from 300-1500 CE.

China and Europe were Centers of Growth: China experienced a burst of technology and inventions, commerce and trade, and growth of cities. It was the largest economy in the world at that time. China exported silks and porcelain ("china") and imported goods such as spices from India and Southeast Asia. China's economy affected production and trade all across the hemisphere. With the growth of towns and trade, Western and Central Europe increased production, population, trade, and military strength. European military and political power challenged Muslim control in the Mediterranean region during the Crusades and the Reconquista in Spain. Europeans joined the arena of trade and commerce, and travel. These increased contacts exposed Europeans to cultural influences as well, such as scientific, philosophical, literary and artistic ideas from other parts of the eastern hemisphere.

The Spread of Islam and Muslim Civilization: During this time, Islam and Muslim civilization spread widely in Afroeurasia. The continuing spread of Islam had nothing to do with Muslim conquests. Migrations of Turkic soldiers and herders, and later Mongol armies, did spread Islam to other conquerors, however. Islam spread through traders and others who traveled the trade routes at this time. By about 1400 CE Muslim societies stretched across two-thirds of Afroeurasia. In West and East Africa, Central Asia, India, and Southeast Asia, Muslim trading towns and ports grew up. A common set of beliefs, Arabic as a common religious and commercial language, and Islamic laws of trade helped Muslims act as cultural middlemen in the exchange of goods, ideas, and technical innovations across regions of Afroeurasia.

Mongols Build an Empire: From the middle of the 13th century, the Mongols under Chinggis Khan conquered several regions of Eurasia to build the largest land empire the world had ever seen. Their terrible war machine used no gunpowder, but showed tremendous skill on horseback and organization of its armies conquests. The destruction of cities and irrigation works caused devastation and population decline, but recovery under Mongol rule led to a century of commercial and cultural interchange across the continent. During the 14th century, the Black Death spread rapidly along these trade networks, with a dramatic effect on Europe, the Islamic world, and probably China.

Civilization in the Americas: The Aztecs in Central America and the Incas in Peru built states and established trade networks. They built cities, monuments, agricultural works, roads and developed scientific and engineering knowledge. They did this without iron tools or wheeled transportation. Elsewhere in the Americas, indigenous American societies followed varied ways of life in grassland, forest, mountain and coastal regions, trading locally and across regions.

Contents

Unit One
Southwest Asia Before Islam

Contents

Unit Two
Muhammad, Messenger of Allah

Contents

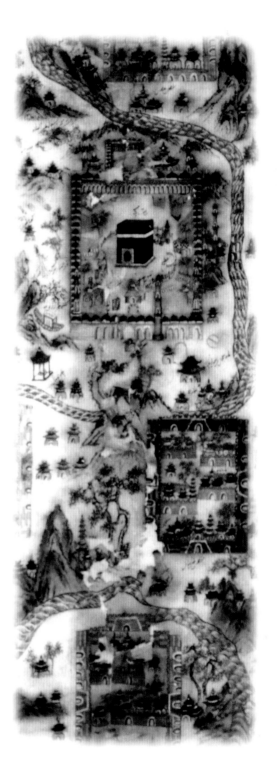

Unit Three
The Era of the Khulafa ar-Rashidah

Contents

Unit Four
The Clan of Umayyah

Unit One

Southwest Asia Before Islam

Chapter
One

Setting
the
Stage

Lesson One

What is History?

Looking Ahead

As you read this lesson try to understand the importance of learning about human history.

Preview Vocabulary

Geology
Archeology
Historian
Evidence
Vicegerent
Khalifah

When you read history books, questions such as "what is history?", are bound to come to mind. You may also ask why do we even need to study history. History is another subject of learning such as mathematics, languages, geography, and physical education. We study mathematics in order to know addition, subtraction, multiplication, division, and many other methods of calculation. We learn languages to know how to read and write better and to communicate with others. But what do we gain by studying history? We will try to answer these questions in this lesson.

History contains stories about the past: What happened in the past? How did it happen? Why has it happened? Who did it? What is the result of it? History generally discusses these questions. Let us look at one example that we are all familiar with -- Muhammad Ali is one of greatest sportsman in history. Some of us may remember that he had the honor to ignite the Olympic flame for the 1996 Olympics held in Atlanta, Georgia. But why was he chosen for this extraordinary honor? After all he was not the *only* famous sportsman in America. So in order to understand why he was chosen we need to know about the achievements that Muhammad Ali reached in his life before the 1996 Olympics.

Cassius Clay (as he was called before he became Muslim) was born in an Afro-American family in the United States. He won his first gold medal in the 1960 Rome Olympics. Remarkably Cassius was only 18 at that time. One day after his return to America Cassius went to a restaurant with a friend where he was denied service. He was denied service only because he was a black. At that time in the United States, Afro-Americans did not have equal rights and opportunities. They were not allowed to eat at restaurants that were marked only for White people. As Cassius and his friend left the restaurant a gang of White youths followed them uttering abusive racial remarks. Cassius Clay, who had brought pride to all Americans, was hurt by this treatment. In anger he threw his Olympic gold medal into a nearby river. He later said that he wanted to protest against America's injustices committed against the Afro-Americans. He strongly believed that America's White-dominated society treated Afro-Americans as less than human beings.

The gang left him alone but Cassius Clay became more determined to succeed in life. He did not just sit, feeling sorry for himself. Instead he made up his mind to fight injustice in America. He became deeply influenced by the Islamic faith. Cassius was impressed by the teachings of Elijah Muhammad and Malcolm X, men who were not only Muslim but also fought for the improvement in the condition of Afro-Americans. Cassius decided to become a Muslim and changed his name to Muhammad Ali.

In the meantime Muhammad Ali won the professional heavyweight boxing championship title in 1964. Despite earning this honor, Ali did not end his struggle against injustice. In 1967 he was drafted in the US army to fight in Vietnam. But Muhammad Ali felt that US military involvement in Vietnam was not right and he declined to enlist in the army. The government reacted by taking away his heavyweight championship title. Millions of Americans from all races joined Ali in condemning American involvement in Vietnam. Muhammad Ali went to court and regained the championship title. But he decided to establish his credibility in the boxing arena. He again fought and won the same title. He established himself on his own merit. After he retired from the boxing arena, Muhammad Ali went on to use his fame to spread a message of peace and goodwill to the people of the world. The life struggle of Muhammad Ali encouraged hundreds and thousands of people all over the world. As recognition to this, Ali was given the honor of igniting the Olympic flame in Atlanta. Also his gold medal from 1960, which he had thrown in Ohio River, was replaced with a new medal.

Lessons from History

Do you think that Muhammad Ali was a born hero or became famous because of noble birth? No, he was a common man like most of us. He became famous because he stood for justice. He thought all human beings should be equal, no matter the color of his or her skin. He stood firm on what he believed, and he won in his struggle. That is why many people appreciate him.

In the Yugoslavian province of Kosovo people were also discriminated against because of their ethnic background. Although it was under the control of Serbia, nearly 95% of the inhabitants of the province are Muslim Albanians. The Albanians could not attend good schools, could not go to good hospitals, and could not use their language in public simply because of their ethnicity. The Albanians of Kosovo suffered for many years. But some courageous people stood against the discriminatory system. One of these men was Adem Demaci. Demaci was put into jail for nearly thirty years by the Yugoslav government, but the struggle of the people of Kosovo continued. At last the people of Kosovo succeeded in changing the unjust system. Adem Demaci came out of the jail to become one of the leaders of a new, free Kosovo.

It is interesting to know that it was due to struggles of people like Muhammad Ali and Adem Demaci that many people around the world achieved rights to be equal with others. People became equal before the law, they received rights to education and jobs. In history we study stories that bring changes to societies.

Although in history we read stories of the past, we should not confuse history with stories told in movies, or in comic books. Such things are often based on the imagination of their creators. They may be inspired by some events in history, but they are not necessarily true. History, on the other hand, reports the real events as they had occurred in the past.

An Albanian father and son look for relatives killed in a Serbian-led massacre. The Muslim people of Kosovo suffered for decades under severe oppression.

History is Human

Many people are interested in the study of the past, all the way back to the creation of the universe. Because there are different ways and approaches to studying the past, we often use different words when we talk about them. Studying about the formation of the earth is called geology; studying past human remains often found long lost and buried is called archaeology. Studying the past of human beings is called history.

Human activities generally include ideas, events and achievements. A historian is the one who writes about history. But a historian cannot write just anything about history. He has to prove that what he writes is correct. He has to support his writings by providing evidence or proof. This is what distinguishes a historian from a fiction writer. Historical evidences that a historian uses include old writings, paintings, and the remains of human activities. Sometimes historians find evidences only by digging in the earth because the people and their remains have been buried by earthquakes, floods, or even volcanoes.

History tells us about who we are as individuals, as part of families, or as a part of larger communities and societies. It tells us about who our forefathers were. Where they were born? How they came from elsewhere to a new land. If they have been living in one area,

how long have they been living here? If they came from another area, where did they come from and when and why did they move? History informs us about these true events.

History teaches us about the people around us. It tells us about our neighbors next door and people in other countries. It helps us explain why we look different from each other and why we behave differently. We learn answers to these questions through our study of history.

A Representative of God on Earth

In the Qur'an we are told that Allah created human beings to fulfill a special role. However the Qur'an does not provide us with many details about early human history, so scientists have had to look at other evidences and try to figure out more about the earliest period of life on earth.

Nevertheless we can still find important information in our religious books. All major religions have the idea that our world was created by One Creator and that Creator often speaks to mankind through religious books.

Our planet is an island of life in an immense universe. According to Islamic teachings, God entrusted humanity to take care of Earth.

Muslims believe that the Qur'an is the book of guidance, while Hindus believe in the Vedas, Jews in the Old Testament, Christians in both the Old and New Testaments. None of these books tell us about the exact date when the earth or the universe was created. But they respond to many other questions, including how and why human beings were created. They also tell us about the purpose for the creation of human beings.

The Qur'an is the last and best preserved of all religious books known to man. We can say this because compared to other religious books it is most recent and it has been preserved in its original text. Other religious books have often been changed or destroyed for various reasons. However, there have been no changes in the text of the Qur'an. It is the same as it was recited by Prophet Muhammad. That is why we, as Muslims, depend more on the Qur'an for information about human beginnings.

The Qur'an introduces the story of the creation of mankind through a conversation between God and angels. From the Qur'an we know that angels are spiritual beings made of light. God created them before He created man, and they live in dimensions other than ours. They act as messengers of God. The Qur'an tells us that God called the angels and told them that He was going to create humans to be his vicegerent on earth. The word vicegerent means representative. The Arabic term for this is *Khalifah*.

This is a great honor for humans. It means that man has power and potential to do great things. But as soon as God expressed His plan to create man, the angels cried out, "Will You make a creature that will shed blood on the Earth and kill each other?" In response God said, "I know what you do not." And the angels kept quiet, knowing that God's plan was far above their knowledge. From this story in the Qur'an we know that God created us for a special purpose and by studying history we can come to understand that purpose.

An Islamic View of History

God created Adam from the elements of the Earth and taught him things which were not taught to any other creatures before. God then called Adam and all the angels and asked questions about those things that He taught Adam. The angels failed to answer to those questions. Then God asked the same questions to Adam who answered correctly. This means that the original man was more knowledgeable than any other creation of God. Then God asked the angels and other creatures to recognize Adam's superior knowledge. He commanded them to prostrate (*Sajdah*) in front of Adam. All did so except one Jinn (a creature of the element of fire) named Iblis.

Iblis refused to carry out God's command saying, "Why should I bow down to Adam when he is made of clay and I am made of fire? Am I not superior to Adam?" Actually Iblis was, in a way, a racist; he was proud of his origin from fire. He thought fire was superior to clay, and that one's superiority lies in physical make-up. Iblis did not want to accept the fact that Adam, though made of clay, was more knowledgeable, more intelligent and humble before God than he. This behavior of Iblis did not please God. He was hence cursed for disobeying his Creator and from then onwards called Shaitan. Shaitan swore to be the enemy of Adam and all of his descendants forevermore.

God then created Eve as Adam's female partner and they were asked to dwell in the Garden, enjoying all the luxuries in it. But they were asked not to approach a certain tree and eat the fruits of that tree. They happily accepted God's instruction and began to live in the Garden. But Shaitan did not like this situation. He began to make plots against Adam and Eve to deceive them and to end their happy life in the Garden.

Shaitan eventually succeeded in taking Adam and Eve to the forbidden tree. Adam and Eve forgot about the instruction from God on this matter. As soon as they followed Shaitan and ate the fruits, they lost the favor of God. Adam and Eve immediately understood their mistake. They sought God's forgiveness saying, "O God, we have done a great injustice on ourselves by disobeying you. Please forgive us." And God responded, "I forgive you, but I shall send you and Shaitan to earth, where you will be each other's enemy, and you shall live there for some time."

With this Shaitan said, "I shall continue to deceive Adam and his children from your way. I shall do so in the same manner as I have done to Adam. I shall cause them to be cursed as you have cursed me."

In response to this God proclaimed, "Yes, I shall let you mislead the children of Adam, but you will be able to mislead only those who are careless." Then God told Adam, "Your life on earth will be a testing ground for you where Shaitan and your children will be enemies to one another. Iblis will try to mislead your children the way he misled you. However, I shall send my messengers to guide and remind them of my way — the way of living in peace. If they follow my guidance, they will live peacefully on earth and will be rewarded and will again be allowed to live in the heavens. But they will suffer both on earth and later in the Hell if they follow evil."

The Qur'an tells us that human life on earth will last only for a certain period of time. Islam teaches that every human will return to God after his or her life on Earth has ended. The Qur'an also tells us that every human being will be responsible and accountable for all actions on Earth, and they will be rewarded or punished accordingly. They will be re-admitted into the heavens if they follow God's guidance and live peacefully on Earth. If they follow Shaitan and the path of corruption, they will be punished.

Despite this sacred account of the creation of human beings no where in the Qur'an or in any other religious book is it clearly indicated how long ago man was created and began to inhabit Earth. It is, however, clear that the earth was already full of plants and animals when mankind appeared on it. We gather this knowledge from human experience. The study of history provides us with this knowledge.

Lesson Review

1. In what ways can understanding history help you make decisions in your life?

2. Write a short report on Muhammad Ali. Focus on the factors of his life that made him an important figure in history.

3. Most religions teach that humans were created by a higher power. According to Islamic belief, God created mankind for a certain purpose. What is that purpose?

Lesson Two

Defining Civilization

Looking Ahead

As you read this lesson keep in mind the various factors that gave rise to major civilizations.

Preview Vocabulary

Prehistoric
Ibn Khaldun
Tribe
Chatal Huyuk

*Nicaen Creed
*Sects
*Fertile Crescent
*People

Do you think that mankind was disciplined from the very beginning of life on earth? Did they choose to accept division of labor without any organized government? If you look around you will easily discover that no organization of activities occurs without a leader or some form of government. Imagine what would happen if in your school there was no principal and no teachers to guide students. Do you think that students would discipline themselves automatically? What would happen if there was no teacher in your class? You would probably come to realize that the stronger students in the class would try to dominate and rule over the whole class. Do you think that similar situations might have occurred in early human communities that lacked an organized government?

Historians will often use the term Prehistoric. Prehistoric means the time in human existence before written records were kept. Forms of writing only came into existence about 6,000 years ago. Before that time historians have to rely on non-written records, like pottery, burial chambers or the remains of buildings.

Archeologists and anthropologists believe that all prehistoric communities had some form of government. They believe that the leaders of these community governments were also some type of religious teachers. They used to pray for the general well-being of the community: for health, rich soil, strong animals, and rain. But the most difficult job of the chief was to administer land-ownership. Since people's lives were dependent on the use of land, disputes often arose over who owned it. Of course most people wanted the most fertile land. The main job of these early governments was to handle these disputes and to guide the people so that they did not fight against each other. This helped communities develop stability, which in turn encouraged growth and prosperity.

How did these early humans choose the leader of their village? Archeologists have found villages that existed about 10,000 years ago. Remains of these villages do not provide us with an answer to this question. One of the earliest villages that has been excavated by archeologists is located near the Palestinian town of Jerico. Another such village has been found in Syria. But the archeologists have not been able to find any evidence suggesting an election or selection process for the leadership of these villages.

Some anthropologists believe that during this early period of human culture people selected their leaders out of necessity. They had to do it, because without a leader they could not have survived. But how could they do it without any formal education or guidance. Does such a thing happen now? Imagine your class without your teacher. Would you automatically nominate a teacher? Would the teacher be knowledgeable enough to teach the class? Would this new teacher be fair to everybody in the class? This is very unlikely. From your studies of history you will know more about how people have fought other people over very small issues. But now our question in consideration is: How did prehistoric people organize themselves? Anthropologists cannot provide us with a clear answer, but you

can find an answer to this question in religious books.

Remember what God said to Adam when he was sent to Earth. God promised Adam that He would guide his descendants by sending prophets, and these prophets would teach people how to live peacefully. Although we don't have any solid historical evidence suggesting prophets existed in prehistoric times, our common sense suggests that people simply could not have learned to organize and discipline themselves under one leader without any Divine guidance. Prophets taught humans how to show justice to each other and how to live peacefully on earth. People must have learned to discipline themselves and to organize themselves under a government through the guidance of the prophets.

* About 600 years ago there lived a Muslim historian by the name of Ibn Khaldun. He explained how humans formed communities and governments. Ibn Khaldun said that men and women within one family naturally love one another. Because of their feelings of love for one another they cooperate among themselves in order to grow food, to construct houses, and to secure themselves against attacks from animals or from other groups of people. These feelings gradually lead them to form larger groups. Close relatives formed these groups. These groups were known as tribes. Usually the most capable and senior man (or woman) within these tribes became leader. God selected prophets from among the leading individuals within the society. These early prophets were also probably tribal leaders. As you read history, you will learn that religious institutions were later responsible for keeping records of births, deaths, and marriages. These were done in order to keep

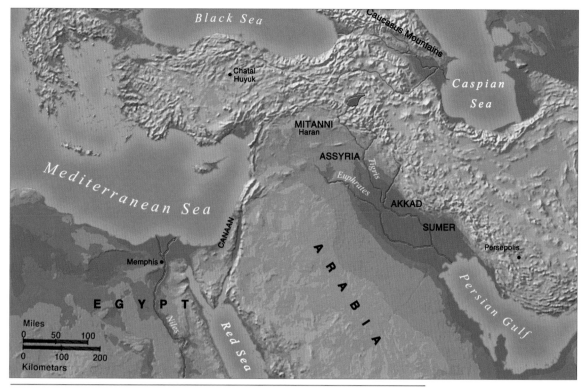

Located in what is now central Turkey Chatal Huyuk is the earliest example of a town so far uncovered by archeologists.

proper records of properties and belongings of particular individuals and families. •

The Earliest Known Society

Archeologists have found more historical evidence of human activities in another village called Chatal Huyuk which was located in present-day Turkey. Experts believe that this village existed about 7,500 years ago and for some unknown reason was destroyed by fire. Because of the fact that this village was destroyed by fire many material such as wood and cloth became blackened. This enabled these things to survive to this day and we are able to understand life during those times better.

By digging the earth in that area, archeologists found out that flat-roofed houses in Chatal Huyuk were made of oak and sun-dried mud brick. Each house had two or three rooms but there were no doors at all in these walls. They had holes on the roof, and it seems that people used ladders to get in and out of their houses. They must have done this in order to protect themselves from dangerous animals. Archeologists believe that at the height of its development, about 3,000 to 6,000 people lived in Chatal Huyuk.

The people of Chatal Huyuk grew wheat and barley and raised sheep and cattle. They also hunted wild animals. They used to produce finely woven cloth from wool and maintained contact with other villages a distance away from their own. They used to import marble, metal, and expensive rocks from far away places to make jewelry, mirrors, and knives. Many of these items have been found in their graves.

Archeologists have found colorful decorations on the walls of Chatal Huyuk. They believe that much of the art and decorations had religious meaning. According to some archeologists and anthropologists, the people of Chatal Huyuk believed in many gods. Some buildings in the village were decorated in plaster carvings and statues of clay, marble, or limestone. Experts believe that these buildings were religious shrines where one of the main goddesses was the goddess of the harvest. Archeologists cannot explain why the village was destroyed by fire. Perhaps we will find an answer to this dilemma in the future when we will have more evidence. But one thing can be learned from this: All civilizations eventually come to an end.

The Rise of Culture & Civilization

As villages grew up in various parts of the world, people developed a distinct identity with the passage of time. Differences in identities developed mainly because of climatic differences. They wore different clothes in different parts of the world because of variances in weather patterns. Some areas had more rainfall than others, some areas had snow, others had deserts. People ate different types of food because the weather allowed for particular types of foods. Some ate barley, others ate rice and cereal; some were happy with fish and vegetables, while others needed beef, mutton and chickens to eat. These differences created cultural differences among people in various parts of the world.

Ancient people also moved from one place to another for various reasons. Sometimes they

Most humans have a natural desire to live with others. Societies provide its members with security as well as a sense of belonging.

moved for an easier and better life; other times they moved to avoid natural disasters and some other time they moved due to war. Most of these people settled near river banks where fresh water was in constant supply. As time passed these groups of people increased in number and established villages and cities. Slowly they adjusted with the local weather and developed a culture which suited that area. Gradually these cultures grew into a civilization.

• About five to six thousand years ago civilizations established themselves in various places of the world. Villages grew into cities. The first civilizations developed in four great river valleys in Asia and Africa. The first one developed between the rivers Tigris and Euphrates in modern Iraq. In Egypt another civilization emerged on the Nile river. On the Indus river valley another civilization developed, while another civilization took shape on the banks of Huang Ho river in China. •

• Why did these civilizations develop on river banks? Because rivers provided food and fresh water for both people and animals. Rivers also supplied water to irrigate lands for agricultural products. Also travel by water is easier than travel by foot, and as a result rivers encouraged trade.These civilizations also learned to make use of wheels. But most important of all writing developed during this period. As a result we know more about these civilizations than the people during prehistoric times.

Historians can explain how civilizations grew and flourished. Ibn Khaldun himself gave interesting ideas about this. He said human beings naturally need the cooperation of each other. This is because people cannot survive alone. They also need security, and they need this for their progress. This sense of cooperation is stronger within the family because they are related by blood ties. As the family gets bigger and stronger, it takes the form of a tribe.

According to Ibn Khaldun, when many tribes cooperate, people can divide work among themselves. Some people specialize in pottery, some in carpentry, and others in different professions. When they specialize in specific professions, they are able to produce better products in less time. Therefore they move to produce necessary goods to luxurious goods. They gradually build cities in place of villages. When a city establishes its own government, it is called a city-state.

Understanding Culture

Differences in food, dress and other aspects of life are called cultural differences. Our styles of behavior, our daily activities, and our means of communication are generally described as culture. Culture changes with the passage of time. It also changes with education and learning or lack of it. There was a time when people traveled on animals. They rode on horses, camels and elephants. The rich used to ride on carts pulled by animals. But now we travel by cars, trains, and aircraft. We now know how to travel in space. All these developments have brought many changes in culture. In history, we learn about culture itself and also cultural changes and their impact on the people and society.

History also teaches us about the relationship between different cultures. How is German culture different from the Mexican culture? How different is the Turkish from Indonesian culture? You will find many similarities as well as differences among cultures. This comparative study of culture leads us to learn about civilizations. A civilization is composed of many cultures over a long period of time. There can be many cultures within the same civilization. For example, French and Dutch cultures belong to European or Western civilization while the Pakistani and Turkish culture belong to Islamic civilization.

There have been many civilizations in history: the Mesopotamian, the Greek, the Chinese, the Indian, and many others. Some of these civilizations survive today and some are already lost in history. Studying history we can learn about rules and principles of the rise and fall of civilizations. What inspired certain people to rise and spread their rule over others? What was the main force behind their success? How did they prosper? We also learn how after certain time in history civilizations fall. They become victims of decline, poverty, and sometimes perish. In other words, in history we learn about ourselves, about our fellow human beings — how they behave individually and collectively — and why and how they sometimes cooperate with one another and fight against one another at other times. From history we can learn how to draw good lessons from experience and avoid previous mistakes of those who have been destroyed and how to live peacefully on Earth. History explains how changes occur in the society with the passage of time.

Lesson Review

1. What is culture? Write some of your own thoughts about the culture you live in. How is it different or similar to other cultures around the world?

2. Briefly summarize the theory that was developed by Ibn Khaldun regarding human history.

3. Explain why ancient civilizations developed around the great rivers of the world.

4. Write a short one-page report on one of the early centers of civilization.

Ancient Civilization in Southwest Asia

L ooking Ahead

As you read this lesson, think about factors in the world of pre-Islamic Southwest Asia that made the later spread of Islam so rapid.

Preview Vocabulary

Fertile Crescent
Polytheism
Ziggurats
Semitic
Empire
Cuneiform
Communication system
Hellenism

(mesopotamia + nile)

The location of the area called Southwest Asia (or more commonly the Middle East) has made it one of the most important regions on Earth. It is located at the conjunction of three continents - Asia, Africa and Europe. Despite common perceptions of Southwest Asia as one vast desert, the region varies considerably in physical geography. However, great deserts do extend from the Sahara all the way across the Arabian Peninsula to the Persian Gulf. In fact about three quarters of the Arabian Peninsula is covered by desert, but fertile coastal and mountainous areas, in addition to steppe and oasis regions, help break up the arid regions.

The two river valleys of the Nile (in Egypt) and the Tigris-Euphrates (in Iraq) made large areas of Southwest Asia very hospitable for human life. Throughout recorded history mention has been made of the large region of fertile land that stretches all the way from the head of the Persian Gulf through Iraq, Syria and into Egypt. This stretch of land is known as the Fertile Crescent because on a map it forms a rough crescent shape. Bordering the Fertile Crescent on the north and east are high mountains that lead to the plateaus of Anatolia (modern Turkey) and Iran.

Since prehistoric times the lands of Southwest Asia have been home to many different cultures and peoples. The lands that lay on

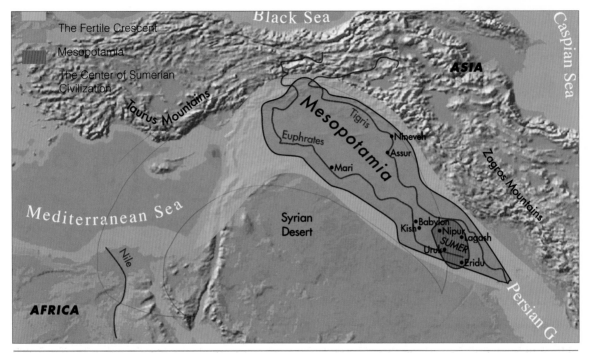

The Fertile Crescent
Mesopotamia
The Center of Sumerian Civilization

Black Sea

Caspian Sea

ASIA

Taurus Mountains

Mesopotamia

Tigris

Euphrates

Nineveh

Assur

Zagros Mountains

Mari

Mediterranean Sea

Syrian Desert

Kish
Babylon
Nipur
Lagash
SUMER
Uruk
Eridu

Persian G.

Nile

AFRICA

This map shows the extent of inhabitable land in ancient Southwest Asia. Find the city of Ur. In ancient times it was a port on the Persian Gulf. Why is it now so far inland?

— Tigris-Nile-Euphrates = Fertile Crescent.

the banks of the Tigris and Euphrates Rivers provided a source of fresh water and fertile land for farming. The lands between these two rivers are known as Mesopotamia. Archaeological evidence shows that people began to live in small farming villages that slowly developed into towns by 5,000 BCE. As these towns grew in population and prosperity, great cities soon began to develop.

The earliest cities in southern Mesopotamia belonged to a civilization known as Sumer. Historians do not know exactly where the Sumerians originated from; some tend to believe they were related somehow to the ancient people who inhabited the Indus River valley in modern-day Pakistan.

The cities of the ancient Fertile Crescent were quite large for their time. The city of Ur (which was then a port on the Persian Gulf) was believed to have had a population of some 25,000. These cities were highly organized. Each city acted as an independent state with a king as its leader. At the center of Sumerian city life was the temple. The Sumerians were polytheists, meaning they believed in many gods and goddesses. Temples to the gods often sat on top of ziggurats, or pyramid-shaped mounds. Religion was very important to these early cultures and the temple priests held very powerful positions in society.

Mesopotamian Empires Grow

Because of the wealth and stability they produced, Mesopotamian cities attracted people from surrounding regions. More primitive people were amazed by the riches of the towns and cities. Over the centuries tribes began to move northward out of the arid Arabian Peninsula into the fertile plains of Mesopotamia. Among these tribes were a people known as Akkadians, whose language and writing system would become very influential in Southwest Asia. Another group of migrants (who were related by race and language to the Akkadians) were the Hebrews, from whom the family of Abraham (ar. *Ibrahim*), the great spokesman of monotheism, descended.

Unlike the Sumerians, the people of the Arabian Peninsula spoke languages that belonged to the Semitic language family. The term Semitic refers to people who spoke related languages that are the roots of modern Arabic, Hebrew, and Aramaic. The Semitic peoples settled in large numbers throughout central and northern Mesopotamia (modern-day Iraq) as well as Syria and Palestine. Over time the Semitic-speaking peoples mixed with the Sumerians, producing a blend of the two cultures. An important aspect of this was that the Akkadians adopted the Sumerian writing system known as cuneiform to write their own language, leaving behind written records of their achievements.

Over time the Akkadians became the most important group of Semitic peoples to settle in Mesopotamia. Eventually the Sumerians were completely absorbed by the Semites and their language disappeared. The Akkadians built one of the world's first empires around 2,300 BCE. An empire is a state made up of many conquered groups. The first great ruler of the Akkadian Empire was King Sargon, who incorporated all of the important Sumerian cities to his realm.

Although the empire that Sargon established lasted several centuries, it gradually weakened and was replaced by a strong state centered on the city of Babylon. Like the Akkadians, the Babylonians were a Semitic people. One of Babylon's greatest rulers, King Hammurabi ruled around 1750 BCE. He was a skilled military commander who expanded his empire's borders northward up the Tigris and Euphrates Rivers. Hammurabi governed his empire using the organizational skills that had been built upon throughout centuries of civilization. The code of law he developed had a lasting impact on ancient Southwest Asia. Hammurabi became known throughout history for his set of laws, known as the Code of Hammurabi, by which he successfully governed his empire.

Babylon's power ended soon after Hammurabi's death. Shortly thereafter, people from the highlands of Anatolia and Iran began to filter into Mesopotamia. Indo-European people from Anatolia and Iran carved out small states in Mesopotamia. These invasions further added to the mixing of ethnic groups that had been a feature of Mesopotamian culture since the dawn of history, a feature that would continue long into the Islamic period.

Assyria and the Chaldeans

Mesopotamia was dominated by several Iranian ethnic groups for centuries. Despite the fact that they dominated the land, they were still a minority in a sea of Semitic peoples. Gradually a new power arose out of the semi-independent Semitic city-states in northern Iraq. The need to acquire land for growing populations, the rulers of these cities began to expand outward. In 1000 BCE, a people known as the Assyrians began to expand their control throughout much of Mesopotamia. The Assyrians were successful in subduing the Indo-European invaders and the region fell once again under the domination of a Semitic power.

Iraq/Iran/Pakistan

Semites, Indo-Europeans and Others

These terms were developed by scholars of the modern age to describe groups of languages that developed from a single "mother" language. They often tell us how these groups of people spread out from a common region. For the Semitic peoples this area was probably somewhere in the southern portion of the Arabian Peninsula. The Semitic family of languages includes tongues that are no longer spoken, such as Akkadian, Babylonian, Assyrian and Phoenician. Today the largest representative of a Semitic language is Arabic, which is spoken as a first language by more than 220 million people. The two other surviving languages from this group are Hebrew and various dialects of Aramaic (which was the main tongue of the Middle East on the eve of Islam).

Of all the world's many language groups, Indo-European is the most widespread. Some form of it is spoken on every continent by half the world's population! The original Indo-European peoples came into existence somewhere on the flat lands between Eastern Europe and the Caspian Sea. Indo-European languages descend from one common ancient language known as Proto-Indo-European ("proto" means first or original). Proto-Indo-European is thought to have been spoken about 3000 BCE.

The nine surviving branches of Indo-European today are: Indo-Iranian, from which come the Indic languages (such as Sanskrit, Hindi and Urdu) and Iranian languages (Farsi and Kurdish); Baltic (including Lithuanian and Latvian); Slavic (including, among others, Bulgarian, Russian, Polish, and Bosnian); Armenian; Albanian; Greek; Celtic (which includes Irish, Scottish, Welsh); Italic (including Latin and its descendants, the Romance languages of Italian, French, Spanish, Portuguese, and Rumanian); and Germanic (which includes German, English, Dutch, and the Scandinavian languages). At least two branches of Indo-European have died out, Anatolian (which included Hittite); and Tocharian which was spoken in Central Asia and the very west of what is now China.

A few other language and cultural groups played an important role in the history of Southwest Asia. The Sumerians spoke an ancient tongue so different from either Semitic or Indo-European that scholars don't know exactly where to place it. Much later, in the period known as Late Antiquity (which lasted roughly from 200 CE to 632 CE), a group of peoples from the Ural-Altaic language family began to spread out from their homeland in the area of what is now Mongolia and central Siberia. The Ural-Altaic peoples would come to play an important role in the history of Islam, for from them came the Turks and the Mongols.

The Assyrians were well known for their advanced military skills, which included the improved use of the war-chariot and effective siege engines. With this skill they were able to easily overcome their neighbors. By 639 BCE, the Assyrians controlled Southwest Asia and Egypt. Their empire stretched from Iraq to Syria, Lebanon, and Palestine and into Egypt.

In 605 BCE, the power of Assyria came to an abrupt end. A people known as the Chaldeans had been a thorn in Assyria's side since they began migrating out of the Arabian Peninsula. Assyria was able to keep these people under often brutal control during the height of their power and the Chaldeans resented being subjected to harsh oppression. In 689 BCE, the Assyrian king devastated the Chaldean city of Babylon, an act that was never forgiven.

As the Assyrian state weakened because of continual warfare and rebellion, a Chaldean chief by the name of Nabopolassar entered into an alliance with the Medes, an Iranian people who lived in the mountains east of Mesopotamia. In one swift blow the allies captured the Assyrian cities of northern Iraq and brought an end to their empire. The Chaldeans soon embarked on their own period of expansion. Chaldean armies moved to occupy the Assyrian provinces all the way to Egypt.

But the conquered people of Southwest Asia held the same resentment towards the Chaldeans that they held for the Assyrians. In

As you can see in the map , both the Assyrian and Babylonian Empires allowed for the Semitic domination of the Middle East in the ancient period.

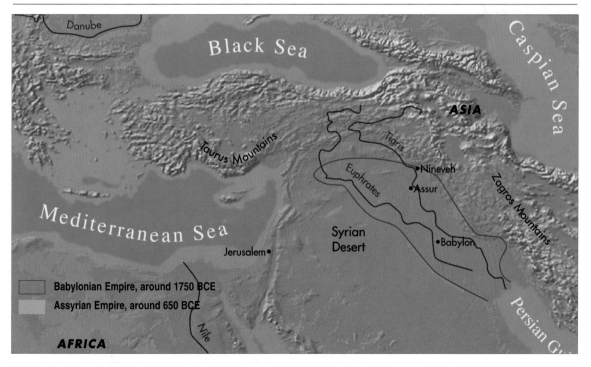

Babylonian Empire, around 1750 BCE
Assyrian Empire, around 650 BCE

Nomads from the Arabian Peninsula were a constant threat to the settled peoples of Southwest Asia. In this wall carving Assyrian warriors fend off a raid by Arab raiders.

586 BCE a rebellion broke out among the Hebrews who lived in what is now Israel/Palestine. The Hebrews had been conquered by the Assyrians and they had a strong desire to restore the kingdom that was founded by David (ar. *Dawud*) centuries earlier. The Chaldean King Nebuchadnezzar sent a huge army to subdue the Hebrews. During the struggle the sacred city of Jerusalem was sacked and the temple built by King Solomon to the One God was destroyed. The entire Hebrew population of Palestine was thrown into chains and deported to Babylon. There they suffered in slavery until the Chaldeans themselves were vanquished by an energetic new force: the Persians.

The Persian Empire

The exact identity of the original inhabitants of ancient Iran is unclear. But historical research has shown that an Indo-European people known as the Aryans began migrating from their homelands in southern Russia into the Indian subcontinent and modern-day Iran nearly 3,000 years ago.

The Aryans had a strong warrior tradition and were masters of the horse. Their Indo-European language set them apart from the other peoples of Southwest Asia. Their arrival in the area south of the Caspian Sea, where modern Iran is located, can be taken as the starting point of Persian Civilization.

The first of the great Iranian Dynasties,(the Medes and the Persians), united much of Southwest Asia into a single empire. From 550 to 525 BCE the kings of the Achaemanid Dynasty spread their control over lands from the Nile to the Indus. Unlike their Assyrian and Chaldean predecessors, the Persians were able to gain control over Anatolia and parts of the Balkan Peninsula in southeastern Europe. More importantly the Persians were generally more tolerant and just to their subject peoples.

The Persians maintained control over such a vast area of land by developing communication systems. The kings improved roads and established an efficient network of couriers that allowed for the quick relay of messages. It was said that a message could travel more than 1,500 miles in seven days, a truly incredible feat!

On several occasions, the Persians tried to conquer the city-states of Greece and failed. These wars with the Greeks were never forgotten, and they would eventually prove to be the undoing of Persia's empire. In the northern regions of Greece, the Kingdom of Macedonia was on the rise. In 334 BCE the young king of Macedonia, Alexander the Great, crossed from Europe into Asia with the goal of destroying the power of Persia.

The Spread of Greek Culture

The Persian Empire collapsed in 331 BCE, following a series of stunning defeats at the hands of Alexander. Like most conquerors, Alexander did not set about creating a new empire from scratch. In most cases he kept the old administration in place. But the few places he destroyed included the Persian capital Persipolis where his army burned the royal palace along with important Zoroastrian shrines. This was an act that Alexander was said to have later regretted. Following his conquest of Persia, Alexander marched through

Where Mesopotamia *is and* *Who was Alexander The Great*

Afghanistan and Uzbekistan and into what is now Pakistan. Many of his soldiers settled down in these areas adding Greek, or Hellenistic cultural influences into the local cultures.

The empire that Alexander forged stretched from the Balkans in Europe to the Indus River in India and up into Central Asia. But it did not survive him. Following his untimely death in 323 BCE, his generals began to quarrel over the division of the new empire, and as a result it broke up into several competing states. These Greek kingdoms, called the Successor States, ruled the Middle East and Egypt until the growing power of Rome and Parthia destroyed them.

The conquests of Alexander the Great in the 3rd century BCE opened Iran and the Middle East to the ideas and culture of the Greeks. Because of Alexander's conquests, a mixture of

Greek and Roman cultural influences were deeply embedded in pre-Islamic Southwest Asia. This mosaic floor panel depicts a rural scene in Roman Syria.

Greek culture with the older Semitic and Iranian cultures developed, thus adding one more element to a region of racial, linguistic and cultural diversity.

The Rise of Rome

As Greek power throughout the Mediterranean began to collapse, a new force was emerging in the Italian Peninsula: Rome. The political system set up by Rome would last for nearly 500 years. Historians usually date the start of the Roman Empire from 27 BCE when the Roman Senate proclaimed Augustus the undisputed emperor after many years of bitter civil war. At its peak the empire included all the lands throughout the Mediterranean world. Rome had initially expanded into other parts of Italy and neighboring regions during the period of the Roman Republic (509-27 BCE), but made wider conquests and strengthened control of these lands during the empire. The Roman Empire lasted until the massive invasions by Germanic tribes, economic decline, and internal unrest in the 4th and 5th centuries CE ended its ability to dominate such a large state. But the Romans and their empire gave cultural and political shape to the history of Europe and Southwest Asia from the Middle Ages to the modern day.

In 44 BCE Julius Caesar, a man who governed the Roman Republic, was assassinated. Rome plunged into more than a decade of civil war. After Caesar's heir Octavius defeated his last rivals, the Senate in 27 BCE declared him 'Augustus', meaning the 'exalted one'. Augustus then established a monarchy that became known as the Roman Empire. The Roman Republic, which had endured for nearly 5 centuries, was forever dead, and the new empire would endure for another 500 years.

The emperor Augustus reigned from 27 BCE to 14 CE. He ruled with complete power. He restored political and social stability and launched two centuries of prosperity known as the *Pax Romana* (Roman Peace). Under his rule the empire began its transformation into one of the finest and most influential political institutions in world history. During the first two centuries of the Christian Era the empire grew and added new territories: Britain, North Africa, and large parts of Palestine and Syria. People from these provinces poured into Rome where they became soldiers, bureaucrats, senators, and even emperors. The city of Rome evolved into the social, economic, and cultural capital of the Mediterranean world. Most Rome's emperors ruled wisely until military and economic disasters brought on the political uncertainty in the 3rd century CE.

Though the Roman Empire embraced a huge amount of territory, it allowed people of many different cultures to retain their native heritage. The empire helped to preserve the art, literature, and philosophy of the Greeks, the religious and ethical system of the Jews, the new faith of the Christians, Babylonian astronomy and astrology, and cultural trends from Persia, Egypt, and other eastern civilizations. In return, the Romans gave their own peculiar talents for government, law, and architecture and also spread their Latin language. In this way they created the Greco-Roman synthesis, the rich blending of cultural elements that for two thousand years has shaped what we call the Western tradition.

who was Augustus*

Lesson Review

1. How did migration affect the culture and politics of the Fertile Crescent in ancient times?

2. What were the causes for groups clashing with one another in this region?

3. What was the geographic origin of Iranian or Persian civilization?

4. How did the conquests of Alexander the Great affect culture in Southwest Asia?

5. Do a mini-research project on one of the early empires that arose in the Fertile Crescent. Map the extent of its territory, describe the groups who were prominent in the state, and select one or two features such as art, architecture, or warfare that were important. Profile one ruler or other leader.

6. What geographic features help to explain the movement of people in the Fertile Crescent and Southwest Asia? How did this movement affect the languages, arts, technology and spread of religions in the region?

7. Select one of the prophets of the monotheistic tradition and show how their story fits into the historical setting of their time and place.

   (Examples: the journeys of Ibrahim (Abraham) and the response to his belief in One God in Sumer; or Yusuf (Joseph) and his brothers' migration to Egypt.

Chapter Two

Southwest Asian Religion at the Dawn of Islam

Lesson One

The Ways of the Old Gods

Looking Ahead

As you read this lesson think about how ancient religions and practices left influences in society and culture long after they died out.

Preview Vocabulary

Pantheon
Monotheism
Mystery Religions
Initiation
Demiurge
Gnostic

Along with the varied and colorful mingling of cultures and peoples that took place as human civilization developed in Southwest Asia, religious life likewise reflected a wide multitude of beliefs and practices. Artifacts belonging to many periods and cultures, and written historical records, have provided historians with much evidence for this diversity of faiths. Various forms of polytheism as well as early monotheistic trends can be seen in ancient Southwest Asia. Out of the prophetic tradition of monotheism, which extended back to Abraham, both Judaism and Christianity developed over a long period from 3000 BCE to 500 CE.

As Christianity established itself as the dominant force in the Mediterranean world in the 3rd century CE, this diversity sharply decreased. Later Roman emperors upheld the supremacy of Christianity, while other ancient faiths were championed by states, such as Zoroastrianism in Sasanid Persia. Minority faiths such as Jews, Gnostics, and polytheists existed in pockets scattered widely throughout Southwest Asia.

Religious Freedom in the Roman World

The Roman Empire was comprised of many different peoples, and it contained an even wider variety of religious beliefs and practices. Traditional Roman beliefs centered around a pantheon (a group) of gods and goddesses that was similar to those of the Greeks. More importantly, the emperor of Rome himself was viewed as a god. Because of this belief it was the duty of every Roman citizen to pay respect to their emperor and offer sacrifices in his name.

As long as citizens remained loyal to the emperor, they were generally free to practice whatever religion they chose. Trouble only came when a members of a specific religion refused to acknowledge to the divine position of the emperor. As we shall see later on, many religious Jews as well as early Christians would not compromise their monotheistic beliefs to accept the Roman emperor as a god. This often brought heavy punishment for a crime that was seen as treason. It should be stressed, however, that Roman officials really did not care what Jews and Christians believed in their hearts as long as they acknowledged the authority of the empire through lip-service.

> "If it had been your Lord's will, all who are on the earth would have believed, altogether. Will you, then, force the people to become believers? No soul can have Faith except by the will of Allah."
>
> *the Qur'an 10:99-100*

The Mystery Religions

The concepts of savior, incarnation, rebirth and resurrection were ideas held in common by many religious movements in the Mediterranean region that came into being in the decades before and after the birth of Jesus Christ. The vast majority of people living in Southwest Asia at this time followed some form of polytheism. These traditional beliefs and practices focused on the "here and now". Gods and goddesses were prayed to when some worldly need arose and the thought of an afterlife was not a reality for most.

This type of traditional polytheism would soon be overshadowed by a new wave of spirituality. Several religious movements that were popular in the Roman Empire during the first and second centuries before and after the birth of Christ were known as Mystery Religions. They were called this because their beliefs were often based on secret teachings that were passed on only to initiated members of the sect. The Mystery Religions differed in many ways from traditional polytheism.

Mystery Religions typically promised good both in this world and the next, beliefs that helped common people face the harsh realities of everyday life in ancient times. They also gave members a deep personal relationship with the god or goddess worshiped. During the centuries in which the Mystery Religions flourished, there was a general decline in the value placed on logic and reason. People expressed increasing concern about life after death and how to prepare for it. They often viewed the activities of this life trivial and a distraction from the true goal of the everlasting next world.

Participation in the ceremonies of the Mystery Religions required initiation. Priests conducted ceremonies and secret rituals that allowed a person to become a member and share in group worship. The sense of belonging to a special select group was an important part of the religious experience of the Mystery Religions.

Many people from the lower classes of society and soldiers in the Roman military (who faced death daily), found spiritual satisfaction in

This remarkable Roman painting shows the Egyptian goddess Isis receiving a blessing from the Greek god Pan. This shows the remarkable exchange of religions and cultures during Roman rule over Southwest Asia.

the Mystery Religions. The most well-known of these was a faith of Iranian origin called Mithraism. Many soldiers of the Roman legions took this religion when they were stationed in the provinces that bordered Persia. As they retired from service and returned home, these men brought Mithraism with them.

Modern scholars believe that the Mystery Religions may have influenced early Christian teachings and practices. For instance, Mithraists believed in the constant death and resurrection of their god. Many believers saw signs of this in the cycle of the seasons, where the "dead" earth of winter was reborn again in spring. The doctrine of resurrection can be seen in many other Mystery Religions such as in the worship of the goddess Cybele, who was known as the "Great Mother". During a great celebration in honor of the "Great Mother" a bull (that represented one of the husbands of Cybele) was sacrificed and the crowds smeared its blood on their foreheads. This blood was believed to clean the believer of all past sins.

The Gnostics

Another religious trend widespread in the Roman Empire and Southwest Asia was that of the Gnostics. The name of this school of thought came from the Greek word for "one who knows", *gnostikos*. The Gnostics came into existence during the same period in time that the Mystery Religions began to spread throughout the Roman world.

On the surface the teachings and beliefs of the Gnostics appear to have been deeply influenced by forms of Zoroastrianism. Like the Zoroastrians most Gnostics believed that the universe was a battleground between good and evil forces. They taught that there was one supreme God of Goodness and Light. This High God, however, was so unlike man that he was beyond the comprehension of the human mind. Gnostics believed that all of the material universe was created by an evil, lesser god (called the *Demiurge*) to trap light of the good God in flesh and earth so that it could be corrupted. The souls of man (which were originally particles of the light from the Good God) were entrapped in corruptible, decaying flesh. The ultimate goal of the Gnostic was to liberate the soul from this trap and return to the original source of light.

In many instances Gnostic, Jewish, and early Christian ideas overlapped. Gnostics often described their beliefs in Biblical terms. They taught that the "evil god" was in fact the deity described in the Old Testament of the Bible and that the God of the New Testament was the High God. The reason for this was that they recognized serious differences in the characteristics and behavior of the God mentioned throughout both sacred texts.

In addition many Gnostics claimed to be followers of Jesus. These Gnostics Christians

Mithras: An Iranian Deity Moves West

One of the best known of the Mystery Religions was centered on the figure of the god Mithras. This deity had it origin in the Zoroastrian faith of ancient Persia. In this tradition Mithras' job was to aid the supreme creator Ahura Mazda in the struggle against the forces of evil.

From his homeland in the Iranian highlands Mithras moved west into the Roman Empire when Roman soldiers carried his legends back with them from their campaigns in Iraq and eastern Anatolia. Temples dedicated to Mithras have been found all over the Roman world. Archeologists have uncovered hundreds of these temples in locations along the Rhine River in Germany, the border between England and Scotland, Austria and Rumania, and even in North Africa.

The beliefs and practices of Mithraism provided a way for people to overcome their lower desires and purify themselves. The bull was seen in Mithraic myth as a symbol of the sinful desires of the world. In mythology, this cosmic bull was killed by the god Mithras to erase the sins of people. Mithras' temples were often built in caves. Where there were no caves, the holiest part of the temple was built under a special dome called an *aveh*. A sacred table, an altar, was set in the temple. Wine, bread and sometimes meat were placed on it to symbolize the blood and body of the bull that was slain for the sins of man. This was called the 'good food', which in old Persian is *hu khoresht*, and in Greek *eucharist*. The worshippers ate this food to achieve oneness with Mithras. When Christianity became the official religion of the Roman Empire in the fourth century, the faith of Mithras disappeared. However, the similarities in many aspects of belief can be easily noticed.

believed that the Supreme God sent Jesus to Earth to provide mankind with the "knowledge" (*gnosis*) of how to obtain salvation from the evils of the material universe and its devilish creator. Since all body and flesh was believed to be the creation of the evil god, Gnostic Christians believed that Jesus only appeared to be a man, and was in fact a pure spirit. Rejecting the belief that Jesus was crucified they claimed that the entire event was merely an illusion.

As the Christianity rose to power throughout the Roman Empire, organized Gnosticism gradually declined. However Gnostics left a recognizable mark on early Christian thinking. Like Gnostics, many Christians believed that the world was primarily an evil place. In fact Paul, who was perhaps the most influential of the early Christian thinkers, wrote "Satan is the god of this world", which echoes the Gnostic concept of an evil creator god. To escape the traps of this world, many early Christians sought to isolate themselves from life by living in monasteries. Here they completely devoted their lives to worship and study, relying on the general population for food and supplies.

Lesson Review

1. Compare and contrast beliefs about good and evil, sacred and worldly in the Mystery Religions and Gnosticism with your own ideas about these subjects.

2. List five beliefs that the religions described in this section have in common with what you know about Christianity.

Lesson Two

Judaism In the Roman World

Looking Ahead

Think about how the Judaism of today differs from the Judaism of the first century CE. Understand what happened to the various sects that once existed in the Jewish community.

Preview Vocabulary

Rabbi
Proselytization
Autonomy
Sadducee
Pharisee
Talmud
Synagogue
Essene
Zealot

Of all the religious groups that co-existed within the Roman Empire, the Jews alone tried to maintain a strict belief in One God. Many Jews, however, did not necessarily regard this God as one who could be worshiped by non-Jews. A traditional belief in the concept of "the Chosen People" led many Jewish religious leaders to conclude that the Jews alone were worthy of bearing the message of the One God. This belief prevented widespread proselytization (trying to spread their faith) of non-Jews. In spite of this cases of conversions to Judaism did occur in Roman times. It was common for Jewish masters to encourage their servants and slaves to embrace this ancient monotheistic faith. The widespread distribution of Jewish communities throughout the Roman Empire also allowed many non-Jews to become accustomed with Jewish beliefs and practices.

When the Persian emperor permitted the Jews to return to Palestine from their slavery in Babylon in the year 536 BCE, they rebuilt the temple of Solomon and re-established Jerusalem as the center of their community. While they were still subjects of the Persian Empire, the Jews were given a fair degree of autonomy, or permission to govern some of their own affairs. Many Jews remained in Persia and Mesopotamia, while

The Hebrews

The long and rich history of the Hebrews (whose descendants came to be known as the Jews) revolved around their relationship with the One God. Originally a nomadic Semitic tribe, the Hebrews moved into Palestine during the time of Prophet Abraham (ca. 2500 BCE) and established a loose tribal community. Following a long period of slavery in Egypt, they were led back into Palestine by Moses (ar. *Musa*). The Hebrews, under the leadership of King David, established a powerful state around 1000 BCE, which gradually declined until it was devoured by a succession of outside empires.

others established communities throughout the towns and cities that dotted the Mediterranean coast.

In the 4th century BCE, Alexander the Great destroyed Persia's power and established a new empire. Despite Alexander's brief rule, the spread of Greek culture (Hellenism) had long-lasting influence throughout the whole of Southwest Asia. The adaptation of Greek culture and ideas extended to the Jews as well. To keep their privileged positions under Greek rule, many wealthy and upper-class Jews openly adopted the culture of their overlords.

This trend caused a backlash from those Jews who remained attached to the old traditions. Many Jews found the infatuation by many in their community with foreign ways upsetting, much like many in today's world who worry that the spread of Western culture will threaten to extinguish their own traditions and beliefs.

Tension grew between the Greek rulers and Hellenized Jews on one hand, and conservative, pious Jews on the other. This tension eventually broke into violent rebellion against the Greek governors and the Hellenized Jewish allies. The most famous of

Following the death of King Solomon (ar. Sulaiman), the Hebrew kingdom began to weaken to the point that it was constantly threatened and occupied by outside powers. This ancient relief carving shows a Hebrew king submitting to the Assyrian Emperor around 800 BCE.

This mosaic from the 3rd century CE shows a Jewish synagogue. Found in the ruins of the city of Dura Europos (in northern Iraq), it shows a great deal of Eastern influence. The long shirts and baggy trousers were the customary dress in the Persian dominated areas of the Middle East.

these revolts was that led by Judah Maccabee, who successfully freed most of Palestine from Greek rule for some time. But before any hopes of Jewish independence could be realized the Greeks were replaced by the Romans. The Jews of Palestine would again become just a part of another world empire.

Bound to the Torah

During the time when Jesus Christ lived (roughly between 6 BCE and 34 CE), the Jews of Palestine were divided into several different sects: the Sadducees, the Pharisees, the Essenes, and the Zealots. The Sadducees were comprised of wealthy, educated Jews who belonged to the priestly families. They oversaw the sacred Temple of Soloman in Jerusalem and the complex rites of worship performed there. Many Sadducees had assimilated much from Hellenistic and Roman culture. They dominated the administration of Jewish Palestine and controlled the main religious council of their people. Nevertheless they had very little contact with the common people and the

Sadducees gained a dubious reputation for cooperating openly with Roman authorities.

The Sadducees followed a literalist interpretation of the Torah, the sacred text of the Jews. They refused to believe in any aspect of faith that was not explicitly mentioned in their sacred literature. For instance they did not accept the Day of Judgment and life after death because such concepts were not clearly defined in the Old Testament of the Bible.

A more influential religious group than the Sadducees were the Pharisees, a name that literally meant "the Separated Ones". They were a scholarly, middle-class group of Jews who followed their religious rituals with great passion. The Pharisees were well known for their dedication to Torah and its interpretation by their teachers. Unlike the Sadducees, they believed in life after death and hoped for salvation as a reward for strict obedience to religious laws. Also unlike the Sadducees they were much more in touch with the common people that lived in the small towns and villages. Avoiding trouble with the Roman authorities, the Pharisees refused to become involved in the political disputes that raged through Palestine during the Roman period.

Members of the Pharisee movement spent much of their time in the study of sacred writings. Their religious teachers were known as rabbis (masters). The sayings, traditions and teachings of the rabbis, along with their interpretations of the Torah, were collected into a colossal work known as the Talmud. For the Pharisees the Talmud held a place of great veneration and it would grow in an importance that even surpassed the Torah. The Pharisees developed the concept of focusing worship around synagogues, gathering places where rabbis and their students came together to study and worship. After the destruction of the Temple in Jerusalem by the Romans and the scattering of the Jewish population of Palestine, it would be the Pharisees who preserved what we now know of Jewish belief and practice today.

An Otherworldly Outlook

The members of the Essene movement in Roman Judaism were men who devoted their lives to fasting, praying, and studying sacred scripture. They were a group who sought to detach themselves from society by living in isolated communes. There they shared their food and possessions with one another. The Essenes despised wealth and cared little for what went on in the world around them.

One of the more well-known rituals practiced by the Essenes was called baptism.

"Before this, We had bestowed on the Children of Israel the Book and the Command and the Prophethood, and provided them with good things, and favored them above the nations."

the Qur'an 45:16

Akin to the Islamic practice of *ghusl*, or washing before prayer, baptism was a symbolic washing away of sins by submersion in water. One other interesting doctrine of this group was a belief in the imminent coming of the Messiah, the 'anointed one', a man divinely inspired who would establish God's rule on Earth.

A group believed to have had their origins in the Essene movement were the Zealots. Unlike the Essenes who chose social isolation, the Zealots were men of action. But like the Essenes, they hoped for the coming of the Messiah. They saw him coming as a great military leader who would free the Jews from their conquerors and who would establish a powerful nation similar to the ancient kingdom of David. Unlike other Jewish sects the Zealots openly espoused rebellion against Roman rule and saw it as their religious duty to struggle against the foreign occupiers of their land. They assassinated Roman soldiers and government officials in Palestine, as well as Jews who collaborated with the occupiers. Such acts that would be called terrorism today brought tremendous retribution down on the heads of all Jews.

Roman Retribution

The aggressive acts of the Zealots eventually brought disaster to the Jews of Palestine. In 70 CE a major revolt broke out only to be brutally crushed by Roman might. The Temple of Solomon, (which was until that time the spiritual focal point for the Jewish people) was flattened and Jerusalem ransacked. Six decades later, in 132 CE, another attempted rebellion was crushed and as punishment the Romans expelled the entire Jewish population from Palestine. This blow was tremendous. Religious life was so disrupted by the expulsion that all of the varying expressions of Judaism (with the exception of the Pharisees) withered and died out.

In time the Romans rebuilt the city of Jerusalem, but Jews were forbidden to live within its walls. This policy continued long after the Romans embraced Christianity. Jews would not be permitted to live in the city until Muslim Arab rulers granted them that right five centuries after they were expelled by the Romans.

Having been brutally removed from their homeland, the Jews established scattered communities throughout Southwest Asia and the Roman world. It is believed that during this period in time small groups of Jews began to move into the Arabian Peninsula. There they established small settlements around the town of Madinah, the oasis of Khaibar and further south in Yemen.

In time these communities expanded in size, adopted the language of the surrounding Arab peoples, as well as many aspects of the tribal Arab social structure. Some Jews in the Arabian Peninsula encouraged the spread of their faith among non-Jewish Arabs (as will be seen in the last chapter of this unit) and one of these Arab converts would go on to establish a Jewish kingdom in Yemen.

Saducees- wealthy, hellinistic culture, priest, literal meaning of Torah

Essenees - lived in social isolation, believed in Messiah, practiced baptism, spent life praying, fasting, etc. (studying)

Zealots- men of action, believed in Messiah

pharisees- believed in life after death, Middle Class, Torah, Interpreted by teachers, not in politics

Lesson Review

1. How did the different sects within Judaism reflect a variety of responses to life under Roman rule?

2. How did the spread of Hellenistic culture affect Jewish traditions and attitudes?

3. Explain for whom the word "Zealot" is used in our modern vocabulary.

Lesson Three

The Beginnings of Christianity

Looking Ahead

As you read the lesson look for the points that explain how the religion of Christianity evolved from a Jewish sect into a new world religion.

Preview Vocabulary

Gospel
Canonical
Injil
Nazarene
Universalization
Original Sin
Christian

One of the most profound individuals to shape both the religious and historical landscape of the pre-Islamic world was a Jewish holy man by the name of Jesus. However the exact details of this man's life remain to this day far from clear. The only documents that offer us a glimpse of his biography and teachings are from conflicting accounts that were written well after his life. But even these works provide only a sketch of the life of Jesus. For instance, these accounts provide little information about Jesus' childhood, the narration of which comes to a complete stop after the age of 12. The texts then resume their biographical narrative when he initiates his mission at the age of 30.

The sayings and teachings of Jesus were passed down orally in the first decades after his mission came to an end. Numerous scribes began to write these out starting around 70 CE or 80 CE. These written documents attempted to capture a record of Jesus and became known as the Gospels (a word which originated from the Greek meaning "good news"). Before 325 CE there were hundreds of these Gospels in existence, many of which presented conflicting and contradictory portraits of Jesus. Over time only four of these Gospels (commonly known as Matthew, Mark, Luke and John) became part of the Church's canonical, officially accepted, text called the New Testament.

blessed water for constant struggle sustenance

A Glimpse at the Teachings of Jesus

"A rabbi stood up and wanted to test Jesus. He said, '*Jesus, what shall I do to receive eternal life?*' Jesus said, '*What does it say in the Torah? What do you read there?* The rabbi answered, '*One shall love the Lord God with all of the heart, the soul, strength and mind and love your neighbor as you love yourself.*' Then Jesus replied to him, '*You have answered right. Do this and you will live eternally.*' But the rabbi wanted to test Jesus further and said, '*But who is considered my neighbor?* Jesus replied, '*Listen. A man was traveling from Jerusalem to Jericho and was jumped by bandits. They stripped him, beat him and left him for dead. Now by chance a Jewish priest was going down the road. When the priest saw the poor man on one side of the road he passed by on the other. So also did a rabbi who passed along the same way. But then a Samaritan, as he journeyed, came to where the poor man was and when he saw him, he had compassion. The Samaritan went to the poor man and wrapped his wounds, pouring olive oil and wine to heal them. Then the Samaritan set the man on his own donkey and took him to the nearest inn, and there took care of him. The next day the Samaritan took out two dinars and gave them to the inn-keeper saying, 'Take care of this man. Whatever extra you spend I will repay when I come back.'* Then Jesus said to the rabbi, '*Which of these three Jews do you think proved to be the real neighbor of the man who was attacked by bandits?*' The rabbi said, '*The one who showed mercy.*' Then Jesus said, '*Go and do the same.*' "

-The Gospel according to Luke 10:25-37

These four Gospels, along with the writings and letters of early Christian leaders, make up the text of New Testament, which has traditionally been believed by Christians to be the Word of God. This document is the most sacred scripture in Christianity and forms the basis of most Christian belief.

A Historian's Puzzle

Like the intimate details of his life, what Jesus exactly taught has presented modern scholars with a puzzle. One impediment to understanding Jesus has to do with language. Palestinian Jews in the time of Jesus spoke Aramaic as their native tongue, an ancient Semitic language related to both Hebrew and Arabic. If there were any written records of Jesus' statements in Aramaic they have now been completely lost; only fragments of Aramaic phrases can be found in the Gospels today.

The New Testament that Christians have been using for the last seventeen centuries was based almost entirely on documents written in Greek. The words Jesus spoke to his people in their original form cannot really be retrieved, only approximated. The Qur'an refers to these now lost teachings as the *Injil*.

Scholars cannot hope to achieve a full reconstruction of the original message of Jesus, but they have been able to verify common historical elements and themes. We know that the earliest followers of Jesus were not called Christians but rather Nazarenes (Hebrew *Netzarim*). This term may have simply meant "the followers of the one from the region of Nazareth" (i.e. Jesus). But the Nazarenes chose to describe themselves as "Followers of the Way." These early disciples of Jesus differed in many ways from later Christians. They were all Jews who strictly kept the laws of the Torah. They also did not believe Jesus to be the incarnation of God the key belief of Christianity. They simply believed him to be the Messiah, the one chosen by God, to lead the Jewish people into a new period of spiritual growth. The first leader of this group was James, a man believed to have been the half-brother of Jesus. Until the great Jewish rebellions James and his followers played the leading role in the movement. However like other Jewish movements in Palestine, the Nazarenes were all but wiped out in the tribulations brought down by the Romans.

Enter Paul

From the beginning of their movement the followers of Jesus suffered opposition from the mainstream Jewish community. Many of the Pharisees and Sadducees despised Jesus' revolutionary ideas that called for a reinterpretation of Judaism. The Nazarenes were often openly mocked and harassed. But the Jews could only go so far. As long as the Nazarenes did not pose a threat to the Roman government, those who opposed them could take only limited action.

One man who was well-known for his persecution of the Nazarenes was a Jew named Paul. Paul was raised in the Greek-speaking city of Tarsus in Asia Minor and was very familiar with Greek philosophy and culture. In Paul's day Tarsus was a center of activity for the Mystery Religions. It can be said with a fair degree of certainty that Paul must have been well aware of the ideas that were conveyed by these non-Jewish faiths and ideas.

For several years Paul was engaged in harassing those who believed Jesus to be the Messiah. But in the midst of his persecution an event occurred that would forever change his life. According to the accounts preserved in his own writings, Paul claimed to have had an unearthly vision of Jesus while on his way to the city of Damascus in 36 CE. This experience caused him to have a complete change of heart. Following an order from this phantom Jesus, Paul became a devoted missionary who spread his personal view of Christ throughout the Roman world. Many scholars believe that it was Paul who singlehandedly transformed

An early Christian image of Paul of Tarsus, one of the major shapers of Christian thought.

the Jesus movement from an obscure Jewish sect into a world religion.

Unlike the Nazarenes, Paul believed that Jesus' message was not only for Jews. Paul universalized the Christian faith, and he made Jesus available for everyone. But Paul realized that if this new faith was to be attractive for non-Jews, its teachings had to be modified to fit Greek and Roman worldviews. Since Paul and those who embraced his ideas found it difficult to convey the concepts of Jewish monotheism to polytheistic non-Jews, they reshaped the core beliefs held by James and the Jerusalem community. In doing so Paul changed the meaning of terms and phrases. For example the term 'Son of God' in Jewish tradition meant simply a righteous or pious person. But the phrase was further interpreted by Paul as meaning an actual offspring of God. Pagan mythologies contained many examples of humans who were fathered through the intervention of the gods. This fact made Paul's concepts easy for non-Jews to believe but nonetheless very difficult for Jews to swallow.

Paul also gave new meaning to the death and resurrection of Jesus. Through the crucifixion (execution by nailing to a wooden cross) and subsequent death of Jesus, Paul claimed that all of mankind was freed from sin and given a chance to gain eternal salvation. This concept later developed into a theory known as Original Sin. This doctrine states that all human beings are by nature evil due to Adam's disobedience before God, when he and Eve ate from the forbidden tree. The stain of this error was passed on to all of Adam's descendants from the time of birth. It was a sin held so great that it could only be wiped out by the self-sacrifice of Jesus on the cross, who Paul taught was both the Son of God and God at the same time.

Even on every-day issues Paul and the Nazarenes clashed. Paul gave little importance to the laws of Judaism that the community under James held dear like circumcision and abstention from pork. Paul went so far as to condemn any follower of Jesus who continued to keep the laws of the Torah. He taught that these laws were abrogated by the sacrifice of Jesus and had to be abandoned. Such flagrant disregard for Jewish religious practices encouraged non-Jews to follow Paul's teachings as they were not forced to abandon elements of their pagan cultures.

Christianity Takes Root

The process by which the teachings of Paul became official doctrine of the Christianity was tied to the way in which the faith spread and how it was transformed from the persecuted faith of a small community into the official religion of the mighty Roman Empire.

Although it is difficult for modern scholars to trace history of the myriad beliefs and teachings that developed around the figure of Jesus, they are certain that most of those who followed James (a group that included many of Jesus's actual disciples) challenged Paul's doctrines. The tension between Paul and the companions of Jesus can be seen in Paul's own letters preserved in the text of the New Testament.

The Life of Jesus Christ (ar. 'Isa al-Masih)

Outside the New Testament and the Qur'an, information on the life of Jesus Christ is virtually non-existent. The traditional account of his life states that he was born sometime around 6 BCE to a young Jewish woman named Mary in Roman Palestine. According to both Muslim and Christian teachings, Jesus was born without the biological intervention of a male. When the Roman-backed king of Israel, Herod the Great, heard a prophecy that a *new* King of the Jews would soon be born, he ordered all infant boys born in the town of Bethlehem (where the new "king" was to arise) to be killed. As a result, Mary and her husband, Joseph, fled with the baby Jesus to the neighboring province of Egypt. There they stayed until Herod died some years later. Jesus and his family then returned to their native town of Nazareth, which lay on the Sea of Galilee.

Jesus was known in his youth for his remarkable knowledge of the Torah and he would often engage the rabbis of the Pharisee sect in debate. What occurred during much of the early adult life of Jesus is unknown. Nothing in the New Testament provides information regarding these important years. There are many theories about Jesus' life during this time and a few modern historians have even put forward the idea that Jesus traveled to India where he studied under Buddhist monks!

In the New Testament account we next hear of Jesus when he was about 30 years of age. He traveled from his home in Nazareth to be baptized by John the Baptist (ar. *Yahya*), a man of great piety who most likely was a member of the Essene sect. It was during this time that Jesus came to understand his special position as a Prophet of God and he set about preaching in his native region of the Galilee. He gathered about him a number of followers, who are traditionally called the disciples.

Jesus brought a new interpretation of Judaism that, while still obeying the laws of the Torah, was deeply spiritual in nature. Jesus taught that the Judaism of his day had grown too dry and heartless. Of course this angered many of the priests and rabbis, who were concerned with the minute details of Jewish law and ritual. The leaders of the Jewish community soon began to complain about Jesus and eventually convinced the Roman governor of Palestine to have him arrested. According to the New Testament and Christian belief, Jesus stood trial and was convicted of the serious crime of trying to rebel against the Empire. This was a treasonable act punishable by death. Following the trial he was executed by crucifixion. Three days after his death, he was resurrected and walked among his disciples. Jesus then rose up to heaven where he sits at the right side of God. However Muslims differ with this account. In the Qur'an, God states that Jesus escaped the initial arrest and at some point in his life (the majority of Muslim scholars believe it was during the arrest attempt) he was raised to Heaven. Thus Islamic belief denies the event of the crucifixion. Nevertheless both Muslims and Christians share the belief that before the last day, Jesus will return and rescue the Earth and its people from impending disaster.

Paul traveled widely throughout the eastern provinces of the Roman Empire in an effort to spread his faith to the world. During these journeys he established Christian communities that were centered on houses of worship called churches. Paul wrote long letters to some of these communities elaborating his religious ideas and warning against those who taught other "versions" of Christian belief, mainly the Nazarenes.

To the dismay of the Nazarene leaders in Jerusalem, many of the non-Jewish churches broke completely with the Jewish heritage of Jesus. People who accepted Paul's ideas came to be known as Christians, the followers of Christ. By the time he died in 65 CE, Paul's version of Jesus had become so widespread that it eclipsed those followers who held true to the Torah.

Paul's interpretation of Christianity eventually gained the upper hand over the Nazarenes. Aided by the troubles that continued to torment Roman Palestine, the Jewish successors of Jesus soon had no chance to voice their opposition to Paul. The Nazarenes were almost completely wiped out during the Jewish rebellions against Rome in 70 CE and 132 CE. A few modern historians have theorized that remnants of these Nazarenes settled in southern Iraq, where they evolved into a religious group known as the Sabaeans. With this last thread of what was most likely the original path of Jesus severed, those who followed Paul could teach without opposition coming from their own ranks.

Paul's faith expressed in terms of ideas familiar to the pagan Greeks, Romans and adherents to the Mystery Religions, help explain how his teachings spread so rapidly among non-Jews. Much like the followers of Mystery Religions, early Christians tended to be from the lower class, particularly craftsmen, women and slaves, all of whom were powerless members of the Roman Empire. These people found Christian concern for the poor and downtrodden as well as promises for eternal salvation appealing.

As the Christian faith spread throughout the 2nd and 3rd centuries, Roman authorities began to clamp down on it (often with excessive violence) because Christians refused to perform ritual sacrifices to the emperor. Many of the early followers of Christianity suffered persecution and this only served to intensify the importance of redemption and the life to come. The martyrdom of these early believers made an enormous impact on society at the time and established a legacy of those who imitated Christ in their willingness to endure suffering.

Lesson Review

1. What difficulties do Biblical scholars have in reaching conclusions about Jesus' life and teachings?

2. Which sections of Roman society were the first to accept Christianity? Why do you think this is true? From what you know of Islamic history, can you say the same thing about the early Muslim community in Makkah?

Becoming a World Faith

Looking Ahead

Why do you think Christians were so divided in their beliefs about Jesus? Note the influence the Imperial government had in backing one school of thought against the others.

Preview Vocabulary

Colosseum
Edict of Milan
Pope
Nicean Creed
Celibacy
Trinity
Excommunication
Heretic
Schism
Infallible
Patriarch

The Roman Empire saw the rapid spread of Christianity as a threat to long-held traditions as well as the authority of its leaders. The refusal of Christians to honor the emperor as a god greatly angered the government. Roman authorities viewed this stubbornness more as a sign of rebellion against the state than as a theological issue. But whatever the reasoning, this act brought the empire and its Christian community into open confrontation.

From Official Persecution to Official Religion

Near the end of the 1st century CE the faith taught by Paul became so widespread that Roman officials began to persecute Christians in an attempt to curb its growing influence. Many Christians living in Asia Minor (modern-day Turkey), North Africa and other provinces were arrested, tortured and put to death, often in the cruelest manner. Christians who refused to sacrifice to Roman gods or accept the emperor as more than a man were often sentenced to be devoured by wild beasts in front of huge audiences in the colosseums (sport stadiums). They became martyrs whose actions would be a source of veneration for devout Christians.

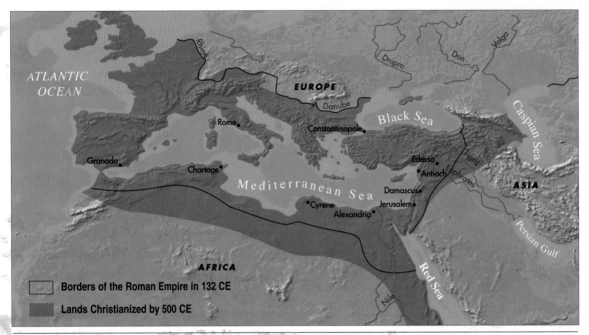

The spread of early Christianity went far beyond the borders of the Roman Empire. Even so, it took many centuries for it to win the hearts of the peoples of Western Europe. Christianity was only beginning to take hold in some areas of Europe at the birth of the Prophet Muhammad in 570 CE.

This policy of violence toward the new religion, however, completely backfired. Many non-Christians were impressed by sights of martyrs patiently enduring torture through their strong faith and often became Christians themselves. Others who did not share the faith, became sympathetic to the sufferings of Christians and called for tolerance.

After nearly two centuries of persecution, this situation changed drastically. A Roman general by the name of Constantine accepted the Christian faith in 312 CE after he defeated rivals for the throne. One year after he became emperor, Constantine issued the Edict of Milan, a document that forever ended the oppression of Christians in the Roman Empire.

In the decades following the Edict of Milan Roman subjects practiced both Christianity and the old religions side by side. But the age of polytheism in the Roman world was soon drawing to an end. In 381 CE, the Emperor Theodosius proclaimed Christianity as the official religion of the Roman Empire. Theodosius closed all pagan temples and places of worship and outlawed customs that were offensive to Christian sensibilities, such as the Olympic Games (which were often performed in the nude). As Christians had been persecuted in the preceding centuries, non-Christians who did not conform to the new state religion now faced the same.

In time, the suppression instituted by Theodosius extended to those Christian groups that differed in their beliefs from officially accepted doctrines. The tremendous diversity of doctrine among early Christian sects narrowed sharply as the price for official acceptance in the Empire rose. Over the next several centuries, imperial and church officials sought to stabilize Christianity by establishing a unified set of beliefs and practices.

Practice and Policy Develop

In the decades and centuries following Paul's death the far-flung Christian communities developed variant interpretations of his message, especially in regards to the nature of Jesus. The dominant community had its center in the city of Rome, the capital of the Roman Empire. Many Christians saw this city as sacred because Paul and other early missionaries had once visited the Christian communities that sprang up there. As the influence of Christianity grew in the city so too did its religious importance.

The leadership of the Christian community in Rome developed into a very structured hierarchy with a pope (a Latin term meaning "Father") at the top. The pope was viewed by people in Latin-speaking regions of the empire as the supreme leader of all Christians. In the eastern provinces of the empire, where the Greek and Aramaic languages dominated (and where Christian practices still displayed great diversity) the reverence for Rome and its Latin-speaking pope did not exist.

Beneath the pope were officials and priests of various ranks who took care of their local communities. These priests held great authority over the spiritual lives of their flocks. In communities far from Rome, and especially as Roman authority weakened in Western Europe, the Church took over many functions of community organization and became a force for social stability. The Roman Church ordered

The Nicean Creed

The main reason for the Council of Nicea was the concern among many about the growing influence of the teachings of a man named Arius of Alexandria, Egypt. Arius taught that Jesus was not equal with God, which was not a popular view among many well-established bishops (high level priests). The Emperor Constantine called for the convention to settle the issue of Christ's nature once and for all. As a result, the doctrines of Arius were officially banned and the following creed became the official belief of all "true" Christians to be followed without question:

"I believe in God, the Father Almighty, maker of heaven and earth and in all things visible and invisible. And in one Lord, Jesus Christ, the only-begotten Son of God. Born of the Father before all time. God of God, light of light, true God of True God. Begotten not made, being of one substance with the Father, by whom all things were made. Who for us men and for our salvation came down from heaven and was incarnate by the Holy Ghost into the Virgin Mary and was made man. He was crucified for us, suffered under Pontius Pilate [the Roman governor of Palestine] and was buried. On the third day he rose again according to the Scriptures, and rose up to the heaven. He sits at the right hand of the Father and he shall come again with glory to judge both the living and the dead. His kingdom shall have no end. And I believe in the Holy Ghost, the Lord and Giver of Life, who issues from the Father and the Son, who together with the Father and the Son is worshiped and glorified and who spoke through the Prophets. And I believe in one, holy catholic and orthodox church. I acknowledge one baptism for the forgiveness of sins and I look for the resurrection of the dead and the life of the world to come. Amen."

its priests to adopt the practice of celibacy, abstaining from marriage and sexual relationships. This shocked many who belonged to Eastern branches of Christianity, where priests and religious leaders were free to marry.

Unifying Christian Belief

Because different doctrines and practices existed among Christians, disputes (often violent) broke out throughout the empire. The Emperor Constantine was the first to prevent further chaos and confusion by using the power of the state. Constantine realized that an unstable and disorganized religion would affect the stability of the empire and could eventually lead to its downfall. Constantine ordered all church leaders to attend one huge assembly in an attempt to resolve differences in both doctrine and interpretation.

In 325 CE this assembly was convened in the small town of Nicea (the modern Turkish town of Iznik). The religious leaders who attended this council defined a set of statements to express the beliefs of Christian faith. A creed, or list of beliefs, was collected and published after long, heated debates. This list is called the Nicene Creed, and it was to be accepted faithfully by all those Christians who did not want to earn the anger of the imperial government and its church.

One important result of the Council of Nicea was its endorsement of the doctrine of the Trinity. The Trinity is the belief that God, though One, is made up of three distinct personalities who are both different and identical at the same time. These three persons are the Father (God), the Son (Jesus) and the Holy Spirit. Since the Father, Son and Holy Spirit are one in the same, Christians believe that God took on an earthly presence in the bodily form of Jesus. Thus Jesus is believed to be God Himself as well as the Son of God, joined by the Holy Spirit, the third part of the Trinity.

The beliefs laid down in the Nicene Creed were not accepted by all. But with the official backing of the emperor and the church the doctrine of the Trinity was spread throughout the empire. Church officials, educational institutions and local priests were all required to teach it.

Those individuals who did not completely accept the Nicene Creed could be excommunicated, expelled from the community of believers. They were considered to be heretics, or deviants, by the government-approved church. Excommunication was not to be taken lightly since it had serious consequences in terms of personal life. It could mean that an individual could not be legally married, could not inherit from relatives, and would not be given the rites of burial. To a believer, it meant exclusion from one's community in this life and from eternal salvation in the next. Such sanctions became even more important as the authority of the church grew while that of the empire declined.

Despite these government-sanctioned attempts to unify Christian belief, a serious division began to form after the Council of Nicea. Hostility began to grow between the head of the church of Rome and religious leaders in Constantinople. The roots of this split were found in the differences between the Greek and Roman cultures that each group represented. The Greek-speaking leaders of Christianity refused to accept the authority of the Latin-speaking pope in Rome. Worship services sanctioned by Rome were to be conducted in Latin and it was forbidden to allow worship in any other language. The leaders in Constantinople, however, permitted services in Greek, and later, in the native languages of the people where the church spread: in Serbian, Bulgarian (and later Russian) as well as into Semitic-speaking Southwest Asia. Friction continued to increase, often enhanced by very minor disagreements over religious doctrines, until the 6th century CE, when the division became a lasting split, or schism.

Another point of contention between the Church of Rome and that of Constantinople was that the Greeks refused to accept the absolute and unlimited power of the pope in Rome. The Romans felt that the pope should be head of all of Christianity. Those who followed the pope believed he was infallible, that he could not make mistakes. His decisions had to be taken without question. Since he was seen as the true successor of Paul, the pope's orders were to be accepted immediately as part of belief and practice. The church headquartered in the old imperial capital came to be known as the Roman Catholic Church.

The church that was centered in Constantinople, however, became known as the Greek Orthodox Church. It was called this because the world in which it developed was a world of Greek language and Greek culture. Its followers lived in the provinces in the eastern Mediterranean, parts of North Africa, Asia Minor and the Balkans, lands with close connections to Constantinople. The emperor, who appointed a patriarch to lead this branch of the faith, was viewed as the head of Christianity rather than the pope.

The differences separated the two bodies of believers proved to be insurmountable and led to final separation in 1045 CE, when the two churches mutually excommunicated each other. Each side declared the other as unbelievers and thus doomed to hell.

Early Divisions within Christianity

In the early history of Christianity there were many groups that had disagreements with the main churches of both Rome and Constantinople. While some of these differences regarded questions of leadership, most revolved around views on the nature of Jesus. Below is a list of some of the most important rival interpretations that both the Roman Catholic and Greek Orthodox Churches had condemned and tried to stamp out through preaching and occasional violence.

Arianism: The founder of this group, an Egyptian bishop named Arius, taught that Jesus could not be God since he was a created being. This meant, said Arius, that since there was a time when Jesus did not exist, and since God has always existed the two cannot be equal. The teachings of Arius were outlawed by the Council of Nicea in 325 CE since it denied belief in the Trinity. In the 4th and 5th centuries CE Arian teachings spread among many of the Germanic tribes that had moved into Europe. This caused the Roman Catholic Church to launch an all out effort to convert the rulers of these tribes to the mainstream interpretation of Christianity. They were eventually successful in this effort and by the 6th century Arianism completely died out.

The Coptic Church: This was the main Christian community in Roman Egypt. The Copts held to the position of their priests that Jesus Christ was of only one nature; that he was completely God and not a man. This was opposed to the Nicean Creed and other officially approved creeds, because they stated that Jesus was both God *and* man at the same time. The Copts underwent severe persecution under the Byzantines because they refused to conform to Orthodox belief. The Coptic Church survives to this day in modern Egypt.

Docetism: This very early Christian group was deeply influenced by the Gnostics. They believed that Jesus was simply a "disguise" used by God to cover Himself while he dwelled among men. The Docetians believed Jesus' sufferings were not real but an illusion. Some even taught that he was never crucified at all but escaped and that a man named Judas was nailed to the cross in his place. This school of thought was eventually crushed by the official Church in the 4th century.

Donantism: was followed by the majority of Christians in North Africa and was established around 305 CE. Although the Donantists upheld the authorized view of the Trinity, their refusal to acknowledge the official leadership in Rome brought about their bitter repression by the Imperial government in 412 CE.

Montanism: This group was founded by a Christian named Montanus around 170 CE and spread throughout eastern Asia Minor. Their main difference with the official body of Christianity was that they believed that God spoke directly through their leaders and they allowed women to hold high positions in their churches (something unheard of in the mainstream Church). The Montanist movement gradually lost popularity after the Council of Nicea in 325 CE.

Nestorianism: took shape through the work of a priest named Nestorius of Syria (who died in 450 CE). He taught that Jesus Christ was made up of two persons; one human and one Divine, whereas the official position was that Jesus was both man and God in one. Another difference was that the Nestorians rejected the Catholic and Orthodox belief that the Virgin Mary was the "Mother of God". He believed that Mary was only the mother of Christ the human, not Christ the God. The Nestorian Church later fled eastward into the lands of the Sasanid Persians to escape persecution by the Byzantine government. It flourished in Iraq and Iran where its followers can still be found.

Lesson Review

1. How did the persecution of Christians affect people's attitudes toward Christianity?

2. How did Constantine help the spread of Christianity in the Roman Empire?

3. What role did Church organization play in the Western Roman Empire, especially in the lives of ordinary people?

4. Why did officials in Constantinople want to make Christian beliefs more uniform, and how did they try to achieve this goal?

5. How did the separation, or schism, between the Western and Eastern branches of Christianity occur?

Chapter Review

1. Discuss the causes and effects of religious tolerance in Rome. What do you think caused intolerant reactions by the government?

2. Do you think there might be a connection between the spread of "Mystery Religions" and the decline of the Roman empire? Give reasons for your answer.

3. Research and summarize evidence of various cultural influences on religious practices among various groups of Jews during the Hellenistic and Roman periods.

4. Do additional research about the split between Judaism and Christianity. Role play a debate or discussion among members of the two groups to show why the split occurred.

5. Trace the steps taken by the Roman government at Constantinople to narrow the diversity of Christian beliefs and practices. How might this process have been related to the needs of the empire?

Chapter Three

Faith Beyond the Euphrates

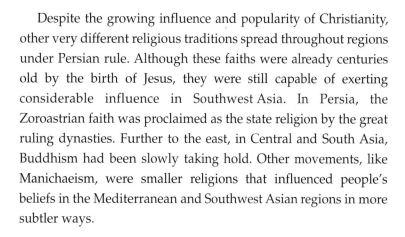

Lesson One

The Zoroastrian Faith

Looking Ahead

Keep in mind the religious diversity that was prevalent in the pre-Islamic Middle East. Can you identify Zoroastrian concepts in other religions?

Preview Vocabulary

Magu
Ahura Mazda
Mazdayasna
Amesha Spenta
Yazata
Gatha
Angra Manyu
Dualism
Avesta

Despite the growing influence and popularity of Christianity, other very different religious traditions spread throughout regions under Persian rule. Although these faiths were already centuries old by the birth of Jesus, they were still capable of exerting considerable influence in Southwest Asia. In Persia, the Zoroastrian faith was proclaimed as the state religion by the great ruling dynasties. Further to the east, in Central and South Asia, Buddhism had been slowly taking hold. Other movements, like Manichaeism, were smaller religions that influenced people's beliefs in the Mediterranean and Southwest Asian regions in more subtler ways.

"Thus Spake Zarathustra..."

Since the dawn of recorded history, the ancient Indo-European inhabitants of Iran worshiped many different deities believed to control the forces of life and nature - wind, fire, sun, and water. To appease these gods the early ancestors of the Persians performed animal sacrifices and made offerings using intoxicating drinks. The priests who performed these rituals, known as the *magus*, and they were believed to hold the power to drive away evil. The *magus* held considerable control over their people, who held them in great awe. So when a new religious message appeared among

The life of the Persian Prophet

Shrouded by the mists of time, few concrete facts can be gathered regarding the life of Zoroaster. According to traditional accounts, he was born in eastern Iran some six centuries before Christ. Zoroaster was raised in a family of priests that followed the old Iranian religion. It is said that as a youth he began to contemplate to search of a deeper meaning to life. Then, in his thirtieth year, as he was fetching water to perform a religious ceremony, the angel Vohu Mana (which means "Good Purpose") appeared to Zoroaster and led him to the presence of the One God, Ahura Mazda. The new prophet's message of the One God was met with rejection by his own people and eventually Zoroaster and his small band of followers were forced to flee to the lands of King Vishtaspa (in modern Afghanistan). Despite the opposition of the king's priests, Zoroaster presented his religious message and King Vishtaspa embraced it. With a secure base from which to practice their faith, the Followers of Zoroaster spread the belief in the One God to other parts of Iran. According to tradition Zoroaster was tragically killed by marauding Turkic tribesmen who attacked the city of King Vishtaspa.

the Iranian peoples sometime between 1000 BCE and 600 BCE, the *magus*, as to be expected, were the first to oppose it.

Zoroaster (*Zarathushtra* in the original ancient Persian language) was a man who brought a radically new belief system to the people of Iran. He was considered a prophet who, at the age of thirty, claimed to have been given revelation from the One Good God, called *Ahura Mazda*. Like many other prophets in history, Zoroaster was harassed and ridiculed by his people. But Zoroaster's message dramatically changed the beliefs of those who accepted it. Had Zoroaster never lived, the Iranians may have continued in their religious development in a way similar to their cousins who settled in India, a people who gave rise to Hinduism.

Zoroaster taught that there was only One God named *Ahura Mazda*, who was the source of truth, goodness and light. He stated that it was the responsibility of each human being to choose a path of good or evil. Serving the forces of Light meant promise of happiness in this life as well as the next. This righteous path was called *Mazda-yasna* or "worship of God, Ahura Mazda." This term is what Zoroastrians have used for their faith from ancient times.

According to Zoroaster the old gods of the Iranians (called *daevas*; many of whom are present in Hinduism) were evil demons whose worship was to be shunned. He opposed the polytheistic rituals and practices of the ancient Iranians, openly condemned the sacrifice of cows, and the use of alcoholic drinks.

Zoroastrian Religious Concepts

Zoroaster taught that *Ahura Mazda* was surrounded by seven attributes or characteristics to help in the battle against evil. The seven together were known as the *Amesha Spenta*. These are

1) Splendid Mind, 2) Righteousness, 3) Holiness, 4) Love, 5) Flawlessness, 6) Timelessness, and 7) Creativity. Later, the _Amesha Spenta_ were given individual personalities and were accepted by Zoroastrians as archangels.

Other positive feelings and thoughts were called the _yazatas_, the adored ones or minor angels. Like the _Amesha Spenta_, these characteristics gradually took on personalities and became objects of worship. The most famous of these _yazatas_ were the three "brothers": _Sraosha_ (God's hearing), _Rashnu_ (God's justice) and _Mithra_ (God's all-seeing eyes; the same _Mithras_ mentioned in the previous chapter). Several historians think that these _yazatas_ represented old gods worshiped by the Iranians, that were incorporated into Zoroastrian belief to make it more understandable to common people.

In opposition to _Ahura Mazda_ and his angels was _Angra Manyu_, the originator of Evil. He is the cause of all wickedness and pain, and all who commit immoral acts are his soldiers. Like _Ahura Mazda_, _Angra Manyu_ fashioned his own twisted versions of the _Amesha Spenta_ and the _yazatas_ who were sinister in character.

The original words of Zoroaster are believed to be contained in a short book known as the _Gathas_. The _Gathas_ describe the noble acts of "good thoughts, good words and good deeds" which

lead to salvation for the individual and humanity both. Those who followed these precepts would be rewarded with Paradise after their deaths. People who opposed the spread of goodness would be doomed to the punishment of Hell. In Zoroaster's words we find the earliest recorded mention of concepts like the Day of Judgement, Heaven and Hell among mankind.

The Evolution of Zoroastrianism

Like Judaism and Christianity, the Zoroastrian religion underwent changes through the centuries of its existence. Many of these modifications actually came to contradict the teachings of the _Gathas_. For example, many people began to worship the _Amesha Spenta_ and the _Yazatas_ as deities and even made idols to represent them.

There were several factors that caused the gradual evolution of Zoroastrianism. During the period of the Achaemanid Persian Empire (which lasted from 539 BCE to 330 BCE), Zoroastrianism began to gain converts from among the Persian nobility. Seeing this success, many of the priestly class of the _magus_ (who had originally opposed Zoroaster's teachings) began to accept the religion. The _magus_ introduced in their interpretations many old practices and concepts. Modern scholars believe that during this religious evolution, Zoroastrianism evolved from an essentially monotheistic faith to a dualistic one. _Dualism_ is the belief in two equal opposing forces of good and evil, represented by _Ahura Mazda_ and the wicked _Angra Manyu_ would later influence Gnostic thought.

With the growing dominance of the _magus_, Zoroastrianism began to develop a priestly class that built temples to house the sacred fires. Fire was used as a symbol of _Ahura Mazda's_ light. The

---

Excerpt from the Gathas of Zoroaster

"When I thought of You, O Mazda, as the very First and the very Last, as the Most Precious One, as the Originator of all Good Thought, as the Creator of the Everlasting Law of Truth, as the Lord Judge of our actions in Life, then I made a place for You in my eyes."

(Gathas, Yasna 31-38)

priests made no sacrifices on these sacred fires, for burning flesh in the fire would pollute its sacredness. Only the choicest of woods would be used to keep these fires fueled. When Zoroastrianism became the official state religion, a great temple was built over a fire believed to have been lit by Zoroaster himself that was kept burning for centuries!

✦ As time progressed Zoroastrians began to collect the *Gathas* and other holy writings into a volume called the *Avesta*. This book consisted several parts, including the *Gathas*, which are believed to contain the original words of Zoroaster. Like the Jewish and Christian Bible, the *Avesta* was compiled over a long period of time. But unlike the Bible (about which modern scholars have studied in great detail) historians can only guess about many aspects of the *Avesta*.

The *Avesta* was thought to be a much larger text than the one known today, since it was believed lost when Alexander the Great destroyed the Persian capital of Persipolis in 331 BCE. In addition to this other portions of this sacred text have been lost since then, and some historians say that the book was four times the size that it is today before the Muslim conquests.

Other sacred Zoroastrian texts include the *Zand*, which is a commentary on the *Avestas* that was written during the Sasanid period (between 200 CE and 500 CE). Written in the old Persian language called Pahlavi, the *Zand* reflects very different ideas from those found in the original *Gathas* of Zoroaster, as it nearly endorses polytheism. Thus the *Zand* clearly shows the influence of the *magus*.

An Imperial Faith

Despite the ancient and deep roots of the faith, it was only in 500 CE (less than a century before the birth of the Prophet Muhammad) that the religion became the official religion of Iran. Zoroastrianism formed one of the pillars of Sasanid power and one Zoroastrian high priest of the Sasanid period wrote that the "*Mazdayasna* Faith and the State are born from one mother, never to be separated." Like the emperor of Rome, the Sasanid *shah* (emperor) was seen as a son of God. He was expected to uphold the faith and crush its enemies.

Sasanid society was hierarchical, meaning that it was made up of many ranking classes. The most powerful group in the empire, of course, was the *shah* and his relatives. This was followed by Zoroastrian *mobads* (high-priests), and then the powerful nobility. Under these classes were scribes and secretaries who served the government bureaucracy, followed by merchants and craftsmen. At the bottom of the social ladder were peasant farmers, who were held in virtual slavery by the upper classes.

The Zoroastrian priests became powerful leaders of the Sasanid religious establishment. The priests received huge estates from the *shah* and their temples demanded lavish gifts and taxes from the devoted masses. While there were certainly pious men among them, many used their power and wealth to exploit the common people, which in the end caused deep resentment.

Just as Sasanid society was divided into a rigid class system, so to were the priests of state Zoroastrianism. The head of the church was the *Mobad Mobadan*, who controlled the affairs of all the empire's *mobads* and represented the faith in the imperial court. He held a position that was equivalent to the pope or patriarch in Christianity. It was the duty of the *Mobadan*

Mobad to root out deviation from officially sanctioned doctrine. At any time harsh brutality or general tolerance might be shown to those who would not conform depending on the political circumstances at hand.

During periods of intolerance, followers of other religions were declared supporters of *Angra Manyu's* kingdom of evil. The *mobads* encouraged the *shah* to eliminate the followers of heresy by any means. One famous *mobad* named Kirder noted the measures taken by Emperor Shahpur against non-Zoroastrians with these words, "Great blows came upon *Angra Manyu* and his devils and his beliefs fled our land and were no longer accepted by our people. Buddhists, Hindus, Mandeans, Christians and Manichaens are now crushed in the realm."

Minority faiths were generally tolerated as long as their influence did not go beyond the walls of their communities. Jews, who had lived in Persian lands since the 4th century BCE, were shown relative degrees of leniency. Because the Jews did not have a rival state and showed little desire to spread their faith among the local

A letter from Shah Khusrow regarding the Mobad Mobadan

"The Mobad Mobadan brought to my attention several people whom he named and who belonged to the nobility. The religion of these people was contrary to the faith which we inherited from our fathers and learned men. He warned us that these people were preaching in secret for their religion and inviting people to embrace it. I gave orders to have these heretics brought into my presence to debate with them. After that I ordered that they should be expelled from my capital, my country and my empire and that all those who shared their beliefs should follow them."

populations they were not seen as a threat to social stability.

However two other religious movements - Christianity and Manichaeism - posed more serious challenges to the Zoroastrian leadership. Both actively sought converts among the population. These faiths were seen as threats to the national religion and to the empire's security as well and the Sasanid government dealt with them accordingly.

Christianity was seen as a particularly menacing threat. From the time of its establishment in the 3rd century CE, the Sasanid Empire was locked in mortal combat with the Roman (and later Byzantine) Empire on its western borders. When Christianity was still persecuted by Rome, the Sasanids allowed Christian refugees to settle in their realm, in keeping with the old saying, "the enemy of my enemy is my friend." But once Christianity was adopted as the official religion of the Roman/Byzantine State, tolerance was no longer viewed as such a good policy. The Sasanids now saw their Christian minority as potential traitors in any war against Byzantinum. The *shah* imposed hardships on Christian citizens, increasing their taxes and even conducting mass executions. In turn, Christian Byzantium responded by persecuting those Zoroastrians who lived in its Asian provinces.

Zoroastrianism was the dominant faith in the lands east of Mesopotamia. It often had to compete with other faiths for followers. This Zoroastrian temple is located in modern Iran.

Lesson Review

1. In what ways did Zoroastrianism differ sharply from earlier, Iranian beliefs and practices?

2. Describe the basic teachings of Zoroaster.

3. How did Zoroastrianism change when it became associated with the authority of the Sasanid Persian Empire?

Lesson Two

Alternatives of Faith

Looking Ahead

How did the established faiths of Southwest Asia react to new beliefs and teachings?

Preview Vocabulary

Mobad
Khan
Bogomil
Sanskrit
Mani

In addition to Christianity and Zoroastrianism, several smaller, (though none the less influential) religious movements existed in Southwest Asia. The ancient faith of Buddha was aggressive in spreading its message to the world. It gained a large following among the peoples of Afghanistan, Eastern Iran and Central Asia. Another significant religious movement known as Manichaeism arose out of the Sasanid province of Iraq, and it grew to challenge the very foundations of Zoroastrian Persia. Nevertheless despite the spread of these and other universal faiths there still remained countless villages that lived in isolation from the flow and interaction of cultures and religions. Here the people continued to honor the religions of their ancestors, which was more often than not polytheism in its simplest form.

Mani's Faith

In the last lesson we read about how the Sasanid state displayed open hostility towards Christianity and its followers. But Christians were not the only religious community affected by officially sanctioned intolerance. In 240 CE a man named Mani claimed to have been given revelation by a being said to be an angel. Born into an Iraqi Gnostic family, Mani began to teach an ideology based on elements common to the various spiritual traditions present in the Mesopotamia of his day. He accepted the dualist belief in the eternal war between good and evil. He also taught that the material world was the creation of evil, showing strong Gnostic influence. In addition Mani also recognized Jesus as a messenger from the Supreme God sent to liberate mankind from the prison of physical body and the clutches of the evil creator-god

Mani began preaching his message in Iraq and then traveled as far as modern-day Pakistan and India. His followers established communities in Egypt and North Africa. Eventually Mani's faith became so popular that it won the favor of three Sasanid rulers. Mani was invited as a dignitary to the imperial palace on many occasions.

With the rise of the powerful *Mobad Mobadan* Kirder, Mani fell out of favor with the Sasanid government. Kirder saw in the spread of Manichaeism an open threat to the Zoroastrian faith. He put tremendous pressure on Shah Vahram to end the tolerance shown towards Mani and his followers. The ruler had Mani imprisoned, where he died in 279 CE. His followers were severely persecuted, and many fled to Central Asia, where they spread Manichaeism among the Turkic Uygur people who lived in what is now western China. The faith was welcomed and Manichaeism soon became the official religion of the Uygur *Khans* (kings). It thrived in this part of Central Asia until the 13th century CE when the Uygurs converted to Islam. Some Manichaeans continued to live in Iraq after the Muslim conquest, but the religion had gradually died out by the 10th century CE.

Manichaeans also traveled west into the Roman Empire. They established communities that were not welcomed by Christian churches. During the early period of Christianity, Manichaeans were viewed with great hostility and were seen as serious rivals. When Christianity triumphed over the empire, the Manichaeans were driven into hiding. Dualist tendencies, nonetheless, persisted in Christian

The first images of the Buddha originated in modern-day Afghanistan and eastern Iran and were not made until nearly 300 years after his death. The famous statue of the Buddha once located in Bamiyan, Afghanistan. Having stood through 13 centuries of Muslim rule it was only destroyed recently by religious zealots. This colossal carving was heavy influenced by Greek styles. How did Greek influences appear in Afghan culture?.

lands. A heretical group known as the Albigensians thrived in southern France until the 13th century CE when the pope sent a crusade against them and wiped them out. Another sect thought to have been influenced by the Manichaeans were the Bogomils. This dualist group thrived in the rural areas of Macedonia and Bulgaria. Despite continued harassment from the Orthodox church, they endured until the Ottoman conquest of the region in the late 14th century, when most of them converted to Islam.

"Verily We sent many a Messenger before you; of some We have already related to you the story, of others We have not. Yet it was not in the power of any Messenger to bring a sign without Allah's permission. Then when Allah's command came, the judgement was passed with justice and those who followed falsehood then incurred loss."

the Qur'an 40:78

Buddhism spreads West

Buddhism is usually associated with eastern lands like China, Japan, Burma, Thailand, Laos, Tibet and Cambodia, where, in fact, most Buddhists today live. But just as early Buddhist missionaries trekked out of India to the lands of the Far East, they also headed west.

Buddhism became prominent in the northwestern part of the Indian subcontinent during the first and second centuries CE, when its ideology was adopted by two important rulers, Ashoka (born ca. 300 BCE) and Kanishka (ruled 70-144 CE). With royal backing, Buddhist missionaries set out to mountains of Afghanistan.

Several important centers of Buddhist learning sprang up in this mountainous region,

the most famous being the city of Balkh. From such centers, Buddhism spread along Central Asian trade routes into China, and Sasanid Persia. These regions became important for the cultural exchanges that occurred in them. One example of this can be found in certain stories of Buddha's life that were translated from Sanskrit (an ancient Indian language) into Pahlavi, an old Persian language. They were later rendered into Arabic after the Muslim Arabs conquered Iran. These legends were modified to fit Islamic cultural and religious concepts, stand as an excellent example of how cultures borrow and interact with each other.

Iran was not the end of the westward journey of Buddhism and the faith made modest inroads into the Roman Empire. Written evidence has been found showing the presence of Buddhist missionaries in the city of Rome during the reign of Augustus, who ruled at the time of the birth of Jesus. The ancient historian Philo (20 BCE-50 CE) spoke of a Buddhist monastery near the Egyptian city of Alexandria. The fate of these Buddhists is unknown, but certain similarities between Buddhist traditions and early Christian institutions, like monasteries and monks, provide fascinating material for thought.

Lesson Review

1. What beliefs did Manichaeism share with monotheistic faiths of the Abrahamic tradition? How did they differ?

2. What was the response to Manichaeism from established religious authorities in East and West?

3. What evidence do we have for the westward spread of Buddhism?

Chapter Review

1. Compare beliefs about good and evil in Zoroastrian and other world religions. What symbols are used for this struggle in each tradition?

2. Why do you think abstract ideas (such as good actions) often appear as symbols or personalized beings that become transformed into objects of worship in various religious traditions?

3. Research the spread of Buddhism and in a brief report, describe the manner and routes of its spread. What ideas and practices may have contributed to its acceptance?

4. Compare the spread of Buddhism and early Christianity. What economic and geographic factors might have aided the spread of religions during this period?

5. Explore the relationship between governments and religious movements using the examples presented in this chapter. Discuss resistance to change, persecution, acceptance by those in authority, and changes to beliefs and practices that resulted from the close association of power and the religions discussed here.

Chapter
Four

The Rule
of Kings

The Byzantine Empire

Looking Ahead

How was the Byzantine Empire a continuation of the Roman Empire? What factors made it thrive while the western provinces fell into chaos?

Preview Vocabulary

Justinian Code
Artisans
Icon
Iconography

When the Prophet Muhammad was born in 570 CE, two great empires controlled most of Southwest Asia. The Sasanid Dynasty, upholders of the ancient Zoroastrian faith, established an empire that had been in existence since the second century CE. Their rule stretched from the Amu Darya River in the east, to the Indus River in the south, and westward to the Tigris-Euphrates River. In Southwest Asia, they were locked in a constant struggle with their age-old rival, the Byzantine Empire.

Imperial Origins

Byzantium carried on the legacy of the Roman Empire, which had dominated much of Europe, Southwest Asia and North Africa for centuries. But by the fifth century CE, barbarian tribes that originated on the fringes of Eastern Europe began to migrate into the Roman provinces of France, Italy and Spain. These invaders spoke Germanic languages and possessed a level of cultural development much more primitive than Rome's. The empire tried to resist these migrations, but the shear numbers of barbarians forced the Romans to allow these tribes to settle. Often seen as uncivilized, these German tribes changed the political and social structure of the provinces they occupied. As Roman power began to decline, the maintenance of law and order in the provinces fell

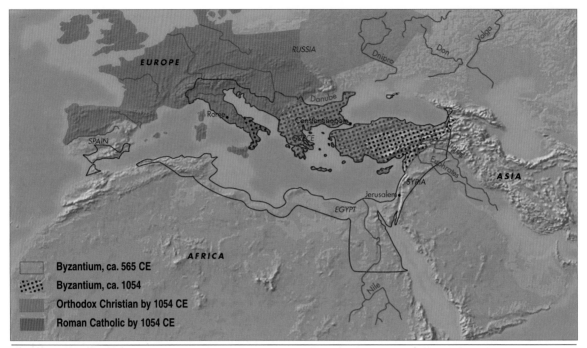

The Byzantine (or Eastern Roman) Empire was locked in a deadly struggle with the Sasanids for nearly four hundred years. The borders between these two super-powers constantly shifted east to west and visa versa.

Legend on map:
- Byzantium, ca. 565 CE
- Byzantium, ca. 1054
- Orthodox Christian by 1054 CE
- Roman Catholic by 1054 CE

on the shoulders of the barbarian tribal chiefs. The chiefs used their new-found authority to establish their own kingdoms on Roman land. For instance the tribe of the Franks dominated what is now France, the Visigoths over Spain, the Lombards in northern Italy and the Anglo-Saxons in England.

In the eastern provinces (which included Anatolia, Egypt, Syria, and the parts of the Balkans) the impact of the German migrations was not as great. Here Roman ways continued for several more centuries, albeit set in a Greek and not Latin-speaking culture. It is this part of the old Roman world that came to be called the Byzantine Empire. A strong army, good government and a productive economy helped allow it endure despite being surrounded in a sea of change.

Historians generally date the beginning of the Byzantine Empire to 313 CE, when the Emperor Constantine moved his capital away from Rome.

He looked for a city that would be safe from invaders and centered on important trade routes. The location Constantine chose was an old town known as Byzantium, located where the Black and Aegean Seas met in a narrow waterway that divided Europe from Asia. This excellent site was easily defendable and it dominated the major water and land routes between the two continents. In 330 CE, Constantine renamed the town Constantinople in his own honor. The town rapidly expanded and it endured as the capital of the empire until 1453 CE, when it fell to Ottomans, who in turn made it the center of their own state.

Emperor Justinian

The Byzantine Empire reached the height of its power two hundred years after Constantine moved the capital eastward from Rome. In 527 CE Justinian took the throne along with his intelligent and powerful wife, Theodora. Together, they reconquered large expanses of Roman territory in the west that was under the control of the Germanic kings. Following this Justinian turned east and brought his empire into a series of protracted wars against the Sasanid Persians. The conflict between Byzantium and the Sasanids continued for over a century, draining the populations and economies of both states.

In addition to his military exploits, Justinian and his advisors developed a legal system to strengthen the government, and hence society at large. These laws were interpretations of earlier Roman codes, rewritten in a language that was easier to understand and better suited to the changing times. In addition the Empress Theodora made sure that many of the old restrictive laws regarding women were removed.

This body of legal work was called the *Corpus Juris Civilis* (Body of Civil Law), more commonly known as the Justinian Code. These laws became the foundation of most European nations' legal systems, influenced American law, and affected many non-European countries that were colonized by Europeans during the 19th and 20th centuries.

The Byzantine Economy

During the early centuries of its existence, Byzantium's economy was both strong and stable. As a meeting place for European and Asian merchants material and cultural exchange flourished in Constantinople. The city dominated overland trade from the Far East, which followed the famed Silk Road, a route long used by merchants that stretched all the way to China.

New industries developed in Constantinople to serve the emperor's court which in turn created wealth for merchants, artisans and craftsmen. The regional silk industry began during Justinian's time and spread throughout the Europe and Southwest Asia. Before this silk could only be imported from China, which made the product extremely expensive. Byzantine merchants were anxious to find new sources for silk, which was rare and had remained a well-guarded Chinese secret. According to legend, a travelling Christian monk smuggled silkworm eggs out of China along with the seeds of the mulberry trees the leaves of which were used to feed the worms. He successfully brought them back to Constantinople starting a revolution in silk production. The ability to produce silk in the Empire ended China's monopoly on this product; for now it was no longer the only place from which silk could be bought. Nevertheless the demand for Chinese luxury products (such as ceramics, spices etc.) throughout Europe and Southwest Asia continued for centuries.

All the regions under Byzantine rule were expected to provide their share of work in maintaining the common prosperity. For instance Egypt and other North African provinces supplied grain for the empire. Nearly all of the yearly surplus grain supply of Egypt went to feed the city of Constantinople alone! Imperial laws and taxes tied farmers to the land they worked and forced them to hand over portions of their crops to wealthy landowners, government officials and the church. Throughout much of Byzantine history there were only two types of landowners: the nobility and Church officials.

Byzantine Society

The city of Constantinople was one of the great cities of the world. It had a well developed water supply system (which included sewers) as well as hospitals, orphanages and homes for the elderly. Education was a priority for the upper-class of society. The children of the nobility were taught by tutors or in private schools. They could attend Christian monasteries or convents (homes for nuns) that were centers of literacy. Studies concentrated on works from the glorious past, such as the classical Greek and Roman authors and, more importantly, Christian religious studies. But for the majority of the people, opportunities for social advancement were quite limited. Any young man who wished to obtain an education could usually only do so by becoming a priest in the Orthodox church.

Byzantine society was deeply rooted in the Christian religion. Greek Orthodoxy influenced the outlook of every walk of life, from emperor to farmer. The emperor was seen as the defender of the Orthodox Christian faith, and he carried with it the responsibility for the well-being of his subjects.

The Orthodox church had a complex relationship with the imperial government. The patriarch, the head of the Orthodox church, lived in the city of Constantinople. He played a role similar to that of the pope in Rome, except that his

The Masterpiece of Hagia Sophia

The Church of Hagia Sophia (Holy Wisdom) in Istanbul was the most important church of the Byzantine Empire for nearly a thousand years. And it is still one of the world's awesome architectural monuments. It was built on the site of a 4th century church that burned to the ground in 404 CE. The church was rebuilt, destroyed in a riot, and again rebuilt as it is today by Emperor Justinian I within the short period of five years (532-37 CE).

Hagia Sophia has a daring and innovative design that features a gigantic central dome, about 30 meters (100 ft) in diameter resting on four great arches that are supported by two half domes. The contemporary Byzantine author Procopius was so much in awe of the structure that he wrote that Hagia Sophia's enormous dome is "not founded on solid masonry, but rather suspended from heaven by a golden chain." The interior of the church was filled with richly colored marble and gleaming golden mosaics that caught the sparkling light through its many windows and openings. These mosaics portrayed religious themes as well as figures from Byzantine history. The huge open space under the vaults and central dome became typical of later Byzantine church architecture, and influenced both Christian and Ottoman Islamic architecture. Byzantine architects and their designs were used both in the construction of great Umayyad Mosque of Damascus and the great Mosque of Cordoba in Spain.

Earthquakes caused the great dome to collapse in 558 CE, 989 CE, and 1346 CE, but it was successfully restored each time. When the Ottomans conquered Constantinople in 1453 CE, they converted this foremost monument of Byzantium into a mosque. In honor of its long and glorious history, the new mosque kept its original name, albeit with the Turkish pronunciation of "Aya Sofia". Follwoing the collapse of the Ottoman Empire, the secular government of Turkey turned the structure into a museum.

A fine example of a Byzantine mosaic. This one shows the Emperor with members of his court.

decisions were not viewed as totally infallible. Also unlike the pope, the patriarch had little say in secular politics. The emperor held the power in that arena. Yet the patriarch could exercise enormous influence over the government and its citizens if he so desired and could raise opposition to any imperial policy that displeased him.

The Byzantine Empire aided the spread of Christianity into the Balkans and Russia, regions where the Orthodox church would eventually dominate. By the late 800's CE, nearly all of the Slavic peoples of the Balkans (the Serbs, Bulgarians and Macedonians) left their pagan religions and accepted the Orthodox Christian faith.

The Roman Catholic church was also active in the Balkans, exerting influence among Croats and Albanians. There was tremendous rivalry between these two branches of Christianity as religious loyalty was sometimes used as a political tool. For example, in the 10th century CE the Bulgarian king considered converting to Catholicism in order to halt the growth of Byzantine influence in his kingdom's affairs.

Regions like Bosnia and Albania were located on the dividing line between territories loyal to the Orthodox and Catholic churches and the two faiths often coexisted side by side. Interestingly, centuries later these areas of mixed religious confession would see the greatest spread of Islam in the Ottoman period.

The Artisans

Skilled artisans in the Byzantine Empire established professional groups (called guilds) for the protection of their crafts. Children born into a family of artisans and craftsmen usually followed in their parents' footsteps, developing strong traditions in each field.

Byzantine artisans constructed splendid public buildings, such as churches and palaces, with elaborate gardens and fountains. They were highly skilled at working gold, jewels, mosaics, and painting. Textiles were an important product, especially luxury fabrics like the brocades and velvets for churches as well as for the imperial court.

Byzantine art was closely tied to the religious demands for public and private worship. Architects were commissioned to design impressive churches and monasteries. Builders worked in the classical Roman style, whose features included huge, heavy, buildings of stone. An architect's highest skill was demonstrated by setting large domes onto square sections of the building and using huge, rounded arches to support doorways and windows.

Mosaics, or murals made from tiny pieces of colored glass or ceramic, decorated the walls, floors and ceilings of churches.

The earliest Christian communities did not include the use of images in their worship. Since Christianity emerged from Judaism, whose religious law and culture considered the making of religious statues and pictures to be a major sin, the use of images was something new. But as Christians began to distance themselves from Judaism, both theologically and ethnically, the old legal constraints were no longer seen as important. Under the influence of Roman, Persian and other Mediterranean cultures, Christians gradually developed an iconography, or means of imagining the way Jesus and other religious figures looked and felt.

Since Christians no longer adhered to Jewish religious law, they freely made pictures of Jesus Christ, the Virgin Mary, the apostles and saints and sometimes even God Himself! These icons decorated the domes and walls of Byzantine churches, as well as the homes of simple peasants, becoming part of the practice of worship.

The insides of churches were covered with dazzling mosaics or tile art. Paintings portrayed individuals and saints of Orthodox Christian tradition. Figures in these images appear tall, usually shown in frontal views. The eyes are wide, with facial features outlined in dark tones.

Special religious images of Jesus, Mary and the saints, called icons, were painted on wooden panels and often decorated with gold and jewels. Figures were carved in ivory or stone.

Lesson Review

1. Compare and contrast Byzantine culture with that of Rome.

2. What was the Justinian Code and why was it important?

3. How did the Empire change after the capital was moved to Constantinople? What were its new borders? What was its dominant language following its moved to the east?

Lesson Two

The Clash of Giants

Looking Ahead

How was the state and society of Sasanid Persia structured differently from that of its rival, Byzantium? What did both of these empires have in common?

Preview Vocabulary

Arsacids

Shah

Dynasty

Relic

The origin of the long conflict between Roman West and Persian East began with the coming of the Arsacid Dynasty which was founded in the 2nd century BCE by an Iranian people known as the Parthians. The Parthians attempted to unite all the different tribes and ethnic groups in Iran. The kingdom they built was stable enough to last for nearly four hundred years. But in 224 CE, a family of Persian noblemen rebelled against the Parthians. The Persians resented being ruled over by the Parthians, a people they saw as barbaric nomads. The head of this family was a prince by the name of Sasan. He gathered support and overthrew his Parthian overlords. The empire that Sasan then set to create lasted until its collapse at the hands of the Muslim Arabs in the 650's CE.

Since the epoch of Alexander the Great, Greek culture had often played a visible role in the societies east of the Tigris-Euphrates Rivers. The Parthians on occasion even encouraged the spread of Hellenism. But this foreign influence was ruthlessly suppressed after the Sasanid Dynasty came to power. Under the Sasanids, Persian culture was re-energized as the rulers looked back to the time when Persia was a great empire, the days long before Alexander's humiliating conquests. Persian art and literature was now less influenced by Greek models than it had been under the Parthians.

In keeping with their desire to revive Persian culture the Sasanids proclaimed the Zoroastrian religion to be the official creed of the empire and it was given the full support of the state. As we read in previous lessons the leaders of Sasanid Zoroastrianism exerted tremendous power in the empire. Their fervent desire to put an end all to foreign faiths in the empire ended a long tradition of religious tolerance that existed in Iranian lands up until the collapse of the Parthians.

A War with No End

As the Romans pushed eastward into Mesopotamia, the Parthians were pushing west into Syria. When these two empires collided, it sparked off a long series of wars between East and West that were to last until the coming of Islam.

The Sasanids picked up this fight where the Parthians had left off and fought against Rome and its Byzantine successor. Battles raged throughout the lands of Mesopotamia and Syria. These provinces were prime objectives as they were extremely rich in agricultural production and sat along important trade routes.

Despite being a traditional rival, Persia was important to Rome and the Mediterranean world for economic reasons. Persia controlled the trade routes leading to and from India and China thus the flow of silks, spices, ivory, perfume and precious stones. In the reverse, Roman manufactured goods like bronze, glass, olive oil and gold were items much desired in Persia.

Combined, Byzantium and Persia controlled a vast swath of the land stretching from Spain to Afghanistan. By the 5th and 6th centuries both empires were under pressure from the migrations of barbarian groups pouring out of the vast steppe lands to the north. As the

Southwest Asia was donimated by two rival superpowers locked in bitter struggle.

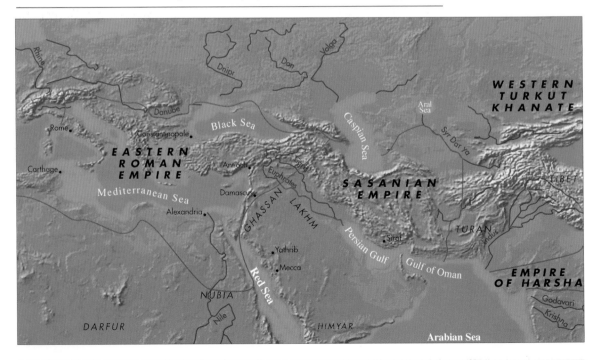

Khusrow Anoshirvan, "The Just" (531-579 CE)

Justinian's Persian counterpart and the most famous of all the Sasanid emperors, was a man named Khusrow I. He ruled during most of the 6th century CE and to his subjects he was called Khosrow 'The Just'. Like Justinian, Khusrow attempted to reform the empire by making taxes more bearable for the common people. He ordered the repair of roads and bridges, improving trade and people's lives in general. Khusrow ordered an imperial census taken that included the population, livestock, and fruit trees. He stationed unruly Iranian tribes on the borders to guard the empire's frontiers.

Khusrow led his armies against the enemies of his empire. He defeated the Byzantines on several occasions and concluded a number of peace treaties with Emperor Justinian, which were favorable to Persia. He sent a fleet down the coast of Arabia to attack the Christian king of Ethiopia, who was expanding his power into Yemen. As a result Khusrow was able to establish Persian control of Yemen that would last until the rise of Islam.

Romans had to deal with migrating Germanic tribesmen, the Sasanids had to come to grips with barbarian peoples from Central Asia who pressed southward into prosperous lands of Persia. These barbarian peoples brought considerable instability to the empire. Like a line collapsing dominos, these migrations caused Sasanid rule to weaken. Internal struggles soon began to break out among the nobility. Unstable government brought a disruption to trade and agriculture and the economy began to suffer. To make up for lost income the Sasanids began to ruthlessly tax their subjects, causing bitter resentment among the population.

Byzantium's Conflict with Persia

In 610 CE, Heraclius became emperor of Byzantium. In that year hundreds of miles to the south of Constantinople an upright Arab merchant by the name of Muhammad received the first revelations of the Qur'an in a cave on the Mountain of Hira.

By this time the period of great expansion that began under Justinian came to an end. The empire now faced attacks from all sides. The greatest threat came from the Persians as Khosrow II, the Sasanid *shah*, launched a offensive attack taking Syria, Palestine and Egypt from Byzantium. His armies sacked sacred Christian sites in Jerusalem and many Christian sacred relics, including objects associated with the lives of Jesus, his immediate followers, saints and martyrs were captured. The Sasanids furthered their success by invading Egypt, capturing the main source of grain for the Byzantine capital. Constantinople itself was besieged by Persia's allies, a Turkic tribe known as the Avars. It seemed that the Byzantine Empire would soon collapse.

Heraclius realized the gravity of the situation and took steps to save his empire. He collected

The Qur'an & the Last Great War between Byzantium and Persia

News of the violent struggle between the two empires of Byzantium and Sasanid Persia between 610-627 CE was well known to the peoples that lived in lands surrounding the main arena of conflict. As far away as Ethiopia, kings and rulers took an active interest in the outcome of this war. In Makkah too, the war became an issue in a great controversy. The opponents of the Prophet knew of the similarities between the Christians and the Muslims having heard Qur'anic revelations. The Prophet Muhammad made it clear that he was the spiritual successor of Jesus Christ who was sent by the same One God. When the pagans of Makkah learned of the seemingly unstoppable Sasanid offensive against Byzantium, they began to chide and mock the Prophet, "Look at your God, he can't even save an empire built in His name!" In response verses were revealed to the Prophet predicting, that despite overwhelming setback, the tables would soon turn and Byzantium would crush the Sasanids.

"Alif, Lam, Mim. The Romans have been defeated in a land near by. But they will, even after this defeat of theirs, soon be victorious, within a few years. With Allah is the control of the past and the future. On that day the believers shall rejoice."

(Surah ar-Rum, 1-4)

Despite this Qur'anic prediction, the unbelievers were so sure of the Sasanid victory they took out a wager on these verses. At first the Prophet was reluctant to enter into such frivolity, but his chief companion Abu Bakr came forward with a sum of money large enough to match their bet. Needless to say the wager was lost by the chiefs of Makkah. News came many months later that Heraclius and his Byzantine army had not only recaptured Palestine, Syria and Egypt but the Sasanid province of Iraq as well!

money from the church and the provinces to raise more troops. He made a separate peace with the Avars. Whatever was left of his army was reorganized and reinforced. Then a surprise counterattack was launched against the Persians. This completely caught the enemy unprepared. The Persians had overextended their lines of supply through their rapid conquests. They were also expecting the Byzantines to collapse, not fight back. But Heraclius did strike back and the Persian army collapsed. The Byzantine army threw the invaders back across the Tigris and were soon occupying the Sasanid imperial capital of Cstesiphon (Mada'in). Amid great celebration and pomp, Heraclius set out on pilgrimage to the holy sites in Jerusalem in an act of thanks to God for his victory over the Zoroastrians.

The long conflict between the Byzantine and the Persian empires exhausted the energy and resources of both, leaving them unprepared to face the force that was rising in the deserts of the south. Within a few decades Arab armies, motivated by the message of Islam, would be standing on the ruins of one and threatening the very existence of the other.

Lesson Review

1. How did the Sasanids try to support their rule with religion (also review Chapter 3)?

2. Describe some of the strengths and weaknesses of the Sasanid Empire.

3. Summarize the causes and effects of the conflict between Byzantine Rome and Sasanid Persia.

4. Contrast the influence of Hellenism on Persian and Roman culture, using examples from art, architecture and other evidences.

5. Compare and contrast the role of religion in the Sasanid and Byzantine empires.

6. How did the persecution of Christians affect Roman attitudes toward Christianity?

5. Using political, economic and physical maps, identify reasons for the conflict between Byzantium and Persia, and hold a panel discussion on the topic.

Lesson Three

Egypt and Ethiopia

Looking Ahead

As you read this lesson think about how the civilizations of Egypt and Ethiopia interacted with Southwest Asia before the rise of Islam.

Preview Vocabulary

Monophysite
Coptic
Nagasi
Muqawqas

The history of Egypt in the ancient world is so extensive that any discussion of it in detail would be well beyond the pages of this volume. A few important points, however, are relevant to our study of the centuries before the coming of Islam. Throughout its 5,000 years of recorded history Egypt relied on one thing: the water of the great Nile River. It is the Nile that provided a year-round source of water for crops. The fertile land along the banks of the Nile was an island in a sea of sand. Except for its northern coastline on the Mediterranean Sea desert surrounded Egypt on all sides. In the early period of its existence, before the rise of powerful empires in Mesopotamia this geographic reality shielded Egypt from frequent invasion.

As powerful empires arose in surrounding lands, with strong military organizations, the security that Egypt had enjoyed for centuries came to an end. Late in the 8th century BCE the Assyrian Empire added Egypt to its domains. A little over a hundred years after that the Persians destroyed Assyrian power and inherited control over the land of the Nile. The Persian were soon replaced by the Greeks in 332 BCE who were supplanted by the Romans, who added Egypt to their empire in 30 BCE.

Egypt under Byzantine Domination

With the conquests of Alexander the Great in the fourth century BCE, Greek culture had spread throughout the Mediterranean. The large Egyptian port city of Alexandria (which was founded by Alexander himself) served as a base for the spread of Hellenism throughout the land. As a port city it had a diverse population as traders and merchants who came from all over the known world to buy and sell. Alexandria was then regarded as one of the most important cities in the world. Trade flourished as luxury goods came up the Nile from the heart of Africa to be sold in the markets. People from all over the empire came to Alexandria to partake in its riches and its many centers of learning.

Despite the occupation of their land by foreign invaders, the peasant farmers of the Nile continued on with their lives as they had done since ancient times, setting their days to the rhythm of the river's annual floods. Most people in Roman and Byzantine Egypt were the descendants of the original ancient inhabitants and they spoke a language (Coptic) that originated in ancient times. The dominance of

the Arabic language that we see today in modern-day Egypt came only centuries after the Muslim conquest.

Before the spread of Christianity, Egypt was home to several different branches of Mystery Religions. Manichaean churches and at least one Buddhist monastery were also found here. An important center of Jewish culture was located in the city both before and after the Romans

Egypt of Antiquity

This ancient land along the Nile developed a centralized civilization long before anything comparable grew in Mesopotamia. Strong pharaohs began ruling the land from 3,000 BCE. Around 1,500 BCE Egypt became an imperial power by occupying Palestine and parts of Syria. This was the high point of Egyptian power. In the first millennium BCE, the empire began to lose its hold over its Southwest Asian provinces and suffered from invasions made by Libyans and Nubians as well. Finally, in 671 BCE the Assyrian army defeated the last pharaoh, Tirhaka. Egypt would remain under foreign rule for the next 2,000 years.

expelled the Jews from Palestine. But by the period of the Byzantine Empire the majority of the people of Egypt embraced Christianity.

"He is of but One Nature..."

Christianity took root in Egypt during the early second and third centuries CE. Most Egyptian Christians followed the Monophysite branch of Christianity. Monophysites differed from the official creed of the Roman Catholic and Greek Orthodox Churches on one issue: they believed that Jesus was wholly God, having no aspect of human nature, whereas the official church taught that Jesus had two natures, both human and divine.

Following the Council of Nicea in 325 CE, all who disagreed with the "two natures of Jesus" doctrine were excommunicated and persecuted. Holding fast to their beliefs, Egyptian Christians refused to accept these restrictions as well as the authority of the patriarch in Constantinople. Their priests formed their own organization, called the Coptic Church.

From its stronghold in Egypt, Monophysite Christianity spread into Sudan and Ethiopia. The Coptic Church became famous for the monasteries it built in the surrounding deserts, and for churches carved out of solid rock in Ethiopia.

The independence of the Coptic Church disturbed the Byzantine government. The Orthodox Church in Constantinople tried to eradicate Monophysite doctrines, often resorting to violence to bring conformity. The Copts nevertheless stood firm in their beliefs about Jesus. Between 616 and 623 CE, the Sasanid Persians captured Egypt from the Byzantines and openly allowed the Copts to practice their faith.

This relief did not last long. Heraclius' armies soon recaptured Egypt from the Persians, the persecution resumed. In 631 CE, the Byzantine emperor appointed a bishop by the name of Cyrus the Caucasian (known in Arabic sources as the *Muqawqas*) to preside over all of Egypt's Christians regardless of sect. Cyrus began to brutally suppress the Copts, closing their churches and killing their priests. This torment was only to be relieved with the Muslim invasion ten years later, an event which most of the Coptic population supported.

Kingdom of the Nagasi

By the 4th Century CE, Christianity had spread up the Nile River from Egypt into the highlands of Ethiopia. The kings of the city of Aksum officially adopted this faith and established up a large state that controlled much of the Horn of Africa and southern Arabia. The kings of Aksum were known as the *nagasi* (in Arabic sources *Najashi*).

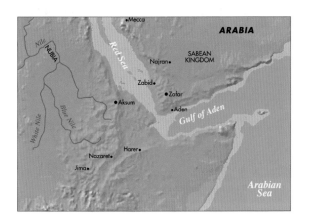

The great empire that was centered on the city of Aksum spread throughout the Horn of Africa and across the Red Sea to Yemen and southern Arabia. How would the empire's geographical location make it rich?

This photograph shows a young Emperor Haile Selassie the last in the very long line of monarchs to rule over Ethiopia. The monarchy ended in the 1970's when a communist-led revolution plunged the nation into turmoil and civil war.

Because of its geographical position, Aksum became a wealthy and influential state. Ethiopian ports were bustling with merchants who stopped to trade while traveling the sea lanes between India, Arabia, Egypt, and the Mediterranean. Foreign goods and cultures (notably the Greek language) were brought into Aksum along with products from the interior of Africa (like rare incense and ivory). The thriving Ethiopian economy allowed the *nagasi* of Aksum to mint fabulous coins that reflected the people's profound comprehension of economics.

Aksumite Ethiopia was also an imperial power. The powerful *nagasi*, 'Ezana (who began his rule around 320 CE), sent armies out to subdue an expanse of territory reaching from modern Sudanese city of Khartoum to Lake Rudolf to Somalia and further across the Red Sea into Yemen. 'Ezana was the first Ethiopian king to embrace Christianity. He outlawed the worship of the gods that his people had prayed to in the past.

All subsequent *nagasis* saw themselves as defenders of the Christian faith. In 523 CE, when the prince of the Yemeni city of Najran, Dhu-Nuwas, converted to Judaism and began to persecute his Christian population, 'Ella-Asbeha sent out an enormous army that defeated the Jewish prince. Then he placed a governor named Abraha to rule Yemen in his name.

The move to expand into the Yemen brought the Empire of Aksum into the struggle between Byzantium and Sasanid Persia. The *nagasis*, who were Christians, naturally allied themselves with the Byzantines. There were several skirmishes between the Sasanids and the Ethiopians in Yemen. The Persians supported the pagan Yemenis against the growing influence of Aksum. Eventually the power of Aksum began to decline and the Persians were able to take Yemen from the hold of the *nagasis*.

Lesson Review

1. How did the split between the Coptic and Byzantine Churches take place?

2. Describe Monophysite beliefs as compared with other Christian branches.

3. Why did Aksum become an important regional power? What geographical factors helped its rise to power?

Lesson Four

The Land of Arabia

Looking Ahead

What are the ways in which Arab culture differed from that of the more settled peoples of the Middle East?

Preview Vocabulary

Commerce
Adobe
Monsoon winds
Frankincense
Arabia Felix

Any description of the Arabian Peninsula presents us with a certain paradox. How could an area of the planet so barren and desolate be at the same time a center of commerce and a cradle of religious thought and culture? While much of Arabia is covered in inhospitable desert, it is neither totally barren nor desolate. Large portions of the peninsula can actually support limited human activity. But life here is fragile, with a narrow space between life and death. The loss of a single caravan, or a slight change in rainfall, could make the difference between prosperity and famine.

For thousands of years humans had been living in the Arabian Peninsula. In fact, there is evidence that this land was much more fertile in pre-historic times than it is now. There were tribes of Arabs living throughout the peninsula when Abraham and his son Isma'il settled in the barren valley of Makkah some time in the 2nd millennium BCE. Settlements based on commerce developed on the long coastlines of the Arabian Peninsula, and became stops on the sea routes to Asia. These towns supported the villages that were found further inland. In the regions of Yemen and Asir in the southwest, rainfall was sufficient enough to support agriculture which in turn supported fairly large populations.

Farming and Trade in Yemen

The geography of southern Arabia differs sharply from the rest of the peninsula. Benefiting from the monsoons that brought ships and rainfall to the coasts, Yemen had relatively fertile land unlike the dry deserts that covered the rest of the peninsula. Agriculture flourished in the rain-fed, terraced slopes of Yemen's rugged hills. Centuries before the birth of Jesus, organized states existed in Yemen. One of the best known of these was the Kingdom of Saba' with its famous queen, Bilqis, who was known as the Queen of Sheba in Biblical lore, and who is also mentioned in the Qur'an.

The ancient Yemenis showed great skill in agriculture and architecture. Throughout Yemen, cities were established with multi-storied buildings of clay bricks called adobe. They once constructed a remarkable earthen dam near a place called Ma'rib. Behind this dam rainwater was stored, allowing people to irrigate the land and increase crop production. Farms and orchards flourished, creating a wealthy, organized and powerful society.

Over the course of time focus on the agricultural activities of Yemen grew less important as trade and commerce between distant lands increased. Sea trade was encouraged by one important discovery. By the 1st century CE, sailors had learned to master the monsoon winds. With these winds they could travel speedily from India to Arabia in the winter, and return just as quickly in the summer, with the winds in reverse behind them. Egypt and India were only four months apart, and in those ancient days as many as 100 ships regularly traveled between the mouth of the Indus River and the Red Sea. Many of these stopped in the Yemen for both rest and trade.

The monsoon winds affect the entire Indian Ocean region and much of Asia. The monsoon results from the heating of masses of air being heated over the Asian land mass during the summer months from April to August. This creates a low-pressure zone that draws in moist air from the Indian Ocean, creating the monsoon rains. During the months from December to March, high-pressure systems force the air masses to flow southward from the Asian continent. During the cool months, the monsoon winds would carry ships from East Africa and Southern Arabia toward ports in India. During the warm months ships returned from India.

The Yemen merchants began carrying on extensive trade with India and East Africa. They produced and traded precious spices, scents and oils, particularly myrrh and frankincense, made from the sap of a small tree. Because of the sweet scents and other luxuries associated with it, southern Arabia became known to the Romans as *Arabia Felix*, or 'Pleasant Arabia.'

Trade in spices and other items from India made Yemen important to the societies of the Mediterranean and the Fertile Crescent. Trade

GEOGRAPHY & THE QUR'AN

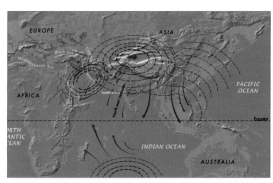

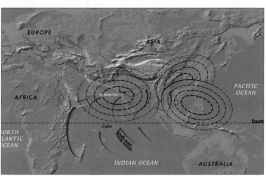

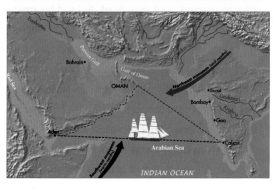

"For the Familiarity of the Quraish. Their Familiarity with the Journies by winter and summer. Let them worship the Lord of this House [The Ka'bah], who provides them with food against hunger and with security against fear."

(Qur'an 106:1-4)

The regular trading caravans mentioned in this surah were a vital part of life in Makkah and many other towns and tribes in the Arabian Peninsula. *Surah al Quraish* mentions the regular journeys in summer and winter upon which the Makkan tribe depended for its livelihood. These annual journeys were timed to the monsoon winds, which brought ships and their trade goods to the ports of Yemen during the winter season. The caravans traveled there to purchase goods, including incense from southern Arabia, silks, spices and perfumes, luxury good which they transported northward across Arabia for sale in Syria on their summer season voyage. This, in addition to the annual pilgrimage, was the source of Makkan wealth & power.

These vessels, known as dhows, still ply the Indian Ocean loaded with goods as they have done since time immemorial.

routes were established going north from the port of Aden up along the coast of the Red Sea towards Syria. All routes funneled goods back and forth between the southern ports and the large and ancient city of Damascus in Syria. Several towns sprang up along these paths and their economies were heavily dependent on the camel caravans going and coming from south to north to south. The largest and most important of these were the towns of San'a in Yemen, Makkah and Yathrib in Central Arabia, and Tabuk far to the north on the Syrian border.

The importance of sea trade routes increased with the continual fighting between the Sasanid and Byzantine Empires. These wars made land routes between China, India and the West so dangerous that more and more traders traveled by sea to southern Arabia and then had their

goods packed to the north. The need for this was increased by the collapse of the Kushan Empire in Afghanistan during the third century. The resultant unrest and disorder made the Silk Road virtually impassible.

Overland Routes & Northern Towns

The leaders of the empires centered on the fertile lands of Southwest Asia, and the Mediterranean viewed the Arabs as somewhat insignificant. Their arid homeland lay beyond the reach of imperial armies, and besides the random bedouin raid there was confidence that the tribes were completely unable to raise a force that could seriously threaten imperial interests. Apart from occasional service of its tribesmen in Byzantine and Sasanid armies and as a source of camels and horses for war, the desert had little to offer to these powers with their vast fertile lands and enormous wealth from the trade routes at their doorstep.

As with the Roman Empire before them, both the Byzantine and the Sasanid empires did hold some influence over the Arab tribes that lived close to the borders of their empires. The Byzantines were closely allied to the Christian Ghassanid tribe, whose lands were in the Syrian Desert. The Sasanids similarly allied themselves with the predominantly pagan Lakhmid tribe, which made its home in the regions now called Iraq. Northern Arab caravan towns like Palmyra and Petra had played important roles in Roman history and became important centers of trade.

This region was important to the Roman and Byzantine economies, and also to East Africa and other caravan cities in Arabia. It was becoming a key link in the ancient Indian Ocean basin trade. It was easier for Byzantine merchants to travel through the Red Sea and into the Indian Ocean than to risk sending goods overland through hostile Sasanid territory. Persia too, wanted to control the Yemen in order to block Byzantine trade and ruin their opponent's economy. Neither empire could exert much control over the Yemen, though a neighboring power briefly dominated the Yemen. During the 300's CE, Yemen and the Kingdom of Aksum became bitter rivals in dispute over trade, and Ethiopian troops invaded and occupied much of the Yemen for about forty years.

Religious tension in Southern Arabia

The main effect of the Ethiopian invasion was to introduce Christianity to the Yemen. Many Yemenis embraced the Ethiopian branch of Christianity forsaking the pagan faith of their forefathers. The town of Najran became an important center of Yemeni Christianity in the fifth century CE and it maintained close contacts with the churches in Ethiopia and Byzantine Syria.

As Christianity began to take hold in Yemen another religious group became influential in Arabia. In the ghastly aftermath of the anti-Roman revolts in Palestine of 132 CE, small bands of Jews migrated southward into the Arabian Desert via the existing trade routes. Some Jews traveled on to Yemen where they established settlements and influenced several local princes one of whom actually converted to Judaism. His name was Yusuf Ash'ar, better known in history as Dhu-Nuwas. After taking the throne, Dhu-Nuwas embarked on a campaign to eliminate Christianity from his kingdom. Because of their continued persecution by the church in Byzantine lands, many Jews view Christians with hostility and suspicion. Exercising their influence over Dhu-Nuwas, the Jews of Yemen exacted vengeance.

In 524 CE Dhu-Nuwas sent an army against the Christian tribes in northern Yemen and eliminated them with great ferocity. Encouraged by victory, Dhu-Nuwas marched to Najran and besieged the city. When the town surrendered Dhu-Nuwas announced that all Christians had to choose between conversion to Judaism or death. Most of Najrani Christians stood their ground and chose death.

Dhu-Nuwas' tyranny proved to be his undoing. News of the terror in Najran quickly spread to the Christian powers of Byzantium and Ethiopia. The emperor Justinian took action in his role as protector of Christianity, and entered into an alliance with the *nagasi* of Ethiopia, 'Ella-Asbeha. Their adherence to different branches of the Christian faith seemed less important than the massacre of Yemeni Christians by Dhu-Nuwas.

In 525 CE, the *nagasi* sent an army across the Red Sea to strike at Dhu-Nuwas, who was then defeated and killed. The Ethiopians placed a governor to rule over Yemen, although the Yemenis later rejected this foreign influence. Around 545 CE, a man from the nobility named Abraha gathered supporters and threw out the Ethiopian governor, declaring himself king of Yemen.

As soon as he took power, Abraha began a policy of persecuting Jews and pagans in revenge for the atrocities of Dhu-Nuwas. Despite his moves to strengthening Christianity in southern Arabia, Abraha spent much of his early reign developing the economy of the kingdom, which was centered on the city of San'a. He spent a considerable amount of money on irrigation and damming projects that improved the kingdom's agricultural wealth. Abraha also developed close relations with the Christian rulers of Byzantium and Aksum.

One of Abraha's more ambitious projects was the construction of a dazzling cathedral in the city of San'a. Abraha wanted to establish it as a center of pilgrimage, to gain from the prestige and commerce it would certainly attract. Over the mountains far to the north however, lay a rival town: Makkah. Located in a barren valley on the north-south trade route, Makkah was the site of the Ka'bah, a small, stone cubical shrine, a monument to Abraham's faith in one God. Despite its monotheistic origins, Makkah had become the center of polytheistic worship in the Arabian Peninsula. Together with the prestige and spiritual importance of its association with its religious heritage, the city's location on the trade routes contributed to its wealth.

In 570 CE King Abraha decided to march northward, subjugate Makkah and tear down the Ka'bah. But his attempt ended in utter failure as his army was stopped in its tracks at the outskirts of the town. The Yemeni army was beset by a plague that is attributed in the Qur'an to God's direct intervention to protect the house of worship that He commanded Ibrahim and Isma'il to build.

The attack on Makkah marked the end of Abraha's power and of Christian domination over Yemen. While Abraha was marching north against pagan Makkah, pagan and Jewish Yemeni tribes plotted to rid themselves of their Christian king. The Sasanids, always eager to tip the balance of power with Byzantium, sent a naval force to aid the rebellion. A detachment of their troops landed near the town of Aden, marched inland, and with the help of pagan and Jewish Yemenis, destroyed Abraha's kingdom. The Sasanids quickly placed their own governor in power over Yemen.

Lesson Review

1. What two sources of wealth helped Yemen prosper at different times in its history?

2. What groups and regional powers were involved in the episode of Dhu Nuwas?

3. What chapters of the Qur'an describe the incidents related to Dhu Nuwas and Abraha? Compare and contrast Qur'anic and political/historical views of these conflicts.

The Arab Heartland

Looking Ahead

Keep in mind the geographical effects that Arabia had on the people that live there. What are the ways in which lives and culture was shaped by the desert?

Preview Vocabulary

Sedentary
Pastoral
Infanticide
Bedouins
Zamzam
Hanifs

Central Arabia was populated by sedentary (settled townsfolk or farmers) and pastoral desert dwellers, people who moved from place to place tending herds of animals. They followed the seasonal vegetation and water supplies upon which they and their animals depended for survival. For them knowing the environment was crucial for survival. A portion of central and southern Arabia is called the *Rub'al-Khali,* the 'Empty Quarter', a deadly wasteland of shifting sands that has no water and can hardly be crossed even by the most experienced trackers. In other parts of central Arabia, however, pleasant oases of water and trees made agriculture and towns possible.

Rough Land, Rough Life

Land that might seem barren to the untrained eye was a place of comfort and beauty to the pastoral Arab. They were skilled in finding gullies where sufficient water collected to nourish grasses, flowers, or even thorny vegetation on which goats and camels could survive. The nomadic life made it a necessity to have knowledge of changes in the weather, wind, water, plant cycles, the needs of animals and people. They lived with few material possessions, all of which, after quickly breaking camp, could be transported on their animals.

In many rural parts of the Arab world, the camel is still an important animal in daily life.

The Bedouin Tradition

Nomadic Arab groups, often called Bedouins, lived in extended family units made up of near relatives that made a clan. Groups of related clans formed a tribe. Tribal leaders were generally the older and more experienced men, the most senior of whom was called *shaikh*. The *shaikh* made final decisions in all tribal matters, but not before the men had met in council to discuss and debate. Women generally did not meet in the men's councils. However they might influence events through their husbands by working within their clans. Arab women did not enjoy secure rights to life, status and wealth under the nomadic tribal system. Women did not always enjoy decision-making authority even over their own marriage or divorce.

Bedouins did not establish permanent dwellings, but rather lived in tents made of goat or camel hair. They wove bags, decorative rope and made rugs and tent cloth. Their diet consisted mainly of milk as well as yogurt and cheese, made to preserve the milk. They ate meat occasionally, especially for celebrations. In towns or oases, they traded sheep and goats, wool and leather for dried dates, vegetables and grains such as barley used for bread. Seasonal market fairs supplied metal goods such as brass tools, cooking pots, weapons and jewelry.

Part of the bedouins' relationship with the townsfolk was their ability to supply riding animals for trading caravans and for war. In addition, they supplied guides and protective forces traveling merchants. Traditional alliances frequently developed between certain tribes and towns, or between traders and the tribes along a given caravan route. Perhaps the alliances involved a branch of the tribe that had settled but traced its earlier roots to the desert life. In any case, sedentary and pastoral folk shared complementary ways of life.

The bedouins developed a culture that suited their isolated and often dangerous life. In a man they looked for bravery and strength in battle, intelligence, generosity and hospitality to the guest. Eloquence in Arabic language was also highly prized. For them, the greatest qualities in a woman, aside from producing sons, were obedience, loyalty and strength.

Unrestrained Freedom

Their greatest treasure and source of their honor was freedom. They were fiercely independent, and did not easily fall under the rule of settled powers or empires. Arab tribesmen or entire tribes served on occasion in the armies of

The Wondrous Physiology of the Camel

The camel is an amazing creature that is perfectly adapted for travel in the harshest desert regions. First, it can store water in the fat of its hump, drinking over 50 gallons at one time, then going up to 8 days without. Its eyelids and nostrils can close to protect it from blowing sand and dust. It has long legs and wide, tough, cushioned footpads that allow it to walk or run on shifting sand or stony ground—as much as 20-25 miles in one stretch. Its thick light coat of hair insulates against both cold and heat, and makes fine woolen cloth. It gives vitamin-rich milk, and its meat is very tasty and nutritious, providing food for the people who tend the herds. Finally, the camel has very strong bones, with an arched spine that allows it –properly loaded and saddled – to carry much bigger loads than other pack animals—between 400 and 600 pounds or more. What is more, the camel has a generally gentle nature that allows as many as six animals to be managed in a string by one person. Because they are large, tall, swift, and very maneuverable by a skilled rider, they can be very effective military mounts as well.

It is not fully certain where and when camels became domesticated for herding and transportation, but they certainly appeared more than one millennium BCE, both in Africa, the Arabian Peninsula, and Asia. In the Middle East, camels were certainly being raised by many tribes around Syria and Mesopotamia by 700 BCE. Its increasing use for trade and transport between 500 and 100 BCE means that the pastoral desert tribes breeding camels were becoming fully integrated into these cultures' economies, politics and military. Roman and Nabatean coins and other pictorial sources tell historians that one clue to this development might have been a simple technological invention: a new type of North Arabian saddle that fit over the camel's hump. This allowed a rider to hold fast, and pack weight to be distributed onto the animal's strong rib cage. Historians think that this type of saddle was important to the rise of nomadic Arabian tribes and Arab cities shortly before the rise of Islam.

For thousands of years dates have been a staple source of food in Arabia. Even today dates are harvested with great skill.

great powers, but usually on their own terms, and only when they saw the possibility of material gain. Arab nomadic tribesmen excelled as warriors because of their skill in riding and hunting, and their endurance under harsh conditions. Generosity to guests was both a virtue and a necessity. In the desert, a stranger - whether friend or foe - was welcomed with food, lodging, conversation, and protection. Arab legends feature amazing feats of hospitality and bravery. One of these figures was the famous Hatim al-Ta'i, who once gave all he possessed to a stranger who stopped at his home for dinner.

Tribes did not always co-exist in harmony. Each group of tribes inhabited traditional grazing lands known to others, and interlopers were fair game. Drought conditions might force nearby tribes to compete for scarce water and grazing. In such cases, loyalty toward one's own tribe won out over other impulses. Competition and complex tribal relations included frequent raiding. One tribe's men mounted their fastest animals, made a lightning attack on another

tribe's camp, grabbing what they could carry - including animals and women - and raced away.

Though injury or death might result, the point was merely plunder. Each side knew that a raid would sooner or later be avenged. Mutual raiding was part of the bedouin way of life, and seeking reprisal was also part of the code of honor for a tribe or individual. If they were not ransomed with goods or money, captives became slaves. Thus the son of a tribal chief might become a slave overnight, as was the case of Zaid ibn Haritha, a tribesman who came to live in the house of the Prophet Muhammad. Feuds and rivalries among tribes might go on for centuries, causing great bloodshed and community friction.

Oasis Towns: Makkah & Yathrib

Oasis were sometimes little more than a spring where underground water bubbled near the surface and fed a few palms, or they may have been seasonal wells with brackish water. Some oasis, however, supported villages and towns. Water was seen as a blessing and oases were the key to survival for desert dwellers and traveling merchants, who knew exactly where they were and how many days travel lay between them. Men knew how to read the signs of nature such as storms, stars and animal traces.

Oases were places of exchange and rest. Even now, the English word 'oasis' means a place of beauty and rest. The inhabitants of most oasis traced their roots to desert tribes whose ancestors had settled to cultivate the land, but maintained relations with their nomadic cousins.

The central Arabian towns of Makkah and Yathrib played a crucial role in the history of Islam have been of great interest to historians, so more is known about these towns than others. Makkah was had an oasis with a famous source of water. According to traditional sources, the Arab tribe of Banu Jurhum, was migrating in search of water when they saw birds circling over a barren valley of then known as Bakka. There the Banu Jurhum found Hagar, wife of Abraham, and her son Isma'il living in the vicinity of a well now known as Zamzam. Marveling at the appearance

of the woman, her son and a spring that seem to have appeared in the desert, they asked permission to remain there. The Bani Jurhum tribe stayed, married one of their women to Isma'il, and a settlement grew up around the oasis. The spring called Zamzam, however, was never used for agriculture. Makkah drew its livelihood from from the trade passing between the Indian Ocean, Africa and the Mediterranean.

Makkah was also the site where the Ka'bah, a simple stone house of worship, was constructed by Abraham. According to tradition, Abraham and his son Isma`il had constructed and dedicated the Ka'bah to the worship of the One God. Yet in the centuries that followed, the monotheism of Abraham was corrupted by the introduction of idols and pagan rites, which turned the Ka'bah into a well-known polytheistic temple.

About 250 miles north of Makkah was the town of Yathrib, a collection of several large villages, some with fortresses-like, multi-story dwellings each having large, heavy doors and windows only in the upper parts. The town was

Settled tribes in the Arabian Peninsula often lived in communities comprised of several walled compounds.

so spread out that it took half a day to walk from one end to the other. Yathrib was encircled by a lava field whose fertile volcanic soil and ample water supported orchards and gardens. The city's date palms are still famous today.

Settled Life of Central Arabia

Desert Arabs were not fond of townspeople and viewed the settled lifestyle as soft, unmanly and unhealthy. While they might sometimes envy the wealth of townsfolk, the bedouin loved the freedom that their sedentary brethren sacrificed in pursuit of material comfort. In any case, both groups benefited from the other. Townsmen needed the bedouin for pack animals and for their skill as desert guides. Passage of the caravans depended on good relations with the bedouins to prevent banditry. The bedouins gained from the townsfolk's skill in trade, and drew a share of the wealth for their services.

The central Arabian towns drew substantial wealth from trade routes that crossed the peninsula, both the north-south routes and the less important east-west routes from Iraq and the Persian Gulf to Egypt and Ethiopia. Merchant traders in the towns grew skillful in the arrangement and management of the trade caravans. Relations between the settled and nomadic Arabs were sometimes peaceful and on occasion erupted into strife. In time, the more powerful tribes in the wealthy towns, such as the Quraish at Makkah, made efforts to head alliances of tribes.

Though many townsfolk thought of the bedouin as ignorant and crude, they held a deep respect for their own desert roots. It was the custom of noble families to send small children out to be raised in bedouin families for the first few years of their lives. The urban Arabs believed the bedouin lifestyle to be closer to the original Arab character, and healthier in a time when plagues and epidemics could strike down whole populations in a short time. Because of this practice, many Arabs of noble families had two mothers, one in the city and one in the desert, having been nursed by both.

Makkah and Yathrib were small compared with great cities in Iraq or Syria. Makkah housed many pilgrims during the Hajj season, but the usual population might be counted only in the hundreds. During four sacred months, raids and fighting were forbidden. This period was important to Makkans because it protected trade and the flow of pilgrims.

Unlike the bedouins, townsfolk lived in houses. These were made of mud brick or stone. Depending on wealth and status, an Arab house might be an elaborate dwelling or a one-room hut. Wood was extremely scarce, and roof beams and pillars were made of palm branches. A wooden door or chest were considered valuable treasures. The wealthy, of course, enjoyed luxuries from Syria, Ethiopia and India.

The diet of the townsfolk was simple (even among the rich): dates, barley bread, vegetables, and occasionally meat. They drank beverages made from milk, dates and grain, some of which were alcoholic. Milk from goats, sheep, and camels was readily available. Like other inhabitants of harsh lands, they were used to surviving on little food. But when the caravans arrived, food might be plentiful for a while: spices from the south or from India, strange fruits, dried ginger, and even sugar.

The Arabs dressed simply. Men wore a long ankle-length shirt, much like today's *thaub* or *jalabiyyah*. Another common form of dress was simple cloth wrapped around the waist. In

The Pre-Islamic Poetry of the Arab People

Arabic poetry, the highest art form of a people whose libraries were the oral tradition housed in their collective memory, used the rich vocabulary and grammar to portray the landscape, the values and the experiences of the desert Arabs. The tradition of Arabic poetry that continued in the towns, where competitions were held and poets were highly esteemed. At the fairs, the local market towns and in Makkah during certain seasons, poets were heard to recite stories of their tribe's lineage, its exploits in battle, the landscape and seasons in their territory, as well as romances of love and heroism. Expressions of love, respect and stories of great women are known in the tradition of poetry from this period. The tradition of Arabic poetry became an important feature of Muslim culture in lands as far from Arabia as Central Asia and Spain. Many scholars of literature and culture trace a link between Arabic poetry and the knightly literature of romance and chivalry, which originally means horsemanship. The beauty of the Arabian horse, among the world's finest breeds, was a common subject of pre-Islamic poetry in itself. In the European knightly tradition, chivalry meant the conduct and bravery of a warrior as his lady's champion, his skill in battle and his refinement, which were much influenced by contact with Arab culture in Spain. The following is a brief sample of pre-Islamic Arabic poetry featuring some of these themes:

Early in the morning, while the birds were still nesting, I mounted my steed.
Well-bred was he, long-bodied, outstripping the wild beasts in speed,
Swift to attack, to flee, to turn,
Yet firm as a rock swept down by the torrent,
Bay-colored, and so smooth the saddle slips from him, as the rain from a smooth stone,
Thin but full of life, fire boils within him like the snorting of a boiling kettle;
He continues at full gallop when other horses are dragging their feet in the dust for weariness.
A boy would be blown from his back,
And even the strong rider loses his garments.
Fast is my steed as a top when a child has spun it well.
He has the flanks of a buck, the legs of an ostrich, and the gallop of a wolf.
From behind, his thick tail hides the space between his thighs,
And almost sweeps the ground.
When he stands before the house,
His back looks like the huge grinding-stone there.
The blood of many leaders of herds is in him,
thick as the juice of henna in combed white hair

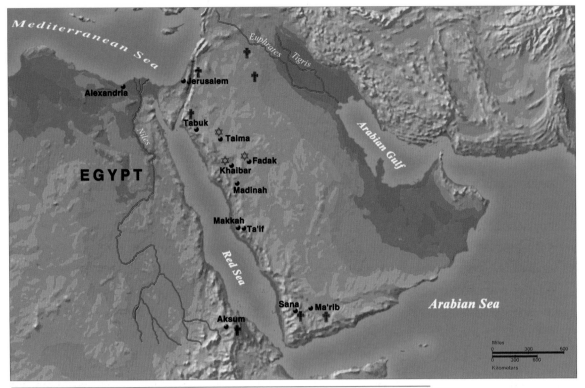

The Arabian Peninsula was dominated by ancient pagan religious traditions. However scattered communities of Jews and Christians could be found.

winter or on cold evenings, people wrapped themselves in woolen blankets or cloaks. Arab men wrapped turbans to protect their heads from the harsh desert sun, or draped a cloth into a sort of hood. Both men and women often braided their long hair.

Women wore simple long robes, embroidered or plain. Women and men wore leather or woven belts and leather sandals or boots, while the accessories of the poor were made from palm fiber. Jewelry might be worn, with gold and jewels only for the wealthiest. Fine, tightly woven textiles were imported from Syria, India, Africa or even China, but only the wealthy could afford such luxury fabrics.

Social Structure in Arabian Towns

The tribe and family were the only social institutions in Arab life. Business ventures, marriages, and travel were undertaken with the advice and consent of tribal elders. Nearly everyone who lived in Arabian towns was under the protection of some tribe and clan. If a person such as a foreigner or slave had no family ties, he needed affiliation with an existing tribe and clan. Such persons became confederates, (or in Arabic, *mawla*), meaning that they enjoyed the protection of a clan without which he was an unprotected outcast. This system lasted well into the early Islamic period, when most non-Arab converts, attached to one of the Muslim Arab tribes, were known as *mawalis*.

Leading male clan members managed the affairs of town and tribe. From about 400 CE, the Quraish had become the most powerful tribe in Makkah and the surrounding area, with, the clans of Makhzum, 'Abd al-Dar and Hashim as the strongest. The chiefs of these families met near the Ka'bah to consult about business, care of the pilgrims, and other matters. Their decisions were the law of the city. Power might shift among the members of this group based on family prestige, wealth or personality. Wealth was not always decisive, and a poorer member of a prestigious clan might influence the council more than a rich clansman of less important family. In traditional Arab life, family honor and genealogy were very important.

Since Makkah was not a farming society, class was based not on land ownership but on the business of trade and the wealth it brought. A clever businessman who employed an agent or accompanied the caravan himself, might gain a fine profit and a respectable name. Townsmen owned property in the city, but the rights in the desert were governed by traditional use and sometimes force of arms.

The annual pilgrimage was the other source of income for the Makkans. During the month of Hajj, and three other months of safety, people could travel without fear of armed attack. During those months the city was crammed with Arab pilgrims and merchants from near and far. Then as now, while they attended to the rites of worship, they purchased supplies, paid for lodgings and food, and often bought and sold goods in the city's markets.

The Makkans offered food and water to the pilgrims as a special privilege and duty, but the pilgrims paid for many other services. The Quraish's role as custodians of the Ka'bah and its sacred statues were the basis of their prestige, honor, and wealth. Combined with their prominent role in long-distance trade, it also gave them a position of influence among the tribes of the peninsula.

Crudely carved stones like this one were worshiped throughout Arabia.

Other than the merchants, crafts-persons like tailors, leatherworkers, potters, metalworkers and bakers pursued their livelihood, but generally had little influence and enjoyed few rights. Slaves occupied the lowest ranks in urban Arab society. Slaves were persons captured in raids, kidnapped, or purchased elsewhere. Some slaves were trained in a craft and put to work for their master. Others made domestic life easy for the master and mistress of the household. Some masters treated slaves like members of the family, while many suffered mistreatment. Regardless of the treatment, however, slaves were considered property and lived without social rights or rank. Male or female, they could be married off, bought, or sold, beaten, tortured, or killed, and no one else could do anything but disapprove.

As we have read above the status of Arab women was lowly compared to men's. Nowhere did females enjoy the same rights as males. They could easily be divorced, and men often married many wives at the same time and kept the company of slave girls. Daughters were viewed by many Arab men as an unneeded burden on the family and a risk to its honor, since sons were prized above all else. Female infanticide, the killing of newborn baby girls, was common as having too many daughters was seen as something less than manly. Women did sometimes inherit wealth, however, and a woman of good family could become quite wealthy and powerful even though she remained under the command of her husband or other males in her family.

It is probably unwise to generalize about the lives of Arab women in the towns and desert tribes, however, since the scant clues about ancient Arab social life show quite a lot of variety. For example, there may have been situations in which women had children of various fathers, and stayed with their own family rather than their husband's. Morals were an outgrowth of the social situation. The men could do nearly anything except damage the honor of their family or their city. Mistreating a person of lower status, visiting a prostitute, or cheating at business may not have affected personal honor in every case. Honor came from lineage, generosity to family and guests, bravery in battle and often, but not always, wealth.

Arabian Religious Beliefs

In the centuries after the time when the Prophet Ibrahim established monotheism, Arab religion degenerated into a primitive form of polytheism. While the pre-Islamic Arabs seem to have vaguely acknowledged the God of Ibrahim, Allah, they claimed that other gods, angels and *jinn* might be worshiped as a way to approach the All-Powerful Creator. Because of this, 'Abd al-Muttalib, the grandfather of Prophet Muhammad, did not contradict himself when he told Abraha that Allah was the God of the Ka'bah, even though he also believed in Hubal. The Arabs claimed that Allah had entrusted certain powers to others, such as the goddesses, al-Lat and al-'Uzza and Manat. The Ka'bah was still honored as an ancestral holy place, a site of pilgrimage for tribes in Arabia, but by then it housed hundreds of idols.

The Arabs also adopted gods from neighboring cultures to which they had been exposed. Thus the goddess al-'Uzza, who was like the Roman Venus, had a central shrine in the valley of Nakhlah, south of Makkah. The god al-Lat had a large temple in Ta'if in the mountains east of Makkah. Hubal had a distinctive image inside the Ka'bah and was the favorite deity of the Quraish.

Veneration of these gods and goddesses took many forms. Most people worshiped the forms of their deities in wood, stone, or clay. They included singing, dancing, sacrificing of animal and various prohibitions and taboos. Arab culture entertained many superstitions. People used to consult magicians, shamans and oracles about the future and for protection against evil.

Arab religion related mostly to securing the fortunes of life as it acknowledged that greater, unseen powers that deeply affected their lives. Arab polytheism was not tied to a strong ethical and moral system, nor did it emphasize reward or punishment in any but the most materialistic terms. The world beyond the visible was viewed as a realm which might speak through magic, dreams and omens. They worshiped the gods for good luck, protection from disaster, and as a link to their ancestors, providing a constant thread that bound together tribal and family life with the natural and spiritual world around them.

Despite the depth of paganism and superstition among the Arabs few individuals upheld a simple, pure faith in the God of Abraham. These men and women were known as the *Hanifs*, or righteous ones, and they did not associate any of the pagan gods or idols with Allah. Some of the *Hanifs* were familiar with revealed scriptures, while others sought more personal paths to God, often in isolation from society. The *Hanifs* (like many Christians and Jews) believed that the scriptures contained news of a coming Prophet and each generation awaited his arrival.

Jews and Christians in Arabia

Although they were never numerous in Central Arabia, three Jewish tribes existed in and around Yathrib, and by 600 CE large Jewish settlements were found north of Yathrib at the oasis of Khaibar and Fadak. The Jews living in Arabia were mostly farmers and craftsmen. Their way of life was much like that of the Arabs around them, but they kept to their own religion, looking down on the Arabs with contempt because of their polytheism.

Few Christian lived in Central Arabia, and those who did lived as hermits or monks devoted to spiritual exercises. Others, like Khadijah's cousin Waraqa, strove for a devotional life more satisfying than the idolatry of their fellow Arabs. Christianity barely penetrated Central Arabia, perhaps because of the Jewish and Persian influence that was strong there. Many Arabs openly sympathized with the Sasanids in their hostility towards Christianity, and the Sasanid leaders exploited these sympathies as a buffer against Byzantine expansion.

Jews, Christians and the occasional *Hanif* do not seem to have suffered persecution by the Arabs, who valued individuals much less than the tribe. As long as the stability of society was intact, they were ignored. Jews and Christians established places in the local society and did not disturb the established order. The value placed on freedom might even grant a person some degree of respect for the strength of their convictions.

Lesson Review

1. Describe the relationship between tribes of the desert and the towns. What causes for conflict or cooperation were present among tribes, among towns, and between nomadic and settled groups?

2. Why did the desert tribes place such a high value on honor, generosity and freedom?

3. How might women of the towns or the desert tribes have been more influential in their societies? Why?

4. How was knowledge of the history of the Arabs and of the Ka'bah transmitted even though most Arabs practiced polytheism. What importance did this heritage hold for them?

Chapter Review

1. Describe the goods and routes involved in from southern to northern Arabia. What other hemispheric trade routes led into northern cities like Palmyra and Nabatean Petra?

2. Explain the roles of pastoral nomads, farmers and merchant groups in defining the situation in the Arabian Peninsula before the rise of Islam. In what ways were their ways of life complementary.

3. Compared with the frequent conflicts among the civilizations in the Mediterranean region of Southwest Asia and North Africa, why did Central Arabia and the Yemen usually remain free of interference from regional powers?

4. Do a research project on areas that are currently being farmed in modern countries in the Arabian Peninsula. What sources of water are being used for agriculture, and what crops are being raised.

5. In what ways did the Arabic language contribute to cultural and artistic life among the Arabs of town and desert. Why was it so important.? Compare this trait with the use of language among other peoples with pastoral roots.

6. Compare and contrast pagan or polytheistic practices among Greeks, Romans, Persians and Arabs. What elements of monotheism appear in all of these, and how are they expressed?

Unit Two

Muhammad, Messenger of Allah

Chapter One

The Early Years

Lesson One

The Year of the Elephant

Looking Ahead

Recognize the religious and political influences in the Arabian Peninsula that provoked the "Year of the Elephant"

Preview Vocabulary

Zamzam
Shaman

'Abd al-Muttalib's Test

One night a man of Makkah named 'Abd al-Muttalib had a dream in which he was commanded to search for the long lost well of Zamzam, which according to legend, was once found in the vicinity of the sacred Ka'bah. The next morning 'Abd al-Muttalib began his search. Doing so he not only found the ancient spring but a treasure that Banu Jurhum had buried when they were forced out of Makkah many generations before. The main tribe of Makkah, the Banu Quraish, made a claim to the ownership of the well, but 'Abd al-Muttalib refused, because he claimed that the God of their ancestor Abraham had purposely singled him out.

But the chiefs of the town refused to relent on their claim. So to settle the dispute, they agreed to consult a shaman, a person regarded as having access to the world of unseen spirits. But when they did they found that the shaman agreed with 'Abd al-Muttalib's position and the chiefs reluctantly conceded. In a show of gratitude 'Abd al-Muttalib made a vow to sacrifice one of his boys at the Ka'bah if he ever should father ten sons.

The years went by and 'Abd al-Muttalib was eventually given ten strong sons. When they had all reached adulthood, he told them of the vow he made many years before. Being dutiful sons, they told their father that they would do whatever he wished. 'Abd al-Muttalib had all of his sons' names written on arrows and given to a priest of the god Hubal. The arrows were shuffled and drawn. Then whoever's name was on that arrow would give up his life to preserve his father's vow and his honor. The result indicated that the youngest son 'Abdullah was to be sacrificed. The venerable tribal chief reluctantly took his son to the Ka'bah to be sacrificed. However this was easier said than done. Realizing that 'Abd al-Muttalib was really going to go through with the act 'Abdullah's uncles and as well as his brothers scurried to stop the murder. They suggested to 'Abd al-Muttalib to again consult a shaman to see if there could be a way to override the vow. Needless to say 'Abd al-Muttalib eagerly accepted this suggestion.

The shaman ordered that arrows be drawn again. A bundle of arrows was brought in with one having the young boy's name etched on it. Every time 'Abdullah's name was picked ten camels were to be sacrificed and the drawing repeated. This was repeated until the number of the camels amounted to one hundred. Then in place of his youngest son these 100 camels were to be sacrificed. The entire process was completed and the 100 camels were taken out and slaughtered. For a week the whole town of Makkah feasted on roasted camels and 'Abd al-Muttalib rested with the satisfaction of having fulfilled his original vow of gratitude. The young 'Abdullah survived, for he was destined to play a greater role in history: He was to become one day the father of Muhammad.

A New Power Rises in Yemen

As 'Abd al-Muttalib uncovered the ancient well of Zamzam the Ethiopian Empire became embroiled in Yemeni politics. As we have read in the previous unit, the Ethiopians invaded southern Arabia to protect the Christian population from continued torment inflicted upon them by Yemen's Jews and their pagan allies. But Ethiopian

dominance over Yemen did not last long. Some time around 545 CE, one of the *nagasi's* governors in Yemen (a man named Abraha), threw off Ethiopian rule established himself as king.

As a devout Christian, Abraha desired to spread his faith. He order the construction of a massive church in the city of Sana'. He desired for it to become such a spiritual and economic attraction that it would rival the Ka'bah in Makkah.

Much to Abraha's disappointment his church did little to assist in the spread of Christianity throughout Arabia. Most Yemenis remained followers of the polytheistic religion of their forefathers. Christianity was only practiced by the people who lived along the Red Sea coast and in a few large towns. For these pagan Yemenis, and for most Arabs, the center of their religion remained the Ka'bah.

Angered at the failure of his building project, Abraha plotted to destroy the Makkan rival of

The Assault of King Abraha in the Qur'an

The Qur'an mentions the failed attempt of Abraha to destroy the ancient shrine of Abraham in Makkah. It stood as a reminder to the pagan Makkans of the Prophet's time as to the power of God to overcome anything.

"Have you not remembered how your Lord dealt with the people of the Elephant? Did He not make their plans useless? And sent against them flights of birds; Which pelted them with stones of clay; And He made them shrivel up like dry leaves."

(Qur'an 105:1-5)

his great cathedral. He believed that if the ancient shrine of the Ka'bah were to be torn down, all would be forced to focus their spiritual attention on his cathedral, drawing prestige and income to his kingdom. A call went out to gather for war. Though now well advanced in years, Abraha led his army north toward Makkah in 570 CE. His forces included his loyal Ethiopian bodyguards, Yemeni tribesmen and one or more war-elephants.

The Attack on Makkah

After several weeks march up the Red Sea coast, Abraha's army finally reached the outskirts of Makkah. Upon hearing of the impending attack, the Makkans abandoned the city days earlier in great terror. The people fled to the rugged hills that surrounded the town and prepared themselves to witness the destruction of their sacred site. But one brave soul stayed on: Abd al-Muttalib.

In an attempt to ward off the assault Abd al-Muttalib came forward to open negotiations with Abraha. The two men met and Abraha, impressed with 'Abd al-Muttalib's integrity, asked him to state the terms of surrender. 'Abd al-Muttalib made only one condition: that Abraha pay for the sheep that his men requisitioned from the townsfolk for food. Abraha expected the old chief to beg that the Ka'bah be spared from destruction. When asked about this 'Abd al-Muttalib explained, "I am the protector of my people's sheep. I am responsible for them. However Allah is the owner and protector of the Ka'bah. He will take care of it Himself."

The negotiations ended and Abraha ordered his men to begin the attack the next day. But when the time came the assault ran into unforeseen problems. The war-elephants refused to budge, despite all efforts to prod them forward. Abraha's men began to worry that this was some evil omen. According to both traditional sources and the chapter of the Qur'an called "The Elephant" (al-Fil) a vast flock of birds suddenly swooped down over the Yemeni army, pelting it with small stones, decimating the ranks. Unable to withstand this supernatural force, the power of Abraha's army melted away. Many men died (including of Abraha) from some untold disease that was thought to be contained in the small stones. The threat to the Ka'bah came to an end. Word soon spread far and wide of how Allah saved His sacred house and the reputation of the Bani Quraish being a special people went with it.

Following the collapse of the Yemeni assault on Makkah, Abraha's two sons took control of his kingdom. They were less talented than their father in preserving Christian rule. Soon pagan and Jewish Yemenis overthrew these two incompetent rulers with the help of the Sasanid Persians. Yemen once again shifted its loyalty, this time from the Christian Byzantine Empire and Aksum to the Zoroastrian Sasanid Empire.

Lesson Review

1. What are the benefits for any city of attracting visitors? List several sacred sites in the world that continue to draw people. What modern sites and events do cities try to attract?

2. Why do you think the Makkans reacted to the invasion by retreating to the hills? How did 'Abd al-Muttalib's reaction differ?

Early Life of the Prophet

As you read this lesson, think about the social standing of the Prophet among the people of Makkah. What his personal qualities that would later benefit the credibility of Islam.

Preview Vocabulary

Year of the Elephant
al-Sadiq
al-Amin
War of Fijar
Abu Talib
Khadijah

Muhammad was born in the same year that Abraha's army failed to destroy the Ka'bah. This year came to be known in Arab tradition as the "Year of the Elephant". Muhammad's father 'Abdullah, was one of the ten sons of of the city's patriarch 'Abd al-Muttalib. Like many Makkans 'Abdullah engaged in trade and during one of his business trips to Madinah he died in the months before Muhammad was born. His young wife Amina would now be forced to raise their son on her own. In keeping with Arab custom the infant Muhammad was sent by his mother to live with a wet-nurse who lived among local bedouins. Muhammad returned to his mother at the age of five or six years only to have her die shortly thereafter. The orphaned lad was taken in by his distinguished grandfather, who cared for him with great love. But after two years 'Abd al-Muttalib succumbed to his advanced years and Muhammad was again left alone. Fortunately Muhammad had plenty of uncles and he went to live with another son of 'Abd al-Muttalib, Abu Talib, a man who looked after him until he was married.

From Child to Man

Abu Talib cared for Muhammad as if he were his own child. Despite the fact that Abu Talib's clan, the Bani Hashim, enjoyed

An Event that Changed the World

"During this year a most dread event took place. For the sun gave forth its light without brightness ... and it seemed exceedingly like the sun in eclipse, for the beams it shed were not clear." [Procopius 536 CE]

Less than 30 years prior to the birth of the Prophet Muhammad something very drastic happened to the planet that effected the entire course of history. Climate changes do not just make sea levels rise in a few unfortunate locations or make life miserable for El Niño victims. They have the capacity to change the economic, political and demographic shape of the world. According to historian David Keys, the last time global climate changes transformed our planet in this way was back in the sixth century CE. In today's world climate change is mostly a result of man-made polution. But 1,500 years ago it was triggered by a massive volcanic eruption (believed to have occured in 535 CE) in Southeast Asia. Following this event the sky went black and winter gripped the earth for two years causing famine, drought and the spread of disease. The old way of life was swept away, setting in motion a chain of events which included plague, barbarian migrations and social revolution.

We have several eyewitness accounts describing what might in our time be call a "nuclear winter", a phenomenon caused by the atmosphere being so choked with ash that the sun becomes completely blocked out. According to the Syrian Bishop, John of Ephesus *"The sun became dark...Each day it shone for about four hours, and still this light was only a feeble shadow."* An Chinese chronicler from the same period stated that: *"Yellow dust rained like snow. It could be scooped up in handfuls."*

One example of the environmental change can be seen with the spread of the plague. It seems that the disease had long been present among rodent populations in East Africa, but it was the climactic disaster following 535 CE which enabled the disease to spread outside its normal territory. Cooler weather increased the population of the fleas that carried the plague. Once the disease had broken out of its normal territory, it appears to have spread throughout much of Africa – and northward into the Mediterranean world. Its journey to Europe and the Middle East was by way of the Red Sea. It was probably the ivory-trade vessels which introduced bubonic plague into the Mediterranean world. The plague also fundamentally changed the culture and the economy across vast swathes of eastern and southern Africa. Agriculture declined in many areas because plague-carrying rodents were more attracted to agricultural settlements and their stores of grain.

One interesting note is the fact that all of the traditional accounts of the birth of the Prophet Muhammad mentioned that this event was tied to very visible and unusual natural phenomena, like the shaking of the earth, blotting out of the sun and the like. Perhaps these new scientific and historical discoveries will lend credence to these accounts.

Muhammad spent much of his childhood as a shepherd. Years later he was reported to have said, "Allah did not send any prophet who did not tend sheep."

great prestige in Makkah, it was not particularly wealthy or politically powerful. Nevertheless the young Muhammad was well cared for. As a young boy he was not like the other children of town. While the upper-class Makkan youths spent their time indulging in material luxury and the pursuit of pleasure, Muhammad worked as a shepherd and gave what little he earned to his uncle. He did not take part in the moral decay that engulfed Arab society. Muhammad was an individual with a character of kindness, politeness and respect.

As Muhammad grew into adulthood, people became deeply impressed with his honesty. His reputation for trustworthiness became so widespread that when someone asked for *al-Sadiq*, the truthful one, or *al-Amin*, the trustworthy one, people would know that he was asking for Muhammad. The townsfolk often entrusted their valuables to him for safekeeping simply because they knew he would honor their trust. They would ask for his judgment on important issues as he was known to be wise beyond his age, fair and unselfish.

Muhammad's blood-relationship with 'Abd al-Muttalib also added to his reputation in a society where tribal lineage was extremely important.

As a young man, Muhammad witnessed the disruptive effects of the constant feuding that afflicted the many, often rival tribes of Arabia. One of these conflicts was so extensive that it came to be called the War of Fijar. It was fought between two large and influential tribes: the Quraish and the Qais. Muhammad accompanied his uncles to one of the battles and observed first hand the senseless bloodshed.

Like most men of importance in Makkah Muhammad's uncle Abu Talib was a businessman. He often took Muhammad with him on the long caravan trails, teaching him the rules of trade. It was not surprising then that when Muhammad grew into manhood he too entered into the business of trade. But he had no money of his own and his uncle's deteriorating financial condition was of no help. Muhammad's glowing reputation soon came to his aid. As soon as it became well-known that he wanted to start his own trade people wanted him to use their money for investments and they allowed him to take a share in whatever profit was gained.

At that time there was a rich widow living in Makkah named Khadijah. She was one of those who asked Muhammad to do business on her behalf. He agreed and shortly there afterwards took one of her caravans to Syria. When Muhammad returned to Makkah several months later he was carrying a large profit for Khadijah. She was so impressed by Muhammad's hard work and integrity that she proposed marriage to him.

Khadijah was forty years-old living with the three children from her first husband and Muhammad was twenty-five and still unmarried. He desired a wife who was honest, well-mannered and of respected standing, all qualities that were present in Khadijah. The match was blessed and the two remained married and committed to each other for nearly 25 years when the death of Khadijah finally separated them. The union gave Muhammad four daughters and two sons, all of whom, save Fatimah, would not outlive him.

Although the marriage with Khadijah provided Muhammad with the financial opportunity, he was not consumed with material gain. He constantly gave whatever he could to help the poor and dispossessed of Makkah. When Khadijah presented Muhammad with a servant named Zaid, who had been made

> "Did He not find you an orphan and give you shelter? Did He not find you wandering and guide you? Did he not find you needy and enrich you? As for the orphan, do not oppress him; and as for the beggar, do not repel him; and as for the bounty of your Lord, proclaim it."
>
> *the Qur'an 93:6-11*

prisoner in one of the feuds that plagued the tribes., Muhammad freed the young man and told him to go back to his parents. Zaid's parents received word of their son's location and came to take him home. But Zaid had became so attached to his kind master that he never left. Another addition to the household came a few years after his marriage to Khadijah. Muhammad's young cousin 'Ali came to live with the family when a drought made it difficult for Abu Talib to support his children.

The Search for Truth

Despite the respect and admiration his tribe and his town showered on him, Muhammad was deeply troubled with his people and their outlook on the world. Since childhood he shunned the worship of idols, the greedy, heartless and often lawless approach to business, and the widespread sexual immorality. He was distressed with the social inequality that forced many people into poverty and with the inhuman way in which slaves and servants were often treated.

In a search for answers to these social ills Muhammad began to keep seclusions in a cave high atop one of the rugged mountains that surrounded the city. There he meditated and fasted hoping to gain clarity of mind. Calling to mind the old tradition regarding the the Lord of the Ka'bah, the One God of is forefather Abraham, Muhammad sought His help.

Lesson Review

1. What aspects of Muhammad's character prepared members of his clan and tribe to accept that his claim to be a prophet was sincere and genuine?

2. Describe Muhammad and his social position in Makkah.

Chapter Review

1. Research and read to the class a story from Muhammad's youth.

2. Research and write a brief biography of one of the persons mentioned in this chapter.

3. What is the significance of the story of 'Abd al-Muttalib, 'Abdullah and the ten camels?

4. What is the significance of 'Abd al-Muttalib's rediscovery of the well of *Zamzam*?

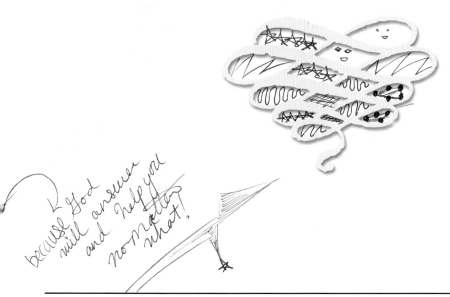

because God will answer and help you no matter what!

Chapter
Two

Revelation

The Call to Prophethood

Why was the Message of Muhammad viewed so negatively by many of the upper class in Makkan society?

Preview Vocabulary

Hira
Jibril
Meditation
Preach
Luminous

The Cave of Hira'

High on the Mountain of Hira Muhammad sat locked in meditation and fasting, hidden away from friends and family. Early into the evening of one of these seclusions a strange unearthly glow began to fill the cave. In shock Muhammad could at first make out the shape of what vaguely appeared to be a tall man whose stunning beauty was bathed in a blinding light. With a thundering voice the towering figure commanded, "Read!" Muhammad, like the vast majority of people in his time, was not literate and replied, "I cannot read." Three times the command was given for him to read and then the figure moved forward to embrace the bewildered Muhammad. The luminous shape was the Archangel Jibril (Gabriel) who then pressed the first revelation of what would be called the Qur'an into the heart of Muhammad;

"Read in the name of your Lord Who created! Created humans from a drop of blood. Read! And your Lord is most Bountiful. He who taught humans by the pen, taught humans that which they did not know."

After this first revelation from the One God, which occurred near the end of the Arab lunar month of Ramadan in the year 610 CE, a period followed in which the Angel Jibril brought no further messages. The utter strangeness of the encounter caused Muhammad to think he might be going mad or that he was

The very first verses (ayat) from the Qur'an revealed to the Prophet Muhammad commanded Mankind to "Read!".

somehow possessed by a *Jinn*, an malevolent spirit. Khadijah, who was his main support during this trying period, reassured him as best as she could.

The First Muslims

Muhammad was frightened and worried about his experience. He kept himself covered with blankets somehow trying to hide any further unearthly visitors. Khadijah tried to assure him that his noble character certainly would never earn Allah's displeasure. "How could God abandon such an upright man like you?" she said, "Surely this is something good." It was not long after this that Jibril appeared again with the command for Muhammad to commence with the prophetic mission:

O you, wrapped in the blankets
stand up and warn!
Magnify your Lord, clean your clothes and
keep from all unclean practices.
[The Qur'an 74:1-5]

Muhammad now understood the meaning of these visits and took heart. In the beginning, the new Prophet taught the message of the One God only to his closest family members and friends. Khadijah, his wife of many years, became the first person to embrace the message of Islam with 'Ali, Zaid and his four daughters quickly following. Outside of the immediate household, Abu Bakr, Muhammad's long-time companion

and wealthy Makkan merchant, was the first adult male to embrace Islam. A few others who held the Prophet in high regard also entered Islam. For nearly three years the Prophet taught his small band of followers in private. Those who had accepted Islam did not talk about it unless asked.

In 613 CE, the Prophet was ordered through revelation to make the message of Islam public. He invited all of the people of Makkah to assemble near a local hill called Safa. The Prophet stood on the hill and asked those gathered, "What do you think of me?" Everyone responded "You are *al-Sadiq* and *al-Amin*, one of our city's finest men."

The Prophet then asked, "Would you believe me if I told you that there was an army behind this hill ready to attack you?" "Yes, of course, we would. You have always spoken the truth and have always held our trust," the people answered.

"Then listen!" the Prophet said, "I now warn you of even greater danger. There will come a day when you will be judged for all of your beliefs and actions. I invite you to believe in one God, and give up these helpless idols. Leave wicked manners and do good." Then one of Muhammad's uncles, Abu Lahab retorted, "Is that what you wanted to tell us? You have only wasted our time!" The crowd dispersed, disappointed over what they thought were foolish words.

Although people still respected Muhammad for his truth and honesty, it could not help his call. Many thought he had gone insane talking of such unheard things. Few were willing to accept what he asked for and his opponents began to spread slander and rumor.

The chiefs of the Bani Quraish were, for the most part, very hostile to the message of Islam. The social and religious changes that the Prophet called for were far too drastic for their tastes. The chiefs feared Muhammad's call because of its challenge to the existing order of Makkan society. To replace the many gods of the Ka'bah with One would ruin the income from the yearly pilgrimage, since the Arabs came to pray to many dieties. In addition Islam's demand for human dignity would certainly end their exploitation of the poor and powerless of their community.

Nonetheless Muhammad continued to preach openly. This caused his rapidly expanding circle of enemies to increase their opposition. One day the Prophet went to the Ka'bah and openly invited people to accept Islam. People had gathered there in their customary idol worship. They were enraged by

Mount Hira lies on the outskirts of the city of Makkah. Though not required by Islamic practice, many Muslims visit this sacred site in order to connect with the Prophet's life.

his remarks and physically attacked him. His followers, however, came to his timely rescue.

Despite the opposition of the rich and powerful, the lowest classes of Makkah were attracted to Muhammad's message. The poor, the slaves, the powerless unattached to tribe and clan and, more importantly, the young, found in Islam an answer to the ills of injustice and social turmoil.

Lesson Review

1. What effect did the pause in revelation have on Muhammad and his immediate family?

2. How did the leaders of Quraish react upon hearing the first news of the revelation?

Lesson Two

Boycotts and Persecution

Looking Ahead

What where the responses that the early Muslim community gave to the increasing hostility of Makkah?

Preview Vocabulary

Boycott
Year of Sorrow
Ta'if
Distressed
Tribal

Two matters in particular bothered the chiefs of Makkah with Islam. First, they observed that the town's youth, women, and slaves were attracted to the Prophet and his message of compassion and justice. They saw their authority over these groups under threat. Secondly, they were distressed that the Prophet not only criticized the worship of the traditional Makkan gods, but that he rejected them outright. To admit that these gods were false would be to admit that all of their forefathers had been in error, something unthinkable in a tribal society where lineage and ancestry played an important role. They also realized that their forefathers had built up a trading empire based on worship of the many gods of the Ka'bah. The status of the Quraish as the preeminent Arab tribe was tied to their prestige as custodians of the venerated Ka'bah in Makkah, and to their role as hosts of the pilgrimage which drew people from all over the Arabian Peninsula. The spread of the Prophet's message would certainly undermine the foundations of the tribe's prestige and wealth if left unchallenged.

Persecution and Persuasion

It did not take long for the chiefs to become convinced that the Prophet's message was turning into a threat that had to be

Ja'far ibn Abi Talib and the Nagasi of Ethiopia

Ja'far bore the harsh treatment and the persecution of the Quraish with patience and steadfastness, but before the boycott or the Hijrah, Ja'far went to the Prophet and sought permission to take his family and a small group of the Companions to the land of Ethiopia. But the Quraish made plans to travel to the court of the Nagasi to convince him to turn the immigrants over to them. Sending two people skilled in diplomacy, 'Amr ibn al-'As and 'Abdullah ibn Abi Rabi'ah, the Quraish provided them with rich presents for the Nagasi and his bishops.

In Ethiopia, 'Amr and 'Abdullah then went to the Nagasi himself and presented him with gifts which he greatly admired. They said to him: "Your Majesty, there is a group of evil persons from among our youth who have escaped to your kingdom. They practice a religion which neither we nor you know. They have forsaken our religion and have not entered into your religion. The respected leaders of their people - from among their own parents and uncles. and from their own clans - have sent us to you to request you to return them. They know best what trouble they have caused."

The Nagasi looked towards his bishops who said: "They speak the truth, O King. Their own people know better with what they have done. Send them back so that they themselves might judge them."

The Nagasi refused to turn them over before he had given Ja'far a chance to answer the charges against them. "If what these two men have said is true, then I will hand them over to you. If however it is not so, then I shall protect them so long as they desire to remain under my protection. Then Ja`far began to speak, "O King, we were a people in a state of ignorance, worshipping idols and eating the flesh of dead animals, committing all sorts of shameful deeds, breaking the ties of kinshipand the strong among us exploited the weak. We remained in this state until Allah sent us a Prophet, one of our own people whose lineage, truthfulness, trustworthiness and integrity were well-known to us. He called us to worship One God alone and to renounce the stones and the idols which we and our ancestors used to worship. He commanded us to speak the truth, to honor our promises, to be kind to our relations, to be helpful to our neighbors, to abstain from bloodshed. to avoid obscenities, not to appropriate an orphan's property nor slander chaste women. We believed in him and what he brought to us from Allah and we follow him in what he has asked us to do and we keep away from what he forbade us from doing. After that, O King, our people attacked us, tortured us to make us renounce our religion and take us back to the old immorality and the worship of idols. They oppressed us, made life intolerable for us and obstructed us from observing our religion. So we left for your country, choosing you before anyone else, desiring your protection and hoping to live in Justice and in peace m your midst."

The King of Ethiopia was so moved by these words that he allowed the Muslims to remain in his realm under his complete protection.

completely eradicated, and eradicated with violence if need be. They were thoroughly embarrassed by the spectacle of a divided city that visitors arriving for the annual pilgrimage would witness. Outsiders often mocked them for not being able to control their sons and slaves. The chiefs worried that the appeal of Islam would spread to tribes living outside Makkah, an event that would threaten the Quraish's lofty reputation that ranked it above all of the Arabs.

This led the leaders of the Quraish to take moves to actively suppress the spread of Islam before it could further upset the stability of Makkan society. While many were initially cautious in their opposition, some (in particular Abu Jahl and the Prophet's own uncle, Abu Lahab) were exceedingly aggressive in their attacks and slander. Abu Jahl would hire thugs to beat and harass all Muslims who lived without the protection of a powerful clan. This meant that the poor and slaves became prime targets for abuse. The most notable of these was a man named Bilal ibn Rabah, who was tortured by his master for refusing to give up his faith in the Prophet. Fortunately he was ransomed by the Prophet's close companion Abu Bakr and freed.

Other individuals fared worse and died under torture: the first martyrs of Islam were the husband and wife Yasir and Sumayyah. Muslims like Abu Bakr and the Prophet himself, were too highly connected with important families to be physically attacked. But this did not prevent them from being insulted, shunned and openly slandered.

Despite the growing use of physical violence some of the pagan leaders tried to exert subtler means of persuasion on the Prophet. They kept continual pressure on Abu Talib to control his

> Al-Mughira once said: "The Blessed Prophet stood so much for prayer that his feet became swollen. Someone said to him, 'Why so you do this Messenger of Allah, when you are purified of sin?' To this he replied, 'Should I not then be a grateful servant?'"

nephew's outspoken critique of Makkan society. Through Abu Talib they unsuccessfully tried to bribe the Prophet with offers of money and leadership if he only he would give up preaching Islam or at least come to some sort of compromise with the old ways. However these non-violent pressures, as well as the violent ones, only served to strengthen the resolve of the Muslims

Ethiopia, Boycott and Relief

The wave of repression that was growing daily in Makkah eventually became so unbearable that many of the Muslims who lacked strong clan protection asked for the Prophet's permission to leave the town. The Prophet gave his approval and advised these Muslims to go to Christian Ethiopia, where the ruler Armah would surely protect them because of a shared belief in One God. About forty of the Prophet's followers (including one of the Prophet's own daughters) left on the long journey under the leadership of Ja`far, a cousin of the Prophet. On their arrival the *Nagasi* welcomed the Muslims and offered them his protection despite the protests of the Makkans. Ethiopia became a refuge for persecuted

Muslims, and until his dying day the Prophet thought highly of that land and its ruler.

Frustrated by their failed attempts to quell the growing influence of Islam in their town, the pagan chiefs decided to resort to a form of collective punishment that would touch all who supported or sympathized with the Prophet. After much deliberation a proclamation was hung up in the Ka'bah forbidding anyone to do business with, marry, or have social interaction with the clan of Bani Hashim, the clan of the Prophet. All of the Bani Hashim, Muslim and non-Muslim were forced to live in a desolate valley on the edge of the city. There they suffered great hardship and misery. For three years the Prophet, his clan and their sympathizers endured this cruel boycott. They were only saved from complete starvation by non-Hashimite friends who broke the boycott to provide them food and water.

Because of the great physical and mental stress caused by the imposed isolation, Khadijah and Abu Talib weakened and died shortly afterwards. The Prophet was deeply saddened by their deaths, and in Muslim tradition this year became to be known as the Year of Sorrow. Abu Talib's death meant that the one man who stood between Muhammad and the rage of the Makkan chiefs was now gone. The Prophet was now an open target.

With Makkan resistance to Islam stiffening, the Prophet began to look elsewhere for a community that would be more receptive to the Divine Message. He visited the neighboring town of Ta'if hoping to win over its inhabitants. Ta'if was the center of the tribes of Thaqif and Hawazin. They were a rich and proud people who firmly believed in their gods. The town even housed a huge temple dedicated to the goddesses Lat.

Despite the best of hopes the people of Ta'if proved to be even more resistant to Islam than those of Makkah. When the Prophet met their leaders and invited them to Islam, they mocked him and had their children chase him out of town, stoning him along the way.

Though severely injured by the incident the Prophet did not curse the people of Ta'if or lose heart. On the roadside outside of Ta'if he sat, covered with blood and dirt. He reflected on the happenings of the day, then looked to the heavens and prayed, "O Allah, You are most Merciful, the Lord of the helpless. In whose hands will I find help if you abandon me to the unsympathetic and an unkind?"

At that moment a great angel appeared and said, "If you wish O Messenger of God, I will bring these mountains down upon the inhabitants of Ta'if." The Prophet, whose only purpose had been to be a mercy for all mankind, replied as he wiped the blood from his forehead, "No, do not punish them, rather let Allah guide them and their children to Islam."

> "If you punish, then punish with the like of that wherewith you were afflicted. But if you endure patiently, this is indeed better for those who are patient. Endure patiently; your endurance is only through Allah."
>
> *the Qur'an 16:126-127*

Lesson Review

1. What steps did the leaders and other members of Quraish take to stop the challenge presented by Prophet Muhammad, and why did they choose such methods?

2. How did the deaths of Khadijah and Abu Talib in the Year of Sorrow increase the difficulties for the Prophet and the Muslim community?

Chapter Review

1. What steps did Quraish take to bribe Prophet Muhammad into giving up his claim to the truth, and why were they willing to do this?

2. Research the stories and lives of two strong Quraish opponents, either men or women. How did their social position affect their reaction to Islam?

3. Knowing that Quraish was an influential tribe in central Arabia, role play a conversation between members of two outlying tribes upon hearing of the boycott against the Muslims. How does this act affect the respect other tribes hold toward Quraish?

4. Trace the journey taken by Ja'far and the other emigrants on a map; how far did they travel, what means of transportation would they have used, and how long do you estimate the journey took? What does the emigration signify?

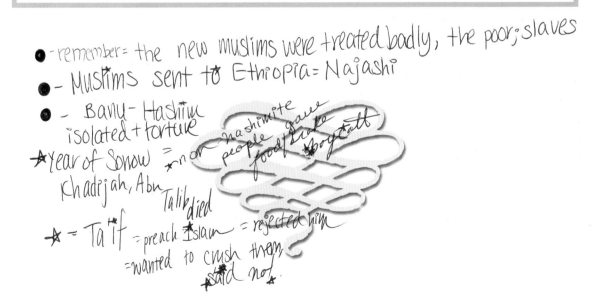

- remember = the new muslims were treated badly, the poor; slaves
- Muslims sent to Ethiopia = Najashi
- Banu-Hashim isolated + torture
hashimite people gave food/water boycott
★ Year of Sorrow = non
Khadijah, Abu Talib died
★ = Ta'if = preach Islam = rejected him
= wanted to crush them, said no.

Chapter
Three

The Hijrah

Lesson One

"The Full Moon Rose Upon Us…"

Looking Ahead

What were the difficulties facing the Muslim community in their new home at Yathrib?

Preview Vocabulary

'Aws
Khazraj
Bay'at
Madinat an-Nabi
Prosperous
Feud

Yathrib presents Itself

Yathrib was an oasis town some 250 miles to the north of Makkah, a distance that required two week's journey by camel. Yathrib's many wells and springs enabled its inhabitants to cultivate productive gardens and orchards, especially in the volcanic soil that lay between two stretches of jagged, impassable lava rock that almost completely surrounded the town. Unlike Makkah, Yathrib's economy was primarily focused on agriculture and not trade. But Yathrib was important for its position along the vital trade routes that linked Syria and Yemen, and merchants often stopped to rest and trade.

Although Yathrib enjoyed many natural blessings, its people were bitterly divided. In addition to pagans Yathrib was home to several large Jewish tribes. Bloodshed was a daily occurence. The major tribes that lived in the town, the 'Aws and the Khazraj, were locked in seemingly endless feuds. Their struggle grew bitter with time, fed by the cycle for revenge caused by the constant killing. The Jewish tribes of Yathrib were no better united and they too occasionally fought among themselves. In addition their chiefs often encouraged feuds among the pagan Arabs to keep them from threatening their own positions.

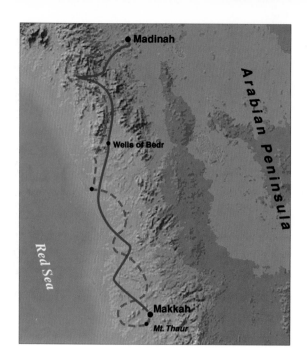

At the time that the Muslims of Makkah were suffering through the boycott, many of the inhabitants of Yathrib had grown weary of the constant strife that afflicted their community. They sought a final solution to the self-destruction. They began to look for an individual of such character and strength that he would have the power to unite the tribes of Yathrib, both pagan and Jewish. An influential chief of the Khazraj by the name of 'Abdullah ibn Ubayy was considered the likely candidate. However, before Ibn Ubayy could be officially nominated, six men from his own tribe traveled to Makkah to attend the annual pagan festivities. Just as the Quraish had feared, the Yathribi men met with the Prophet and were so impressed with his character and message they entered into Islam. They soon returned home and told of a man who had a solution for the town's troubles.

The next year the Yathribi men returned to Makkah with all who had embraced Islam at their hands. Their sole intention was to meet with the Prophet. In a narrow valley called 'Aqaba just outside of Makkah, 72 men and women of Yathrib pledged their allegiance (bay'ah) to obey the Messenger of God in every aspect of their lives. They also promised to defend him if need be. "Even if all Arabia unite against us," they said, "we shall support the Prophet and the cause of Allah."

The Prophet was deeply moved by sincerity and faith of the people of Yathrib. He honored them with the title of Ansar, the Helpers of Allah. The people of Yathrib were delighted by this blessing and forevermore were they known.

The Ansar invited the Prophet and the Muslims of Makkah to immigrate to Yathrib. With this assurance of protection, the Prophet granted permission to the Muslims to leave the torture and ridicule of Makkah for the safety of Yathrib. Slowly all of those who professed Islam packed whatever little belongings they could and left for Yathrib, where they were warmly received.

The chiefs of the Quraish responded to this migration with alarm. They prevented some Muslims from leaving by force as Arab tradition and tribal loyalty did not allow any individual to make such important decisions like moving without the permission of his or her clan. The Muslims of Makkah, however, had accepted a faith that superceded tribal custom and consequently the split between many families deepened.

With Makkah nearly emptied of its Muslim population the Prophet prepared for his own departure. This was done under cover of night since the chiefs of the Quraish had laid a plan for his assassination. The Prophet eluded their plot and escaped northward with his close companion Abu Bakr. After weeks of travel through the desert they finally reached Yathrib. Needless to say they were received with great joy and celebration. This migration, known as the *Hijrah*, would later mark the start of the Islamic calendar.

Following the arrival of the Prophet, the name of Yathrib was changed to *Madinat an-Nabi*, which literally meant the "City of the Prophet". This name was (and is) more commonly shortened simply to Madinah.

> The Prophet Muhammad once said,"On the Day of Judgement I shall come to the Gates of Paradise and call to have them opened. The gatekeeper will cry out, 'Who are you?' To which I will reply, 'Muhammad!' Then the gatekeeper will say, 'I have been ordered not to open these gates to anyone but you."
>
> *(Sahih Muslim)*

The spiritual importance of Madinah ranks second only to Makkah. Every year millions of Muslims visit the City of the Prophet to pay their respects to his grave.

Lesson Review

1. Contrast the geography of Yathrib with that of Makkah, including the way of life of the inhabitants.

2. What problem did the people of Yathrib want to solve by inviting Muhammad to live there? What risks did this decision involve?

Lesson Two

The Community of Madinah

Looking Ahead

Understand the many components that made the Islamic state of Madinah successful.

Preview Vocabulary

Masjid
Jum'ah
Muhajirun
Ansar
Sahabah
Ummah
Dustur al-Madinah

In Madinah, the Muslims were finally free from torment and Islam could now become the foundation for a functioning society. The persecution and harassment of Makkah left little opportunity for social activity and organization. But despite the almost unbearable hardships, life in Makkah had served to strengthen the commitment and determination of the Muslims.

The First Islamic State

Upon his arrival, the Prophet organized Madinah according to the code of ethics and behavior that was revealed to him by God. Devotion to the One God and the moral obligations towards community became the focus of life. Not surprisingly the first building ordered constructed was a *masjid*, or place of worship. Although at the time it was the simplest of buildings, this *masjid* was to be the center of the city's activities. In the *masjid*, the five daily prayers (*salat*) were held, as well as the *Jum'ah* or the Friday obligatory communal prayer. In addition, it was a place where ideas were shared, plans were made, and disputes were judged and settled. The Prophet's *Masjid* at Madinah, made of sun-dried mud bricks and the trunks of palm trees, was the prototype of an institution from which Muslim civilization would blossom.

Following the completion of this important community structure the Prophet then implemented a social change that would shake the very foundation of Arab tribal structure. To solidify the bond between the Muslims of Madinah and Makkah, he joined the two groups in a relationship of brotherhood. Every man from Makkah (a *Muhajir*) was bound to an *Ansar* man, a Madinan Muslim. This move allowed the more experienced *Muhajirun* from Makkah to teach the Madinans more about Islam. In return the Madinans helped their refugee brothers and sisters establish themselves in their new environment. In one stroke the new reality of a kinship based on faith replaced loyalty to tribe and clan.

The *Muhajirun* were primarily merchants, not farmers like the Madinans, and had much to learn in order to make a modest living in their new environment. Many had left all of their money and property behind in Makkah as a condition for being allowed to depart unharmed by the Quraish. Seizing the opportunity to prove

Where did the word "Mosque" come from?

How did the word "mosque" come to be used to describe an Islamic place of worship instead of the original name *masjid*? *Masjid* is a form of the Arabic word *sujud*, meaning prostration. Prostration is the position in Islamic prayer when the worshipper's forehead, hands, knees and feet touch the ground in humility and submission to Allah. Adding "M-A" to the word makes the place-form of the word, "a place of making *sujud*" or house of worship. The word "mosque" is a French word used to mean masjid. It is what word-historians call a corruption , or a changed form that happens when an unfamiliar word in one language gets mispronounced or misspelled in another, and the new version becomes common. The word "mosque", however, is a double corruption, since "mosque" originally came from the Spanish word for "mosque", which is *la mesquita*. It makes geographic sense that Spanish would be the first European language to have a word for *masjid*, since Spain was home to a Muslim civilization from 711 CE until 1492 CE. When you pronounce the Arabic and the Spanish versions of the word, you find that they are very similar. Patterns of transfer, or translation, between Spanish and French, however, caused further change to the word "mosque", which doesn't even have the same number of syllables. It is not known exactly why the French version passed into English unchanged. Since Islam has become more familiar in places where English is spoken, however, many Muslims are trying to re-introduce the original Arabic word, *masjid*, which neither difficult to pronounce nor to spell, and helps people to better understand the Islamic concept of worship. This same type of corruption will be found later in Muslim history with the name 'Ottoman', which is an Italian mispronunciation of the real name of the dynasty the 'Uthmaniyyah.

their commitment, the *Ansar* opened their doors, houses, lives, and property to the service of fellow believers.

The formation of this brotherhood was a very practical system for integrating the new residents into Madinan society. Although it tapped into the Arab tradition of hospitality toward guests and travelers, it demonstrated that in the new Muslim community, bonds of faith were now more important than tribal ties based on blood relationships or lineage.

In practice, the *Ansar* and *Muhajirun*, worked well together, although overcoming the deeply ingrained tribal consciousness was not always easy. For the *Ansar*, the sharp rivalries between 'Aws and Khazraj were diffused in a new common purpose, although the Prophet still was requested to intervene in occasional disputes between the two. Over and over the Messenger of Allah emphasized that tribal loyalties and feuds were now completely abrogated by Islam. The Prophet elaborated on this when he said, "He is not of us who upholds the cause of tribalism and he is not of us who fights in the cause of tribalism; and he is not of us who dies in the cause of tribalism." When he was asked to explain the meaning of tribalism, he answered, "It is helping your clansmen in an unjust cause."

Whether *Muhajirun*, *Ansar*, or people who later accepted Islam, those Muslims who lived, worked and sometimes fought alongside the Prophet are called his *Sahabah*, or Companions. This term came to be applied to those believers who met him, saw him or worked with him, even for the briefest of moments. But in its narrowest sence it refers to those men and women who took an active part in the development of the Islamic community, or *Ummah*, with the Prophet.

Despite the growing Muslim presence in Madinah there was still a sizeable non-Muslim population in the town formed predominantly by the Jews. As an important part of establishing Islamic rule, the Prophet presented a treaty to the Jewish tribes of the Madinah, which they willingly accepted. This agreement, known as the *Dustur al-Madinah*, or the Constitution of Madinah, was agreed upon by all the tribal chiefs of Madinah, Muslim, Jew or other.

Through this pact Jews and Muslims were formed into a single community that promised freedom for each's others religious and social traditions. Muslim and Jew were to be held equal under the law. If one wronged the other, everyone had to help the wronged one to obtain his or her rights, regardless of religious affiliation. More importantly the pact called for mutual defense of the town. If outsiders waged war against Madinah, all of its people would fight together to defend their city, and neither Muslim nor Jew was allowed to make a separate peace with an enemy.

According to the *Dustur al-Madinah* all disputes were to be referred to the arbitration of the Prophet, whether or not individuals recognized his sacred position. The Jewish tribes were not forced to acknowledge Muhammad as the Messenger of God, but they did have to agree to accept him as the highest authority in Madinah's affairs.

With the acceptance of this treaty by all of the significant quarters of Madinah, the Prophet became the unifying force that the people of Madinah were searching for. Well aware that the Jews were the recipients of previous revelation, the Prophet hoped they would eagerly support his mission. But as it turned out, most Jews in Madinah could not accept the possibility of a prophet of non-Jewish origin. They clung to their belief that as the "Chosen People" they and they alone were the recipients of such heavenly honor.

This artistic reconstruction of what the Prophet's Masjid in Madinah may have looked like shows the simplicity in which he and his followers lived. This masjid became the focal point for Muslim life during the lifetime of the Prophet.

A few did however embrace the message of Islam, including the one of the chief rabbis of the Banu Qainuqa, a man named 'Abdullah ibn Sallam.

The Revelation Continues

The nature of the revelation that the Prophet Muhammad received in Madinah was markedly different in character from that revealed while the community was growing in Makkah. Early revelations stressed the existence of One God, Allah, presented His attributes, and laid out basic elements of social and personal morality. These Makkan verses gave inspiring examples of the prophets of the past, warned of the coming of Final Judgment and the Last Day, pointed out the moral ills that plagued mankind and encouraged believers with the good news of a better future. These revelations redirected the individual from materialistic goals to a life dedicated to worship and the care for relatives, neighbors and the downtrodden. These revelations directed the soul to concentrate on

the ultimate end of things, as well as on Allah's justice and mercy.

In contrast, Madinan revelations, while holding the same themes, became more practical, laying down regulations applicable to daily life in the newly established Islamic community. Verses taught the specifics of worship such as *salat* (the prayer) and *zakat* (charity) and *saum* (fasting), and later, the *Hajj*. The Prophet was given revelation that concerned issues of inheritance, marriage and divorce, and proper social interaction as well as other legal matters. The status of women was greatly enhanced. They were given rights unheard of in Arabia before. Women could now inherit and divorce. They were to be treated as complete human beings and spiritual equals with men.

Aspects of social justice, crime and punishment, the conduct of business, employment and financial arrangements were revealed on the occasion of a question brought to the Prophet for judgement or advice. Issues arose naturally in the daily life of Madinah, as the town

The Pact of Madinah

The Pact of Madinah was one of the most important documents of the early Islamic State. Its goal was to solidify the different communities that lived in and around the city of Yathrib. One of the more remarkable features of the pact is that it allowed for complete religious freedom for the Jewish tribes.

In the name of Allah the Compassionate, the Merciful.

This is a document from the Prophet Muhammad governing the relation between the Believers from among the Quraish and the residents of Madinah and those who followed them and joined them and strived with them. They form one and the same community as against the rest of men...No Believer shall oppose the ally of another Believer. Whosoever is rebellious, or seeks to spread injustice or sedition among the Believers, the hand of every man shall be against him, even if he be a son of one of them...Whosoever among the Jews follows us shall have help and equality; they shall not be injured nor shall any enemy be aided against them.... No separate peace will be made when the Believers are fighting in the way of Allah....The Believers shall avenge the blood of one another shed in the way of Allah ....Whosoever kills a Believer wrongfully shall be liable to retaliation; all the Believers shall be against him as one man and they are bound to take action against him.

The Jews shall contribute with the Believers so long as they are at war with a common enemy...The Jews shall keep to their religion and the Muslims theirs. Loyalty is a protection against treachery. The close friends of Jews are as themselves. None of them shall go out on a military expedition except with the permission of Muhammad, but that person shall not be prevented from taking revenge for a wound...The Jews shall be responsible for their expenses and the Believers for theirs. Each, if attacked, shall come to the assistance of the other.

The valley of Yathrib shall be sacred for all that join this Treaty. Strangers, under protection, shall be treated on the same ground as their protectors; but no stranger shall be taken under protection except with consent of his tribe....No woman shall be taken under protection without the consent of her family....Whatever difference or dispute between the parties to this covenant remains unsolved shall be referred to Allah and to Muhammad, the Messenger of Allah. Allah is the Guarantor of the piety and goodness that is embodied in this covenant. Neither the Quraish nor their allies shall be given any protection.

The contracting parties are bound to help one another against any attack on Yathrib. If they are called to cease hostilities and to enter into peace, they shall be bound to do so in the interest of peace; and if they make a similar demand on Muslims it must be carried out except when the war is against their religion.

Allah approves the truth and goodwill of this covenant. This treaty shall not protect the unjust or the criminal. Whoever goes out to fight as well as whoever stays at home shall be safe and secure in this city unless he has perpetrated an injustice or committed a crime.... Allah is the protector of the good and God-fearing people.

and its people became involved in events that would eventually direct the course of world history. As the community in Madinah developed relationships with neighboring Arab tribes, and later with leaders of states and empires, the guidelines revealed in response to early situations would become the basis for the principles of international relations.

Madinah's citizens lived with the Prophet, and had (in addition to the Qur'anic revelation from God) a continuous source of guidance in him. But the Prophet's words were clearly distinguished from Qur'anic revelation. Many of the details regarding Islamic practices and moral values were expounded not directly in verses of the Qur'an, but rather through the living example of the Prophet. From the time of Adam, revelation had been an interactive process teaching through the lives and examples of prophets who put revelation into practice. These men were the ultimate interpreters of Divine revelation. In this sense, the Prophet Muhammad was viewed as Qur'an in human form.

The commands given by the Prophet were binding on Muslims, unless otherwise stated. The totality of the Prophet's example and experience is known in Islamic theology as the *Sunnah*, or practice. The *Sunnah* would later develop into the second source of knowledge about Islam, the first being of course the Qur'an.

The *Sunnah* was transmitted to us today through written records of the Prophet's words and deeds. During his lifetime, the followers of Muhammad were encouraged to observe and to commit his words and deeds to memory. These accounts were eventually put into writing and passed through the generations. These written accounts of the *Sunnah* are called the *Hadith*, a word that can literally mean "tradition" or "saying". Transmission, verification and recording of the *Hadith* were among the most important activities during the earliest period of Islamic history. This resulted in the creation of the important *Hadith* collections that theologians have relied upon to this day.

The believers who lived during this remarkable period realized the importance of the Prophet's words even as they bore out the hardships of life in 7th century Arabia. They listened, observed and tried to emulate the Prophet's noble example in every aspect of their lives. Many of these individuals attained high degrees of piety and selflessness. Accounts of their lives stood as an inspiration to later generations of Muslims. After the death of the Prophet, one of the Prophet's companions, a lady named Barakah, was asked why she always had tears in her eyes. She explained that it was not for the passing of the Prophet, but rather because channel through which divine revelation came was no longer among them.

Lesson Review

1. What was Prophet Muhammad's first major act upon entering Yathrib? What was the importance of the site and its selection?

2. What steps were taken to adjust the social organization of the city to the new arrivals?

Battles and Treaties

Looking Ahead

Note the circumstances that finally led Muslims to resist oppression by force of arms.

Preview Vocabulary

Armed Conflict
Battle of Badr
Abu Sufian
Munafiqun
Uhud
Persecution
Stipulation

Living in Madinah, the *Muhajirun* faced many problems such as lack of housing and food shortages. Madinah was primarily a farming community and the people of Makkah were expert merchants. Those who were successful merchants in Makkah now lacked the financial ability to start new businesses. The resources of the *Ansar* alone could not cover all of the expenses of the *Muhajirun*, and needy Muslims were arriving from Makkah on a constant basis. The city's finances were stretched to the limit. Despite the fact that the pagans of Makkah remained dangerous enemies no revelation had yet allowed the Muslims to take up arms to reclaim the goods and homes that were forfeited when they fled Makkah.

The chiefs of Makkah had long been contemplating a move to wipe the Muslims out once and for all. During the first year of *Hijrah*, Madinah anticipated attack from the Quraish. The Prophet sent out scouting parties to look for any developing hostile activity. One of these bands took matters into its own hands and attacked a small Makkan caravan that passed near the outskirts of Madinah. It was hoped that the goods taken from the caravan could help alleviate the economic plight of the *Muhajirun*. The men did not have permission from the Prophet to fight, and the attack took place during one of the traditional sacred months of the Arabs in which fighting was forbidden. One man was killed

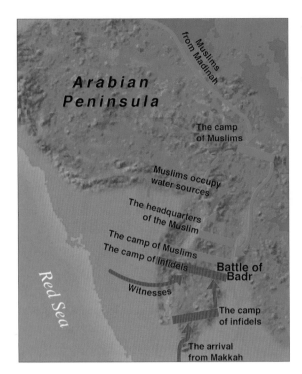

Arabian
Peninsula

The camp
of Muslims

Muslims occupy
water sources

The headquarters
of the Muslim

The camp of Muslims

The camp of Infidels

Battle of
Badr

Witnesses

The camp
of infidels

The arrival
from Makkah

Red Sea

Muslims from Madinah

The march to the Wells of Badr was planned to be a raid on an armed Makkan caravan. The two armies clashed in a battle that was to prove disastrous for the Quraish.

and and the goods were seized. Returning to Madinah the group quickly regretted their rash action when they found the Prophet waiting with displeasure. Not long after that incident, however, a revelation was delivered, and the Muslims were given Divine permission to defend themselves:

> *"Permission to fight is given to those who fight because they have been wronged...those who have been unjustly driven from their homes for no other reason than their saying, 'Our Sustainer is Allah!'"*(Qur'an 22:39)

This verse however was not blanket permission given to launch an all out attack on their enemies. Later revelations, as well as statements made by the Prophet restricted the rules of military engagement and outlined clear moral principles to be followed in warfare. For example, an attack could not be undertaken without being provoked by the enemy. Likewise,

if the enemy inclined towards peace, the Muslims were obliged to accept.

At the start of the second year of the *Hijrah* (624 CE), the Muslims were hoping to seize yet another Makkan caravan and scouts soon delivered news that a large one would soon be passing near Madinah as it traveled back from bustling marketplaces in Syria. Unknown to the Muslims was that this caravan was led by Abu Sufian, one of the leading opponents of the Prophet.

However Abu Sufian's scouts were also busy. and he came to know that his caravan was spotted. He dispatched a rider to alert the chiefs of Makkah and call for their immediate help. In a move to put distance between itself and Madinah Abu Sufian shifted his route further to west hugging the Red Sea coast. By doing so he hoped to buy time until help from Makkah arrived.

Word that the Muslims were heading into armed conflict could not have pleased pagan Makkah more. The enemies of the Prophet would be handed the opportunity to finish Islam off once and for all on the field of battle. Within days after the arrival of Abu Sufian's rider, the Makkans had mobilized a force of over 1,000 warriors. They quickly set out northward confident of total victory.

As Abu Sufian's dispatch reached the ears of the leaders of Makkah the Prophet set out from Madinah at the head of little more than 300 men. Their goal was a place known as the Wells of Badr some 80 miles to the southwest of their beloved town. Badr was a popular resting post on the long caravan route between Makkah and Syria and they quite naturally assumed that Abu Sufian's caravan would have to stop here for water and they hoped to capture it as it rested. But during their march to the wells the Muslims received word that a large force from Makkah was headed their way.

The Muslim army arrived at Badr days before the Makkans and they were able to take control of the wells and set up their defenses. This, of course, meant that the Makkans would be deprived of water after weeks of marching through the desert. If they wanted water, they would have to fight for it.

Within days the Makkan army, large, confident and well-equipped, finally arrived at Badr. Many of the chieftains who had violently opposed the Prophet from the very beginning of his mission were present, hoping to gloat over his demise and the destruction of his movement. The two forces quickly lined up for battle, facing each other in full array. In keeping with the traditional way of Arab warfare, the champions of each side were sent out to engage in individual duels. These went well for the Muslims and the pagan champions were slain. After the duels were finished battle was joined. Combat was fierce and for the *Muhajirun* it was full of bitter emotion. Many of them now faced not only former tormentors, but family members as well. During the fighting several of the Prophet's bitterest foes, including Abu Jahl, were slain.

Despite being outnumbered 3-to-1 the Muslims fought with enthusiasm and fearlessness for they were convinced that death would only open greater rewards in the Hereafter. As the fighting raged, the Makkan ranks began to buckle and break. They retreated from the field in disarray and despair, leaving their dead and dying where they lay. Those who did not leave in the route were taken prisoner.

The Muslims gained tremendous confidence from the Battle of Badr. Their faith in the Prophet reached new heights as Allah's hand was seen guiding the victory. As word of the astounding victory spread throughout Arabia, outlaying tribes began to take notice of Islam. But defeat only increased the hatred and rage in pagan Makkah. They could not comprehend how a small band of poorly equipped men could have defeated the most respected and well-equipped tribe in Arabia. The fact that it was at the hands of people who were once at their complete mercy made it all the more unbearable. In keeping with old Arab tradition, they vowed revenge.

Plots of Treachery

The Prophet now turned to a problem that had been simmering since his arrival in Madinah nearly two years earlier. The Jewish tribes that lived in and around the city began to express growing discontent having such a strong leader in their midst; one whose power and influence was growing daily. They witnessed how the faith of Islam forged people of the various feuding tribes into a single brotherhood. The three Jewish tribes of Madinah - the Banu Qainuqa, Banu Nadir, and Banu Quraizah - believed that their own security and well-being was best preserved when the Arab tribes were divided among themselves.

In an attempt to counter the growing power of the Muslims, several prominent Jewish chiefs began to conspire with 'Abdullah ibn 'Ubayy (a man once considered to be the leader of Madinah) to find ways to weaken Muslim power. Ibn 'Ubayy became the head of the *Munafiqun,* or hypocrites. The *Munafiqun* were those disgruntled members of the Madinan populace who felt displaced by the Prophet and the *Muhajir* newcomers. Although they openly professed Islam, inwardly they waited for the opportunity to exploit any weakness in the new community for their own benefit.

Despite the fact that individuals among the Jewish tribes recognized Muhammad as a prophet and embraced his message, most kept to the faith of their ancestors. The Qur'anic revelation during this period counseled the Jews to look into their own sacred books to find signs pointing to the Prophethood of Muhammad. But such advice did little to ease the strain that was starting to appear in the daily interaction between Muslims and Jews in Madinah.

Despite their initial satisfaction with the *Dustur al-Madinah*, the Jewish tribes began to reassess the communal ties and obligations that were demanded by the pact. The first tribe to openly discard the provisions of the treaty were the Bani Qainuqa. Many of their members began to openly mock the Prophet in the weeks following the victory at Badr. Words soon escalated into violence and scattered fistfights broke out between individual Muslims and Jews. The Banu Qainuqa refused to go to the Prophet for mediation in one of these fights that escalated to such an extent that it caused the death of a Muslim and a Jew, despite the stipulations present in the treaty they initially agreed upon.

With this tension growing, the Banu Qainuqa decided the time had come to take up arms and expel the Prophet and his followers from Madinah. Needless to say the *Munafiqun* wholeheartedly (though secretly) encouraged this rash move. The Banu Qainuqa sent out messengers calling on the surrounding pagan tribes for support. They then withdrew into their heavily fortified houses that lay among their fertile date orchards and made ready for impending battle.

For the Muslims this breach of the *Dustur* was seen as an open declaration of war. The Prophet quickly ordered warriors to surround the settlements of the Bani Qainuqa. When this was accomplished he went forward to their gates and demand their immediate capitulation. As the Bani Qainuqa initially refused to lay down their arms and open their gates they were placed under siege. But the help that they had expected from their pagan allies never came. Word had spread regarding the outcome of the Battle of Badr, and none of these tribes would dare engage the Muslims in open combat.

Realizing that outside aid was not coming the Bani Qainuqa finally decided to surrender and face the consequences for arbitrarily breaking their pact with the Prophet. In retaliation the entire tribe was expelled from Madinah being allowed to take with them all the property they could carry on the backs of their camels. Their houses and date groves were to be handed over to the Muslims.

Quraish Marches Again

Having to shoulder the disgrace from the defeat of Badr the chiefs of Makkah began to look for any opportunity through which they could exact revenge on their Muslim enemies. In the third year of the *Hijrah*, they sent out a second military expedition with the goal of assaulting Madinah directly. This time the Makkan army numbered 3,000, including 200 horsemen.

As word of this huge army arrived in Madinah, the Prophet ordered all able-bodied

Muslim males to take up arms. Not wishing to subject Madinah to a bloody siege, a plan was devised whereby the Muslim army would march out and meet the Quraish in open battle. The Muslims amassed a force of nearly 1,000 made up of both *Ansar* and *Muhajirun*. There were also some 300 *Munafiqun*, who later broke rank and went home. Despite the provisions in the *Dustur* that called for mutual aid in wartime, only one man from the Jewish tribes came forward to fulfill his obligation.Of him the Prophet spoke with glowing praise.

The opposing forces met at the foot of the Mountain of Uhud, a location less than 10 miles outside Madinah. The battle went well for the Muslims in the beginning, and the pagans began to break under fierce onslaught. The flow of combat, however, soon turned. A group of Muslim archers had been personally ordered by the Prophet to guard the rear approaches of the Muslim position, telling them that under no circumstances were they to leave this post. During the initial retreat of the Makkans these archers abandoned their position and started to search for booty scattered about the battlefield. With the rear of the Muslim lines left unguarded, a band of Makkan horsemen under the command of Khalid ibn al-Walid took the chance to strike. This attack on the rear of the Muslim army threw its ranks into confusion. The fleeing Makkans soon rallied and turned to face their pursuers.

Unable to hold back a foe coming in from two directions, the Muslims fled up the slopes of the mountain. The Prophet was injured during the counterattack, and many Muslim were slain. Fortunately the Makkans were in no condition to exploit the favorable turn of events, and their assault soon ran out of steam. Satisfied that they had avenged their humiliation at Badr, they withdrew from the field.

The Muslims were at first discouraged by the defeat at Uhud, but it ultimately served to strengthen their resolve. It taught a hard lesson about the importance of obedience to the Prophet and showed that self-discipline was a part of overcoming evil at a personal, communal and universal level.

In the following year, the Muslims again marched out of Madinah to meet a rumored Makkan assault, but it was a rumor that was proved false. Many neighboring Arab tribes were impressed by the steadfastness and strength of the Muslims in their struggle with the Quraish. As the reputation of the Muslims spread over the peninsula, so too did their message.

Situation of Badr/Uhud

Lesson Review

1. What are the limits placed on warfare as set down in the Qur'an?

2. During wartime, treason is considered a crime punishable by death in nearly all countries of the earth. How did the Prophet Muhammad deal with treason during the years of war with the Quraish?

3. Give the main reason for the defeat of the Muslims at the Battle of Uhud.

Lesson Four

The Confederates and Conspiracies

Looking Ahead

What were the dangers the Muslim community faced during this period? How did they deal with these problems?

Preview Vocabulary

'Umra
The Battle of the Ditch
Banu Quraizah
Co-religionists
Siege

After the Battle of Uhud, the Prophet went to the chiefs of the Banu Nadir (one of the two remaining Jewish tribes in Madinah) to have them account for their absence during the battle. The *Dustur al-Madinah* stipulated that the Muslims and Jews would assist each other in times of war, and the non-participation of both Jewish tribes was suspect. We read in the previous lesson that relations between Jews and Muslims had been slowly deteriorating in the aftermath of the Battle of Badr. Worried about the growing influence of Islam, the Jewish chiefs began to look for ways to withdraw from their obligations and return the town to its pre-Islamic *status quo*.

Unknown to the Muslims was the fact that several Jewish chiefs in Madinah had begun to enter into negotiations with the leaders of pagan Makkah. It was hoped that through these negotiations common cause could be made against the Muslims. The Makkans encouraged the chiefs of Bani Nadir to assassinate the Prophet, knowing very well that his death would throw the Muslims into crisis and confusion. But the plot was foiled and the hostile intentions laid bare. In response the Prophet ordered the fortified compounds of the Bani Nadir surrounded.

'Abdullah ibn 'Ubayy, the leader of the *Munafiqun*, sent secret word to the Bani Nadir that if they would hold out against the Muslims he would personally come to their aid. The Bani Nadir

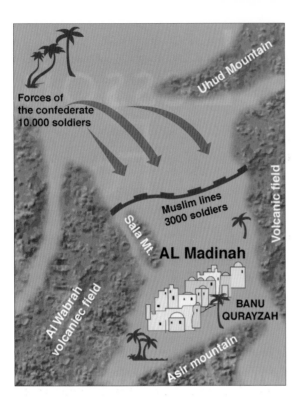

Forces of the confederate 10,000 soldiers

Uhud Mountain

Sala Mt.

Muslim lines 3000 soldiers

Volcanic field

AL Madinah

Al Wabrah volcaniec field

BANU QURAYZAH

Asir mountain

The Quraish and their allies tried in vain to storm the city of Madinah.

likewise looked to the Bani Quraizah, the only other remaining Jewish tribe in Madinah. Their headman Huyay was convinced that if he threw his warriors behind those of Bani Nadir and the *Munafiqun*, the combined force could easily defeat the Muslims.

The Muslims mobilized and encircled the strongholds of Banu Nadir, causing Ibn 'Ubayy to have second thoughts about his plan. In a blatant display of his own character he went back on his pledge to the Bani Nadir and failed to deliver his promised assistance. When the Bani Quraizah came to learn of this they too decided to avoid all involvement in the conflict.

Seeing that their position was now completely lost, the Bani Nadir chose to place themselves at the mercy of the very man they had sought to kill. In return for their willful violation of the pact with the Prophet (an act that would have brought certain execution in any

other society) the entire tribe of Bani Nadir was evicted from Madinah with whatever goods of theirs they could carry on their camels.

The Battle of the Trench

In the fifth year after the Hijrah (627 CE), the pagans of Makkah prepared for what they hoped would be a final assault against Madinah. Jewish leaders from an area to the north of Madinah known as Khaibar journeyed to Makkah to strengthen their contacts with the pagans. The two parties were united in their determination to destroy the Muslims. Despite their own unquestionably monotheistic faith, the Jewish chiefs convinced the pagan leaders that their polytheism was better than the teachings of Muhammad. The chiefs of the Makkah,were taken in by this approval and formed a coalition with the Jews.

The Jews and the Makkans sent their emissaries to every tribe known to hold animosity towards Muslim Madinah. They were either persuaded or bribed into joining in an alliance. The Bani Ghatafan, with their 2,000 warriors, were promised half the date harvest of Khaibar by the Jewish chiefs if they were to march against the Prophet. In this manner a great anti-Islamic alliance quickly took shape. The gathering of the pagan and Jewish tribes, the Confederates (*Ahzab*) as they were called, mobilized well over ten thousand men. They were confident that an army of this size would be able to eradicate the message of the Prophet once and for all.

Concern and worry gripped the Muslims when they learned of the force that was being sent against them. They were faced with the task of defending their homes against an army they could not hope to match with numbers alone. After discussing various plans, the notable *Sahabah* Salman al-Farsi (who was a freedman of Persian origin) suggested digging a trench across the area of Madinah that lacked any natural defensive barrier (it should be remembered that much of the town was surrounded by impassable lava fields). While such defensive tactics were readily employed by the kingdoms and empires far to the north, they were anything but heard of among the Arabs. Nonetheless the idea was accepted, and work began on the trench immediately.

The communal effort of constructing the trench unified the Madinan community. The Prophet himself participated in the work alongside his *Sahabah*. One *Hadith* tells how during the digging a huge boulder was uncovered which the workers could not break. The Prophet went to the giant stone and hit it three times with his own pick axe. With each strike, brilliant sparks went up from the rock - one south, one north, and one east. Salman al-Farsi saw these and was amazed. The Prophet said, "Did you see them, Salman? By the light of the first I saw the castles of the Yemen; by the light of the second I saw the strongholds of Syria; by the light of the third I saw the white palace of Khusrow at Mada'in. Through the first Allah has opened the Yemen to me; through the second He has opened Syria and the West; and through the third, the East."

The trench was completed just as the Confederate scouts began to appear around Madinah. Those who lived in the outlying villages took refuge in the center of the town. With only 3,000 men under his command, the Prophet lined the Madinah side of the moat. The main body of Confederate army took up positions and prepared to take the town by storm.

But the assault of the Confederates was brought to a complete halt when it reached the edge of the trench. The attack was thrown into confusion as the Arabs had never faced such an obstacle in their traditional methods of warfare. Trying to cross such a deep ditch would make the army very vulnerable as it climbed into and out of it. Where ever the Confederates tried to cross the Muslims were quickly able to concentrate their forces at that one spot and push them back. All the Makkans and their allies could do was to set up camp and wait, hoping to starve out the city through siege or perhaps find some unknown pathway to get around the defenses.

Although the Muslims were able to hold the defense lines along the trench, trouble was brewing in the rear. The last remaining Jewish tribe in Madinah, the Bani Quraizah, had remained true to their pact with the Muslims (although they never assisted in any military operations) up until the Confederates appeared outside Madinah. Their fortified houses were closer to the center of Madinah than those of the other Jewish tribes, and their buildings actually formed part of the defenses of the city.

As the Confederates laid siege to Madinah the stance of the Bani Quraizah began to shift. The headman of the Bani Nadir secretly crossed over the lava fields to visit the Bani Quraizah. He encouraged them to breach their pact and attack the Muslims from the rear. He assured them that the Muslims would not be able to

Focus on History Writing:
The Prophet and the Sahabah as Historical Figures

Many people who read introductory accounts of the rise of Islam in Western languages might gain the impression that Prophet Muhammad single-handedly founded the Islamic community, originated its beliefs, forms of worship, laws and government. Two major elements of the story are missing. First, these accounts are written from a secular point of view. This means that the historian seeks explanations of events solely in terms of worldly motives, causes and effects. Secular explanations exclude the concept of God as an active agent in human history. Second, the actions and personalities of the Sahabah are often practically missing from such accounts. The entire story of Islam revolves around the person of Muhammad.

In writing about the rise of Islam, many Western, or European historians of the past two centuries often turned to a "Great Man" explanation. According to this view, Muhammad was such an outstanding historical figure, or great man, that his genius and charisma (gift of attracting people) is sufficient (or complete enough) to explain the rise of Islam as a historical force and origin of a civilization. According to this viewpoint, Muhammad composed the Qur'an out of his own mind, gathered and held a group of followers around him and planned every move with a clever eye to winning them over and overcoming any and all obstacles. In such histories, the Sahabah barely figure in the story of Islam until after the death of the Prophet, when those Sahabah in ruling positions are cast in the role as Great or Lesser Men.

Such writings may be contrasted sharply with earlier, medieval Western writing about Prophet Muhammad which were intended as polemics, or arguments against the Islamic religion, and contained many falsehoods and inventions interspersed with half-truths. For example, centuries ago, some of these writings used to state that Muslims worshiped Muhammad—even in the form of an idol—and they accused him of all sorts of criminal or insane behavior. Of course, the goal was to "prove" that Muhammad could not have been a prophet of God. In a sense, however, while many more modern historical writings about the rise of Islam actually praise the Prophet Muhammad and recognize his greatness, they in fact reject the idea that he was a prophet, just as the more extreme writings from long ago. Some historians reject the idea of prophethood altogether except as something that people believe in, but which has no basis in "reality," except in the human mind. Fortunately, some modern writers have demonstrated that they can lay aside their secular prejudices and tell the story from a point of view that takes into account both religious and secular, or worldly, sides of the story.

withstand such an assault, with forces coming in on two fronts. He encouraged his proposal with an added threat: if they sided with the losers the Bani Quraizah could expect to share their fate. Reluctantly the chiefs of the Bani Quraizah acquiesced. But cautiously they withheld their warriors, waiting to see which way the tide of the battle was going before making a move.

Despite the secrecy of the negotiations with the Bani Quraizah, the Muslims soon found out about the seditious plot through certain *Munafiqun*, individuals who were often willing to leak the secrets of both sides. With such a serious menace at their very backs Muslim warriors now had to patrol the streets of Madinah as well as the frontline, keeping one eye on the Confederates and another on the Bani Quraizah. This stretched their already thin ranks even further.

The Confederates continued the siege of Madinah for two weeks. But things were not going their way. Whenever they attempted a crossing of the trench they were beaten back. Demoralization spread through the ranks of the Makkans and their allies. Eventually one Muslim sympathizer in the Confederate ranks made his way into Madinah to present a plan that would cause a rift between the Confederates and Banu Quraizah. The strategy proved successful and Banu Quraizah locked themselves in their walled villages refusing to come to the aid of the Quraish and their allies.

Despite the military stalemate it would be the bitter cold of the desert winter that brought an end to the Confederate attempts to take Madinah. A freezing gale came out of the desert blowing apart tents, putting out fires and scattered horses and camels. Abu Sufian (one of the major leaders of the Makkan pagans) became so fed up with the lack of progress in the assault that he packed his belongings, took to his camel and set out for

The Camp at Hudaibiyah

The chiefs of the Quraish sent several of their own to the Prophet to negotiate the entry into Makkah as he stayed camped at Hudaibiyah. One of these envoys was a man named Urwa ibn Masud. Urwa stayed several days among the Muslims noting their behavior not only with each other but with their prophet. When he returned to Makkah, he reported his observations to the chiefs of the Quraish:

"O people, I have been sent as an ambassador to kings, to Heraclius and Khosrow and the Nagasi, and I have not seen a king whose men so honor him as the companions of Muhammad honor Muhammad. If he commands anything, they almost surpass his word to fulfill it; when he performs his ablutions, they nearly fight to touch the water of it; when he speaks, their voices are hushed in his presence; they will not look him full in the face, but lower their eyes in reverence for him. He has offered you a worthy concession; therefore accept it from him"

Makkah. The warriors of the Bani Quraish were quick to follow his example and by morning the entire Confederate army had melted away.

With the main threat gone the Muslims turned their attention to the problem of the Bani Quraizah. Their strongholds were surrounded and they were ordered to throw open their gates and lay down their weapons. They refused these demands and were then placed under siege for nearly a month. With food supplies running out, the chiefs of the Bani Quraizah finally agreed to come out, but only with the condition that they be allowed to choose the man who was to judge their attempted treason. They did not want to put their fate in the hands of the Prophet, despite the fact that he had dealt leniently with the other two Jewish tribes of Madinah. The Prophet agreed and the Bani Quraizah chose Sa`d ibn Mu`adh to decide their punishment since he had been a friend and ally long before Islam was established in Madinah. They were sure that he would rule in their favor

The story of what followed next has proven to be quite controversial. The earliest detailed account of the trial of the Bani Quraizah was given by the historian Ibn Ishaq (who died nearly 150 years after the event) and many later theologians disputed its actual occurrence. According to Ibn Ishaq the Bani Quraizah did not receive the lenient ruling they were expecting. Sa`d condemned the tribe to the fate that all nations of all times have given to traitors in times of war: death. The Prophet reluctantly accepted this verdict, and the Bani Quraizah resigned themselves to the fate they could have easily avoided. According to Ibn Ishaq's account the women and children were taken into servitude, and all adult males were put to the sword, except three who embraced Islam.

The defeat of the Confederates did not end anti-Muslim hostility. The Jewish tribes that lived in the oasis settlement of Khaibar encouraged their pagan allies to continue the fight. This time however the Muslims resolved to strike before another threat could be formed. The Prophet led an army of 1,500 men northward to deal with this growing threat. They understood that this would

not be an easy task. The fortresses of Khaibar were so solidly constructed that they were believed impenetrable and the Jewish tribes of Khaibar had great wealth generated primarily from their extensive date groves.

Trusting with confidence in their own strength, the Jews of Khaibar believed that the Muslims would not dare move against them. So when they awoke one morning to find a large army waiting outside their gates in complete silence they were completely taken by surprise. The Jews decided to man the ramparts of their strongholds rather than face the Muslims in the open field. The Prophet then ordered that the fortresses be put under siege.

The campaign stretched on for many days as the Muslims assaulted one fortress after the other. At last the Jews of Khaibar laid down their weapons and flung open their gates in defeat. Unlike the Jewish tribes of Madinah, the Jews of Khaibar were given a choice as to their fate: they could leave with all they could carry on their camels or they could continue to remain in their homes and farm the land. If they chose the first option the Muslims would acquire control of all property left behind. If they chose the second they would have to pay half of their yearly income to the Muslims. The capture of Khaibar did much to increase the wealth of the Muslim community and uplifted many of the needy and dispossessed.

The Treaty of Hudaibiyah

After the threat from the Confederates fell apart but still prior to the campaign against Khaibar, the Prophet received inspiration to visit the sacred shrine of the Ka'bah in Makkah. He and his *Sahabah* set out to perform the lesser pilgrimage, known in Arabic as *'Umrah*. They went completely unarmed seeking no confrontation with their opponents. Since this took place during one of the sacred months of the Arabs bloodshed was forbidden and an armed attack by the Makkans would be unthinkable.

But as the Muslims approached the holy city, a major dilemma confronted the pagan chiefs of the Quraish. Their position as caretakers of the Ka'bah meant that they could refuse no one entry into Makkah, even sworn enemies. On the other hand, if the Muslims came and made the pilgrimage it would be an affront to their honor and an admission of the legitimacy of the Muslim community.

In their desire to preserve face the chiefs of Makkah chose to break with tradition and block the Muslims. They sent out the celebrated warrior, Khalid ibn al-Walid, with a force of some 200 heavily armed horsemen to block the Muslim pilgrims before they reached the limits of the holy city. But many Makkans had by now grown cautious of Muslim power and were worried about provoking any violent clash.

The Muslims neared the city and the Prophet received word that the Makkans had dispatched Khalid to stop their pilgrimage, he ordered his followers to prepare to defend themselves. The pilgrims proceeded to a dry gulch known as Hudaibiyah where they hoped to resist the impending attack. Upon arrival at this place the Prophet's camel sat and refused to rise. "He who holds her once held the elephant," he said.

A message was sent to Makkah stating that the Muslims had come unarmed and desired only to visit the hallowed sanctuary. The

> "The first sanctuary ever built for mankind was that at Makkah, a blessed place, a guidance to the peoples; in it there are plain signs; the place where Ibrahim stood. Whoever enters it is safe."
>
> *the Qur'an 3:96-97*

Prophet sent his son-in-law, 'Uthman ibn 'Affan, to negotiate with the the the chiefs of Makkah. 'Uthman was well received by the pagans since his strong family connections still gave him much prestige. Despite the opening of communication and overtures of goodwill the Bani Quraish remained unwilling to allow the Muslims into Makkah. If they wanted to visit the Ka'bah, they stated, the Muslims would have to fight their way through. Since the Muslims had come unarmed, this was certainly not an option.

'Uthman did manage to persuade the chiefs to arrange a peace treaty with the Prophet. Its points were agreed upon and written down on parchment. This treaty stipulated that Prophet and those with him were to return to Madinah immediately without being permitted to enter Makkah at all. They would be, however, allowed to perform the 'Umrah the following year, during which time the Quraish would put the city at their disposal. But the treaty also secured a 10 year period of peace between the Muslims and the pagans of Makkah. During this time the two parties were prohibited from carrying out violence against the other in any shape or form.

On the surface the treaty signed at Hudaibiyah appeared to give the upper hand to the Makkans. In actuality it held a number of beneficial aspects for the Muslims. Firstly, it created a binding peace in Arabia. Tribes could now visit Madinah with ease, visit the Prophet and observe firsthand the implementation of Islam. Many would come to see a community united behind a leader who was powerful and

The Text of the Prophet's Letter to the Byzantine Emperor

In the name of Allah, Most Compassionate, Most Merciful.

It is from Muhammad who is Allah's Messenger and servant. It is for the Roman ruler, Heraclius. Peace is upon him who follows guidance. I invite you to Islam. If you prefer peace and safety, you should accept Islam. If you embrace Islam, Allah will confer upon you a double reward. However, if you refuse, you will be held responsible for the error and misguidance of your people.

O people of the Book! you should disregard all controversial issues and gather together on the point that is recognized as valid both by you and us - that we will not worship any one other than Allah. Nor will we attribute any partner to Him. We shall not take any as our Lord other than Him. If you disagree on this point, you should realize that both of us nonetheless share the belief in the Oneness of God.

Muhammad, Messenger of Allah

---

charismatic, but yet at the same time modest, wise, and deeply loved.

In the two years after the signing of the treaty with the Makkans the number of Muslims had more than doubled, and many of them were from the ranks of the enemy. And for the first time the Prophet began to look beyond the borders of Arabia. He sent forth emissaries to the powerful states that surrounded the Arabian Peninsula. Sealed letters were handed to Khusrow the *Shah* of Persia, to Heraclius, the emperor of Byzantium, and the *Muqawqas*, the Byzantine governor of Egypt, inviting them all to the message of Islam. The Prophet also sent communications to the Persian governor of Yemen and the *Nagasi* of Ethiopia.

These rulers responded with a wide range in attitudes, from hostility to sympathy. According to traditional accounts, Heraclius showed curiosity with the possibility of a new prophet rising in the deserts. However he dared not openly express such feelings in the face of the tremendous power that the Orthodox Church held in his domains. The *Muqawqas* was said to have remained committed to his faith, but seeing the Prophet as an influential new leader, sent gifts. The reaction of the *Shah* of Persia was very different. He tore the letter to shreds and rebuked the Arab emissary. When the Prophet heard this news weeks later he responded, "As he tore the message, Allah will surely tear his kingdom."

In Yemen (a land that had been under Sasanid domination for decades) the rulers were more open to the Prophet's call, perhaps due to a shared Arab heritage. The Sasanid governor of Yemen converted to Islam after having witnessed the Prophet's prediction of the assassination of Khusrow. The pagan tribes entered into the community of Islam and several *Sahabah* were sent to teach the people the principles of their new faith.

Lesson Review

1. Why did the polytheists of Makkah think that the Battle of the Trench would be the "final assault against Madinah"? What actually happened?

2. What was the goal of the Treaty of Hudaibiya for the Muslims, and why do you think the Quraish leaders were willing to sign it?

Chapter Review

1. Make a chart to help analyze the Constitution of Madinah. In 5 columns, list the provisions of the document that discussed *Establishment of Leadership*, *Cooperation Among Diverse Groups*, *Defense*, *Individual Rights*, and *Responsibilities of Muslims Toward Each Other*. Research the opinions of several historians about this document and discuss their views.

2. Compare and contrast both the campaigns of Quraish and of the Jewish tribes against the Muslims of Madinah.

Chapter Four

Mission Completed

Lesson Four

Home to Makkah

Looking Ahead

Despite gaining victory over his enemies, the Prophet showed great kindness and mercy.

Preview Vocabulary

Adhan
Mut'ah
Bani Ghassan

In the year after the signing of the treaty in the valley of Hudaibiyah, the Muslims of Madinah set out once again to perform the pilgrimage to Makkah. In keeping with their agreement, the Bani Quraish abandoned the town to the pilgrims and watched the visitors from the mountaintops surrounding the city. Following three days of ritual, the Muslims left Makkah and returned to Madinah.

A Glance North

Soon after the return to Madinah, several prominent men of Makkah appeared in the Prophet's city desiring to embrace Islam. The transformation of these former enemies only added momentum to the ever-increasing number of Arab tribes that were converting to Islam daily. Among these men was Khalid ibn Walid, the same individual who foiled Muslim victory on the battlefield of Uhud four years earlier. The Prophet embraced him and prayed saying, "O Allah, forgive Khalid for all of his obstructing of Your path." We shall read in later lessons how Khalid ibn Walid would become one of the greatest military leaders in early Muslim history.

During this time the message of Islam began to take hold among the tribes of the northern Arabian Peninsula, a region

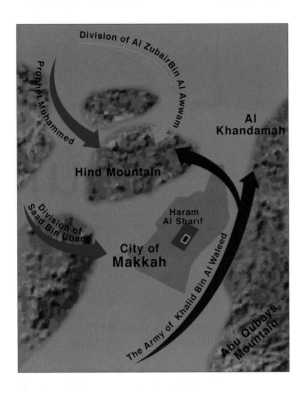

Division of Al Zubair Bin Al Awwam

Prophet Muhammed

Al Khandamah

Hind Mountain

Division of Saad Bin Ubade

Haram Al Sharif

City of Makkah

The Army of Khalid Bin Al Waleed

Abu Qubays Mountain

The march into Makkah was divided into several columns each under the command of a notable Sahabi.

that bordered Byzantine Syria. Any communication between Madinah and the Byzantine imperial administration first had to go through the large Arab tribe of the Bani Ghassan. These were a people who had been Christian for centuries and they were deeply attached to their faith. As people with extensive tribal connections, the Bani Ghassan were very well informed about the rise of Islam way to the south. It was something that caused great worry and they were quick to inform their Byzantine overlords of the power that was growing among the Arabs.

Late in the eighth year of the *Hijrah* the Prophet sent another letter to Emperor Heraclius inviting him to accept Islam. However this message was intercepted by the leading chief of the Bani Ghassan. Fearing any further spread of Muslim influence he had the

emissary executed, an act that caused outrage among Muslims. This cold-blooded murder was completely unprovoked and tantamount to a declaration of war, for the Muslims had never made any hostile moves towards those tribes they were at peace with. In response to the killing the Prophet ordered the mobilization of 3,000 men and instructed them to march against the Bani Ghassan. At the head of this force he placed his adopted son Zaid.

When the Bani Ghassan came to know that a Muslim army was heading their way, they immediately sent word to the Byzantine governor of Syria and a large contingent of imperial troops was dispatched to reinforce the Bani Ghassan. When Zaid arrived on the southern borders of Syria a few weeks after having left Madinah he found his army vastly outnumbered by the enemy (according to some accounts at least 35 to 1!). Near a place called Mut'ah the Muslims would meet for the first time the forces of the superpower, triggering a struggle with Byzantium that would last seven centuries.

Battle was quickly joined as the Byzantines and their Arab allies pressed the attack. The Muslims did their best to hold the line but the valor and bravery of the Muslim warriors gradually buckled under the sheer weight of numbers and the experience of the Byzantine army. Zaid and several prominent *Sahabah* fell in the initial onslaught causing panic to spread through the Muslim ranks. It was only the quick thinking of Khalid ibn al-Walid that saved the army from total annihilation. He rallied the breaking lines and quickly pulled the army back into the desert. Khalid knew full well that the Byzantines, despite their experience in warfare, would dare not follow into the vast waterless expanse. Although they were defeated, the battle gave Muslims insight into the military tactics and organization used by armies outside the Arabian Peninsula. It was quickly understood that the traditional tribal way of warfare would have to be modified.

Return to Sacred Makkah

Less than two years after the Peace of Hudaibiyah was signed conflict again broke out between Madinah and Makkah. Although they certainly were in no position to break the treaty and challenge the Muslims once more, certain individuals began to assist an allied tribe that was locked in a bloody feud with a tribe that was allied to the Muslims. However this aid was in open violation of the stipulations laid down by the treaty signed at Hudaibiyah. When the Prophet received word of the Quraish's involvement in the feud he sent word to Makkah that the treaty was now to be considered breached.

Panic spread throughout Makkah. The chiefs of the town realized the extent of the spread of Islam. The Muslims could now gather such numerical strength that the thought of resistance was futile. As the leading individual in Makkah, Abu Sufian went to Madinah to attempt to renew the treaty and ward off the threat of war. But this move was of no use as the Muslims refused to listen to his apologies and excuses.

At the beginning of the month of Ramadan in the tenth year after the *Hijrah* 10,000 warriors gathered in Madinah ready to march against Makkah. The Prophet did not immediately inform his men as to their goal but soon it became quite clear that it was their sacred home. The Makkans were completely unaware of the huge army that was heading towards them until it had reached within a days march of the city. In desperation Abu Sufian again went to the Prophet to negotiate some form of an agreement. But seeing the strength of the Muslims he realized that the Makkans were now completely at their mercy. He went to the Prophet and declared his conversion to Islam. He returned home to his town and informed his people that resistance was useless and that they should prepare for the bloody retaliation that was sure to come.

The day after Abu Sufian's visit the Prophet and his army began to pour into Makkah. Despite the worst fears of the Makkans he had it announced to the inhabitants of the town that all of its inhabitants would be spared if no resistance was offered. He magnanimously addressed those Makkans who dared venture out of their homes, "How do you expect me to treat all of you, my kinsfolk?" "You are a noble man, and a son of a noble man, so what less should we expect?", answered the Makkans. The Prophet then forgave a people who had spent the best part of twenty years tormenting both him and his followers. He bade them to go about their business freely absolving them of their past transgressions, as the Biblical Joseph had once done with his estranged brothers centuries before.

One act that the Prophet proceeded to do without delay was to clean the Ka'bah of its idols. The old gods of the Arabs were swept away with one stroke and the worship of the One God of Abraham restored. The notable companion Bilal climbed to the roof of the sacred building and made the *adhan*, the call to prayer. Most of the city's population, including those who had been harshest opponents of the Prophet, came forward and embraced Islam. For them Muhammad's beneficent display of mercy and clemency was proof enough of the truthfulness of his claim.

Lesson Review

1. Why do you think that amnesty was granted to those members of Quraish who had fought so long against the Prophet and the spread of Islam?

2. Compare and contrast these three events: (a) the *Hijrah* to Yathrib; (b) negotiation of the treaty of Hudaibiya and the following year's Umrah; (c) the victory over Makkah. How does each event reflect change in the circumstances of the Muslims and the Quraish?

Lesson Two

Unifying Arabia

Looking Ahead

Notice the reaction among the remaining pagan tribes to the Muslims' continued victories.

Preview Vocabulary

Tabuk
The Battle of Hunain

The Battle of Hunain

Shortly after the taking of Makkah, the Muslims prepared to confront the powerful pagan tribes of Bani Hawazin and Bani Thaqif that lived in the regions just to the east of the town. On hearing of the destruction of the idols of the Ka'bah these two tribes mobilized a force of 20,000 warriors and planned to recapture the city for the old gods. In response the Prophet gathered his original army of 10,000, along with 2,000 warriors of the Makkans who had recently embraced Islam. In a barren valley ten miles outside of the Holy City, at place known as Hunain, the two forces met for battle.

As the clash began, the Muslim forces were almost smashed by the fierce assault of the Bani Hawazin. The Prophet nevertheless succeeded in rallying the army of Islam and urged his followers forward. This counterattack was successful and the pagans fled the field. With victory in the hands of the Muslims, the champions began to collect the property abandoned on the field. But the Prophet wanted to win the hearts of his enemies and he ordered all captured livestock, property, jewelry, and prisoners handed back to the defeated Banu Hawazin. This display of reconciliation went far in speeding up the conversion of the remaining pagan tribes of Arabia. Such a gracious victor must truly be from God, they thought. Among the freed prisoners taken at Hunain was Malik

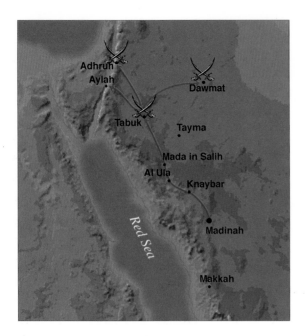

The campaign against the Byzantines and their Christian Arab allies took place in the 9th year after the Hijrah. One detachment of Muslims even reached the shore of the Dead Sea.

ibn 'Awf, the chief of Banu Hawazin. When all of his property was returned in front of his face he became Muslim on the spot.

With the threat of the Bani Hawazin subdued, the Muslims marched to the town of Ta'if, which was not only the abode of the Bani Thaqif but home to an important pagan shrine as well. The Bani Thaqif put up stiff resistance and the Muslims were unable to break through the town's walls. In frustration, someone in the Muslim ranks asked the Prophet to curse the town and its people for their tenacious resistance. But instead of invoking Divine retribution, the Prophet prayed, "O Allah, guide the people of Ta'if and bring them to us." The siege of Ta'if continued without let up for over forty days. But with the Bani Hawazin now Muslim, Ta'if no longer really posed a serious threat to the security of Makkah. The Prophet departed from Ta'if and left for Makkah, leaving behind a small band of warriors to continue the siege.

The Prophet's stay in the sacred town was short. He appointed a governor to rule over the affairs of Makkah before leaving for Madinah. Soon after arriving in Madinah, a delegation from the people of Ta'if arrived. They stated that the Bani Taqif would be willing to surrender the town and embrace Islam if they could only be permitted to drink alcholoic beverages. The Prophet was happy at their coming but of course was unwilling to compromise on the Qur'anic prohibition of strong drink. The delegation from Ta'if rescinded their demand and stated that they would abstain from liquor. But they did request to be exempted from participating in *jihad* and from paying *zakat*. To these requests the Prophet agreed. Those Muslims present asked in wonder, "O Prophet of Allah! How is it that you have exempted these people from *jihad* and *zakat*?" The Prophet replied, "First let faith enter into their hearts, for they will soon become aware of the importance of these commands and then they will willingly carry them out." Seeing the Prophet's lenience the delegation from Ta'if declared, "O Messenger of Allah we are ready with our hearts and souls to pay *zakat*, observe the fast and participate in *jihad*."

Tabuk Campaign

In the 9th year of the *Hijrah*, the Prophet received word that the Byzantines and their Arab allies were massing a large army in Palestine. The Byzantine governor had previously sent word to the emperor regarding the rapid spread of Islam in the peninsula. The Battle of Mu'tah that took place three years earlier was thought to be just an oversized bedouin raid. But now with the growing power of Islam at the very doorstep of the empire, alarm spread throughout those provinces that bordered Arabia.

During the season of the date harvest (which coincidentally was the hottest time of the year), the Prophet gathered 30,000 warriors to march north and challenge the growing might of Byzantium. The *Munafiqun* in Madinah took advantage of the timing of the mobilization to spread dissension in the Muslim ranks. They told the people that the date harvests would be left to rot if they went out on campaign. They were also sure to remind the Muslims of the power of the Byzantine army they had to face at the Battle of Mu'tah. But they were unable to succeed in discouraging the warriors and had to settle with offering excuses to stay behind.

Since the Muslim army was not a professional army every man had to provide his own weaponry as well as supplies of food and water. Many of the poorer Muslims could not afford the cost of these things so those who had the financial means came forward with huge donations. One prominent *Sahabah*,'Uthman ibn 'Affan, gave enough money to equip several hundred men. Yet compared to the Byzantine army the Muslims could hardly be called a match.

In the blazing heat of the desert sun the Prophet led the army 500 miles north toward the boarders with Syria. After a march of several weeks, the army arrived at near a place called Tabuk. The Prophet ordered the Muslim army to encamp and wait for the expected Byzantine army. As they waited he sent out emissaries to make alliances and treaties with tribes that lived in that region. The emissaries proved to be successful in establishing good relations with the tribes. However the massive Byzantine army never came and battle was avoided. After a two-and-a-half week wait, the Prophet ordered the Muslims back to Madinah.

Shortly after the Prophet's return a flood of delegates began to arrive from all over the Arabian Peninsula. Scores of tribes and clans eagerly entered into treaties with the Prophet and into the Islamic faith. As a religious force, the power of Islam was spreading well beyond the region of the Hijaz and now central and southern Arabia began to adopt the new code of life. All of Arabia had begun to enter into the fold of the *Ummah*, the Muslim Nation.

Lesson Review

1. Why was the year after the Victory of Makkah called the "Year of Delegations," and who were the delegations?

2. Why did so many Arab tribes enter Islam after the Muslims won the Victory at Makkah?

3. What was the importance of the Tabuk campaign, which some people thought might endanger the date harvest?

Lesson Three

Farewell

Looking Ahead

Recognize the final events of the Prophet's life and mission.

Preview Vocabulary

Al-Khutbat ul-Wada'
Usama ibn Zaid
The Plain of 'Arafat

The Farewell Pilgrimage

In the tenth year of *Hijrah*, the Prophet led 30,000 people on a pilgrimage to Makkah. His followers watched him very carefully and tried to memorize everything he did and said in regards to the pilgrimage, the *Hajj*. He stressed that they were in fact re-instituting the ancient rites laid down by Abraham centuries before.

On the plain of 'Arafat, several miles to the east of Makkah, the Prophet stood up on a low hill and gave a speech. Many of his closest companions who listened could hear from the tone of his voice that this was to be his last *Hajj*. In the sermon he encouraged Muslims to overcome tribal rivalries by accepting each other as brothers and sisters, by protecting each other's life, property and honor and by caring for the well-being of humanity. He said, "I have left among you that which, if you hold fast to it, shall preserve you from all error, a clear indication, the Book of Allah and the model of His Prophet. O people, hear my words and take them to heart." He also presented them with a newly received revelation:

"This day the disbelievers have no hope of prevailing against your religion, so do not fear them, but rather fear Me! This day have I perfected for you your religion and fulfilled My favor unto you, and it has been My will to choose submission [Islam] for you as your way of life."
(Qur'an 5:3)

When he had finished speaking, he asked the people, "O people, have I faithfully delivered to you my message?" The multitude present exclaimed, "By Allah you have!" The Prophet said, "By Allah, then I bear witness to this!"

After he returned to Madinah from the *Hajj*, the Prophet ordered preparations for another

The Farewell Sermon
(al-Khutbat ul-Wada')

"Indeed your blood and your property are as sacred and untouchable as the holiness of this day of yours, in this month of yours, in this land of yours. Look! Everything connected with the days of ignorance is under my feet totally abolished. Terminated are also the feuds of the days of ignorance. The first claim of ours on blood revenge which I abolish is that of the son of Rabi'ah ibn al-Harith. And the interest loans of the pre-Islamic period is absolved and the first interest loan I abolish is that of 'Abbas ibn Abd al-Muttalib, for it is all canceled. Fear Allah concerning your wives! Verily you have taken them on the trust of Allah and the Word of Allah has made relations lawful to you. You also have rights over them and they should not allow anyone into your home you don't approve of. But if they do that, then scold them, but not harshly. Their rights upon you are that you should provide them with food and clothing in a fitting manner. O people listen to my words and understand. Know that all Muslims are brothers and sisters to one another. You are one brotherhood all together! Nothing that belongs to someone else is lawful to you unless you are given it. Protect yourselves against committing injustice. Let you who are here tell those who are not. I have left among you the Book of Allah and if you hold fast to it you will never go astray. And when you are asked about me on the Day of Judgement, will you say that I delivered my message?"

Then the crowd said with one voice,

"Indeed you have, Messenger of Allah!"

campaign to be undertaken against Byzantium. At the head of this army the Prophet placed Usama ibn Zaid, even though he was a young man no more than eighteen years-old. Some questioned the Prophet's appointment of someone so young and inexperienced, but the mobilization proceeded any way.

In the days after the call to arms went out, the Prophet became gravely ill and began to suffer from high fever and great pain. He had Abu Bakr lead the congregational prayers in his absence and then retired to his apartment. There he succumbed to his illness several days later. Upon hearing of his death, the people of Madinah fell into deep shock. The Prophet's longtime companion 'Umar refused to believe the Prophet was gone, and threatened anyone who said otherwise. Finally, Abu Bakr came out from the apartment of the Messenger of Allah with tears streaming down his cheeks and said, "O believers, those who worshiped Muhammad – know that Muhammad has passed away from us; and who worship Allah – know that Allah is Ever-Living and does not die!" He then recited the verse from the Qur'an:

"Muhammad is a Messenger, and Messengers have passed away before him. If he dies or is killed, will you run away? Who runs away will not hurt Allah in the least; and Allah will reward the thankful."
(The Qur'an 3:144)

The Prophet was buried where he had died, beneath the floor of his wife 'A'ishah's room. With his passing, the message of Islam was sealed. It was now up to the community, the *Ummah,* to carry the faith to the world, as the Prophet had once stated, "...It is incumbent upon those who are present to inform those who are absent because those who are absent might comprehend what I have said better than the present audience." In this spirit, his companions, the *Sahabah,* exerted themselves to carry on as they had been so carefully taught during the twenty-three years of Prophethood.

Lesson Review

1. List what you think are the three most important points in the Prophet's Farewell Sermon and explain your selection.

2. Do you think that the fact that Abu Bakr was assigned to lead the prayer during Prophet Muhammad's illness was a sign of his coming leadership role in the *Ummah?*

The Message of Islam

Looking Ahead

Recognize and understand
the central beliefs of Islam.

Preview Vocabulary

Shahadah
Shari'ah
'Ibadah
Qadar
Mala'ikah

What do Muslims Believe?

The word *Islam* itself literally means to *"surrender one's own will to that of God"*. There can be no true faith without this surrendering of one's own wants and desires to Allah's commands. Islam in fact is also the only major religion that was not named after its founder or the region where it was founded. Judaism for instance comes from the name of the Hebrew king Judah; Christianity from the name Christ; Hinduism from the old word for the land of India, the Hind; Buddhism from the Buddha and so on. Although Westerners in the past have mistakenly termed Islam as 'Mohammedanism', no Muslim ever would use such a term to describe their faith. Muslims do not 'worship' Prophet Muhammad since he considered to be a human being, albeit one with superhuman qualities.

Every faith has concepts, beliefs and worldviews that are central to its existence and Islam is no different in this regard. The most important belief that the Prophet conveyed to mankind was that God is One, indivisible and all-powerful. This doctrine is carried in an expression known in Arabic as the *Shahadah*. This simple phrase states that God is One with no partners and that Muhammad is His Messenger. In Arabic this is *La ilaha il Allah, Muhammad ar-Rasul Allah*. Once any individual has said this with conviction and sincerity, he or she has entered into the worldwide community of Islam.

Every Muslim (regardless of sect or denomination) is required to believe in seven essential points that comprise the Islamic creed. The most essential of these is the belief discussed above: the Oneness of God (who in Arabic is called *Allah*). The Arabic word for this monotheism is *Tawhid* and to believe in *Tawhid* means recognizing the Oneness of God by means of devotion and refusal to compromise this belief. Muslims believe that it is beneath the majesty of God to have physical offspring or parents. Islam teaches that God is everlasting and He existed before there was a beginning and He will exist beyond the end. He has no form or shape (although this issue was a point of debate with certain fringe groups) and is so great that nothing can contain Him.

Muslims are required to believe in the existence of angels (*Mala'ikah*). According to the text of the Qur'an the primary purpose of angels in relation to humans is to act as emissaries between God and Mankind. The belief in angels is, of course, a belief shared with Zoroastrians, Jews and Christians. However unlike in the Biblical tradition where angles can disobey the will of God, the Qur'an depicts angels as being pure and good in nature having various tasks and jobs to perform in the seen and unseen universe. Thus in Islam there is no concept of "fallen angels" as in Judaism or Christianity because it would be impossible for angels to disobey God by their very nature.

Community life for Muslims all over the world traditionally revolved around the Masjid. Below we see the congregation of a Masjid in China finishing one of the five daily prayers.

Islam was the first world faith to recognize the validity of other religions and the central figures in those religions. All Muslims are commanded to accept all revelation that came prior to the Qur'an. Prophet Muhammad was in fact the last in a long line of men commissioned by God, beginning with Adam, and proceeding on through the centuries. Some of these prophets had scripture revealed to them that was later compiled into book form. Muslims believe in these early messages but that the centuries of human history people had allowed their sacred texts to become distorted, changed and even corrupted. This is not the case with the Qur'an however which has been preserved for the last 1,400 years free of change or error. Muslims believe that being free from error is a necessity of this particular revelation, as the Qur'an and the Prophet Muhammad are the last of God's books and messengers that will be sent to man.

Islam teaches that the human soul continues to live on despite physical death and that there will be a final Judgment Day during which Allah will judge every human being according to his or her conduct and belief in this life. Those who were faithful and obedient will be rewarded while those who did evil and rejected belief in the Creator will be punished.

Muslims believe that God knows everything. This means that nothing in this world happens without God's permission and that in reality He controls everything. This belief in Arabic is called *Qadar*. For the Muslim it brings great peace of mind knowing that in the end every event is part of God's plan. This does not, however, mean that people should just sit back and let whatever happen happen! Islam also teaches that everyone is responsible for his or her own actions.

How Do Muslims Worship God?

It is not enough for a Muslim to believe. Faith requires obedience to God's commands in both understanding and action. In Islam, being a Muslim consists of faith, or *iman*, and worship, which is called *'ibadah*. This *'ibadah* is made up of 'Five Pillars' or components. Every Muslim must carry out these duties as part of their religious obligations. These 'Pillars' are:

* *Salah*: This is what may be called 'prayer' in English, but it is certainly more than what most of us would consider to be 'prayer'. *Salah* consists of various bodily postures, which include standing, bowing and prostration. Though to many modern Westerners this way of praying may seem strange, it was in fact a way many of the Biblical prophets prayed! *Salah* is so important that it must be performed five times a day. Muslims are required to perform *salah* at pre-dawn, noon, mid-afternoon, sunset, and night.

*Sawm : This is the act of fasting during the month of Ramadan. The *sawm* is a month-long, daytime fast. From before dawn until sunset those who are observing the fast are forbidden from eating, drinking, smoking, and marital relations. Ramadan is the month during which the first verses of the Qur'an were given to the Prophet. Fasting is not unique to Islam and many other religions also use fasting as a way of finding inner purity. For instance Jewish practice contains several fasting days, and it is known by the New Testament that Jesus himself fasted for forty straight days.

* *Zakat*: This is a minor tax on the property of all adult Muslims who meet certain requirements. It is to be paid once a year to any organized body that collects the tax. *Zakat* is an offering of a portion of one's wealth that is considered part of one's service to God. *Zakat* is a religious duty and is not

considered voluntary charity, which is also highly recommended for Muslims to give. *Zakat* money that is collected goes to help those in need and to the upkeep of the community and general welfare of society.

* *Hajj*: This is the pilgrimage to the sacred city of Makkah, which is now found in Saudi Arabia. It is required to be performed once in a lifetime only if a Muslim is financially and physically capable to do so. Not withstanding the spiritual aspects of the ritual, the *Hajj* is a powerful symbol of the worldwide unity of the Muslim community. During the *Hajj* one can find Muslims from every nation, of all colors, languages, and walks of life. The *Hajj* consists of many different rituals, all of which have deep historical and spiritual meaning.

As a religion, Islam provides its followers with guidance in all aspects of their lives. Many Muslims do not believe that religion should only be practiced on certain days of the week or year.

Allah has given humans a code of life that has to be followed daily in all doings and transactions both private and public.

This is why Islamic Law has regulations for dealing with such topics as criminal justice, marriage, divorce and trade as well as more moral issues like neighborly relations, personal ethics and animal welfare. These laws are called the *Shari'ah*. Taken from the sacred sources of Islam (the Qur'an and the Prophet), the *Shari'ah* has been developed by scholars of the religion over the centuries. But the implementation of the *Shari'ah* was only to be carried out by the state, and traditionally individuals had no authority to take the law into their own hands

Islam teaches that if every person leads a life of belief, virtue and good conduct, human beings will obtain genuine peace and harmony. The Qur'an and the example of the Prophet Muhammad provide Muslims with the foundation on which to build this type of ideal society.

Lesson Review

1. Why is it incorrect to refer to Islam as "Mohammedanism?

2. Describe the different acts of worship required from Muslims.

Chapter Review

1. Explain Islamic beliefs concerning prophethood and Divine revelation.

2. Discuss the concept of submission. How does surrender to God's will differ from submission to worldly authorities?

3. What is the difference between the terms Islam and Muslim, or Islamic and Muslim? How should these terms be correctly used? Give examples. Give examples of incorrect use that you have encountered in books, newspapers or other media.

4. Why is Islam called a complete system of life?

Unit Three

The Era of the Khulafa Ar-Rashidah

Chapter One

The Establishment of Succession

Lesson One

A Question of Leadership

Looking Ahead

As you read this lesson look for the events that shaped the succession to the Prophet.

Preview Vocabulary

Saqifah
Fadak
Explicit

The death of the Prophet in 632 CE was a critical moment for the Muslim community. Since the very beginning of revelation, the Muslim community had never been without the strong leadership of one man: the Prophet Muhammad. If ever a problem or question arose people knew where to turn. But now they were without the one man upon whom they had depended on so dearly. For many despair set in as they saw that the Prophet had left no explicit instructions as to the question of succession. In the long hours following the announcement of his death, the issue of succession occupied many Muslims even more so than the funeral preparations. These were handled by the Prophet's immediate family.

As the community grieved the passing of their prophet, a large band of *Ansar* gathered in the council hall of the tribe of Banu Sa'ida to discuss what moves were to be taken regarding their future. When two of the preeminent *Sahabah*, Abu Bakr and 'Umar, heard of this meeting, they rushed to the hall, fearing that any hasty moves would cause confusion and chaos. Abu Bakr and 'Umar realized that it was of the utmost urgency to ensure that the position of leader of the *Ummah* be filled immediately to prevent the community from fracturing. They arrived only to find that the group had chosen one of their own to lead the community of Madinah. The Ansar recommended that other Muslim groups should pick their own leaders, something that would have been a step backwards to the days of the tribes. Abu Bakr and 'Umar

'Umar ibn al-Khattab's account of the events at the council hall of the Banu Sa'idah

"What happened was that when Allah took away His Messenger, the Ansar opposed us and gathered with their chiefs in the *Saqifah* (hall) of the Banu Sa'idah. 'Ali and Zubair and their companions likewise withdrew from us while many of the *Muhajirun* gathered around Abu Bakr.

I told Abu Bakr that we should go to our brothers the Ansar in the hall of Banu Sa'idah. In the middle of them was their leader Sa'd ibn 'Ubaba who was ill. Their speaker then continued, "We are the *Ansar* of Allah and the soldiers of Islam. You, oh *Muhajirun*, are a family of ours and you have come to settle among us." I then thought "they are trying to take our authority from us" and I wanted to speak, but Abu Bakr said, "Gently 'Umar." I did not like to anger him and so he spoke in his unique way better than I could have done. He said, *"All the good that you have said about yourselves is deserved. But the Arabs will recognize authority only in the tribe of the Quraish, they being the best of the Arabs in blood and country. I offer you these two men as choice for leadership. Accept which one you please."* Saying this he took hold of my hand and that of Abu 'Ubaidah ibn al-Jarrah who had come with us. Nothing he said displeased me more than that. By Allah, I would rather have come forward and have my head struck off than rule over Abu Bakr.

Then the Ansar said, *"Let us have one leader and you another, O Quraish."* Dispute grew hotter and voices were raised until when a complete split was to be feared I said, *"O people yesterday I thought that the Messenger would order our affairs until he was the last of us alive. But Allah has left His Book with you, by which he guided His Messenger and if you hold fast to it He will guide you too. Allah has put your affairs in the hands of the best one among you, the companion of the Messenger, 'the second of the two when they were in the cave'. So stand up and give him your bay'ah. Stretch out your hand, Abu Bakr!"* He did so and I gave him *bay'ah*; the *Muhajirun* present followed and then the *Ansar*.

(From the Sirah of Ibn Ishaq)

protested that such a decision would surely divide the *Ummah* between the *Ansar* and the *Muhajirun*. Islam, they firmly held, was to bring people together and not divide them.

Abu Bakr put forward challenges to the propositions of the *Ansar*. Despite Islam's stand against it, tribal affiliation was still an important factor in the minds of most Arabs. It was important, Abu Bakr argued, that the new leader of the Muslims be from a tribe that held the respect of everyone and the Bani Quraish were by far the most respected and praiseworthy tribe in all of Arabia. Were they not the tribe from which God raised a prophet? Had they not been since ancient times the hosts of pilgrims to Makkah and caretakers of the Ka'bah? Did not Allah grace them with divine protection against the army of Abraha? These were a few of the factors that gave the Quraish great prestige in the eyes of the Arabs.

But those of the *Ansar* gathered still seemed determined to go their own path. Heated debate raged until 'Umar raised his voice above the crowd, grabbed Abu Bakr by the hand and raised it. He asked all of the *Ansar* gathered there to name any one among them who could possibly have more standing in the community than the man whom the Prophet had chosen to lead the prayer during the final days of his life. 'Umar then pledged his allegiance to Abu Bakr and asked all present to do the same. Silence settled over the hall until one by one those gathered came forward and placed their hand in Abu Bakr's. The next day, this ceremony of *bay'ah* (allegiance) was repeated in the Prophet's *Masjid* for the whole community, and in this way the overwhelming majority of the Muslims in Madinah, both *Ansar* and *Muhajirun*, swore loyalty to Abu Bakr. He now assumed the post of *Khalifat ur-Rasulullah*, the successor of the Messenger of Allah and the leader of the Muslim *Ummah*.

Disquiet

Although the issue of succession may have appeared to be clear-cut on the surface, it gave rise to disagreement and dispute that has lasted among Muslims to this day. Throughout the centuries historians have tried to reconstruct the events of this critical period in Muslim history but have found the varying and often contradictory accounts offered by early chroniclers bewildering. As a result several interpretations of the events regarding the succession to the Prophet have come down to us today.

It is clear that the selection of Abu Bakr as *Khalifah*, despite being accepted by the vast majority of Muslims, left certain individuals dissatisfied. These were people who declined to give *bay'ah* in protest over what they believed a rash and arbitrary decision. The most distinguished of these dissenters were members of the Prophet's immediate family (the *Ahl al-Bait*) and those *Sahabah* who sympathized with them.

According to various early chronicles the Prophet's family was unhappy with the way the leadership of the community had been determined. The fact that deliberations occurred while they were busy with burial arrangements for the Prophet's body allowed them no opportunity to participate in the deliberation and did not help in smoothing over hard feelings. Furthermore most members of the Prophet's

The palm groves of the oasis of Fadak were a source of contention between Abu Bakr and the the Prophet's daughter Fatimah.

clan, the Bani Hashim, felt that his cousin 'Ali could lay the strongest claim to the leadership of the *Ummah*. It appears that 'Ali too believed that he had been clearly designated by the Prophet to be his successor. Nevertheless, the question of whether 'Ali and the Bani Hashim were out of the decision process at the Hall of the Bani Sa'idah, inadvertently or not, is still subject to controversy.

After Abu Bakr had been chosen to lead the *Ummah*, Abu Sufian went to 'Ali and tried to convince him to put forward his claim. But 'Ali refused to take his advice on the grounds that this would assuredly create divisions among the community. He said, "If I say something about this issue people will say that I am hungry for power. If I remain quiet people will say that I am afraid of death. But people should have known that the son of Abu Talib is as much fond of death as a baby is fond of the milk of its mother. My silence is because of the secret which I alone know. If I utter this secret you will tremble as the ropes binding a bucket tremble when it is lowered in a well." Because of his reservations about the process of selection, 'Ali did not give *bay'ah* to Abu Bakr for nearly six months, until after the death of his wife Fatimah.

The Bay'ah of 'Ali
(According to the History of at-Tabari)

"The Khalifah came alone to 'Ali who had assembled the Banu Hashim in his house. 'Ali got up and after praising Allah said, "What stopped us from giving *bay'ah* to you, Abu Bakr, was neither denial of your preeminence nor consideration of you as undeserving of any gifts that Allah has given you. Rather we held that we had a right in this matter which you all have heedlessly taken from us." 'Ali then mentioned his closeness to the Messenger of God and the right of kin and continued until Abu Bakr wept.... 'Ali promised to give his public *bay'ah* by the evening. When the afternoon prayer was over, Abu Bakr turned to the assembled people and offered some excuses as to why 'Ali didn't take *bay'ah* before. Then 'Ali rose and extolled the right of Abu Bakr, mentioning his excellence and prior merit. He went forward to the *Khalifah* and gave bay'ah to him. The people hastened to 'Ali, congratulating him."

Lesson Review

1. Role play a discussion that might have gone on following the death of Prophet Muhammad among the following groups:

   • *Muhajirun*
   • *Ansar*
   • Leading *Sahabah* of Makkah and Madinah
   • Members of Banu Hashim upon hearing of the succession

2. Why would a candidate from Quraish have been acceptable to all sides?

3. Using the text of Abu Bakr's inaugural speech, describe his vision of an ideal Muslim government. What important principles apply to the ruler and the citizens according to his view?

Lesson Two

The Man Abu Bakr

Looking Ahead

As you read this lesson, make a note of the personal characteristics that signaled Abu Bakr's ability to be a good leader.

Preview Vocabulary

Veracity
Shura
Consolidate
Irreproachable
Qunya

★

The selection of Abu Bakr as *Khalifah* established two important precedents that were eventually accepted by the majority of Muslims: 1) that the *Khalifah* had to be from the tribe of Quraish; and 2) that he had to be chosen from among the most upright of individuals. His authority rested on two foundations: adherence to the Qur'an and the Prophet's *Sunnah*. In addition, the *Khalifah* had to obtain the oath of allegiance from the people over whom he ruled.

As his authority consolidated Abu Bakr followed an important precedent that had already been established by the Prophet. This was the practice of basing those major judgments not covered through revelation on *shura*, a process of seeking advice from the most capable and knowledgeable members of the community. In an ideal *shura* system the *Khalifah*, like the Prophet, reserved the right to make the final decision, but he took into account the qualified opinions of others. We can see this process in the case of the collection of *zakat* from the bedouins of central Arabia, and the subsequent Riddah Wars. In spite of the fact that Abu Bakr was advised by several leading *Sahabah* to be lenient with these rebellious tribes, he insisted that the Qur'an and *Sunnah* required him to be firm in demanding obedience from all who professed Islam.

When he took the position of *Khilafah*, Abu Bakr gained the confidence of those who gave their hands to him. His piety and devotion were irreproachable, and his understanding of Arab society and temperament, combined with his talent for reconciling people, enabled him to sit humbly and effectively in the position of *Khalifah* for the next two years.

The Formation of the Early Muslim Community

Abu Bakr was born into the Quraishi clan of the Banu Ta'im in the city of Makkah during the years following the birth of the Prophet Muhammad. His original name was 'Abdul-Ka'bah (Slave of the Ka'bah), but the Prophet later changed it to 'Abdullah. However it was by his *qunya*, his sobriquet, Abu Bakr, that he would be known forever in the hearts of Muslims.

Abu Bakr had developed a close friendship with Muhammad in the years prior to the revelation of the Qur'an as both men were involved in trading business. He was a moderately wealthy man who gave his wealth freely to those in need. In the years of the *Jahiliyyah*, before the morality of Islam put an end to the often wild and cruel habits of the Arabs, Abu Bakr was a fine example of human virtue. He was well-known and respected in Makkah, and his generosity gained him the admiration of his people. The city chiefs had at one point in time even given him the position of judging retribution in murder cases.

It has been widely accepted that the first people to embrace Islam were the from the own Prophet's household: his wife Khadijah, his adopted freedman Zaid, three of his four daughters and his young cousin 'Ali. Outside of the Prophet's immediate family the first individual to come forward and place his unswerving belief in the hands of Muhammad was his close friend Abu Bakr. Years later, the Prophet recalled the conversion of Abu Bakr and said, "Whenever I had presented Islam to any one, they would always show some hesitation. But Abu Bakr was a man who accepted Islam without wavering." Throughout his life-long friendship with the Prophet, this quality of readily accepting everything from the Messenger of Allah was Abu Bakr's core characteristic and strength.

"Abu Bakr was the most austere man in the Jahiliyyah"
From the Tarikh ul-Khulafa' by Jalaluddin as-Suyuti

Abu'l-'Aliyyah ar-Riyahi said, "It was said to Abu Bakr as-Siddiq in a gathering of the Sahabah of the Messenger of Allah, 'Did you drink wine in the Days of Jahiliyyah?' Bakr said, 'I seek refuge in Allah!' Someone said, 'Why?' He replied, 'I tried to protect my honor and guard my manliness, for whoever drinks liquor surely will lose both his honor and his manliness.' The news of this talk reached the Messenger and he said, 'Abu Bakr has told the truth, Abu Bakr has told the truth.'"

When the Prophet made his *Mi'raj* in the tenth year after the revelation of the Qur'an a great uproar ensued. In the morning following of the miraculous journey the Prophet went out and spoke to the people of Makkah. This caused widespread ridicule from his enemies. "Look what nonsense he speaks! Surely his followers will laugh at him too!" The mob went to Abu Bakr and said, "Do you know what your friend is saying this morning?" They proceeded to relate what the Prophet had said. "Whatever Muhammad says I believe." replied Abu Bakr. When the Prophet learned of this, he exclaimed, "Abu Bakr is *as-Siddiq*." This is a person who's loyalty endures no matter what.

Abu Bakr endured the years of suffering at the hands of the pagans of Makkah along with the rest of the Muslim community. One day a mob had gathered around the Prophet and began to beat him until he nearly lost consciousness. Abu Bakr stood over his body and cried out, "Shame on all of you! Do you wish to kill a man just for saying his Lord is Allah?" Then the mob began to ask one another, "Who is this man? That is Abu Bakr the madman!"

Abu Bakr was a man of great humility and modesty. Ibn 'Umar tells of how the Prophet once said, "Whoever drags his clothing on the ground in pride will not be looked at by Allah on the Day of Resurrection." Abu Bakr, whose covering was then touching the ground, uttered with shame, "O Messenger of God! One side of my garment always drags on the ground unless I constantly tend to it." To this the Prophet responded, "Yes, but you do not do so out of pride."

Abu Bakr never hesitated in sacrificing his all for the cause of his beloved friend. Once in Madinah the Prophet ordered a general collection of charity. Abu Bakr came before the Prophet with every single bit of money and property he had and handed them over. The Prophet said to him, "Is this all you have? What then have you left for your family?" Abu Bakr replied, "I have left them in the care of Allah and His Messenger."

Lesson Review

1. What personal qualities did Abu Bakr possess that helped him to rule during this crucial period? How did his relationship with Prophet Muhammad affect his position?

2. Compare and contrast the ba`yah given to Abu Bakr with the bay`ah given to Prophet Muhammad by the Muslims.

Lesson Three

The Task at Hand

Recognize the challenges that Abu Bakr faced during his short rule.

Preview Vocabulary

Musailimah
Riddah
The Najd
Inviolable

The first decision that Abu Bakr made as *Khalifah* was to send a force of Muslims off to Syria. This army had initially been ordered to mobilize by the Prophet in the days prior to his death. The Prophet put the youthful Usama ibn Zaid (the 18 year-old son of his adopted freedman) as the head of this army. However the movement of the army had been delayed by the Prophet's death.

As the leader of the Muslim *Ummah*, Abu Bakr decided to follow through with the final command of the Messenger of Allah and sent the force to Syria. Many were perplexed by the Prophet's choice of such a young and inexperienced man to lead an army against the might of Byzantium. But Abu Bakr kept the teenage Usama, daring not to challenge the Prophet's final decree.

Before the warriors departed Abu Bakr gave Usama regulations by which he was to wage war: "Be not dishonest. Do not deceive. Do not deny your men their pay. Do not mutilate the bodies of the enemy. Do not kill the elderly, women and children. Do not set fire to date-palms. Do not cut down fruit trees. Do not slaughter any animal except for food. You will also come across men who have given up the pleasures of this life and are sitting in monasteries. Leave them alone." Thus were laid the guiding principles by which warfare was to be pursued.

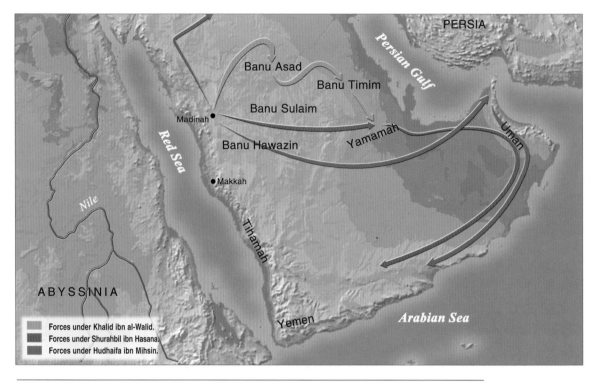

PERSIA

Persian Gulf

Banu Asad

Banu Timim

Banu Sulaim

Madinah

Banu Hawazin

Yamamah

Uman

Red Sea

Makkah

Tihamah

Nile

ABYSSINIA

Yemen

Arabian Sea

Forces under Khalid ibn al-Walid.
Forces under Shurahbil ibn Hasana.
Forces under Hudhaifa ibn Mihsin.

The Riddah Wars were the first crisis to face the Muslim community after the Prophet's death.

The Riddah Wars

Usama and his army set out for Syria and were back within two months without meeting the Byzantines. However while in the north they gave the Arab tribes there a display of Muslim military power. As soon as Usama returned to Madinah a major problem ensued. Prior to the Prophet's death, tax collectors were sent out to the tribes to gather the *zakat*, which was (and is still) mandatory for every eligible adult Muslim to pay. Paying the *zakat* meant that a central government now had the right to inspect all of the property of a tribe to calculate the *zakat* owed. Many saw this as an intrusion into the rights that tribal Arab society had enjoyed since time immemorial where taxation was almost unheard of.

Though the concept of taxation may be comprehensible for us today, for the average Arab of the seventh century it was something quite strange and even alarming. It was in many ways a test of the tribes' attachment to the Islamic community. Had loyalty been to the Prophet alone, people might have felt that any obligation owed to the *Ummah* came to an end with his death. But if loyalty belonged to Islam and to the *Ummah*, then clearly any responsibilities were to be carried out regardless of the physical presence of the Messenger of God.

Those tribes who felt their loyalty was to the Prophet alone, began to turn back the *zakat* collectors sent by Abu Bakr. Although this was a clear challenge to the authority of Abu Bakr as *Khalifah* there was disagreement among the

"And after me will come thirty-three liars..."

This quote taken from the Hadith of the Prophet expresses one of the primary concerns that occurred as the power of Islam strengthened in the Arabia Peninsula. Musailimah, Sajah and others put forward claims to some form of divine revelation and developed religious ideas similar to Islamic ones in hope, according to Muslim sources, of attracting the power and success the Muslim community enjoyed. Although the threat of these early claimants to prophethood was eliminated after the Arabian Peninsula was united under Islam, the notion that revelation (*wahi*) could continue after the Prophet Muhammad arose from time to time. There have been individuals throughout Muslim history that asserted a belief in continuing revelation, often stating that the time of Islam eventually will come to an end and allowing for a new faith to arise. These individuals often completely did away with the *Shari`ah* or Islamic law, or brought a new system, though only few of these individuals were able to produce a scripture to replace the Qur'an. The motivation for such lofty claims varied from person to person. Some were in response to ethnic tensions between Arabs and non-Arabs while others were a direct challenge to social stagnation. However, orthodox Islamic belief, be it Sunni or Shi`i, has taken the explicit statements made by the Prophet regarding the impossibility of further revelation to mean that absolutely no prophets, messengers or divine books will come after Muhammad or the Qur'an. Islam is the final message from God to mankind and is befitting until the Day of Judgment.

Some Famous Claimants to Revelation:

Musailimah   (Arabia, 7th century CE)
Salah ibn Tarif   (North Africa, 8th century CE)
Abu'l Fadl al-Qarmati   (Bahrain/Iraq, 10th century CE)
Fadhlullah Hurufi   (Iran, 15th century CE)
Sayyid 'Ali Muhammad, "The Bab"   (Iran, 19th century CE)
Mirza Ghulam Ahmad of Qadian   (India, late 19th century)
Mirza Husain 'Ali, "Baha'ullah"   (Iran, late 19th century)

Sahabah as how to handle this apparent rebellion. 'Umar (among others) were of the opinion that leniency should be shown. He said to Abu Bakr, "How can we fight these people when the Prophet of Allah said to fight people only until they say: 'There is no God but Allah'? Certainly whoever says this, makes himself and his property inviolable and his reckoning with Allah."

Nevertheless Abu Bakr was determined to enforce the collection. "I swear to Allah," he said, "that I will fight whoever separates *salah* and *zakat*, for *zakat* is an obligation on all property! Were they to withhold even a single sheep, I will fight them." For Abu Bakr the payment of *zakat* was one of the essential pillars of Islam; some tribes might regard it as a form of tribute, but he regarded it as both a moral and social duty designed to spiritually purify people's accumulated wealth. Furthermore the *zakat* was not the property of the ruler but used to uplift the financial state of the entire *Ummah*.

After much deliberation Abu Bakr finally declared non-payment of *zakat* to be comparable to apostasy (*riddah*), or leaving Islam. He saw it as being impossible to accept one component of the Islamic faith and discard another. Eventually all of the leading *Sahabah* who pushed for leniency assented to the force of Abu Bakr's logic and a notice was sent out to those tribes who withheld their *zakat*: either pay or be compelled to pay.

This ultimatum was not received well. Those tribes that had snubbed the first *zakat* collectors strengthened their resolve to defy the central government. These feelings were especially strong among the tribes of the Najd, a region that now lies at the heart of Saudi Arabia. Many of these people were recent converts who had previously "sat on the fence", so to speak,

waiting to see whether it would be the pagan Makkans or the Muslims who would triumph before committing themselves to one side.

Some of these tribes had allied themselves with the Muslims simply because they recognized the growing strength and superiority contained in the community that was taking shape under Islam. As individuals many were impressed with the charisma of the Prophet, with his discernment, nobleness, and his ability to unite so many different and often hostile peoples under one banner. However with his passing from this life many felt that their allegiance to the Prophet had come to an end. They attempted to regain their tribal self-rule and refused to recognize the authority of Abu Bakr.

When word came to the chiefs of these tribes that Abu Bakr was prepared to fight over the *zakat* issue, they started to launch raids against Madinah. Fortunately for the Muslims, the bravery and skill of such individuals as Talha and Khalid ibn Walid (as well as the timely return of the force that had been sent to Syria) repulsed the rebels' attacks.

False Prophets Appear

As law and order started to break down in central Arabia over the *zakat* question, a new and added menace came in the appearance of certain individuals who began to claim that they were receiving divine revelations as the Prophet Muhammad had. The most influential of these individuals was a man named Musailimah. He was the chief of the Bani Hanifah, a tribe that dominated the region of the Najd. Musailimah had watched the rise of Islam with concern. He saw how the Prophet Muhammad united the divided Arab tribes into a well organized, disciplined and powerful force. Musailimah hoped to copy this success and began to proclaim to the people of the Najd that God had made him a prophet. In the final year of the Prophet Muhammad's life a communication was sent out from Madinah inviting Musailimah and his tribe to accept Islam. In response, the Najdi chief agreed to embrace the faith as long as he were recognized as a co-prophet along with Muhammad. The Prophet denounced Musailimah's aspirations and conferred on him the title of *Kadhdhab*, 'the Liar'.

In defiance of the Prophet's admonitions Musailimah began to gather a following. He was an imposing speaker who attracted those tribes of the Najd who rejected Abu Bakr's calls. He formed an alliance with a woman named Sajah who also laid claims to being a prophet.

Abu Bakr sent his armies against Musailimah, and a frightful struggle ensued. It is said that more deaths occurred during these battles in the Najd than during all the battles that occurred in the lifetime of the Prophet. In the end Musailimah was finally defeated and killed. With the death of their prophet the Banu Hanifah admitted defeat, entered into Islam and accepted the full authority of the *Khalifah*.

But even as authority was reestablished in the Najd, other revolts broke out in parts of Yemen, Oman and in the area of what is now Bahrain and Qatar. Rebel tribes began to attack the Muslims and it again took military force to quell the violence. As the threat from the Riddah Wars diminished, a new peril arose in the north. During the course of the Riddah Wars, several of the tribes living in northern Arabia had been drawn into the conflict. This had a ripple effect and the disturbances were promptly noticed by the Byzantines, the Sasanid Persians, as well as their Arab clients.

Lesson Review

1. Why was it important to allow the expedition under Usama ibn Zaid to continue its mission?

2. What caused the Riddah Wars, and why did they not break out during the lifetime of Prophet Muhammad?

3. What threat did the "copycat" prophets in Arabia pose, and how was the situation resolved?

Lesson Four

Into Iraq

Looking Ahead

Understand the reasons behind the Muslim campaign against the Sasanids.

Preview Vocabulary

Bani Lakhm
En masse
Peasant

During the lifetime of the Prophet Muhammad there had been limited contact with the two great empires that lay to the north of the Arabian Peninsula: Byzantium and Sasanid Persia. The expedition led by Usama bin Zaid was dispatched primarily as a show of strength for the northern Arab tribes that were under Byzantine influence. The most powerful of these tribes were the Bani Ghassan, who held a small realm in what is now Syria and parts of Jordan. Since most of them followed Christianity, the Bani Ghassan were natural allies of Byzantium. Their lands sat on the borderline of the two superpowers, and the Bani Ghassan dreaded the Sasanids and those Arab tribes under Persian influence. For this they continually sought Byzantine protection and support. But the Bani Ghassan were powerful enough to dominate several smaller Arab tribes and habitually procured tribute from them. This caused considerable resentment and eventually these weaker tribes looked for any force that could disrupt the influence of their more powerful neighbor.

A comparable situation was developing among those Arab tribes living in Iraq that fell under the sway of the Sasanid. The Persians viewed the growing influence of Islam with great caution and demonstrated their antagonism to it when their ruler, Khusrow, ripped up the letter the Prophet sent him inviting him to accept the faith. Persia's allies in this area were the Bani Lakhm, an Arab tribe who's lands were centered in southern Iraq. Like the

Bani Ghassan (who were their traditional rivals), the Bani Lakhm had close connections with the tribes of the northern Arabian Peninsula. By the time of the birth of the Prophet Muhammad, they had converted to the Nestorian branch of Christianity, a branch not recognized by mainstream Chirstianity.

Despite being under the sway of either Byzantium or Persia, neither of these Arab tribes had any great love for the imperial powers. Constantinople and Mada'in (Cstesiphon) constantly exacted heavy tributes, or taxes, from them and constantly demanded a steady supply of warriors to be used in their never-ending wars of expansion. Knowing this Abu Bakr realized that if the Muslims did not seek to gain influence over the northern tribes, both Byzantium and Persia would use these tribes to contain and counter the growth of Islam.

Following the Riddah Wars in 633 CE, a serious crisis developed in Iraq, one that would draw the Muslims into conflict with the Sasanids. One of the major tribes of northern Arabia, the Bani Shaiba, had accepted the call to Islam in large numbers and took an active part in the Riddah Wars. However, once the fighting had ended they began raiding into Sasanid territory without Abu Bakr's knowledge. Their raids reached as far as the delta of the Tigris and Euphrates Rivers at the head of the Persian Gulf. The chief of the Bani Shaiba, Muthanna, encouraged the local Iraqi people (both Arabs and Aramaeans) to embrace Islam and rise up against their Sasanid overlords. Many of them did, adding to the slowly increasing number of Muslims in Iraq.

When word of these audacious, but unauthorized, actions reached Madinah Abu Bakr called a *shura* council to discuss the new developing situation in Iraq and the inevitability of war with Sasanid Persia. After much deliberation, it was decided that assistance would be given to the Bani Shaiba. According to the reports Madinah was receiving, the Sasanids were offering little opposition to Muthanna's incursions and the people of Iraq, fatigued by centuries of Persian domination, were welcoming the Muslim Arabs with open arms. The *shura* was also aware that the Sasanid Empire was still in a complete state of weakness following the disastrous and ruinous war it fought against Byzantium some fifteen years earlier.

Notwithstanding the initial weakness of opposition it was certain that the Persians would not let these Muslim forays go unfettered. Iraq was the most important province in all of the Sasanid Empire. The bulk of the empire's agricultural and trade activity originated from it. The Tigris and Euphrates Rivers were life-giving waters and provided the lands of Iraq with extremely fertile soil from alluvial deposits. Merchant fleets set sail from Iraqi ports along the Persian Gulf, plying ancient sea routes through the Arabian Sea to the lands of the Indian Ocean basin. Iraq was a prize that had been passed back and forth many times between the Romans (along with their Byzantine heirs) and the Persians.

The population of Sasanid Iraq was composed of several different ethnic and religious groups. Semitic Aramaeans (who formed an overwhelming majority) dominated the landscape. Arab tribes roamed the fringes of the desert. An Indo-European people known as the Kurds were found in the hills and mountains that led east into Persia. During this period of history, Nestorian Christianity dominated Iraq, although Zoroastrianism, Manichaeanism and paganism were still practiced in areas. There were also large and ancient communities of Jews, mostly found throughout central Iraq.

Why all this talk of Wars and Battles?
Islam means Peace through Submission to Allah!

It may seem strange to associate the spread of a religion with warfare. These two aspects of human civilization would seem to be completely opposite impulses. Of course, the record of human history is full of wars fought in the name of religion, in opposition to religion and even between sects within the same religion. Yet one of the central tenets of most religions has been brotherhood and peace.

Islam has constantly been singled out for accusation that its adherents, starting with Prophet Muhammad himself, sought to spread Islam by the sword. This is particularly strange in light of the Qur'anic order not to seek conversion through force, *La ikraha fid-din*, or "Let there be no compulsion in religion." Fortunately for serious historians, evidence has been well preserved, and the factual record is clear. Prophet Muhammad can certainly not be accused of being an aggressor. We can remember that he and his followers suffered life-threatening persecution (to which many succumbed) throughout most of the Makkan period. The decision to migrate was accompanied by an assassination attempt carried out by the pagans of the Quraish. The appearance of a secure and growing Muslim community at Madinah was seen by Quraish as a provocation to attack. If they had been unable to stop Muhammad while he was defenseless at Makkah, how much more dangerous to the Quraish's cherished power would they seem living in Madinah.

Around this time, the permission to fight was revealed, and shortly afterward the first of several battles began at Badr, most involving the Quraish and their allies. The battles that followed were struggles for survival waged as defensive wars. As soon as the Quraish realized that they could not easily defeat the Prophet they became ready to recognize him as a negotiating partner, Muhammad concluded a peace treaty with them: the Treaty of Hudaibiya. Even after the treaty was violated by the Quraish, the Muslims' victory over the Makkans was nearly bloodless.

Military engagement was made necessary by opposition, and it was fought according to rules protecting innocent lives and property. Hostilities halted as soon as peace became possible. The same was essentially true for the other campaigns, some of which did not involve the Quraish, but other tribes in the Peninsula. As it turned out, the Quraish accepted Islam, as did most other opponents, but not at the same time, or as a result of coerced conversion "by the sword". Tribes and individuals saw that it was in their interest to join the ranks of the Muslims. The Riddah Wars set down the principle that adherence to Islam was not a trivial matter, a case of pick-and-choose, or a function of loyalty to Prophet Muhammad alone, but a commitment to a complete way of life. But most of these early waverers went on to become loyal and ardent supporters, even on the battlefield.

In order to understand the battles that followed the death of Prophet Muhammad, it is necessary to look at the overall context of life in the world at that time. The seemingly endless wars that went on between the Byzantines and the Sasanids swallowed up many lesser powers, forcing them to become allies or clients of one power or the other. In Byzantium internal conflicts to enforce positions on religious doctrine was often little better than the persecution of Christians that occurred under the Romans. The Sasanids likewise had a mixed history of religious tolerance, sometimes allowing freedom of worship or even encouraging certain sects or groups, at other times not. Tolerance or persecution often depended upon political utility or upon the personal beliefs or whims of a given ruler. Tolerance was not written into imperial laws. As it was and would continue to be for many centuries in many places, the religion of the rulers was generally expected to be the religion of the subjects. In such a world, inviting others to share different beliefs could be hazardous, the best example being the treatment handed out to the early Christians living in the Roman empire. Indeed, if even a small power like the Quraish, who lacked a sophisticated state, could threaten the survival of Islam, how much greater would be the looming threat posed by superpowers and their allies?

In light of this global reality the policy of meeting force with force became one at which the Muslim military had to become adept. The early forays to meet Byzantine forces during Muhammad's lifetime were serious and necessary. While neither the Byzantines nor the Persians believed that the simple people of the desert could ever challenge their authority, they remained alert and sought to contain any challenge that came to their attention. The Battle of Mut'a demonstrated the Muslims' need to struggle for survival, and for the right to spread the message and live an Islamic way of life without hindrance.

The spectacular conquests during the first century of Islam can be understood in this light. Many people think, however, that these lands instantly became 'Islamic' once they came under Muslim rule. This is not the case, and it is important to understand the difference between two distinct historical events; one fast, the other slow. It is true that territory under Muslim control expanded very rapidly, taking in much of the Byzantine empire and all of the Sasanid Empire. Within a century, the Muslim state reached from the Atlantic Ocean to the borders of India and China. The people in these lands did not, however, embrace Islam as a result. There are accounts of a few accepting Islam, of course, but most people continued to live their lives as Christians, Jews, Zoroastrians, or pagans. The conditions for peace with cities such as Damascus and Mada'in allowed for the safety of houses of worship and individual believers. In fact, many religious people, both Jewish and Christian, welcomed Muslim rule as a release from religious oppression, especially in Byzantine areas.

The process by which people in the lands of North Africa, Syria, Palestine, Iraq and Persia became mostly Muslim was a long and complex one. It took as much as two or three centuries before Islam became the dominant religion throughout Southwest Asia. Many Western historians have noted that early Muslims made little or no effort to change the faith of people under their rule, nor did they expect them to change. Whether or not this is true, the thousands and millions of individual decisions to accept Islam were made over a long period, and for many reasons.

The Campaign Begins

Abu Bakr sent Khalid ibn al-Walid to Iraq with a force of 1,200 men to strengthen Muthanna. Khalid moved with great haste, arriving in southern Iraq after a few weeks' march from Madinah. He quickly seized the city of Ubulla that was an important port on the Persian Gulf. From there, Khalid joined with the forces of Banu Shaiba further up the Euphrates. There they met the army of Hurmuz, the Sasanid governor of Iraq.

Before the two forces collided, Khalid sent a letter to the Persian governor. "In the Name of Allah the Most Merciful," it began, "Accept Islam and you will gain salvation. If you choose not to, then surrender and pay the *jizya*. If you refuse this also you will have only yourself to blame. I am bringing against you men who love death as you love life." But Hurmuz disregarded the letter, trusting that his well-equipped army would be more than a match for these uncivilized Arabs.

Unfortunately for Hurmuz these Arabs were not the disorganized bedouin raiders he expected. Also, his confidence in his own army was overstated. The bulk of his army was made up of Aramean peasants who had no desire to give their lives to preserve the privileges of the Sasanid nobility that ruled over them. In fact these peasants were so reluctant to stand against the Muslims that Hurmuz had them chained together to stop them from running away from the battlefield.

Battle was soon joined and Khalid's levelheaded leadership won the field for the Muslims. Khalid and Muthanna's forces struck the Sasanid army and its ranks simply melted away. The Persian governor fell in the midst of the fighting (by most accounts at the very hand of Khalid). What became known as the Battle of al-Firad was important since it marked the end of Sasanid domination over Iraq. The only parts of this wealthy region to remain under Persian control were the imperial capital of Mada'in and its surrounding area.

The Campaign in Iraq as viewed in Muslim Literature

Hurmuz sent his men to trick Khalid and they plotted with him to do that. Thus Hurmuz went forth while different men of his called out, 'Where is Khalid?' Meanwhile Hurmuz made a plan with his cavalry to surprise Khalid. When Khalid showed himself, Hurmuz dismounted and summoned him to a dual. They met, exchanging several blows. When Khalid began to win the fight, Hurmuz's bodyguards attacked and chased Khalid. But that did not keep Khalid from killing Hurmuz. Al-Qa`qa` ibn `Amr attacked the bodyguards, pushing them back while Khalid was fighting them. The Persians were defeated. The Muslims rode in hard pursuit until nightfall. Khalid collected their equipment, which included the chains. These were a camel load, a thousand pounds. The battle was called Dhat al-Salasil."

from Tarikh at-Tabari (vol. IX, translated by Khalid Blankinship)

Lesson Review

1. What events led to the advance of the Muslim armies into Iraq?

2. What was the importance of Iraq in the region and why?

3. In what ways did Khalid ibn al-Walid demonstrate exceptional military leadership?

The Clash with Byzantium

Looking Ahead

Follow the flow of the military campaign in modern-day Syria and Palestine.

Preview Vocabulary

Ajnadain
Morale
Detachment
Vassal
En masse

Unlike the battles with the Sasanid Persians, hostile contact with Byzantium was nothing new to the Muslims. As we read in the previous unit the Islamic State had its first encounter with the Byzantine military during the lifetime of the Prophet. In the eighth year of the *Hijrah* (629 CE) the Muslims clashed with the Bani Ghassan, who were Christian Arab vassals of the Byzantine Emperor. The Prophet sent a force of 3,000 warriors north to deal with the growing hostilities that inevitably led to conflict with Byzantium. Near the settlement of Mut'a (in modern-day Jordan) a vicious but indecisive battle took place, the first between Muslims and a power outside of the Arabian Peninsula. Further threats of a Byzantine counterattack two years after the battle prompted the Prophet to send out another expedition to the north. But the Byzantines failed to send a force into the desert and the Muslim army sat for several weeks at Tabuk, from where the message of Islam spread to the Arab tribes of the region.

The Holy Land

Abu Bakr continued the Prophet's policy of strengthening Muslim influence in the north. He sent the expedition of Usama ibn Zaid to the borders of Palestine according to the Prophet's decision. It did not take long for Byzantium to realize that the Muslim expeditions were not the common raids of desert nomads, but were nothing less than a growing threat to their supremacy in the entire region. To answer the Muslim challenge they began to use their Arab allies to penetrate deep into the desert where their own heavily armed but cumbersome armies could not dare to enter.

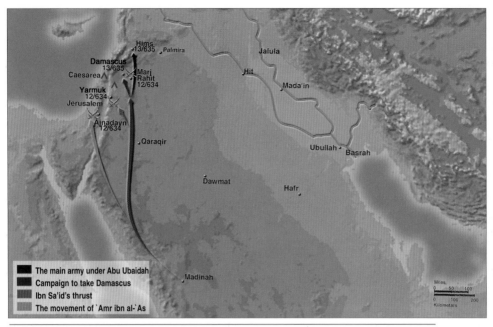

The Muslim campaigns in Palestine and Syria proved to be extremely successful.
Once the large Byzantine army was forced out, the Arabs encountered very little
opposition from the local inhabitants.

In the summer of 633 CE, Abu Bakr dispatched a band of warriors under the command of Ibn Sa'id to scout out the situation on the northern borders. Warriors from various northern tribes who had recently accepted Islam joined in, strengthening the Muslim ranks. Ibn Sa`id and his men camped east of the Dead Sea near a small village known as Taima'. The Byzantine governor of Syria heard of the size of the Muslim force and ordered his Arab allies to engage. These tribes mobilized and sent their men out to meet the army of Ibn Sa'id. But instead of battling the Arab Christians entered into negotiations with the Muslims. Much to the dismay of the Byzantines, the behavior of these Muslims made such an impact on the Christians fighters that they embraced Islam *en masse* and joined Ibn Sa'id's forces!

Despite the desertion of their allies to the enemy, Byzantine troops went ahead and clashed with the Muslims near a place called Taima'. Strengthened with their new allies, Muslim forces easily overwhelmed the Byzantines. Abu Bakr ordered large numbers of

reinforcements to Ibn Sa'id once word was received in Madinah of the victory.

The first of these reinforcements to arrive on the borders of Syria were under the command of Walid ibn 'Uqbah. He and Ibn Sa'id advanced on the important city of Damascus, hoping to gain the type of impressive victory here that Khalid ibn Walid achieved over the Sasanids in Iraq. But their desire for this made them overstretch their lines and Ibn Sa'id fell into a trap. On the plain of Marj al-Suffar just south of Damascus, the Muslim armies were completely routed by a strengthened Byzantine army. In the ensuing panic Ibn Sa'id fled the field and headed south to the Hijaz with some of his officers. It was only through the daring of one of his captains, 'Ikrimah ibn Abi Jahl (who was once a vehement opponent of the Prophet), that complete annihilation of the army was averted.

News of the defeat did not prevent Abu Bakr from exploiting earlier accomplishments. When he received news of Ibn Sa'id's route at Marj al-Suffar, he simply raised a larger army. It was divided into independent detachments, each under the command of a *Sahabi* of the Prophet Muhammad. These men were selected by the *Khalifah* primarily for two reasons; first, they were individuals of considerable standing in the Muslim community and; second (and most important) they were familiar with the lands in which they were to campaign, as they had often traveled the region as merchants. After receiving final instructions from Abu Bakr the force left the Hijaz in the winter of 633/34 CE with the goal of engaging the Byzantines.

The first detachment (which was under 'Amr ibn al-'As) moved north along the Red Sea coast and set up camp near the Palestinian town of Gaza. There it soundly defeated a Byzantine force at the Battle of Dathan on February 4th, 634 CE. Another *Sahabi*, Shurahbil ibn Hasan, raided the Jordan River valley and the lands on both sides of the Dead Sea. Yazid ibn Abi Sufian (along with Abu Ubaidah ibn al-Jarrah) headed straight into Syria. Yazid's force split off from Abu Ubaidah's and headed for the small town of Busra, which was the gateway into Syria for merchants

coming from the Arabian Peninsula and where, it was said, that the Prophet came as a young man.

Abu Ubaidah ibn al-Jarrah was sent out towards Hims, an important city to the north of Damascus. What awaited Abu Ubaidah in Hims was not a local militia but the entire Byzantine army under Emperor Heraclius himself, as news of Muslim successes in Palestine had been arriving in Constantinople for months. To face this Heraclius amassed all available Byzantine forces near Hims and moved south planning to deal with the Muslim threat once and for all. But the emperor must have had some doubts as to his mens' ability to face the Muslims as he declined to lead the army himself and instead placed one of his brothers in command.

As word came from scouts of the approach of this massive Byzantine army, the Muslim commanders in Palestine and Syria sent an urgent request to Abu Bakr for additional men. The gravity of the situation caused the *Khalifah* to order the closest available army to head directly towards Palestine. That army was the force under Khalid ibn al-Walid which was at

After mopping up Sasanid forces in Iraq, Khalid ibn al-Walid marched through the Syrian Desert to relieve Muslim forces in Syria.

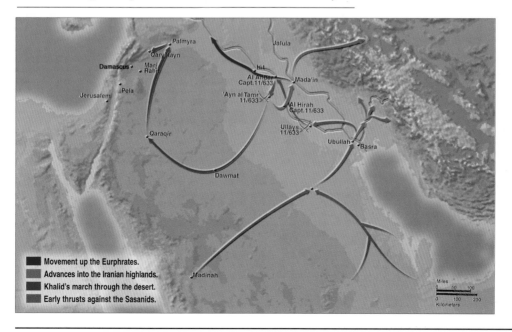

Movement up the Eurphrates.
Advances into the Iranian highlands.
Khalid's march through the desert.
Early thrusts against the Sasanids.

'Ain al-Tamr in Iraq, more than 400 miles from Damascus. As soon as Khalid received the dispatch from Madinah he immediately set out westward with his 1,000 men (all veterans of the year's campaigning in Iraq) to reinforce the Muslim armies.

But the easiest route from Iraq to Syria, up the Euphrates River, would take weeks and that was time that could not be spared. So to cut the marching time in half, Khalid took his men straight into the forbidding Syrian Desert. With such a large number of men, such a move would have been nothing short of suicidal as it would have been impossible to cover water and food needs without a huge supply of slowly moving pack animals. Nevertheless Khalid solved the dilemma by having selected camels drink their fill of water. As the army marched through the scorching desert, these camels were slaughtered; the meat was used as a source of food and the water stored in their bellies was used for water. This move allowed Khalid to get his men across hundreds of miles of desert in less than a week! This astonishing maneuver went down in the annals of military history, and it illustrated the advantage that the tough, lightly-armed desert-seasoned Arab warriors had over the heavily-armed yet cumbersome imperial armies.

On the 24th of April, Khalid's forces suddenly appeared at the Byzantine rear near the town of Busra as the local Banu Ghassan were celebrating the festival of Easter. Khalid ibn Walid linked with the armies of Yazid, Shurahbil and 'Amr. The Byzantines turned to face the bolstered Muslim army and the two forces collided just west of the city of Jerusalem at a place known as Ajnadain. The ensuing battle was bloody and hundreds fell on both sides, including many *Sahabah* whose gravesites dot the battlefield to this day. Despite the vigor of the Byzantine attack the morale of the Muslim forces gave them an upper hand, and eventually the badly mangled Byzantine army disengaged and abandoned the field. What was left of the imperial army fled to the safety of the walled towns and cities.

Lesson Review

1. Contrast the Muslim engagements involving the Byzantine armies with their engagements with the Sasanid armies.

2. Why was the forced march through the Syrian Desert such a famous accomplishment? How does it demonstrate the tactical advantage of the Arabs over their opponents?

Lesson Six

Two Years of Accomplishments

Looking Ahead

Recognize the main events that occurred during the rule of Abu Bakr.

Preview Vocabulary

Central Government
Ayat
Zaid ibn Thabit
Ummuhat ul-Mu'minin

The Collection of the Qur'an

In addition to the military activities of the Riddah Wars and the campaigns in Iraq, Palestine and Syria several other important achievements occurred during the two short years of Abu Bakr's administration. At the time of his rule the Qur'an was compiled into book form for the first time. It has to be remembered that during the lifetime of the Prophet, the Qur'an was preserved in many ways. During the period of his prophethood hundreds and then thousands of people committed the sacred text to memory, reciting it daily in prayers and speech. As individual *ayats* (verses) were revealed, the few *Sahabah* who knew how to read and write copied the words on to any available material - parchment, papyrus, bone, or wood. Some of these individuals had been able to compile their own private copies of the entire Qur'an, most notably 'Ali and Ibn Mas`ud. However, the Qur'an was still widely regarded as most becoming in its oral transmission. Nevertheless the written Qur'an would start to take on increased prominence as Islam began to spread outside the Arabian Peninsula.

During the *Khilafah* of Abu Bakr a serious need to collect the Qur'an in a written form developed. It arose as a direct result of the Riddah Wars during which many of those who had committed the Qur'an to memory were slain. It soon became apparent that losing portions of the sacred scripture was becoming a possibility. To address this concern Abu Bakr ordered Zaid ibn Thabit (who was one of the scribes of the Prophet) to make a complete written copy of the Qur'an, assembling its verses and checking it against the memories of the foremost of the *Sahabah* who had memorized it at the feet of the Prophet. This manuscript was then kept with Abu Bakr and upon his death it was given to 'Umar. After 'Umar's death it went to his daughter Hafsa, who was also a wife of the Prophet. This manuscript furnished the foundation for all copies that were produced and distributed during the rule of 'Uthman.

In the service of the Ummah

The many important administrative reorganizations that were set in motion during the lifetime of the Prophet were hastened during the rule of Abu Bakr. One of these was the weakening of the authority of the tribe to the power of the central government which was based in towns and cities. The entire concept of a central government was unheard of in the history of the Arabs, except for in Yemen where kingdoms had existed in the past. The highest

The Qur'an Brought Together

Zaid ibn Thabit al-Ansari, who was one of the scribes of the Revelation, said once:

Abu Bakr sent for me after a large number of those who knew the Qur'an by heart were martyred at the Battle of Yamamah. 'Umar was there with the Khalifah. Abu Bakr said, "'Umar has come to me and said that the *Ummah* has suffered heavy losses from the memorizers and that a large part of the Qur'an may be lost unless you, Zaid, collect it!"

Abu Bakr then said to 'Umar, "But how can I do something that the Prophet of Allah did not do?" Then 'Umar said to me, "By God collecting it is a good thing Zaid." So 'Umar kept urging Abu Bakr to accept his proposal, until Allah opened his heart and he took this opinion too.

Abu Bakr then said to me, "Zaid, you are a wise young man and we know you as being honest and not forgetful. You wrote down the Qur'an for the Messenger of Allah. Compile it and write it all down in one book." By Allah, if Abu Bakr had ordered me to move one of the mountains from its place it would not have been harder than what he ordered me to do. I said to both of them, "How can you do a thing the Messenger did not do?" Abu Bakr said, "But this is truly a virtuous thing." So I kept differing with him until Allah opened my heart to the idea. On that account I started to locate all of the verses of the Qur'an and collected all the things it was written upon by the people and from those who had memorized it.

(from *Sahih al-Bukhari*)

authority was in the hands of individual tribal chiefs. Every tribe was in many ways an independent country. It was only with the coming of the Prophet and Islam that the Arabs became unified.

In the final years of the Prophet's life, living conditions in Madinah had improved considerably. Trade in commodities increased as the Arabian Peninsula came under central rule. Travel became much more safe and secure and with this came the exchange of goods, information, and money. People felt protected as law and order began to replace the caprice of tribal law.

The collection of the zakat helped the poor and destitute tremendously as considerable effort was made by the government to find and assist them in basic needs. Indeed the old days of meager resources for most seemed to be over. With riches pouring in from the newly subjugated lands money was distributed to any who wished for it. A stipend was set for all the elderly Sahabah, as well as for the wives of the Prophet. The Khalifah also received payment for his expenses. Abu Bakr agreed to take an allowance for himself only after the shura council convinced him he had to rule and not sell rugs in the marketplace for his livelihood. On his deathbed he ordered that all of his possessions be sold to repay this money that was taken from the bait ul-mal, the state treasury.

Spiritual Life

A number of people had been trained by the Prophet to preach and instruct the faith during his lifetime. Great merit was (and still is) attached to the teaching of Qur'an. Those new Muslims who were eager for spiritual knowledge flocked to Madinah to study, and

particular Sahabah became well-known teachers and experts in Islamic belief and practice. Among these were 'Ali, 'A'isha, Ibn Mas'ud, Ibn 'Abbas and Zaid ibn Thabit. Teaching circles were held in the Prophet's Masjid as well as in private homes. Moreover in spite of Islam's undeserved reputation for isolating women from public view the very wives of the Prophet (known affectionately as the Mothers of the Believers - the Ummuhat ul-Mu'minin) were often sought after for their opinions and advice in theological matters.

As these Sahabah, being people who had lived, fought and worked with the Prophet, were consulted on matters new to the rapidly growing community, their judgements and advice formed the foundation of laws and regulations based on the Qur'an and the Sunnah. Because of the town's importance as a center of Islamic learning, Madinah came to be regarded as the example par excellence of an ideal Islamic society. The efforts of those who came to learn in Madinah (a people who transmitted this precious heritage of knowledge) would become more systematic and specialized in the coming centuries, and would eventually become a vast and complex system of Islamic scholarship and law containing many branches and disciplines. For the time being the tradition of oral teaching that began with the Prophet himself and sustained by the leading Sahabah, would remain preeminent.

The Death of Abu Bakr

News of the Muslim victory over the Byzantine Empire at 'Ajnadain reached Abu Bakr as he lay on his deathbed. A week earlier, he had taken a bath in cold weather and developed pneumonia. In the final stages of his

The Call of Belief and Arab Tradition

The message of Islam called people to a state of brotherhood far beyond the old Arab loyalty and pride in tribe and clan. Many of the great Companions grasped this ideal, but most of the later converts, and those tribes who had made political allegiance to the Prophet late in his life did not. They still made much of and took great personal pride in the glory and fabled deeds of their ancestors, and this attitude resulted in vanity, pride, and separatism. This struggle between tradition and the ideal of faith is made plain in the Qur'an, in which Allah says:

O you people! See, We have created you all out of a male and a female, and have made you into nations and tribes, so that you may come to know one another. Verily, the noblest of you in the sight of Allah is the one who is more deeply conscious of Him. Behold, Allah is all knowing, all aware.

The Bedouin say, "We have attained to faith." Say: "You have not attained to faith; you should say, 'We have (outwardly) surrendered' - for faith has not yet entered your hearts. But if you pay heed unto Allah and His Messenger, He will not let the least of your deeds go to waste: for behold, Allah is much-forgiving, a dispenser of grace. Believers are only those who have attained to faith in Allah and His Messenger and have left all doubt behind, and who strive hard in Allah's cause with their possessions and their lives: it is they, they who are true to their word!

Say: "Do you, perchance, inform Allah of your faith - although Allah knows all that is in the heavens and all that is on earth? Indeed, Allah has full knowledge of everything!" Many people think that they have bestowed a favor upon you (Muhammad) by having surrendered. Say: "Deem not your surrender a favor to me: no, but it is Allah who bestows a favor upon you by showing you the way to faith - if you are true to your word! " Verily, Allah knows the hidden reality of the heavens and the earth; and Allah sees all that you do.

mortal illness, Abu Bakr ordered 'Umar ibn al-Khattab to lead the daily prayers in the Prophet's *Masjid* in his stead. During his illness he thought carefully about a successor. He did not favor picking one of his family members, but chose rather a man deemed to be among the most prominent and capable men in Madinah: 'Umar ibn al-Khattab. When some people protested that 'Umar was too tough and harsh a personality, Abu Bakr said not to worry, that the weight of the job would surely soften him.

A few days after selecting 'Umar to be the next *khalifah*, Abu Bakr died at the age of 63, as had his beloved master and friend Muhammad. After the funeral prayers (*salat ul-janaza*) were performed, his body was laid to rest next to that of the Messenger of Allah. Even though Abu Bakr ruled for only two years, they were years of consolidation and strengthening for the new community and its government. They were two years in which a clear decision was made to develop a powerful state out of what had been a small collection of disunited tribes, villages and towns.

When the Prophet died many thought that Islam would only continue to exist as a local faith practiced by the unconstrained and independent Arabs. Abu Bakr's vision, however, went far beyond this, and his legacy was in meeting the early challenges that would have resulted in the collapse of Islamic unity had they gone unchecked. Through his resolute action, the first *khalifah* held together those whose lives had been inspired by the Prophet and returned to the fold of those who apostatized by demanding that loyalty to *Ummah* supercede loyalty to tribe. His resolve truly set the stage for the expansion that was to come.

Lesson Review

1. What evidence of continuity and change in the social and political life of the Arabs in Madinah can you find in the section?

2. List three achievements of Abu Bakr's period of rule.

3. What important precedents did the first of the *Khulafa' ar-Rashidun* set?

Chapter Review

1. In what ways do you think pre-Islamic Arab tribal tradition affected these events:
   • The meeting at the hall of Bani Sai'dah
   • Selection of Abu Bakr as *Khalifah*
   • The failure of some tribes to pay the *zakat*

2. What was the reason for ordering Zaid Ibn Thabit to make an authoritative compilation of the Qur'an?

3. What sources did Zaid ibn Thabit rely on in collecting the written Qur'an?

4. Research Project: Find out more about the Arab tribes in Northern Arabia who were clients of the Byzantines or Persians and prepare a presentation. Use the internet to look up topics like "Christian History in the Middle East", "Bani Ghassan", etc.

Chapter Two

The
Khilafah of
`Umar Ibn
Al-Khattab

The Man
ʿUmar

Looking Ahead

Look for the qualities that made ʿUmar a well-respected leader.

Preview Vocabulary

al-Faruq
Rigid
Leniency

The next man to rule over the Muslims was ʿUmar ibn al Khattab. He had been (along with Abu Bakr) among the advisors and assistants of the Prophet. But ʿUmar had not always been a friend to Islam. When the Prophet made his teachings public ʿUmar stood with those who rejected it. He joined in the harassment and torment of the Makkan Muslim community. But seven years before the *Hijrah* he had a total change of heart. He accepted Islam and became a great source of strength for the early Muslim community.

ʿUmar was a powerful, outspoken, and daunting figure both to those who dared oppose him as well as to those who stood by his side. Before his coming to Islam he was known as a man of powerful passion and often violent temper. Warriors feared his rage, women distressed of his ire, and children warned each other of ʿUmar's wrath if they should be caught doing something wrong. The Prophet had laughingly said once that if Satan were coming along a road and met ʿUmar, Satan would run the other way out of fear.

Yet the years spent by the side of the Prophet softened ʿUmar and his personality became less rigid. People began to develop respect for his character. He did, however, remain strict when it came to enforcing the laws and regulations of Islam, even when they were applied to his own family - he once had his own son flogged eighty lashes - and he was steadfast against those who misused the money of the *bait al-mal* or who sought riches in positions of power. During his reign he tried to remain on the side of the common people, which often meant going against the growing influence some of the nobles

Oil lamps like this one were widely used in ancient times to light up dark nights.

of the Bani Quraish sought to re-establish after they had become Muslim.

As Abu Bakr was bestowed with the title "*Siddiq*" (or truthful friend), 'Umar was likewise given the cognomen "al-*Faruq*", meaning 'the Just'. It is said as *khalifah* he kept two lamps, one filled with oil from the *bait al-mal*, which he used for his public work, and the other with oil he purchased out of his own pocket, to be used on personal time. A man this inflexible with himself was also firm in demanding that others act according to their faith. But there were times when he favored leniency and forbearance. It should be noted that 'Umar had been among those who advised Abu Bakr not to respond harshly with those tribes that refused to pay *zakat* after the death of the Prophet.

'Umar ruled for ten and a half years, a period from 634 CE to 644 CE. During this time, Sasanid Empire was brought to its knees and Byzantium was pushed out of Syria and Palestine. Muslim territory expanded to the frontiers of modern-day Tunisia in the west and the Indus River in the east. In his stay as *khalifah*, 'Umar was noted for being a brilliant organizer and a man continually concerned with the affairs of the *Ummah*. He continually strove to explain that the success of Islam depended upon the righteous behavior of all its people, from the top ranks of the leadership to the warriors, governors, merchants, artisans, farmers and common day-laborers.

By the end of the reign of Abu Bakr confidence in the strength of the central government in Madinah became more and more manifest and tribal feuds quickly became a relic of the past. 'Umar absolved those tribes that had initiated the great *zakat* rebellions and allowed them to join the struggle against the Sasanids and the Byzantines, something that Abu Bakr refused to permit. This did much to overcome the resentment caused by the Riddah Wars.

'Umar's reign witnessed astonishingly rapid territorial expansion and as a result immense wealth began to flow into the *bait al-mal*. This wealth however proved a challenge not only to the uncomplicated lifestyles of the average Arab but to the Islamic principles of faith and material sacrifice as well. The glittering treasures of the world proved to be for many a distraction from the original purpose for military struggle with the great empires. Were men motivated to spread the faith or to acquire riches? The lure of the fertile lands of Iraq, Syria and Egypt and wealth unheard of to the Arabs of previous generations would prove a most difficult test to pass, as the Prophet had repeatedly warned during his lifetime. Wealth and power now bestowed challenges equally as difficult as poverty and sacrifice had been during the times of hardship in Makkah and Madinah many years before.

Lesson Review

1. Compare the circumstances in which Abu Bakr was chosen to be *Khalifah* with the way that 'Umar was selected.
2. List two important challenges faced during the period of 'Umar's rule.
3. What personal qualities did 'Umar bring to the job of leader?

Lesson Two

Expansion Continues

Looking Ahead

Understand the factors that allowed the Muslims to achieve victory over much powerful forces.

Preview Vocabulary

Renounce
Yarmuk
Mawla
Qadisiyyah

The Battle of Yarmuk

The campaign against Byzantium in Palestine and Syria continued to unfold as Abu Bakr's body was laid in his grave. The gifted commander Khalid ibn al-Walid labored to keep the army busy by apprehending several towns and cities in Syria and Palestine. The most important of these was the great and ancient city of Damascus which surrendered after a six-month siege in September of 635 CE. But in the year following the Muslim victory at Ajnadain, there was no major military action. The two superpowers, Sasanid Persia and Byzantium were both smarting from the thrashings inflicted upon them in the last two years by a foe they had once viewed as insignificant. During this time they began to recover their power in a bid to turn the startling successes of the Muslim armies.

Syria was an important province to the Byzantine Empire. Although it could not match Iraq or Egypt in agricultural potential, its ownership was key to controlling major trade routes that generated enormous income for the empire. Consequently, in the spring of 636 CE, Heraclius planned a counterattack to retake this province from the Muslims. Regiments were called up from all parts of the empire; elite troops from the Balkans and Anatolia, mercenaries from Armenia, and warriors from the remaining

Christian Arab allies, now were under Jabalah, a chief of the Bani Ghassan who had once embraced Islam, only to renounce it and returned to Christianity. The emperor then placed an Armenian general named Vahan to command this expansive force.

When this massive force had gathered in southeastern Anatolia (according to some reports nearly a quarter of a million men!) and began to move down the coast of Syria, it raised alarm throughout the Muslim forces that had been scattered about Palestine and Syria on garrison duty. Abu Ubaidah ibn al-Jarrah ordered all officers and their men to assemble in one location, a favorable piece of land some 60 miles southwest of Damascus. The city of Damascus itself was abandoned and, to the amazement of its citizens, Khalid ordered the *jizya* payment returned, on the grounds that the Muslims would no longer be able to fulfill their obligation to protect the city. When this regrouping was complete, it was found that no more than 40,000 men were available. The Muslims now had to face an army more than 5 times its size.

Late in July of 636 CE, the Byzantine army had entered northern Palestine. After much maneuvering the two armies met in the shallow valley of the Yarmuk River. The battle began with the Muslims hopelessly outnumbered. The opening moves went badly for Khalid's men. The Arab Christians began to push hard on the Muslim flanks, threatening encirclement. But the dauntless resolve of the Muslim warriors eventually allowed them to turn the tide of the struggle. The Byzantine lines began to rupture under a vigorous counterattack. When the Muslims saw this they pressed down on the enemy with even greater fury and within a few hours the entire Byzantine army had scattered from the field in chaos.

Because the Byzantines had not expected to lose such a mismatched battle, they made few defensive preparations in the event of defeat. In the days after the battle, Khalid ibn al-Walid retook Damascus and most of the other major towns that had been previously abandoned. There were, however, cities that remained in Byzantine control and continued to resist, such as Jerusalem and the port city of Caesarea.

The Fall of Sasanid Iraq

When Khalid ibn al-Walid left Iraq in 635 CE to strengthen Muslim forces in Syria, he placed Muthanna ibn Haritha in command of the Sasanid front. But not long after, the victories gained there during the previous year were in grave danger of being lost. In the summer of 634 CE the new Sasanid *Shah*, Yazdigird III, took advantage of Khalid's absence to muster a huge army. When Muthanna's scouts brought news of this threatening menace he departed for Madinah to make an urgent appeal to the *Khalifah* for reinforcements.

As Muthanna arrived in Madinah Abu Bakr lay dying and decisions of a military nature now fell on the shoulders of 'Umar ibn al-Khattab. The new ruler of the *Ummah* ordered Muthanna back to Iraq with instructions not to engage the Sasanid army until fresh troops could arrive from Madinah (something that would take weeks to do). 'Umar then sent out word to the Arab tribes to assemble and start moving toward Iraq. However, the tribes that could still provide fighting-age men were hesitant to answer 'Umar's call. So many men had already been sent out to fight and the peninsula was quickly being drained of manpower. A single defeat in Iraq could open the whole of Arabia to Persian invasion. Consequently many chiefs were anxious about Sasanid military power, even though Khalid had exposed its weakness two years earlier.

One of the chiefs to answer the call to mobilize without hesitation was Abu 'Ubaidah ath-Thaqafi, whose tribe dominated the town of Ta'if. 'Umar put him in command of all of the troops bound for Iraq. Ath-Taqafi urged his people to sacrifice for *jihad* and they did. Within days some 10,000 men had rallied in Madinah.

It took nearly a month for these reinforcements to reach Muthanna's positions in central Iraq. Shortly after Abu 'Ubaidah arrived to bolster the defenses the Sasanids hit with unrelenting strength. The Muslim army was caught in a difficult position outnumbered and with their backs to the Euphrates River. The huge Sasanid army soon overwhelmed the Muslims and morale soon broke.

Muthanna tried in vain to disengage his army from the enemy but his men were already abandoning the field. To compound the disaster the Sasanids cut all the bridges across the Euphrates demolishing the only open escape route for the fleeing Muslim army. In desperation many tried to cross the river using the few boats they could find along the banks. Others were not so lucky and hundreds drowned in the river. The two Muslim commanders, Abu Ubaidah ath-Thaqafi and Muthanna were killed as they tried to fend off the Sasanid onslaught.

"And why should you not fight for the cause of Allah and of the weak among men and of the women and the children who are crying, 'Our Lord! Rescue us form this town of which the people are oppressors! Give us from Your presence some protecting friend! Give us from Your presence some defender!"

the Qur'an 8:39

As this appalling reversal hit past successes in Iraq, 'Umar began preparations for a larger campaign that would pluck the province from Sasanid hands once and for all. Governors from all of the provinces under Muslim control were instructed to send to Madinah all of their best available warriors. After they had gathered, several *Sahabah* were commissioned to lead it; notably Talha, Zubair and 'Abd ur-Rahman ibn 'Awf. 'Umar wanted to lead the new army into battle himself, but he was convinced by 'Ali that the *Ummah* would be much better served if he remained in Madinah to oversee affairs. 'Umar placed supreme command of the force in the hands of Sa'd ibn Abi Waqqas.

By the time Sa'd reached the borders of Iraq, picking up men as he went along, his force numbered nearly 36,000 men. In June of 637 CE (14 years after the *Hijra*), it set up camp on a wide and empty plain along the Euphrates River known as Qadisiyyah. By this time a huge army of 100,000 Sasanid soldiers was slowly making its way from the imperial capital of Mada'in (Cstesiphon) bent on inflicting another crushing blow to the Muslims. Sa'd sent messages to 'Umar informing him of the threat. The *Khalifah* sent back instructions that the Muslims were to remain steadfast in their place and that envoys be sent out to the Sasanid *shah* inviting him to Islam before any military action was to be taken.

Complying with these orders Sa'd sent several men of considerable status to meet with Yazdigird III. The *Shah* desired to impress the

Arabs emissaries with an extravagant display of material wealth. They had their imperial tents brimming with jewels, silks and carpets. The courtesans and aristocrats were dressed in their finest clothes. But the Muslim envoys were unimpressed by the glittering exhibition of Persian wealth. They submitted to the Sasanid monarch the only provisions acceptable: he could embrace Islam and keep his empire, he could preserve his ancestral faith and yield to Muslim rule or he could risk annihilation.

The *Shah* then asked the Muslims why they had chosen to invade his domains. Nu'aman ibn Maqran, the leader of the delegation, responded, "O king! Not long ago we were an ignorant, rude and wild people. Then God had mercy on us. He sent to us a Prophet and this Prophet called us toward good and rid us of our wicked habits. He had said that if we accepted his message, we would be successful in this world and in the next. So we accepted his message. He then ordered us to carry his message to the people of the world. His was a message that is a source for all good. O lords of Persia! We invite you to the path of Islam. If you accept it we will leave you alone. We will hand you the Book of Allah and it will be your guide. But if you decline this way, you will pay the *jizya* and live under our rule. We will see to it that there will be no more injustice or evil-doing in your lands. If you refuse this too, then the blade will decide between us."

Yazdigird III was enraged by these men of the desert. He retorted condescendingly, "O Arabs! Not very long ago no people on earth were as contemptible and wretched as you. The scraps from our tables from was enough to win you to our side. Whenever you were naughty, we only had to send a mere garrison captain to set you straight. I advise you to give up your fantasies of conquest. If all of this commotion is because your people do not have enough food we will gladly send you supplies. We will also appoint a good ruler over you, that he may treat you kindly."

One of the Muslims, a man by the name of Mughira, interrupted, "O *Shah*! We were certainly a people as wretched as you have said; perhaps even more so. We ate rotting carcasses and slept on the sands of the desert. But ever since a Prophet appeared among us, we have been transformed. His teachings and his example have made us leaders of men. Exalted monarchs like you now quiver before us. O Shah! Further discussion is useless. We again ask you to either embrace Islam or consent to pay the *jizya*." Both options were rejected leaving only the third: armed conflict. Yazdigird III ordered his most accomplished general, Rustam, to continue to advance to where the main Muslim army was encamped near Qadisiyyah.

For several days the two armies sat opposite one another. Several messages were sent to the general Rustam appealing to him and his army to embrace Islam. In response the Sasanid commander offered the Muslims a proposal to submit to imperial authority and combine with the imperial army. Both proposals were unacceptable to the other and a major battle was now assured.

The battle on the plains of Qadisiyyah raged on for three whole days. During the first two days the tide of battle went in favor of the Sasanids. The Persians were able to make full use of their superior numbers, and for a time it looked as though the Muslims would suffer another defeat like that they faced on the banks of the Euphrates nearly a year earlier. The Sasanids not only had a numerical advantage, but they were far better equipped than the

Garrison Towns in Islamic History

An important development during the time of these early campaigns in Iraq was the establishment in 638 CE of garrison towns, the most important being Kufa and Basra, built by Arab soldiers who had taken part in the fighting against the Sasanids. Garrison towns were established in order to avoid housing the military in the cities. The terms of treaties with such cities as Damascus granted them freedom from providing quarters, or food and housing, for troops. Garrisons provided bases from which to guard against any further Sasanid counter attacks. More important, they provided new homes for the Arab tribes and their families who migrated there from the Arabian peninsula. It was also hoped that these towns would isolate the Arabs from the general population and corrupting influence of Iraqi cities, weakening the rugged lifestyle of the Arab tribesman. Kufa and Basra played an important role in the following decades, contributing both to the development of Muslim culture, and also to the gradual Islamization and Arabization of Iraq.

Garrison towns provided an important link in the development of urban Muslim culture. On one hand, they became early centers of historical writing, as tribal histories of the Futuhat were set down in writing, along with the collection and teaching of *Hadiths*. As outposts for the spread of Arabic language, the garrison towns also became centers of Arabic poetry and philology, the study of words. Kufa and Basra both became well-known for the study of Arabic grammar in the early centuries, and its first systematic grammar books were written there.

On the other hand, the garrison towns became the first points of entry for the earliest non-Arabs who accepted Islam. Becoming closely associated with the tribes through the *Mawali* arrangement, they were probably more rapidly integrated into the culture and language of the Arabs than would have otherwise been the case. Those who had accepted Islam from among the Persians and others migrated to the garrison towns seeking detachment and refuge from their previous religion, customs, and sometimes families who disagreed with their decision. There, the convert might learn more about Islam, seek employment, find a wife, and make his or her mark in Muslim society. These towns became economic magnets to which migrants flocked to sell their goods, to serve the needs of the newly wealthy Arab settlers and their families, and to help build housing, roads, *masjids* and other public buildings. Some of these migrants, and many of their descendants, later accepted Islam.

As Arab and Muslim rule in the cities and territories became a fact of life over time, the garrison towns lost their military character and became more like ordinary cities, playing strategic or economic parts in their regions. Their cultural role as early Muslim cities, as well as the deeds of their founders and famous residents were their lasting legacy to Muslim civilization.

Muslims. In the front ranks fought men clad in chainmail from head to toe who sat on the backs of huge warhorses; on the flanks swarmed bands of nimble horse-archers; and there were even war elephants present in the Persian ranks. Most of the Arab Muslim soldiers would consider themselves lucky if they possessed a simple wooden shield. But the men of the desert held their ground against wave after wave of Sasanid attacks backed by nothing but their confidence in Allah's support.

The flow of the brutal contest began to turn, and on the third day of battle nearly 7,000 Arab warriors arrived to stiffen the Muslim ranks. Galvanized by the fresh troops the Muslims began to punch holes in the Sasanid ranks, which were now fatigued from being on the offensive for two days. The Persians quickly lost heart in the face of the Muslim counterattack and they began to rout from the field. In the pandemonium Rustam was slain and the imperial banner of the Sasanid Dynasty fell into Muslim hands. The Sasanid army was destroyed and now nothing stood in the way of a complete Muslim conquest of Iraq.

Despite being a decisive victory, Qadisiyyah cost the Muslims dearly. Nearly 8,000 of their men lost their lives in the three days of fighting. An even larger number of Persians fell as well. Even though the most important after-effect of the battle was that Iraq lay completely undefended it also had the important consequence of solidifying Muslim unity. A large number who fought at Qadisiyyah were men who had fought *against* Abu Bakr in the Riddah Wars. When these wars came to an end Abu Bakr had decreed that the rebellious tribes were not to be allowed to take part in any military campaigns because their faith in Islam was now in question. But the subsequent drain on Muslim manpower forced 'Umar to change this stance. He forgave the tribes and roused them to go out and render their services in *jihad*. Through the audacity and sacrifice exhibited at Qadisiyyah any past blemishes were rubbed out. Those who had once stood on opposite sides during the Riddah Wars now looked at each other with respect and esteem.

After allowing his troops a brief rest, Sa'd ibn Waqqas pushed on to the imperial capital of Mada'in (Cstesiphon). 'Umar ibn al-Khattab urged him to show clemency to any enemy combatants that fell into Muslim hands. Most of these were subsequently released on promise that they would never take up arms against the Muslims again. This lavish display of benevolence did much to encourage the conversion of many Iraqis (both Persian and Aramaean) to Islam. Those captured Sasanid soldiers who embraced Islam were given commissions in the army. The Muslim *Ummah* was faced with something quite novel: large numbers of non-Arabs now pouring into the fold of Islam.

The message of Islam was meant to be universal, for all the people of the world, but for the Arabs this universality was a new concept. They were a people still unaccustomed to the idea of forming a unified society with people beyond their ancient system of tribe and clan. How would these new Muslims be integrated into traditional Arab social structures? The most appropriate solution would be to merge these people into existing Arab tribes. New converts were to become *Mawali* (sg. *Mawla*), or clients, of a given tribe. Basically this meant that Arab tribes would adopt new converts (including farmers and townsfolk) and they would become members of that tribe. This not only reinforced the religious commitment of the new Muslims but it also intensified the diffusion of the Arabic language.

The Wealth of the Empire

When Yazdigird III discovered that his army had been annihilated, he fled Mada'in for the highlands of Persia. He wrongly assumed that a people only used to the desert would not be able to pursue him there because of its rugged landscape and often bitter climate. From the Persian heartland he hoped to regroup and launch a counterattack.

When the Muslim army entered the Sasanid imperial capital they found it almost completely deserted. The treasure that was abandoned in the palace was beyond the most fantastic dreams of these uncomplicated people. It is said that each Muslim soldier received 12,000 gold pieces and other luxuries as *ghanima* or war booty, even after the required one-fifth had been deducted and sent to the *bait al-mal* in Madinah.

When the riches of Iraq began to flow into the city of the Prophet, it is said that 'Umar wept profusely. Asked as to why he did so he replied that this fortune would soon spawn such rivalry and envy that it would plunge individuals, tribes and eventually the entire *Ummah* into discord. Indeed it did, for in the coming generations, as Muslim power and wealth grew, so too would civil strife.

Lesson Review

1. Why was Syria (which included the areas now known as Palestine, Jordan and Lebanon), so important to the Byzantine Empire?

2. What advantages did the Sasanid Persians have over the Muslim armies and what challenges did they face that may have led to their defeat?

3. Imagine you are a soldier or a migrant to one of the garrison towns of Iraq. Write a message home that describes your life there, and reasons why you would like, or would not like, to bring other members of your family to the town to live with you.

Lesson Three

Jerusalem and Egypt

Looking Ahead

Recognize the importance of Jerusalem for Jews, Chirstians and Muslims.

Preview Vocabulary

Plague
al-Fustat
Hallowed
Quarantine

In the year and a half following the stunning victory at Yarmuk, the Muslims further consolidated their hold over Palestine and Syria. It was during this period that serious differences of opinion arose between the brilliant general Khalid ibn al-Walid and 'Umar ibn al-Khattab that caused the former to be dismissed from his post. Command of the Muslim army in Palestine and Syria was subsequently handed over to Abu 'Ubaidah ibn al-Jarrah.

One serious threat to Muslim control over this area was the port city of Caesarea. Even though the Muslims had completely surrounded the city, it still had an opening via the sea to the rest of the Byzantine Empire. The Muslims were powerless to close this link as they had not yet developed any form of naval power and as a result the Byzantines could land troops into the city with ease. If Palestine was to be made secure, the Muslims would have to take this city.

In addition to Caesarea the other stronghold that held out against the Muslims was the ancient city of Jerusalem. From a military position, Jerusalem contained a large Byzantine garrison that sat behind Muslim lines. It was a threat that easily disrupted Muslim supply lines and communication routes. But Jerusalem was also a city that held great spiritual importance. It was a sight held sacred by both Christians and Jews (although Jews had been

forbidden by the Byzantines to live within city limits). Muslims likewise saw the city as hallowed because of the long line of prophets and saints associated with it as well as it being a place visited by Prophet Muhammad during his supernatural voyage known as the *Isra'* and *Mi'raj*, which took place during the difficult times of persecution in Makkah.

In the spring of 638 CE, it was decided that both of these cities had to be taken. For several months Jerusalem was blockaded to prevent the entry of supplies and reinforcements. One of the most important figures in the city was the Orthodox Christian bishop. He came to the realization that resistance would be futile. Hoping to avoid bloodshed, he entered into negotiations with the Muslims.

Despite the fact that this move was not sanctioned by Constantinople the bishop convinced the city's garrison to lay down its arms and throw open the city gates.On their part the Muslims agreed not to shed any blood or pillage the property of the inhabitants. Churches were to be safeguarded and Christians were to be allowed to worship as they had always done. Only one major condition was demanded from

the Christians: they had to allow Jews into the city once more. Despite the hostility that often marred earlier Jewish-Muslim relations, this opening of their holiest of places so pleased the Jews that several Palestinian rabbis even called the Arabs the forerunners of the Messiah.

Plague & Famine

Two horrible events struck the land as the Muslim armies made further gains in Palestine and Syria. A bitter famine and drought spread throughout the Arabian Peninsula. Hundreds perished for want of food as 'Umar scrambled all available resources to alleviate the starvation. Thousands of Arab tribesmen and their families abandoned their homelands and began to move toward the newly conquered lands of Iraq and Syria. Their presence would strengthen the growing Arab presence in these regions.

But these refugees from famine did not find much relief in Palestine and Syria. In 639 CE a terrible plague broke out near Damascus and it rapidly spread throughout the region. Thousands of the local population perished as did many who served in the Muslim army, including the commander-in-chief Abu 'Ubaidah. To prevent

'Umar's Role in the Taking of Jerusalem

Historical accounts regarding the siege of Jerusalem tell us that the Orthodox bishop of the city agreed to surrender the city to the leader of the Muslims himself. Therefore 'Umar traveled hundreds of miles from Madinah to Jerusalem on camelback with one of his servants. As 'Umar and his man approached the city, it was his servant's turn to ride the one camel they had between them, and the Byzantine aristocrats were surprised to find 'Umar walking, sweaty and covered in the dust of travel, to receive their surrender.

All of the Muslim military officers came out to meet their leader, all of them wearing silk cloaks and bedeck with jewels. Now it is well-known that the Prophet had forbidden men to wear silk and 'Umar was furious. He picked up some small stones, he threw them at his men. "Have you changed so much in just two years?" he yelled, "What kind of dress is this?" The officers replied that they were in a land where people judged an individual by the quality of his clothes. "If we wear ordinary clothes," they said, "We will have little respect among these people!" 'Umar grudgingly accepted the point, but it was a indication of the heavy influence that Byzantine culture, like that of the Persians, was exerting on the Arab Muslims.

With 'Umar's arrival the terms of surrender were drawn up between the Muslims and the inhabitants of the city. It read in part:

> "...The inhabitants of Jerusalem are granted security of life and property. Their churches and crosses shall be guaranteed. This treaty applies to all people of the city. Their places of worship shall remain intact. These shall neither be taken over nor pulled down. People shall be free to follow their religion..."

Once inside the city, 'Umar prayed at the future site of the Masjid al-Aqsa, where the Prophet had prayed on the night of the *Mi`raj*. The area was covered by a heap of garbage, which the *Khalifah* and his men immediately began to clear away. A *Masjid* was then built there. Later it became the site of one of the earliest and most beautiful examples of early Muslim architecture, the Dome of the Rock (sometimes wrongly called the *Masjid* of 'Umar). The *Khalifah* visited the Church of the Holy Sepulcher, a site dear to Christians. When the time came to pray, he refused the offer of its priests to pray inside, fearing that Muslims would later turn the building into a *Masjid*.

further spread of the destructive disease, the *Khalifah* sent instructions that all large troop concentrations were to disperse into smaller formations. These were then quarantined, or sealed off. No one was allowed to enter or leave their camps until the plague subsided. This quick-witted move helped to halt spread of the plague.

By the time the plague ended, two sons of Abu Sufian (the chief of the Umayyad clan) were left in total control of Palestine and Syria. These two were Mu'awiya and his half-brother Yazid. As he lay dying of the plague, Abu 'Ubaidah appointed Yazid to succeed him as commander of of the Syrian front. A year after that his brother, Mu'awiyah, took over. Mu`awiya quickly began to build up a power base in Syria that was centered on the ancient city of Damascus.

To the banks of the Nile

As Muslim armies stamped out the remnants of Byzantine rule in Palestine and Syria, 'Amr ibn al-'As took the 2,000 troops under his command in western Palestine and embarked for Egypt. 'Umar ibn al-Khattab was not enthused with this move, as he did not want to see further bloodshed. He felt that opening a new front was not necessary as the Byzantines would take considerable time to recuperate from the losses that were recently inflicted upon them. But 'Amr was determined to take Egypt, which was a wealthy and fertile province that supplied grain to most of the Mediterranean world. Control of Egypt would open up vast agricultural and economic assets.

Egypt at the time of the Muslim expansion was mostly populated by Christians. The majority of the people followed the Coptic sect rather than the Byzantine, or Eastern Orthodox Church. Byzantine troops were garrisoned throughout the country, and the Byzantine-appointed governor was hated by the Egyptian people.

By the time 'Umar received word of 'Amr's intentions there was little he could do to stop it. Defeating any Byzantine force that stood in his way, 'Amr quickly reached the Nile River. He appealed to the *Khalifah* to send reinforcements so that the province could be completely subdued.

'Umar was impressed by the victories and sent 8,000 men under the venerable *Sahabah* Zubair ibn 'Awwam to bolster the army in Egypt.

Faced with a relentless foe the Byzantine governor abandoned all of Egypt except the strategic port city of Alexandria. In military terms, storming the city seemed a daunting task. It could easily receive supplies and reinforcements by sea, and a large swamp blocked much of the approach from the land side. The city was put under siege for more than six months during which the Muslims made little progress. By the spring of 642 CE the Byzantines began to evacuate their army by way of the sea. They began to see the folly in protecting a population that no longer supported their rule. Gradually the Byzantines withdrew from Alexandria and the local Egyptian population threw open the gates of the city to the Muslim commanders.

As in Iraq, garrisons were established where troops and their families could live apart from the local population. One, al-Fustat (the Pavillion) was established by 'Amr ibn al-'As on the east bank of the Nile. As was the case in other garrisons, permanent structures soon replaced the tents, as houses, shops, *masjids* and other urban structures appeared. Within the coming decades a new city would spring up from this military settlement.

Lesson Review

1. Why was the Muslim victory at Jerusalem especially significant? What historical evidence is there that shows its importance to the Muslim state?

2. How did other religious groups receive the Muslim ruler, and what was their treatment under Muslim governance?

3. Did the conquest of Egypt take place with the full support of the Khalifah? What does the decision by 'Amr ibn al-'As tell about challenges facing Muslim rule at that time?

4. What factors helped achieve victory in Egypt?

The Price of Success

Looking Ahead

Look for the innovations
'Umar made in governing
the Islamic State.

Preview Vocabulary

Amir
Diligence
Precedent
Fiqh

'Umar Appoints His Governors

Every place that held a garrison, a governor, an *amir*, was appointed to represent the *Khalifah*. His responsibilities included leading the prayer, organizing military activities, and collecting taxes (both *zakat* from Muslims and *jizya* from non-Muslims) from his population. The *amir* was expected to keep law and order and to settle disputes that arose among the populace. Additionally the *amir* needed to be capable of handling Arab tribesmen, people who were completely unused to any central control over their lives. Though they were expected to act according to the morals and principles taught by the Qur'an and *Sunnah*, the *amirs* sometimes chose policies that were more practical than moral in securing power and security.

'Umar strove to appoint men from the ranks of the senior *Sahabah* but a great number of these individuals had fallen in battle, and those that were still alive were growing old. Consequently he often had to appoint men whose roots in the Muslim community did not run so deep. These appointees were men of considerable organizational talent and 'Umar constantly inspected their demeanor, making sure they made themselves available to the people, administered justice fairly, and used public funds wisely. If any one of them seemed to be self-indulgent or tyrannical, he was dismissed from his post. None were too far above 'Umar's standards. One governor, Abu Hurairah (a man who had lived in utter poverty during the Prophet's lifetime and who was a very significant *Sahabi*), was dismissed from his post in Bahrain because 'Umar received word that he bought himself a thoroughbred racehorse.

In spite of such diligence, the appointment of suitable and dedicated men to govern the rapidly expanding territories did not always turn out as expected. Communication with Madinah was difficult and it often took weeks to send a message and receive an answer.

Governors more often than not had to make decisions without direction from the *khalifah*. It was only through the strength of his character and will power that 'Umar was able to keep firm control over such a vast dominion.

Precedents Established

The early Muslim community looked to the guiding principles the Qur'an and the *Sunnah* in managing the affairs of the state. Where there was no real precedence to follow, the *Khalifah* (or local leaders) would base decisions upon personal opinion, seeking theological answers most closely relevant to the situation at hand.

Personal Famine Relief

`Umar was a man who tried his best to keep in touch with the people who were under his care. During the great famine that hit the Hijaz in 638 CE, he used to roam the streets of Madinah checking on the welfare of its citizens.

Once, as he was in his nightly rounds, he suddenly noticed a poor woman in a hut looking as if she was trying to cook something to pacify a number of small children. When he approached the woman, he noticed that she actually had nothing in the pot. She was pretending to cook only to show the starving children that she was cooking for them. The woman was hoping that the children would fall asleep, waiting for the food to come.

`Umar was crushed when he saw this pitiful sight. He ran to his home and grabbed the megre ration of milk, bread and dates that he and his family subsisted on. He returned to the woman and fed her children. The poor woman said, *"I don't know who you are, but you are sure better than our leader Umar. He is our khalifah and he doesn't even know that we have nothing to eat. Tell me sir, what kind of leader is this who does not care for us?"*

`Umar nodded in agreement and said, *"Yes you are right! `Umar is responsible for your welfare. Please forgive him this time, for he has learned his lesson."*

During this period Islamic religious scholarship was in the very early stages of development. There were no books of *fiqh* (guidelines on religious judgement and practice), only consultation among those *Sahabah* who had lived through the Prophet's lifetime and had been able to learn from him directly. The judgements of these individuals would later become an important foundation for the expansive majority of future religious scholarship and the development of the *Shari'ah*, or Islamic Law.

By the end of 'Umar's rule certain precedents and standards had been established. As early appointees from among the *Sahabah* were often replaced by less pious men, the temptations of power and wealth (as well as the ancient habits of the people they ruled over) often won out over the need to remain just and fair. Nevertheless 'Umar expected his amirs to live up to ethical standards. A few of these principles and precedents were:

1. *There was to be no hereditary succession.* The leaders and governors were to be selected by the wisest of the *Ummah* from the choicest of individuals.

2. *The ruler(s) should be accessible to all people.* The lowliest of citizens should be able to appear before the governor to voice concerns, complaints, or suggestions. The *amir* should not elevate himself by displaying courtly ceremonies, or by granting favors to the unworthy. Following the example of the Prophet demanded that a ruler eat simple food, wear simple clothing, and not display pride in his rank.

The centuries-old practice of shura is still followed in many traditional Muslim communities around the globe.

3. *The ruler should seek advice, welcome criticism, and take it seriously.* If criticism is well-founded, the governor should admit his mistakes and make amends for it.

4. *The army exists for the protection of peace and security for the Lands of Islam.* The *amir* should never use the military under his command to take advantage of people, destroy their means of livelihood or harm any living thing unnecessarily.

5. *No one is fit to govern who is not a devout Muslim.* The *amir* must strive by word and deed to emulate the lofty example of the Prophet Muhammad. A better person should be sent to replace he who does not uphold the standards of excellence.

Death of 'Umar in 644 CE

There lived in Madinah a Persian by the name of Feroz whom an Arab had captured during the wars against the Sasanids. Feroz became this man's servant and was put to work. One day Feroz complained to the *Khalifah* about the amount of payment he received from his master for this work. Upon investigating the matter, 'Umar ruled against Feroz in the dispute, and the servant became resentful. The following morning 'Umar went to the *masjid* to pray, where Feroz was waiting in a corner, armed with a dagger. As 'Umar began to lead the prayer, Feroz ran out from his hiding place and stabbed him repeatedly. The congregation grabbed the Persian and threw him in chains. 'Umar was taken home, where he succumbed to his wounds several days later. His body was laid next to those of the Prophet and Abu Bakr.

On his deathbed, 'Umar was asked to name his successor. He is reported to have replied while in great pain, "If I do so, I have the example of Abu Bakr before me. If I do not do so, there is the example of the Messenger of Allah." But he then chose six men to form a council that would choose one from among themselves to be the next leader of the *Ummah*. If they could not reach an unanimous decision the majority opinion would decide.

The council was made up of 'Ali ibn Abi Talib, 'Uthman ibn 'Affan, 'Abd ar-Rahman ibn 'Awf, Sa'd ibn Abi Waqqas, Zubair ibn 'Awwam, and Talha ibn 'Ubaidullah. All of these individuals were eminent *Sahabah* and pillars of respect and honor in the Muslim community. 'Umar hoped that their decision would be for the best.

The Council Chooses

Despite the fact that the men chosen by 'Umar willingly performed their task, they could not agree on a candidate without some difficulty. As the council formed, Talha absent from Madinah, so the members began their deliberation without him. It was soon found that there were serious disagreement among the council members on the question of succession. 'Umar ordered that the committee had to reach a final decision within three days of his death. If the debate continued on or if there was a deadlock, 'Abd ar-Rahman ibn 'Awf was instructed to make the final decision.

On the morning of the fourth day following their opening meeting, the choices had come down to either 'Ali or 'Uthman. Since a deadlock now developed, 'Abd ar-Rahman called 'Ali forth and asked him if he would be willing to rule by not only the Qur'an and *Sunnah* but also by the precedents set by the interpretations of

Abu Bakr and 'Umar. 'Ali responded that he was more than qualified to interpret the Qur'an on his own and had no desire to be bound by the opinions of others. 'Abd ar-Rahman then summoned 'Uthman and asked the same question to him. But unlike 'Ali, 'Uthman was willing to include the precedents and opinions of the two previous *khulafa'* in his rulings.

For whatever reason, 'Abd ar-Rahman did not approve of 'Ali's reply. 'Abd ar-Rahman then announced 'Uthman to be his choice as the man to succeed 'Umar ibn al-Khattab. He said to 'Uthman, "Stretch out your hand so that I may give my *bay'ah* to you." 'Uthman then stretched his hand and all those present took the oath of allegiance to him. Despite his dissatisfaction, 'Ali too gave his *bay'ah* to 'Uthman. This was in the 24th year after the *Hijrah*.

Lesson Review

1. Why was the Muslim victory at Jerusalem especially significant? What historical evidence is there that shows its importance to the Muslim state?

2. How did other religious groups receive the Muslim ruler, and what was their treatment under Muslim governance?

3. Did the conquest of Egypt take place with the full support of the *Khalifah*? What does the decision by 'Amr ibn al-'As tell about challenges facing Muslim rule at that time?

4. What factors helped achieve victory in Egypt?

Chapter Review

1. What were the major achievements of 'Umar ibn al-Khattab's rule?

2. Why do you think the Muslim armies were highly motivated? How did this motivation help them in the face of such larger, better-equipped forces?

3. How did the constant military campaigning against Byzantium and Sasanid Persia effect the population of the Arabian Peninsula?

Chapter Three

`Uthman
Ibn `Affan

Lesson One

Leader of the Faithful

Looking Ahead

Recognize the initial impact 'Uthman made in the governing of the Islamic State.

Preview Vocabulary

Overrun
Initiative
Demure
Naphtha
Amiable

The Father of Humility

'Uthman ibn 'Affan was a wealthy member of the powerful Makkan clan of Bani Umayyah. Like most of his kinfolk he was a skillful merchant who often traveled with the caravans to Syria. Once, shortly after Muhammad (who was six years his senior) began receiving revelations, 'Uthman was returning home from such a trip. One night as his caravan camped deep in the desert he perceived an unearthly voice calling out in the star-lit night: "Awake! The Praised One has arisen in Makkah!" Not knowing what these strange words meant, he went to a dear friend named Abu Bakr on his return to the city. Abu Bakr knew exactly what they meant. He took 'Uthman straight to the Prophet, where he embraced Islam immediately.

Despite the dreadful hostility that had already arisen between the clan of the Bani Umayyah and the Prophet, 'Uthman remained faithful to his commitment despite having to enduring ridicule and harassment from his own relatives. He grew close to the Prophet, who gave him the hand of one of his daughters, Ruqayyah. When persecution became almost unbearable, the Prophet ordered some of the Muslims to leave for Ethiopia. 'Uthman and his wife were among their number. They later returned to Arabia only to make the *Hijrah* to Madinah soon thereafter. But life was not without sadness in Madinah and shortly after their arrival, Ruqayyah died. But so deep was the Prophet's affection for 'Uthman that he later gave him the hand of another daughter, Umm Kulthum.

'Uthman was well known for being tremendously generous with his wealth. In Madinah he recommenced his trading business which soon began to flourish again. He paid for enlarging the Prophet's *Masjid* all from his own pocket and gave away a small fortune to equip and supply the Muslim army going off to Tabuk.

> "Those who spend their wealth for the cause of Allah and do not follow their spending with taunts and insults: no fear shall come upon them, neither shall they grieve."
>
> *the Qur'an 2:262*

In addition to his generosity 'Uthman was an amiable man who had an often bashful demure. The Prophet once said of him, "Uthman is the meekest of my Companions." When he accepted his appointment to the position of *khalifah*, 'Uthman was reported to have said, "O people, it will not be easy for me to manage this new responsibility, and I am not even prepared today to speak. There may, God willing, be several occasions for that and if I live, I will address you some other day. But you should know by now that I am not very good at speech-making."

Administration & Expansion

Among the first acts that 'Uthman performed as *khalifah* was to send letters out to all the governors. He instructed them to follow all of the regulations set by his predecessor: to be honest, just, true to their word and to serve those under them. He cautioned that those who did not meet these standards would face dismissal from their positions. 'Uthman did not hesitate to enforce this decree. Sa'd ibn Abi Waqqas, the victor of Qadisiyyah and governor of Kufa, was one of those soon dismissed by 'Uthman. It soon came to the attention of the new *Khalifah* that Sa'd had failed to repay a debt he incurred from the public treasury of his province and hence he was removed from office.

The lands under Muslim rule continued to expand at an astonishing rate. After the annihilation of the Persian army at Qadisiyya, the last remnants of the Sasanid Empire were quickly overrun. Muslim warriors pushed through the mountain passes of the Zagros range and entered on to the Persian plateau. They advanced as far east as the border of today's Afghanistan.

In the west, detachments set out from Egypt and rolled across the Byzantine-held lands of North Africa, reaching as far as modern-day Tunisia. North of Syria, expansion was slowed by both the rugged Taurus Mountains and the still formidable Byzantine Empire. Although this great Christian superpower had suffered a serious setback at the Battle of Yarmuk, it was able to recover from the disaster. Thus Muslim raids into Anatolia (modern-day Turkey) met with stiff resistance. The border between the Muslim world and the Byzantine Empire somewhat stabilized and for the next several centuries little progress would be made on that front.

The societies that the Arabs came in contact with through their conquests were, in many ways, far more advanced than their own simple tribal-based culture. As a result of this cultural imbalance the *amirs* had to rely on the indigenous population to help administer both the urban and rural areas. The Arabs simply had no idea how to govern these ancient and well-organized societies effectively, at least not without the advice of those who grew up in them. In many cases, the Arab governors kept local administrative structure intact along with the local bureaucrats. As a result of this nearly all official documents were written in languages other than Arabic. If they did not conflict sharply with Islamic principles, local customs were readily adapted for use by the conquerors. We read earlier how many Muslim governors began to imitate the dress and courtly rituals of both the Byzantine and Sasanid nobility.

The Muslim Presence at Sea

The Muslims began to realize that in order to safeguard their hold over Egypt, Palestine and Syria, they would have to develop some way to counteract any invasion from the sea. The Byzantine Empire possessed a very powerful navy and they could easily land their troops at any point along the Mediterranean coast. In contrast Arab military tradition had never attended to anything close to warfare on the high seas, this despite the fact that many Arabs lived along the coasts of the Indian Ocean and the Red Sea and were very familiar with sea travel.

For the tribes of the desert, however, the very thought of venturing out into the open sea, especially to fight, was strange and forbidding. It has even been recorded that 'Umar ibn al-Khattab actually discouraged any suggestion that a navy should be built to counter Byzantine threats.

But when 'Uthman came to power this reluctance to look to the sea altered. On the insistence of the then governor of Syria, Mu'awiya ibn Abi Sufian (who was also a cousin of 'Uthman), the very first Muslim naval force was built with the labor of local craftsmen. Mu`awiya then hired any local people, regardless of religion, who were experienced in the art of sailing and familiar with naval warfare.

The Byzantine navy carried on the legacy of the Roman Empire as a Mediterranean sea power. One of their most fearsome weapons was "Greek fire," a naphtha, or petroleum-like compound that could quickly set an enemy ship ablaze.

The presence of Muslim warships on the sea deterred Byzantine attempts to land forces on the coasts of Syria, Palestine and Egypt. Once their confidence in their navy reached high levels, Mu`awiya instructed his ships to go on the offensive during which they managed to land men onto the island of Cyprus and take it from the Byzantines.

The development of a fully functioning navy did much to encourage Arab utilization of the seas. The earlier relationship with sea trade rapidly expanded and Arab ships traveled the Red Sea, throughout the Indian Ocean basin, along the coasts of Africa, the islands of Southeast Asia and even on into China. In the generations to come Arab merchants would perfect navigational skills which in turn brought great advancements to sea travel. They would also bring innovations to ship design, making vessels faster and more efficient. Maps of sea lanes and knowledge of coastlines would later be passed on to the Europeans, who would centuries later, exploit these things to their fullest potential.

Lesson Review

1. What qualities in Uthman gave him great respect among members of the Muslim community?

2. What role did local officials and leaders play in the expanding territories of the early Muslim state?

3. Why did a Muslim presence on the sea become an important goal?

4. What is Greek Fire? What is the source of naphtha?

Lesson Two

Preserving the Word of God

Looking Ahead

Understand the importnace Muslims give to the text of the Qur'an.

Preview Vocabulary

Tashkil
Mushaf
Tabi`in
Sirah

Standardization of the Qur'an

As those individuals who had learned the Qur'an during the lifetime of the Prophet grew older and began to pass away, Islam was spreading into lands far from the Arabian Peninsula. Many *Sahabah* who had memorized the entire Qur'an had either died of old age or fallen in battle. However a new generation of students and scholars was forming (called the *Tabi'in* or "followers"), who, despite having never met the Prophet, were nonetheless just as dedicated to the understanding of Islam. This generation would be a crucial link between their teachers (men and women who sat at the feet of the Prophet) and their future students, individuals who would later lay the foundation for many Islamic sciences (such as *Fiqh*, *Tafsir* and *Hadith* criticism).

During the later part of 'Uthman's rule disturbing reports began to reach Madinah from travelers and officials that inaccurate reproductions of the Qur'anic text were appearing in the new territories. Some of these copies contained variant pronunciations and missing verses that would threaten the very preservation of God's Word to man. For the Arab soldiers on the frontiers of the Islamic state as well as for the new non-Arab converts that were trickling in every day, the distortion of the Qur'anic text could very well mean the distortion of correct belief and practice.

So it was because of this danger that the leading *Sahabah* convinced 'Uthman of the need to standardize the text of the Qur'an. And from this standardized text all other copies would be deemed either fit or innacurate. 'Uthman held deliberations on the plan since the Prophet himself had not set a clear precedent for this action. 'Uthman nevertheless came to see the urgency of the matter and began the task of standardizing the written text of the Qur'an.

For this task 'Uthman commissioned Zaid ibn Thabit, who was a longtime scribe for the Prophet. Zaid was ordered to base all of his efforts in compiling the sacred text upon the earlier collections that had been put together during lifetime of Abu Bakr. This earlier compilation was in the safekeeping of Hafsa, the daughter of 'Umar ibn al-Khattab. Zaid copied this text by hand and began to check it against the memories and recitations of the most authoritative reciters and memorizers he could find.

According to accounts of the day after he completed copying down the Qur'an he recited this text three times in front of a gathering of *Muhajirun* and *Ansar*. When they gave their approval Zaid then compared his copy to the one that was in the possession of Hafsa. He found that the two were exactly the same.

The scribes of Madinah then made five copies (or seven as some say). These manuscripts were then sent to the *amirs* of the provinces, who were to order further copies to be made from these. All existing texts of the Qur'an that did not conform to the standardized text were ordered to be burned. Muslims were well aware of the evolution of earlier revealed scriptures and thier subsequent corruption. Judging by the historical track record of the human memory, there was no guarantee (beyond Allah's will) that such a thing would not happen in this case. Destroying all variant copies of the Qur'an was nothing more than a safeguard for what was believed to be the very Word of God.

The new copies of the Qur'an were made into large, bound tomes, many being several feet wide. They were written in the Arabic script of the time, which was very rudimentary in style. There were none of the vowel marks, or *tashkil*, that we are familiar with today and there was nothing like the beautiful, elegant calligraphy so commonly associated with Qur'anic texts.

Reading the *mushaf*, or printed copy of the Qur'an, of these early times depended a good deal on an individual's grasp of the Arabic language. With a simple misplaced vowel the meaning of a single verse could change signficantly. For instance in Surah 9, verse 3, which reads, "That God and His Messenger annul obligations with the polytheists," can be changed to, "That God annuls obligations with the polytheists and the Messenger," through the misplacement of one single vowel.

Before the invention of the printing press, the only way people could make copies of texts was to do so by hand. This was obviously a very slow and tedious process. Copies of the Qur'an were thus rare and very valuable, unlike today when the book is mass produced and is readily available to even the poorest of individuals. Throughout most of Muslim history memorization was a more common way to connect to the Qur'an than owning a printed copy. Literate Muslims would often make their own personal copies, and wealthy patrons would

Brief History of Compilation of the Qur'an

During the life of the Prophet (570-632 CE)
- The Prophet used to recite the entire Qur'an before the angel Jibril once every Ramadan, but he recited it twice (in the same order we have today) in the final Ramadan before his death.
- Each verse was recited by the Prophet, and its location relative to other verses and *Surahs* was identified by him.
- The verses were written by scribes, selected by the Prophet, on any suitable object - the leaves of trees, pieces of wood, parchment or leather, flat stones, and shoulder blades. Scribes included 'Ali ibn Abi Talib, Ubayy ibn Ka'b and Zaid ibn Thabit.
- Some of the *Sahabah* wrote the Qur'an for their own use and several hundred *Sahabah* memorized it by heart.

During the Rule of Abu Bakr (632-634 CE)
- 'Umar Ibn al-Khattab urged Abu Bakr to compile and preserve the Qur'an. This was prompted after the Battle of Yamamah, where heavy casualties were suffered among the reciters who memorized the Qur'an.
- Abu Bakr entrusted Zaid ibn Thabit with the task of collecting the Qur'an. Zaid had been present during the last recitation of the Qur'an by the Prophet to Jibril.
- Zaid, with the help of the companions who memorized and wrote verses of the Qur'an, accomplished the task and handed Abu Bakr the first authenticated copy of the Qur'an. The copy was kept in the residence of Hafsah, daughter of 'Umar and wife of the Prophet.

During the Rule of 'Uthman (644-656 CE)
- 'Uthman ordered Zaid ibn Thabit to make copies based on the authenticated copy kept with Hafsa. This was due to the rapid expansion of the Islamic state and concern about differences in recitation.
- Copies were sent to various places in the Muslim world. The original copy was returned to Hafsa, and a copy was kept in Madinah.

Three stages of dotting and diacritization
- Dots were put as syntactical marks by Abu'l Aswad al-Dawli, during the time of Mu'awiya (661-680 CE).
- The letters were marked with different dotting by Nasr ibn Asim and Hayy ibn Ya'mur, during the time of 'Abd al-Malik (685-705 CE).
- A complete system of diacritical marks was invented by Khalil ibn Ahmad al-Farahidi (d. 786 CE).

commission calligraphers to produce fine copies with special inks, bindings and illuminations. In fact from the time of the first copied text, a custom of beautifying the Qur'an through calligraphy, or decorative writing, came into being. The tradition of Arabic calligraphy continued to evolve and flourish alongside the well-developed art of vocal recitation. Each enhanced the other as a way of promoting and glorifying the Word of God. These two art forms are greatly treasured in the Muslim world and continue to represent the highest of aesthetic traditions.

A Tradition of Preservation

The primary method in which Muslims learned (and still learn) the Qur'an was by memorization via oral transmission. In all *masjids*, from villages to cities, groups of adults and children memorized verses by repetition under the instruction of a teacher. This was in fact the practice of the Prophet and it continues to be the most common method of learning throughout much of the Muslim world.

Throughout the decades of the rule of the *Khulafa al-Rashidah* the main instructional activity was committing the Qur'an to memory and elucidating on the meaning of its content. Particular *Sahabah* were well known for their great genius in interpreting the Qur'an; most notably 'Ali, 'Abdullah ibn 'Abbas, Ibn Masud, and Abu Musa al-'Ashari.

The *Sunnah*, or record of the Prophet's words and deeds, was also an important component of Islamic learning. Untold numbers of *Hadiths* were repeated and transmitted from the generation of the *Sahabah* to the *Tabi`in*. A custom of narrating, transmitting and sharing *Hadiths* developed in Madinah and later spread throughout the Muslim lands. In the coming decades and well into the following century, the routine of transmitting *Hadith* continued and teachers of the science became very well known and respected. Of course, variant readings, inaccurate memories and deliberate or inadvertent inventions crept into many narrations. For this problem, later generations of scholars would develop complex processes by which to screen out imperfections.

From the Qur'an, *Hadith*, and oral histories, many related branches of knowledge, or sciences, grew. They formed the basis of a strong literate and scientific tradition in Muslim civilization. Alongside the custom of reciting *Hadiths*, the *Sahabah* related information about the momentous events, battles and individual stories surrounding the Prophet. These narrations, combined with existing tradition of Arab oral history, gradually developed into a tradition of historical documentation. Histories began to be set down in writing on the Prophet Muhammad's life. These narrations would form a category of their own and would be called the *Sirah*.

Lesson Review

1. What was the occasion for the decision to standardize the Qur'an based on existing copies and recitation from memory?

2. Who were the *Tabi'in*? What is their importance in the oral tradition among Muslims?

3. List the steps or procedures that were followed to produce the authoritative copy of the Qur'an during Uthman's time.

Lesson Three

Upheaval in the House of Islam

Looking Ahead

Look for the events that led to the murder of 'Uthman.

Preview Vocabulary

Fitnah
Strife
Abu Dharr
Assassination
Dissention

Six years into 'Uthman's rule, arguments over the spoils of the previous fifteen years of campaigning threatened the unity of the Muslim community. The exact causes of this conflict (known as the *Fitnah*) are not easy to unravel. Muslim historians passed down differing and often contradictory accounts of the events that transpired during this great rift in the community. Since these episodes brought about a major split in the *Ummah*, it is natural that those who took one side or the other interpreted these events very differently.

As we read in previous lessons, 'Uthman possessed a personality that was recognized for being reserved, generous and softhearted. He favored avoiding argument and confrontation, often choosing instead making concessions to the offending party. Since the maintenance of family ties (both nuclear and extended) is an important part of the Islamic faith, 'Uthman made sure that many of his kinfolk were taken care of during his administration. He gave many members of his clan, the Bani Umayyah, weighty positions in the government.

Although there were many fair and just men among 'Uthman's relatives, others took advantage of the *Khalifah* to advance their own interests gaining both power and wealth. More aggressive members of the Bani Umayyah had no problem exerting their will over the mild-mannered 'Uthman. His nephew Marwan, for instance, became so emboldened that he regularly sent out letters stamped with the *Khalifah's* seal without permission, implementing numerous decisions and policies in 'Uthman's name, causing considerable unrest and resentment.

Modern historians have concluded that 'Uthman progressively began to loose control over his governors, and too many critical decisions fell completely into their hands. To a large degree this autonomy was both unavoidable and necessary, simply because of the distances between Madinah and the provinces. The drawback was, however, that 'Uthman frequently failed to learn of problems that were brewing in the provinces until the dilemmas were way out of hand.

As a result, charges of incompetency began to be raised against 'Uthman. Even though many of these charges were unwarranted, 'Uthman did little to prove his critics wrong. Popular sentiment began building against the *Khalifah*. Those who raised their voices against 'Uthman's order came not only from those who had converted to Islam after the Prophet's lifetime, but from many notable *Sahabah* as well.

One of these was Abu Dharr al-Ghafari. While living in Syria, Abu Dharr came into open conflict with Mu`awiya, a man who was both 'Uthman's governor and cousin. Abu Dharr openly chastised Mu'awiya's spending on an extravagant new palace paid for by the provincial treasury. Abu Dharr argued that public money was people's money, and should be spent on the people and the welfare of the state. Offended by the pious contempt leveled against his spending habits, Mu'awiya complained to 'Uthman that

Abu Dharr's complaints were stirring up dissension. 'Uthman acknowledged his cousin's concerns and ordered Abu Dharr to return to Madinah. But even there the old *Sahabi* continued to speak out against the corruption he saw developing in the land until he was finally exiled to a remote village.

Strife and Assassination

By 655 CE, charges of corruption and negligence in the provinces began to pour into Madinah. Issues of financial bungling and misappropriation soon exploded into major discontent. The battle-hardened warriors living in the garrison towns of Iraq and Egypt grew furious when they found out that the *Khalifah's* appointees were reallocating land and *ghanima* into their own pockets as well as the pockets of their family members and supporters. The disaffected asserted that they were being denied their fair share pay after having aided in the expansion of the frontiers of Islam through the sacrifice of blood, wealth and families.

In an endeavor to solve these serious problems, 'Uthman called for a meeting of all the governors who were on their way to the *Hajj* of that year. 'Uthman expressed his concern over their behavior. But instead of looking at their own actions, the governors blamed the predicament on malcontents and troublemakers. They pushed 'Uthman to make examples out of these men but, in keeping with his mild nature, he refused to execute any harsh response. He may have felt that the current disruption was nothing more than what the Prophet had foretold, and he would not be one to initiate bloodshed. He told his governors, "I cannot kill a man without sufficient legal reason. These people have some quarrel with me and I will try to address their concerns. I will be kind and forgiving and try to bring them to moderation. If kindness fails to work, I will give myself up to the will of Allah."

But the discontent had spread deep. People in Madinah (including a number of *Sahabah*) who had once supported 'Uthman now distanced themselves from him. In Egypt and Iraq, soldiers began to look at ways to rid themselves of their *amirs* since the *Khalifah* seemed unwilling to do so. Sadly, 'Uthman was left to fend for himself.

Several months after the governors met with 'Uthman in Madinah, a band of soldiers from Egypt and Iraq traveled to Madinah in order to confront 'Uthman personally with their grievances. According to most accounts of the event 'Uthman appeared to have been able assure the men that their complaints were being looked into. Having been given this guarantee, the soldiers departed Madinah. However, it would not be long before they returned.

The Assassination of 'Uthman
From Tarikh ar-rasul wa'l mulk by al-Tabari

Several accounts of the events that led to the assassination of 'Uthman have survived, and though they differ in some details, they allow historians to draw several conclusions. First, there may have been no intent to kill the Khalifah, and it may have taken place in the heat of anger. The accounts also illustrate the depth of anger and division of the community that had developed as a result of the problems. For example, the son of Abu Bakr the first Khalifah, was said to be an active participant in the rebellion.

"Then Muhammad ibn Abu Bakr came to the home of 'Uthman. He threatened Ibn al-Zubair and Marwan and they fled. Muhammad ibn Abu Bakr then came to 'Uthman and seized him by his beard. He said, "Let go of my beard-your father dared not take hold of it!" Muhammad ibn Abu Bakr let it go. But the insurgents rushed upon him, striking him with the iron tips of their scabbards, others striking him with their fists. A man came at him with a broad iron-tipped arrow and stabbed the front of his throat and his blood fell over the Qur'an he was reading. Yet when they were doing this they were still afraid of killing him. 'Uthman was old and he fainted. Others came in and when they saw that they were dragged him by the legs his wife, Na'ila and his daughters began to screamed loudly. Al-Tujibi came, drawing his sword to thrust it into 'Uthman's stomach. When Na'ila protected him, he cut her hand. Then he leaned with the sword upon his chest and 'Uthman was killed before sundown. A crier went about calling that his blood and property were forbidden.

The band of soldiers was only one night's journey away from Madinah when a messenger appeared in their camp. He carried with him a letter addressed to the governor of Egypt stamped with 'Uthman's official seal. The soldiers became suspicious of the messenger and confiscated the letter. What they read in it threw them into a murderous rage. It was an order to the *amir* or Egypt to have these men executed upon their return home.

Understanding that this was how their grievances were to be addressed, the soldiers stormed back to Madinah to challenge the *Khalifah* over the contents of the letter. They went to 'Uthman's home, surrounded it and demanded that he come out. 'Uthman refused to do so sensing the rage that was evident in these men. He insisted that he never issued the letter in question and that he would have never ordered the execution of men who had committed no crime. This did little to assuage the soldiers and they proceeded to blockade 'Uthman inside his home. The people of Madinah, though stunned by the unfolding events, did little to come to 'Uthman's rescue. Other than the few prominent Sahabah who came forward to protect 'Uthman's home, the people of the town stood by and watched.

It has never been determined exactly who wrote the letter ordering the execution of the disgruntled soldiers. Some historians point to Marwan ibn Hakam, 'Uthman's cousin and personal secretary. They argue that Marwan committed a forgery to either further his own power, or because he disagreed with 'Uthman's inaction, believing that only harsh measures against the soldiers would stop further rebellion. Others have played down Marwan's involvement and later Sunni accounts (in an obvious attempt to discredit Shi'i adversaries) often claimed that a pro-Shi'i Jewish convert, 'Abdullah ibn Saba, instigated the entire episode in a bid to stir up chaos in the Muslim community.

The soldiers from Egypt refused to listen to the 'Uthman's pleas of innocence. They contended that even if he had no knowledge of the letter, he had allowed his personal staff unchecked authority, thereby putting lives in grave danger. The men demanded 'Uthman's immediate resignation. But he refused this demand and they decided to draw their swords and storm the house.

'Ali ibn Abi Talib, who initially refused to involve himself in the growing discontent with 'Uthman's authority, sent his two sons to try to hold back the soldiers. But they and their few supporters could do little to hold back the mob and the men broke through the doors and ransacked the residence. They found the elderly *Khalifah* in a room reading his Qur'an with his wife. Without mercy, they proceeded to stab him with their spears and swords. 'Uthman's wife tried in vain to shield her husband with her own body, and several of her fingers were hacked off in the mayhem.

'Uthman did not survive the attack. For the first time since the the Qur'an was revealed, Muslims unleashed their swords against fellow believers. Indeed as the Prophet had foretold, *"When the sword is taken out among my followers, it will be there until the Last Day."*

Lesson Review

1. Look up the word nepotism. Why have some historians applied the term to Uthman's administration?

2. What role did Mu'awiya play in Uthman's administration? Who appointed him, and who was his father?

3. Describe the events which led to Uthman's death.

Chapter Review

1. Why do you think that the problem of governors and the distance of Madinah from the important provinces became acute during `Uthman's time?

2. Research the life and personality of Abu Dharr al-Ghafari. How is he viewed by Muslims in our time? Compare him to a modern figure.

3. What was the relationship between the situation in Egypt and the rebellion against `Uthman? What was happening in Syria at the time, and how does Abu Dharr's complaint illustrate the problem?

4. What role do historians think `Uthman's relatives played in the tragic events that led to his assassination?

5. What role did 'Uthman play in the preservation of Islam?.

Chapter
Four

`Ali Takes
Command

Lesson One

The Aftermath of Assassination

Looking Ahead

Understand how the chaotic situation of 'Uthman's assassination soon spiraled out of control.

Preview Vocabulary

Ahl al-Bait
Nahj al-Balagha
Shi`at `Ali
Untenable
Schism

Brother of the Prophet

It can be argued that no one at the time of 'Uthman's assassination was as better candidate for the *Khilafah* than 'Ali. He was a well respected member of the *Ummah* who had been intimate with the Prophet since childhood. His level of spirituality and knowledge of the Qur'an and the *Sunnah* was vast. Like 'Uthman, 'Ali too had been given the hand of one of the Prophet's daughters, Fatimah. Through this marriage the Prophet's bloodline would continue. The sons of 'Ali and Fatimah, the two brothers Hasan and Husain, were boys deeply loved by their noble grandfather. This family came to be known as the *Ahl al-Bait*, the House of the Prophet.

'Ali was a great warrior who had fought (with one exception) in all the battles where the Prophet was present. 'Ali possessed a powerful personality and upheld his opinions with great forethought. He was known to hold high moral standards by which he measured the actions of not only others but his own self. He was a man who did not like to compromise ideals, but would nevertheless refrain from putting forward his own opinions if they would cause division within the community.

As we read in previous lessons 'Ali's intimate relationship and long experience with the Prophet led him to believe that his knowledge was sufficient alone to make judgments based on the Qur'an and *Sunnah*. He was known for his depth of wisdom, and Abu Bakr and 'Umar would often rely on his judgment when their own knowledge was exhausted. It was narrated of 'Umar that said once, "If it were not for 'Ali, 'Umar would have been ruined." It was primarily for this reason that 'Ali did not agree unconditionally to follow the precedents set by Abu Bakr and 'Umar, terms that 'Abd ur-Rahman had made as condition for succeeding 'Umar.

'Ali was further adored as a brilliant and inspiring speaker. His speeches and letters were later collected and compiled into a work called *Nahj al-Balagha,* the Peak of Eloquence. 'Ali motivated the hearts and minds of many people, attracting many followers who supported him with unwavering loyalty. He was generous and humble and he regularly cared for the needs of the poor even while he denied himself the luxuries his fame could have brought him.

Those who fell in behind 'Ali would eventually come to be known as the *Shi'at 'Ali* (or more simply "Shi'ah"), the Party of 'Ali. Divided with Sunnism over the question of leadership the Shi'i have often been called a sect, and the division has often been called a religious division or schism, despite the fact that they hold essentially the same beliefs as other Muslims. As traumatic as the events of the *Fitnah* were for the Muslim *Ummah,* it was only gradually that the Shi'is and Sunnis developed well-defined positions in opposition to each other. In the coming centuries, whatever political differences there were between the two parties would evolve into differing views on some important religious questions.

The bitterness that enhanced divisions were the result of a failure to come to terms with the collapse of 'Uthman's authority, and these were further complicated by the problems of growing wealth and power struggles in the expanding Muslim state. During the rule of 'Ali, these divisions worsened, despite the tremendous potential that 'Ali might have exercised in better circumstances.

An Untenable Position

Following the slaying of 'Uthman, the insurgents brought about disorder and chaos in Madinah. Deep shock from the preceding days' events, most of the people of Madinah stayed put in their homes. The rebel soldiers grabbed at the opportunity to choose a new *Khalifah,* one who would be more to their liking. But they were divided on exactly who that leader should be. Some proposed 'Ali's name while others supported two other prominent *Sahabah,* Talha ibn 'Ubaidullah and Zubair ibn al-'Awwam. The men then took their choices to the people of Madinah and the majority was for 'Ali.

'Ali initially showed no desire to involve himself in the process and he declined to accept the nomination. But the public continued to press him asserting that there was none better than he to fill the position. So 'Ali entered into consultation with those *Sahabah* still living in Madinah. Without exception they advised 'Ali that he would be the only person who could correct the current situation and save the *Ummah* from further upheaval. Stirred by a sense of duty, 'Ali finally conceded to the pressure and called for a general *bay`at* from the population of Madinah.

Although most Madinans presented their allegiance to 'Ali, a few refused, while still others completely changed their stance on the selection. Talha and Zubair, for instance, had initially encouraged 'Ali to take the *Khilafah* but then chose at the last minute to withhold their *bay`at* for reasons that remain to this day unclear and confused.

Clamoring for Retribution

Upon receiving the *bay'at* from the people of Madinah, 'Ali was faced with two serious predicaments that needed his immediate attention. The first was the apprehension of those who had killed 'Uthman. Yet he realized fully that the assassination was only a symptom of a much larger problem that could not be solved by simply arresting a handful of rebels. Many more people had been directly or indirectly involved, and they were scattered throughout the provinces. In addition much of the anger felt by these men (and many more back in the provinces) was not altogether unjustified.

Against the advice of others, 'Ali sent letters of dismissal to all provincial *amirs* who held power during the time 'Uthman. By doing so he sought to address the roots of the murder, which had been the belief that widespread corruption was responsible for dissent, and that the best possible response would be to remove those charged with misrule.

The second issue that 'Ali had to face was to restore respect for the office of *Khalifah* after it had been damaged by the pessimistic opinions that developed regarding 'Uthman during the final years of his reign. 'Ali tried to address the

> "He who slays a believer intentionally, his reward is Hell forever, and the wrath and curse of Allah are upon him forever, and for him He has prepared a dreadful penalty."
>
> *the Qur'an 4:93*

root of both of these problems by ordering all provincial governors replaced. Needless to say this move alienated and angered these men, and they held substantial power and influence over the areas they ruled.

'Ali's decision to delay retribution for the murder of 'Uthman also angered some influential *Sahabah* like 'A'isha, Talha and Zubair, who wanted justice brought about immediately. They were of the opinion that replacing governors was an issue that could be dealt with much later. Any moves that 'Ali could make were further complicated by the fact that the clan of Bani Umayyah vowed to take revenge for their fallen kinsman and most refused to give 'Ali *bay`at* until this was fulfilled.

The response to 'Ali's plan was mixed. Provinces where complaints against 'Uthman were strong (like Iraq and Egypt) fully supported 'Ali's decision. However in Syria the governor was the noted and powerful Umayyad chief Mu'awiya ibn Abi Sufian. Mu`awiya used the emotional issue of his relative's death to rally support around himself and the other governors under scrutiny.

Mu'awiya sent a message to 'Ali telling him that in Syria the soldiers' beards were wet with tears for 'Uthman and that they would not be dried until his murderers were caught. Mu`awiya and his supporters therefore refused to give *bay`at* to 'Ali until Uthman's murderers were brought to justice. Some historians have viewed this as a ploy to foil 'Ali's chances to organize a stable government. If 'Ali could not establish law and order the same discontent that brought about 'Uthman's downfall would certainly break out. 'Ali could then be easily removed from office and replaced with an individual more favorable towards the Bani Umayyah.

Nevertheless Mu'waiya's reaction to 'Ali's nomination created a serious political dilemma for the *Khalifah*. By refusing to accept 'Ali as leader of the *Ummah* and in refusing to step down from his post as governor of Syria, Mu'awiya was in effect mounting another insurgency against the central government. According to some accounts 'Ali concluded that if Mu'awiya would not submit to the central authorities willingly he must be forced to do so. However as `Ali began to gather an army of his supporters in Madinah a new problem arose in Makkah.

Lesson Review

1. What made 'Ali ibn Abi Talib such an outstanding *Sahabah*? What qualifications did he bring to leadership of the *Ummah*?

2. Why did 'Ali hesitate to accept the *Khilafah* after Uthman's death? How did others react to his selection?

3. Explain the message from Syria stating that "the soldiers' beards are wet with tears for Uthman." What meanings, other than their grief, might it have implied?

The Fitnah

Looking Ahead

Follow the events that led
to the clash between 'Ali
and 'A'isha.

Preview Vocabulary

Basra
Kufa
Battle of the Camel

A Trio in Opposition

The two *Sahabah* who were in Madinah at the time of 'Uthman's
assassination, Talha and Zubair, left for Makkah after having
disavowed their *bay'at* to 'Ali. According to some narratives, both
of these men believed they had legitimate counter-claims to the
khilafah, but that they (so they said) were compelled to give *bay`at*
to 'Ali because of the chaotic situation in Madinah. They resented
the fact that both the murderers of 'Uthman and the people of
Madinah had pushed 'Ali into the position but they were
powerless to prevent it; at least for the time being

The two men found an ally in 'A'isha, a woman of rank and
prominence among the *Sahabah* and great standing in the
community. Not only was she the daughter of Abu Bakr but she
was also the wife of the Prophet. When she received word of the
assassination of 'Uthman and the subsequent disorder that had
broken out in Madinah, she called for the immediate punishment
of all who had a hand in it. Once again several accounts state that
she also to had resented 'Ali's appointment as ruler of the
Muslims because of certain unresolved differences between the
two that went back years before. Preferring either Talha (who was
also a relative) or Zubair for the position, she refused to give *bay'at*

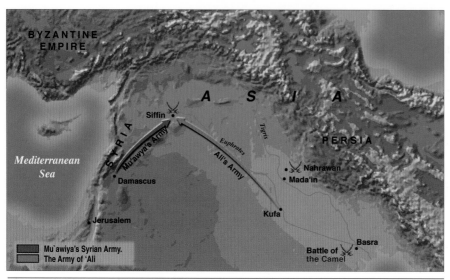

Both sides used Iraq as a base for building support. `Ali was centered in Kufa while 'A'isha stayed further to the south in Basra.

to 'Ali. 'A'isha began to speak out publicly in Makkah against his inaction in punishing the insurgents.

When Talha and Zubair arrived in Makkah, they joined with 'A'isha to openly challenge 'Ali. They gathered a sizable band of supporters in Makkah, and set off for Basra, a city in Iraq that was a stronghold for 'Uthman's supporters. In Basra the trio organized a position where opposition to 'Ali could be mobilized. Within weeks of their arrival in southern Iraq, 'A'isha, Talha and Zubair managed to raise a large army some 10,000 strong.

As challenges to his authority increased, 'Ali sought to secure his own base of support. Makkah offered little help, since most people there either backed the demand for retribution or tried to avoid the dispute altogether. The Iraqi garrison town of Kufa, on the other hand, offered both the support and manpower 'Ali needed to exert his authority. Located some 200 miles north of Basra, Kufa had long resented 'Uthman's

policies. In fact soldiers from Kufa participated in the *Khalifah's* assassination. More importantly, the majority of the garrison town's residents swore *bay`at* to 'Ali and in compliance with his orders forced out the old governor. They seemed to be a people who could be counted upon to support any military action that might be needed.

'Ali proceeded to Kufa near the end of 656 CE and raised an army of his supporters. He took this force to Basra, where he hoped a demonstration of armed force would convince his three adversaries to give up the struggle without bloodshed.

But this did not happen. The tense situation that soon developed outside Basra produced a battle in December of that year. Some accounts claim that some form of agreement had almost been reached when certain malcontents, hiding in the ranks of both armies, triggered battle to cover their own guilt in 'Uthman's murder. Whether or not the principal players intended to fight, a terrible clash ensued and it went down in history as the Battle of the Camel because 'A'isha was at its center, commanding her troops from a litter on the back of a camel.

Though both sides fought with determination 'Ali's army prevailed in the end and the army of Basra fled the field. Hundreds perished on both sides, including Talha and Zubair. Following the rout of her army, 'A'isha was captured. 'Ali sent her back to Madinah with the respect and honor due one of the 'Mothers of the Faithful'. 'A'isha spent the remainder of her long life in regret for having taken part in the bloodshed. She avoided any further political entanglements and concerned herself solely with teaching *Hadith*.

The Battle of the Camel was the first incident of major armed strife between Muslims. Since then, historians have been sifting through accounts of its events trying to untangle the true motives of the of those involved, because the entire incident raises a serious question: Why would these people who had lived and struggled for years with the Prophet suddenly take up arms against each other? This controversy so deeply affected people of that era and of subsequent generations that most avoided discussion of it altogether - either in anguish over the event itself or in fear of passing critical judgment on people of whom the Prophet himself had once spoken so highly of.

The Capital Moves to Kufa

After the Battle of the Camel, 'Ali finished moving his seat of government from Madinah to Kufa. He had a large body of supporters in Kufa who would be needed in the looming conflict with Mu'awiya. One outcome of the Battle of the Camel was that it clearly displayed 'Ali's willingness to fight to enforce his authority. As a result nearly all of the provincial governors gave *bay'at* to him and recognized 'Ali as the legitimate *khalifah*. Only Syria remained outside his control. This was a province whose wealth was equal to nearly double that of all other provinces combined. In addition it offered Mu'awiya a base of support from men whose interests and loyalty were unshakably attached to him alone.

Lesson Review

1. How was the problem of accepting Ali as *khalifah* related to problems in the provinces that began under 'Uthman? How was it related to the murder?

2. Describe Mu`awiya's role in Syria, his background, and his response to 'Ali.

3. Why did Ali move his capital to Kufa? What was happening in Basra?

Lesson Three

Division Deepens

Looking Ahead

Recognize the factors that led to the final collapse of 'Ali's position.

Preview Vocabulary

Khawarij
Negotiations
Battle of Siffin

Mu'awiya Mounts his Challenge

We read in the previous lessons that the powerful governor of Syria, Mu'awiya ibn Abi Sufian, demanded that the killers of his cousin 'Uthman be handed over to him, claiming the right of retribution for near relatives. When 'Ali refused these demands, he mobilized his men into a force that would avenge the death of 'Uthman. Many of Mu`awiya's supporters were convinced that by refusing to prosecute the killers 'Ali had blood on his hands as well.

Mu'awiya entered into a truce with Byzantium and he agreed (obviously without the authorization of 'Ali) to pay tribute to the emperor in exchange for peace. This move allowed him to concentrate all of his military power on the coming struggle with 'Ali. When 'Ali received word in 657 CE that Mu'awiya was moving towards Iraq with a large army, he left Kufa and headed northward along the Euphrates River hoping to engage his opponent and force him to submit to his authority.

In less than two weeks the two forces ran into each other near a place called Siffin, some 250 miles northwest of Damascus. The opposing forces quickly came to blows and a fierce battle raged for several days. As the fighting began to turn against the Syrians, and as 'Ali neared victory Mu`awiya looked for a way to save his position. Fortunately he had in his ranks 'Amr ibn al-'As, an individual of great renown who had a reputation as a keen negotiator. 'Amr instructed the front ranks of the Syrian army to hang pages of the Qur'an from their spears and then march to the enemy demanding a truce, a move that would force 'Ali to turn the dispute over to arbitration. Although the Syrians claimed to be motivated by a desire to halt further bloodshed between Muslims many historians consider this move to have been nothing more than a ploy to allow the Syrians a chance to regroup and save themselves from a defeat that was inevitable.

'Ali hesitantly accepted the call for an armistice and disengaged his forces. Many men in his camp were disheartened by the ongoing fighting with fellow Muslims. They pressed 'Ali to accept any arbitration that would end hostilities. 'Ali appears to have realized that there was more to the call for a truce from Mu`awiya's camp than a simple desire for peace. But he agreed to stop the battle even though he was aware of the possibility that the Syrians could regroup and counterattack.

The two sides then put forward their arbitrators. 'Ali was pushed by many in from his ranks to accept Abu Musa al-'Ashari, a man neither deeply committed to 'Ali nor exceptionally competent. Mu'awiya, however, was able to rely on the sagacity of 'Amr ibn al-'As to present his position. The negotiations went on for days which soon turned into weeks. In the end they proved inconclusive and in many ways only worsened divisions in the Muslim community. The negotiators failed to agree on any matters of real importance. In the end their final judgment was that 'Ali must give up his claim to the *khilafah* and a *shura* council would then decide on a suitable replacement. Needless to say 'Ali refused to accept the judgment, stating that it was completely unacceptable and that it would allow Mu`awiya an opportunity to seize the position through his growing influence. 'Ali decided the only way to bring stability to the Ummah was to physically force Mu'awiya out of power.

The Khawarij Rebel

From the very start of the conflict with Mu`awiya, 'Ali's supporters voiced different opinions regarding what type of response should be given to the difficult challenges that loomed on the horizon. His closest and most ardent supporters had faith in 'Ali's abilities and did not question his authority. Others (especially among some soldiers of Iraq) were not loyal to him personally, but rather united with him out of a dislike for the clan of Bani Umayyah. These were the men who persuaded 'Ali to stop the fighting during the Battle of Siffin as his army stood on the brink of victory.

During the weeks of inconclusive negotiations Mu`awiya was able to regroup and shore up his forces. As this was happening, the very same men in 'Ali's army who pushed him into negotiations now completely reversed their position. They now blamed 'Ali for the lost opportunity to defeat Mu`awiya on the battlefield. They claimed he had been gravely mistaken by opening negotiations with Mu'awiya.

These malcontents began to dispute with 'Ali as he reminded them that he was the *khalifah* and that they owed obedience to him. In protest they left his camp and withdrew to a desert town known as Nahrawan. There, they established themselves as an alternative faction that rejected the positions of both 'Ali and Mu`awiya.

The people who split from 'Ali became known as the *Khawarij*, or 'those who remove themselves'. The Khawarij based their split with

Extremist groups and sects like the Khawarij would make their appearance thoughout Muslim history.

'Ali through religious terminology and claimed that both 'Ali and Mu`awiya had become unbelievers for having used their own opinions in the conflict rather relying solely on the Qur'an. 'Ali tried his best to reconcile with his former supporters but to no avail. But they would have none of that and in their fanatic rage they murdered the envoys sent by 'Ali. The *Khalifah* was now forced to turn both his attention and his army to dealing with this new menace. He marched to the Khawarij stronghold of Nahrawan and dealt them a crippling defeat. Those from their ranks who managed to survive fled into the desert, where they attempted to regroup.

The Khawarij have often been viewed by modern historians as deeply pious men who developed a very literal interpretation of Islam. Because of this mindset they developed a strict, and often harsh, reading of Islam. The Khawarij professed that any Muslim who disagreed with them was no longer considered as one and that the blood and property of all who opposed their views was permissible (*halal*). Over time they formed themselves into a religious sect, one that continued to preach against established authority.

The army of 'Ali, which had been so eager to challenge Mu`awiya before the negotiations, soon lost much of its energy as the Khawarij initiated their dissent. Those who had no real loyalty to 'Ali either went over to the Khawarij or simply deserted rank and went home. Those men who did remained were so demoralized that 'Ali was forced to abandoned plans for a second attack against Mu'awiya. He withdrew his army from northern Iraq and returned to Kufa.

Nearly every Muslim household in Kufa had lost loved ones in the war against Mu`awiya and the Syrians. People began to question 'Ali's ability to deal with the situation. They saw the divisions and desertions in 'Ali's forces as a sign that there would now be little chance for victory. Mu`awiya took advantage of the declining support for 'Ali by sending agents to encourage rebellion and unrest in areas that had given their *bay`at* to the cousin of the Prophet. 'Ali's support soon began to melt away.

Despite the fact that most of the Khawarij had been wiped out at Nahrawan, some of their ringleaders escaped the battle. In their hideouts in the Najd they plotted to avenge their humiliating reversal. The Khawarij chiefs decided that the only way to strike back at 'Ali was to kill him. But in a bid to remove all of their opponents in one swoop their targets not only included their arch-enemy 'Ali, but Mu'awiya and his advisor 'Amr ibn al-'As as well, who were equally guilty of having opposed God's will.

At the start of Ramadan 661 CE (forty years after the *Hijrah*), the Khawarij leaders dispatched three assassins to carry out their revenge. By eliminating these three men they hoped the conflict could finally be ended and a new Islamic government based on their own rigid interpretations could be established. But the two killers that were sent to Egypt and Syria failed in their mission; Mu'awiya was only slightly wounded by the assassin's blade before his guards dispatched the would-be assassin. 'Amr ibn al-'As was never located. Only the man sent to Kufa accomplished his assignment.

'Ali awoke in the morning of the 17th day of Ramadan in the fortieth year of the *Hijrah* to perform his prayers in Kufa's expansive *masjid*. As he prayed the Khawarij assassin struck him

From the Wisdom of 'Ali ibn Abi Talib

- Have hope in Allah and none else. Be afraid of nothing but sins. If you do not know something don't feel ashamed to admit ignorance. If you do not know something do not hesitate or feel ashamed to learn it. Acquire patience and endurance...

- Work! Work! And do good tasks while you still have life, health and opportunities, while there is possibility for you to do good, while your good deeds can still be recorded by the angels and while there is still time for you to repent vice and turn towards virtue and piety

- They [the Prophet's Family] put life into learning and into developing knowledge, and they do their best to remove ignorance. The depth of their patience points to the depth of their knowledge... They understood the real spirit of Islam and its significance by carefully carrying into practice its precepts. Among men there are many that preach good and great things, but very few act upon what they preach.

- Can we not realize the limitations of our knowledge when we see that a very minor and ordinary phase of the marvels of His creations so confounds us that we cannot understand how the beauty, grace and grandeur could be so artistically blended that it bewilders minds and holds intellects spellbound?

- I am less than what you tell about me, but more than what you think about me.

- Whoever keeps his affairs in order with Allah, He will also put his affairs with man in order; whoever makes arrangement for salvation, the Lord will arrange his worldly affairs...

(from Nahj al-Balagha, the collected speeches and sayings of `Ali)

on the skull with a poisoned dagger, inflicting a deep and deadly wound. For three days 'Ali lingered in pain as the poison did its work. His final decree was to name his eldest son Hasan to be his successor.

'Ali had been *khalifah* through five years of non-stop unrest and warfare. Although at the start of his rule many enthusiastically rallied behind him, in the end he died abandoned by all but his closest supporters. His legacy, however, far outweighed the impact he displayed during his short reign. In the future development of Islamic spirituality and in terms of his own thought and achievements, 'Ali would leave a permanent mark in the hearts and minds of millions for generations to come.

Lesson Review

1. How did the conflict over the acceptance of Ali's authority come to arbitration by representatives of both sides?
2. Using his power as governor, what steps did Mu`awiya take to ensure victory, and what enabled him to mount a challenge to 'Ali?
3. Who were the Khawarij, and what position did they take after the defeat of Ali's forces?

Chapter Review

1. Research the lives of Talha and Zubair and present several anecdotes to the class. Include in your research their backgrounds, their roles during the Prophet's life, and incidents surrounding their participation in the *Fitna*.
2. Identify five individuals or members of various groups described in Lessons 2 and 3. Profile each, describing the personal stake or interests they represented. [hints: landowners, governors, *Sahabah* at Madinah, Umayyad clan members, etc.]
3. Write an essay giving your point of view on the end of the period of the Khulafa' ar-Rashidun.
4. Explain the role played by soldiers and garrison towns in the upheaval. What do you think was the effect of the *Fitna* on ordinary citizens living in the Muslim state?

Unit Four

The Clan of Umayyah

Chapter One

The Struggle for Power

Lesson One

Mu`awiya in Charge

Looking Ahead

Look for the characteristics that made Mu`awiya a ruler who was both despised and loved.

Preview Vocabulary

Dynastic rule
Hilm
Constantinople

With 'Ali assassinated, Mu`awiya had little opposition left to stand against his claims. Except for the small group of surviving Khawarij, no one had the ability (or the will) to oppose his power. All political energy was now focused in the hands of Mu`awiya, his clan and his supporters. Having suffered through nearly five years of civil war, the *Ummah* looked for a strong leader who could ensure that it would not completely fracture.

One of Mu`awiya's precedents was that he initiated a new trend in Muslim government: dynastic rule, where the power of the government remains in the hands of a single family. The position of *khalifah* was now inherited rather than being an office open to any qualified Muslim male who was approved by a *shura*. In the system of dynastic rule, the ruler chooses his successor from among his own sons, or if need be, from among his close relatives.

As Mu`awiya tightened his hold over the Muslim community, his own clan, the Bani Umayyah, rose to new heights of power. Before the rise of Islam the Bani Umayyah were a very influential and powerful clan among the Quraish of Makkah. Many members of this clan were upset with the social changes that Islam brought and many of them were instrumental in opposing the spread of Islam. Mu'awiya's own father, Abu Sufian, was one of those men.

Who Was Mu`awiya?

Surely one of the most controversial figures of early Muslim history is Mu`awiya ibn Abu Sufian. Born in 610 CE to the most influential clan of the Quraish, the Bani Umayyah, Mu`awiya followed his father, Abu Sufian, in opposition to Islam. According to traditional accounts, he secretly began to sympathize with Islam after the Treaty of Hudaibiyah (628 CE) but only openly converted after the fall of Makkah two years later.

During the *khilafah* of Abu Bakr, Mu`awiya was sent with his brother to fight against the Byzantines in Syria. It was there that he gradually gained popularity not only among the Muslim Arab warriors, but among local Christian Arab tribes as well. To strengthen these ties, Mu`awiya married a Christian woman, Maisun, who was the daughter of an important tribal chief. Their son Yazid, would later succeed him as ruler. It was in the reign of 'Umar ibn al-Khattab that Mu`awiya was given governorship of the province of Syria. Mu`awiya made the ancient city of Damascus his power center. He was a very skillful politician and administrator. Some of his notable achievements included organizing the first Muslim navy (called the *Dar al-Sina'h*, from which the word "arsenal" comes) and arranging for the regulation and organization of the army.

Muslim opinion remains divided over Mu`awiya's conflict with 'Ali to this day. Shi'is openly condemn him for his wrongful takeover of the *khilafah*. Most Sunni scholars and historians tend to recognize his status as one of the *Sahabah* but generally do not condone his rebellion. Regardless of the debates over the nature of his personality or his actions, Mu`awiya not only built up centralized rule in the Muslim provinces, but he also created the first dynastic rule in Islamic History.

Mu`awiya can also be credited with creating a relatively stable government during his 20-year reign as head of the Muslim state. His style of dealing with opponents can best be described as a mixture of severity and generosity. For instance, in securing the resignation of Hasan, Mu`awiya used bribes and threats that caused Hasan's former supporters to defect. But he then allowed Hasan to live out the rest of his life in relative comfort and security (although Shi`i historians maintain Mu`awiya had Hasan poisoned). One modern historian, Prof. M. A. Shaban, in this regard summarizes best the character of Mu`awiya:

"Mu`awiya was a man of 'hilm'. This word is both complex and comprehensive and is not easily translated, but it is the best if not the only way of describing Mu`awiya's special ability as a leader. However as intimidating the pressures were, as a man of hilm he kept absolute self-control and made decisive judgments. He took decisions after long and judicious thought and whenever possible rejected a show of power as a solution to his problems. He looked squarely at a problem to see what forces were at work so that through subtle readjustment of these forces, he could reach an ingenious compromise. Thus Mu`awiya was always quick to offer reconciliation and treated his fallen enemies with an unassuming generosity and magnanimity which saved their dignity and self respect and gained him their loyalty. His mind was eminently pragmatic and political, characterized by restraint and self-control..."

(Islamic History: A New Interpretation, p.79)

A New Direction

In the weeks following the assassination of 'Ali, Mu`awiya sent 'Ali's son Hasan a message that he was prepared to negotiate some form of compromise. Many accounts portray Hasan as a man who did not want the responsibility that such a post would entail. And the fact that nearly all of those who had initially supported his father had either declared their neutrality or switched sides further dampened Hasan's resolve. He realized that to continue the fight against Mu`awiya would be fruitless and result in nothing but needless bloodshed. After only six months as *khalifah*, Hasan formally abdicated his position to Mu`awiya, under the condition that the name of 'Ali no longer be cursed in the *khutbah* (religious sermons) and that 'Ali's loyal supporters (the *Shi`ah*) be made free from harassment and retribution. Mu`awiya also agreed that upon his own death the office of *khalifah* would return to Hasan and by extension the family of 'Ali. With the terms of the transfer of office agreed upon, Mu`awiya legally became the ruler of the *Ummah*.

The new government formed by Mu`awiya was based largely on secular, or non-religious principles, rather than Islamic ideals. During the many years he ruled over Syria, he and his men absorbed many of the customs of the local population. The province at the time was overwhelmingly Christian and Muslims formed only a very small percentage of the population. Mu`awiya was also very generous to his soldiers and supporters, handing them out land and money as rewards for loyalty. With a trustworthy military and the wealth of one of the richest provinces in Southwest Asia at his beckoning, Mu`awiya was able to successfully exert his power.

In the prior decades, Muslim respect for the office of *khalifah* grew out of an individual's reputation as a long time *Sahabah* of the Prophet Muhammad. There was almost an aura of sacredness around their personalities. But with Mu`awiya it was different. Although he had sat in the presence of the Prophet in the years after the conquest of Makkah, Mu`awiya did not use this fact to increase his reputation. Instead he relied on his own cleverness and shrewd abilities.

One of the first tasks he faced was to restore the political stability of the *Ummah*. To guarantee law and order Mu`awiya did not permit anyone to speak out against his authority without having to face dire consequences. Those who still dared to challenge his power soon found it best to keep to their activities in secret. But overall people of the time generally respected Mu`awiya if for no other reason that he brought an end to the civil wars that threatened the unity of the *Ummah*. Mu`awiya sometimes had to enforce seemingly harsh policies in order to keep society from fragmenting into dozens of warring parties. Once individuals submitted to his authority,

their dignity and freedom were generally respected. He was once reported to have said, "I don't use my sword when my whip is enough, nor my whip where my tongue is enough. And even if there is but one hair connecting me with my people, I will not let it break; when they pull I loosen, and if they loosen I pull."

Continued Expansion

With the political stability brought about by Mu`awiya's strong rule Muslim armies were able to refocus their attention on pressing the war against Byzantium and Sasanid Persia instead of against themselves. With the center of power now in Syria, Mu`awiya concentrated on sending raids deep into Byzantine Anatolia (modern-day Turkey). In 667 CE a combined Muslim army and navy managed to make the nearly 600-mile march from the Syrian border to the very walls of Constantinople. A small naval base was established on the Sea of Marmara near the great city in order to harass Byzantine shipping. In 673 CE, a larger Muslim force arrived and made an attempt to seize the city but failed to do so.

In the east, Mu`awiya ordered the continued demolition of the Sasanid Empire. As Arab forces rolled through the Iranian heartland, they met with little resistance. In many instances, the Persians welcomed the Arabs as emancipators from the harsh rule the nobility had imposed over them. Members of the Sasanid royal family fled Persia to Central Asia where they tried desperately to organize resistance against the invaders, but to no avail. Their subjects simply did not want to give up their lives and property to their former overlords. The swiftness in which the Arabs pursued their enemy also did not allow for the organization of any real army.

Eventually, when the cities of Bukhara and Samarqand fell to Muslim forces in the decade after Mu`awiya's death, the last *shah* of Persia fled to China. Thus ended the four hundred year-old Sasanid empire.

To be able to secure these newly subjugated regions, Mu`awiya began a policy of moving entire Arab tribes to establish settlements in these areas. Whenever a particular region was cleared of armed opposition, tribes from Iraq and the Peninsula would be moved in. These newly set-up colonies were not simply military garrisons. They were entire communities and families. Although their initial purpose was to provide security and control over a given area these settlements would serve as bases from which the spread of Islam and the Arabic language would occur among the local populations.

Lesson Review

1. Describe how Mu`awiya brought change to the government from the way it was run during the era of the *Khulafa' ar-Rashidah*.

2. Give two reasons as to why the citizens of Sasanid Persia welcomed the invading Muslim armies.

3. *"Mu`awiya brought an end to the rule of Shura."* Comment on this statement in light of what you have read in this lesson.

Lesson Two

Challenges Arise

Looking Ahead

Why did revolt and rebellion break out during the rule of Yazid ibn Mu`awiya? Look for the seeds of division within the *Ummah*.

Preview Vocabulary

Karbala
Counter-Khalifah
Husain
Abdullah ibn Zubair

The stability that Mu`awiya imposed on the Islamic State during the 20 years of his rule quickly fell apart upon his death. In the final days of his life, Mu`awiya made it known to the public that his son Yazid would be the one to succeed him. Yazid however lacked any sense of piety and appeared to have over-indulged in the privileges of his rank. He was known to have had a taste for liquor, lavish parties and slave-girls, causing many traditional historians to describe him as a non-practicing Muslim at best. Yet upon Mu`awiya's death the people of Syria were still deeply loyal to the Bani Umayyah and they gave *bay`ah* to Yazid and accepted his rule. There were many, however, who chose otherwise.

The Rising of Husain ibn 'Ali

Yazid's ascent to power stirred opposition from many different circles. Although many people scorned the power and authority of the Bani Umayyah they came to accept the rule of Mu`awiya as the only alternative to chaos. But Yazid was not his father nor did he share his character traits. Many realized that an individual of such notorious repute had no place as ruler of the *Ummah*. Surprisingly Yazid was well aware of these objections. As soon as he took his father's place as ruler he sent his deputies to Madinah to force its

The shrine of Husain at Karbala, Iraq. The current structure was built centuries after the Battle of Karbala. This masjid continues to be an important place of visitation for Shi`is all over the world.

citizens to take *bay`ah* to prevent any rebellion. Few in the city willingly did so. Many of the families of notable *Sahabah* refused to give their pledge to Yazid. Instead they turned to `Ali's second son, Husain and to `Abdullah ibn Zubair (the son of `Ali's onetime opponent) to lead them against the new Umayyad sovereign. The entire city was soon engulfed in anticipation of renewed struggle. Outside of Madinah, other regions likewise showed great interest in dislodging the Bani Umayyah from their position of absolute power. Places like Yemen and Iraq had a considerable presence of Khawarij or Shi`i in their populations, and were naturally hotbeds of anti-Umayyad sentiments.

Needless to say Yazid was furious with the refusal of so many in Madinah to offer their *bay`ah*. He ordered Husain and Ibn Zubair

arrested and forced to give their pledge on pain of death if need be. But the two fled to Makkah before the Umayyad agents could carry out their orders. In Makkah, Husain began to receive hundreds of messages of support from the citizens of Kufa, a city that was once the seat of his father 'Ali's government. The people of Kufa promised to provide manpower to remove the Umayyads if only Husain would come and lead them. Many of Husain's closest supporters were worried that the people of Kufa would not follow through with their pledge. It was known to all that the Kufans had abandoned 'Ali when his clash with Mu`awiya stagnated. There was no guarantee other than their promises that they would not do likewise to Husain.

Despite advice against it, Husain left Madinah for Makkah and from there to Iraq. Yazid's men in

The Death of Husain
Excerpts from *Kitab al-Irshad* of Mufid

The army launched an attack against Husain and cut off his way to his camp. His thirst became severe and he set off, trying to reach the Euphrates River. In front of him was his brother, 'Abbas. However, the cavalry of ibn Sa'd (may God curse him) blocked his way. Among them was a young man from the Bani Darim. He said to the cavalry, "What are you doing? Prevent him from reaching the Euphrates! Don't let him get to the water!"

Then Husain cried out, "O God, I need to drink!" The Darimi man became angry and shot an arrow at him, which lodged in his throat. Husain pulled out the arrow and held his hand below his windpipe. Both of his palms were filled with blood, which he shook away. Then he said, "O God, what is being done to the son and daughter of Your Prophet?!" Then he returned to his position, while his thirst had become even more severe.

Meanwhile the Umayyads surrounded 'Abbas and cut him off from Husain. Single-handed 'Abbas began to attack them until he was killed....

When Husain came back from the river to his camp, Shamir ibn Dhi al-Jawshan advanced towards him with a band of his followers and encircled him. The fastest of them was a man called Malik ibn al-Nusair al-Kindi. He cursed Husain and struck him on his head with his sword. Husain was wearing a cap. The blade went through it right into his skull and made it bleed. The cap was filled with blood. Husain said, "May you never eat or drink with your right hand! May God assemble you with those people who are wrong-doers!" Then he threw away the cap and called for a cloth, which he tied around his head. Then he called for another cap, put it on and tightened it.

Shamir ibn Dhi al-Jawshan and those who were with him fell back from Husain. After a while they came once more and encircled him. 'Abdullah ibn al-Hasan ibn 'Ali came out against them. He was only a boy, not yet mature enough to leave the women. He hurried forward until he stood next to his uncle, Husain. Then Zainab, the daughter of 'Ali came after him to stop him and Husain told her to stop him. However the young 'Abdullah refused and resolutely prevented her. He said: "By God, I will not leave my uncle!"

Abjar ibn Ka'b charged towards Husain. With sword in hand, the young boy said to him: "Woe to you, you son of a foul woman, are you trying to kill my uncle?" Abjar struck at 'Abdullah with his sword. The boy tried to ward off the blow with his arm. The sword cut through to the skin on the other side. There was the arm hanging by the skin. The boy cried out, "O mother!" Husain took hold of him and hugged him. He said to him, "My nephew, try to endure what has come to you and be soothed with the news that God will unite you with your righteous ancestors!" Then Husain raised his hand and said, " O God, even as You have made life enjoyable for them for a time, split them into factions and let their rulers never be happy with them. They called us so that they might support us and then they became turned on us and killed us!"...When nobody except a group of three males of his family was left with Husain, he moved against the people, while the three defended him until all were killed. Husain was left alone. Despite being weighed down by his wounds, he began to strike against them with his sword and they fled away from him.

When Shamir ibn Dhi al-Jawshan realized this he called for the cavalry and they came up at the rear of the foot soldiers. He commanded the archers to shoot at Husain and they showered him with arrows until he became quilled like a porcupine.

Husain drew back from them and they stood facing him. His sister, Zainab, came to the door of the tent and yelled out to 'Umar ibn Sa'd ibn Abi Waqqas, "Damn You 'Umar! Is Abu 'Abdullah being killed while you watch?" But 'Umar did not answer. Then she yelled again, "Curse you all, is there not a believer among you?" But no one answered.

Then Shamir ibn Dhi al-Jawshan shouted at the foot soldiers and cavalry, "What are you waiting for? Attack him!" So they attacked him from every side.

Zur'a ibn Sharik struck Husain on the left shoulder-blade and cut into it. Another struck him on the shoulder. He fell prostrate on his face. Sinan ibn Anas al-Nakha'i stabbed him with a spear and killed him. Khawali ibn Yazid al-Asbahi charged at him and bent down to cut off his head but he quivered. Shamir said to him, "May God rot your arm! Why are you trembling?" Then Shamir bent down and beheaded Husain. He lifted it and gave it to Khawali remarking, "Take it to our commander, 'Umar ibn Sa'd."

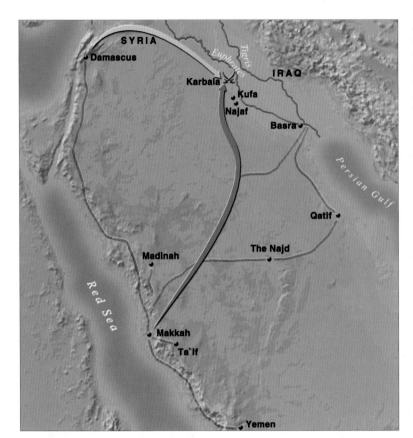

Madinah reported the news of his departure and
the governors in Iraq were put on alert. Through
threats and intimidation the Umayyads beat the
weak-willed people of Kufa into abandoning
their intended support for Husain.

A large Umayyad army intercepted Husain's
small force of 72-armed men (along with their
women and children) as it neared the banks of
the Euphrates River at a place known as
Karbala'. With 3,000 men under his command
the Umayyad governor of Iraq surrounded the
tiny band. A standoff ensued for several days
during which Husain was repeatedly ordered to
surrender. These calls met only with absolute
rejection. On the 10th day of the lunar month of
Muharram the governor grew tired of the standoff and ordered his forces to launch an assault.

Outnumbered 40-to-1, Husain and his band of
warriors were annihilated. All of Husain's sons
were killed, except for the young `Ali (who was
more commonly known as Zain al-`Abidin). The
camp of the Prophet's grandson was looted and
the women thrown into chains. The dead were
decapitated and the head of Husain was taken to
Damascus to prove to Yazid that the problem
had indeed been dealt with.

A More Serious Rising

Following the unsuccessful end of Husain's
attempt to restore his family to the *khilafah*, a
more crucial insurrection broke out under the
leadership of 'Abdullah ibn Zubair. Born nearly
a year after the *Hijrah*, 'Abdullah was the son of
two notable *Sahabi*; Zubair ibn al-'Awwam and

his wife, 'Asma, a daughter of Abu Bakr. 'Abdullah was believed to have been the first baby of the *Muhajirun* born in Madinah.

During the *khilafah* of 'Umar, 'Abdullah went with his father to Palestine and was present at the Battle of Yarmuk. Ten years later he was in the ranks of the army that pushed the Byzantines out of what is now Libya. Following this 'Abdullah took part in the campaign to eliminate Sasanid resistance in the mountains of northern Persia. In the conflict between 'Ali and 'A'isha, Talha and az-Zubair, 'Abdullah naturally sided with his father. He participated in the Battle of the Camel and following the defeat of his father's forces, returned to Madinah.

Although 'Abdullah did not openly object to Mu`awiya's rule, he was not particularly sympathetic to the rise of Umayyad power. Yet when Yazid took the reigns of state 'Abdullah came out in open protest. Like Husain he refused to pledge his *bay'ah* to Yazid. But he refused to join with Husain in forming a unified opposition to Umayyad power. For just as he had qualms with the Umayyads, 'Abdullah also had them with the sons of 'Ali. Instead he organized his own attempt to take the *khilafah* for himself.

After Husain's failed attempt to overturn the rule of Yazid, the inhabitants of Makkah and Madinah quickly fell in behind 'Abdullah. In response Yazid sent an large army to the Hijaz late in 683 CE. The force rolled through Madinah after having met little opposition and proceeded onwards to lay siege to Makkah. It appeared for a while that 'Abdullah's rising would break under the weight of the Umayyad army as Husain's did less than a year earlier.

Fortunately for the insurgents, events in Damascus saved them from certain defeat. News reached the besieging army outside Makkah that Yazid had died and that his young son, Mu`awiya II had been placed on the throne. But the boy died after a few weeks, and the rule of the Bani Umayyah was thrown into chaos as the family began to struggle over the succession. While the sons of Umayyah squabbled over a successor, their army besieging Makkah withdrew back to Syria, hoping to have a say in choosing the new ruler. `Abdullah ibn Zubair took the chance to declared himself the legitimate *amir al-mu'minin*. Throughout the civil war that would follow and that would last for more than a decade, 'Abdullah was recognized as a 'Counter-Khalifah' by his supporters, in direct opposition to the claims of the Bani Umayyah.

Lesson Review

1. Compare the ways in which Abu Bakr was selected as ruler with those of Yazid.

2. Why did Husain decide to leave from Madinah for the Iraqi town of Kufa?

3. Give an account of the circumstances which caused the Umayyad army to lift the siege of Makkah and return to Syria.

4. Read and describe the events of the Battle of Karbala' in your own words.

Lesson Three

Tightening the Grip

Looking Ahead

As you read, look for the reasons that allowed the Umayyads to effectively deal with the challenges to their power.

Preview Vocabulary

Ghanima
Mukhtar al-Thaqafi
Hajjaj ibn Yusuf
Tawwabun
Tyrant
Shurta

As 'Abdullah ibn Zubair laid his claim to the leadership of the Islamic State, the very survival of Umayyad rule was now in question. A large number of people threw their support behind 'Abdullah ibn Zubair. The provinces of Hijaz, Egypt and Iraq were all willing to endorse him. Even the Khawarij (who had been quietly regrouping their strength) endorsed 'Abdullah to some extent. The Muslims of Syria were divided on the issue. Although they had strong ties to the Umayyad clan, many began to question the effectiveness of combating the growing popularity of 'Abdullah ibn Zubair. With Yazid's son dead and no apparent successor available, some in Syria felt that *bay'at* should now be given to the 'Counter-Khalifah'. Before such a drastic step could be taken, one that would have completely extinguished Umayyad rule, the chiefs in Damascus brought forward Marwan ibn Hakam, the elderly but influential cousin of Mu`awiya, and placed him at the head of the dynasty. The question of *bay'at* was therefore settled and all of Syria fell back in line.

Marwan's first task was to get rid of those Syrians who intended going over to the side of 'Abdullah ibn Zubair. The harshness of his methods in doing so, however, caused rebellion among several Arab tribes that had previously been loyal to the Umayyads. Marwan mobilized his army and with it forced these tribes back into the ranks. Where he was unable to use force, Marwan found other ways for expanding power and control. He bribed several high-ranking officials in the enemy ranks (like the pro-Ibn Zubair governor of Egypt) to switch sides. Despite his successful attempts at saving his clan's power, the elderly Marwan could not hold back the inevitable. He died after only a year in power. But before his death in 685 CE, he made it very clear that his son 'Abd al-Malik was to succeed him.

When 'Abd al-Malik took over his father's post as chief of the Bani Umayyah and head of the *Ummah*, the dynasty faced serious challenges. The successes of 'Abdullah ibn Zubair encouraged other groups (namely the Khawarij and the Shi'ah) to rise up in opposition to the Umayyads. During the confusion that engulfed the Umayyads after the death of the young Mu`awiya II, these groups cooperated to a limited extent in ridding themselves of a common enemy. With the reestablishment of strong Umayyad rule and the ascension of 'Abd al-Malik, however, this cooperation fell to pieces and the three opposition factions (Ibn Zubair, the Khawarij and the Shi'ah) commenced fighting among themselves.

The largest and by far the most active of these were the Khawarij. Having been nearly annihilated by 'Ali twenty years earlier, the Khawarij gathered their support in parts of Iraq and among the bedouin tribes of northern Arabia. Interestingly the Arab tribes that supported the Khawarij hailed from the same regions that rose up in the Riddah Wars nearly sixty years earlier. The Khawarij enjoyed popularity among both Arab and non-Arab Muslims in the areas under their control. This was mainly a result of their almost 'democratic' views on the position of the *khilafah,* one that

essentially stated that any man, regardless of social position, could rule the *Ummah*. Still their strict and inflexible interpretation of Islam eventually alienated many of their supporters who began to desert the ranks in droves.

While Marwan and 'Abd al-Malik were busy re-establishing order and control over Syria, the Khawarij began extending their influence into the Arabian Peninsula. This brought them into combat with 'Abdullah ibn Zubair. The Khawarij initially had no real problems with Ibn Zubair, seeing that he too wished to see the Bani Umayyah out of power. But 'Abdullah ibn Zubair later tried to force his authority over them and the Khawarij would have none of it. An insurmountable rift quickly developed.

The conflict with the Khawarij was the first step in the unraveling of 'Abdullah ibn Zubair's power. The Umayyads began to re-establish power and strength, retaking the lands lost during the confusion over succession. Ibn Zubair's supporters in Syria were crushed and Egypt came back under Umayyad control, depriving the 'Counter-Khalifah' of vital resources, both human and financial. 'Abdullah ibn Zubair focused his attention on Iraq, where he still had a solid body of support. But problems were stirring there as well. The Khawarij began to strike against his armies and raid the towns and villages that offered him support.

Not wanting to remain on the sidelines, the Shi`ah began to muster their supporters. Centered around the Iraqi city of Kufa they remained aloof from politics since the death of Husain four years earlier. But many Iraqi Shi'is harbored a deep sense of guilt for having abandoned Husain on the field of Karbala'. When it looked as if Umayyad rule would collapse after the death of Yazid's son, the Shi`ah

The Beliefs of the Khawarij

In early Muslim history no other group was considered as dangerous to the stability of the government than the Khawarij. Not only were the Khawarij a group bent on political domination, they can be considered the first "sect" (meaning "a cutting off" from the main body) in Islam, in the sense that they departed from basic Islamic teachings, as opposed to simple difference of opinion. Their fanatical and uncompromising interpretation of the Qur'an concerning who could be considered a believer, and on matters of worship, separated their views from those of the majority of Muslims. But the Khawarij splintered among themselves over time. By the late 12th century CE, when their influence had greatly declined, there were more than a dozen Khawarij factions. Some of their peculiar beliefs were noted by the great Iraqi scholar, Shaikh 'Abd al-Qadir Jilani in the following text:

They [the Khawarij] have separated themselves off from the religious community, breaking loose from it and from the loyal congregation. They have gone astray from the level course of right guidance and from the True Path.

They have withdrawn their allegiance from the ruling authority and they have unsheathed the sword against the rightful leaders, whose blood they consider it permissible to shed and whose property they consider it lawful to confiscate. They have branded all that oppose them as unbelievers. They dare to heap curses on the Sahabah of the Prophet and on his Ansar. They wash their hands of them, haughtily dismiss them as guilty of kufr and terrible sins and consider it right and proper to contradict them.

They do not believe in the torment of the grave, nor in the Basin, nor in the right of intercession. They offer no one any prospect of deliverance from the Fire of Hell and they profess the doctrine that if someone tells a single lie or commits a sin of any kind, whether it be trivial or serious, and if he then dies without repentance, that person will be counted as an unbeliever and will be condemned to remain in the Fire of Hell for all eternity.

They do not regard the congregational salat as valid unless it is performed behind one of their own Imam, but they do regard it as valid to postpone the salat beyond its prescribed time…

formed themselves into an armed force known as the *Tawwabun*, or "those who seek absolution".

In 684 CE *Tawwabun* made an attempt to push the Umayyad army out of Iraq but were unable to overcome such a large and experienced force. Reinforcements from Damascus were sent into Iraq and they eventually put an end to the *Tawwabun*. However, before their destruction the

Tawwabun managed to kill several of those who led the army against the grandson of the Prophet.

The destruction of the *Tawwabun* was not, however, the end of Shi`i resistance. In 686 CE, a man by the name of Mukhtar al-Thaqafi set about to reorganized the Shi'is of Iraq. Although he himself was not a member of the *Ahl al-Bait* nor even of the Bani Hashim clan, Mukhtar claimed to be acting on behalf of Muhammad ibn Hanafiyyah, one of the sons of 'Ali (but from a wife other than Fatima). In a move to gain wider support for his cause, Mukhtar issued a pronouncement that eventually distanced him from most of Shi'ah living in Iraq. He declared that all who supported the *Ahl al-Bait* would stand on equal footing should a new state be formed. This meant that the *Mawali* (the new non-Arab converts) would be granted the same rights and privileges enjoyed by Arab Muslims.

How could such a desire be so upsetting? Despite the Islamic ideal of equality and prohibition of racism and ethno-centrism, many Arabs saw Islam as a privilege granted to them alone. During the Umayyad period Arabs were normally given favored treatment in administrative positions and in economic advancement. Mukhtar

simply called for an end to discriminatory practices that the *Mawali* had to endure. This egalitarian sentiment caused many Arab tribes (both Shi'i and non-Shi'i) in and around Kufa to break with Mukhtar.

As his support eroded, Mukhtar managed to provoked the animosity of 'Abdullah ibn Zubair by refusing to accept his authority as the sole *khalifah*. 'Abdullah ibn Zubair ordered his governor in Iraq to hunt Mukhtar down and kill him. There was not much Mukhtar could do to stave off defeat. After having been abandoned by nearly all support, Mukhtar met a violent end in 687 CE, not at the hands of the hated Umayyads, but rather the 'Counter-Khalifah'.

The Days of Hajjaj

While the opponents of the Bani Umayyah fought among themselves, 'Abd al-Malik appointed a very effective yet ferocious man to assist in the re-establishment Umayyad dominance. He was Hajjaj ibn Yusuf al-Thaqafi, a member of the Arab tribe of Bani Thaqif, one of the prominent tribes of Ta'if, a town found not far from Makkah. Originally appointed as head of the *Shurta* (the military police) in the province of Syria, Hajjaj's ability to brutally enforce law and order attracted the attention of 'Abd al-Malik. In 691 CE, Hajjaj was put at the head of

Ruins of Umayyad palaces can still be found in the remote areas of Jordan and Syria. These structures were used by the nobility to escape the pressures of the cities as well as for fortified strongholds.

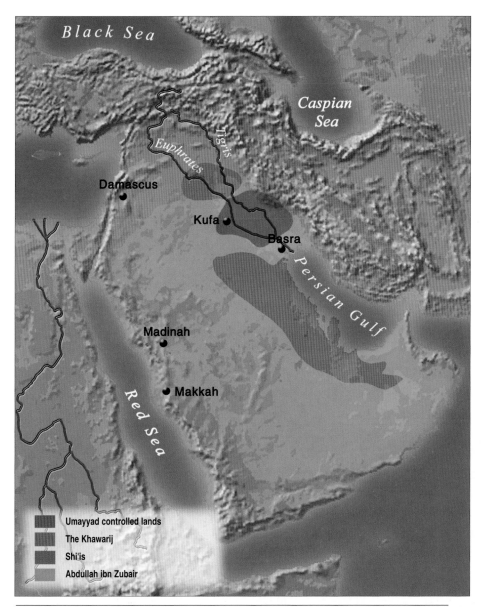

The central Muslim lands during the period of the counter-khalifah Abdullah ibn Zubair.

Umayyad controlled lands
The Khawarij
Shi'is
Abdullah ibn Zubair

the Umayyad army and told to use it to take Iraq back from 'Abdullah ibn Zubair at any cost. This he did with considerable ease crushing all who dared stand against him.

With Iraq now taken from his hand, 'Abdullah ibn Zubair had little to fall back on. He tried to organize further resistance form his base in Makkah. However in 692 CE, Hajjaj and his army entered the province of the Hijaz, took Madinah and encircled the city of Makkah. The Umayyad ruler 'Abd al-Malik desired that Hajjaj negotiate some form of surrender with 'Abdullah ibn Zubair to spare the sacred city scenes of bloodshed. Hajjaj's brutal character would not allow such niceties and he disregarded his master's request. The city of Makkah was placed under siege.

It is said that during the blockade, Hajjaj expressed the desire to perform the *'Umrah*, the customary pilgrimage held outside of the *Hajj* season. 'Abdullah ibn Zubair refused to allow Hajjaj to pass through the lines. Enraged by this apparent affront to his dignity, Hajjaj ordered his catapults to bombard the city, and one of the hurled boulders hit and partially collapsed the Ka'bah. Following the bombardment Makkah was stormed and Ibn Zubair was captured and put to the sword. After nearly nine years, the rule of `Abdullah ibn Zubair had come to a bloody end.

Having eliminated opposition in the Hijaz, Hajjaj turned his attention back to Iraq where the threat of the Khawarij still loomed in the countryside. By 695 CE, he and his men suppressed the Khawarij and chased them into the mountains of Iran. Hajjaj then implemented a procedure that was designed to rid Iraq of all those suspected of disloyalty to the Umayyads: forced resettlement. Hajjaj ordered whole tribes deported to the eastern borders of the Islamic State, where he hoped their energies would be refocused on expanding the borders of Islam rather than used against the Umayyad Dynasty. This program was nothing really new as Arab tribes had been settling on the frontier a generation earlier during the reign of Mu`awiya. Although it rid the central provinces of Iraq, Arabia and Syria of most of its dissidents,

> "And if two parties of the believers fall into mutual fighting make peace between them. And if one party of them does wrong to the other, fight that which does wrong until it returns to the command of Allah. Then if it returns, make peace between them justly and act equitably. Allah loves those who do justice."
>
> *the Qur'an 49:9*

Hajjaj's resettlement program concentrated opposition in the east, and, as we will read later, did little more than sow the seeds of future Umayyad destruction.

Having cleared Iraq of most of its anti-Umayyad elements, Hajjaj set about rebuilding the countryside. The region suffered terribly throughout the two decades of civil war. The rich farmland of Mesopotamia lay abandoned and peasants were suffering under the heavy taxes that were raised to pay for the various armies. Cities became crowded with refugees, all of which added to the general discontent of the population, Muslim and non-Muslim alike.

Hajjaj knew that groups like the Khawarij and Shi'i benefited from such social discontent. With the approval of 'Abd al-Malik, he ordered all peasants to return to their farms. Any who refused, he proclaimed, would be put to death. With his well-earned reputation for brutality, few resisted his command. Hajjaj was a man who made people well aware of the consequences of going against his authority. According to legend, he once came into Kufa disguised by a face-veil. As he made his way to the *masjid* he asked the citizens of the town what they thought of the "great tyrant Hajjaj". Not knowing this veiled person was that very man, the people spoke their minds quite freely. Hajjaj then went to the *masjid*, summoned the townsfolk, stood on the *minbar* (pulpit) and removed his face-veil. He addressed the stunned crowd, "I see your heads like fields of wheat, ripe for harvesting. People of Iraq, I shall not let myself be crushed like a soft fig. The *Amir al-Mu'minin* has drawn the arrows from his quiver and tested the wood, and has found that I am the hardest…And so, by Allah, if you cross me I will strip you as men strip the bark from trees and I will beat you as straying camels are beaten."

And Hajjaj meant every word. In 700 CE, an army of Arab tribesmen that had been sent out of Iraq returned without his prior permission. They had been sent on a disastrous campaign to subdue the pagan mountain people of Afghanistan. When the battle-weary men entered into Iraq, Hajjaj met them with an army of his own and had all of their leaders crucified. Needles to say, for the next 14 years of his governorship, Hajjaj never faced serious problems in Iraq again.

By creating a climate of security through such severe methods, Hajjaj was able to encourage growth in the economy of Iraq. This of course, benefited other provinces, like Syria and Egypt. With the turmoil of rebellion brought to an end and financial abundance beginning to rise, the average person became more willing to put up with Umayyad rule. Attention could now be focused once more on the frontiers of the *Dar al-Islam*.

Lesson Review

1. Given the chaotic situation that engulfed the Muslim world of the time, do you think Hajjaj was justified in using brutal methods to bring about law and order?

2. Explain the positions of the various factions that sought to gain dominance over the Muslim world.

Chapter Review

1. Why do you think people grew disaffected with the Umayyad regime following the death of Mu`awiya?

2. Think about what life must have been like for an average person during this disruptive period of Muslim history. Do you think Muslims and non-Muslims would have been effected by it equally or in different ways and why?

Chapter Two

Later Umayyad Rule

Lesson One

Forging an Empire

Looking Ahead

As you read, look for the ways the Muslims interacted with the native populations of the region that were conquered.

Preview Vocabulary

Transoxiana
Steppes
Turks
Silk Road
Qairawan
Kahina
Berber

In keeping with the principle of dynastic rule, 'Abd al-Malik was succeed on his death in 705 CE (some 86 years after the *Hijrah*) by his eldest son, al-Walid. Thereafter, as was the custom, all the governors of the provinces procured *bay`at* for al-Walid from their constituents. The consolidation of the Umayyad Dynasty that was completed during the final years of 'Abd al-Malik's reign continued on with al-Walid. His reign was to witness spectacular military expansion into Central Asia and North Africa and it was a time when Muslim warriors first stepped foot both in Spain and on the Indian Subcontinent.

Transoxiana & the East

With Iraq pacified largely due to the efforts of Hajjaj, a policy of conquest was launched in Central Asia. The lands of Central Asia were called Transoxiana in classical sources, a Greek word meaning 'lands over the Oxus River'. By the time al-Walid took the throne Muslim armies had already established garrison towns throughout the province of Khorasan, a region in the far eastern part of modern-day Iran. These strongholds were continually reinforced by tribes that arrived either because Hajjaj had forced them to or simply for the lure of better economic circumstances through the acquisition of *ghanima*. During the great rebellions

After coming into contact with Islam and Muslims in the late 7th century, the Turkic peoples of the steppes of Central Asia would be destined to play a tremendous role in the history of Islamic civilization.

that hit Iraq and Arabia, these garrisons were not seriously effected because they were simply too far away to become involved and were busy fighting other enemies.

The majority of the people living in Khorasan and Transoxiana on the eve of Muslim conquest spoke languages closely related to Persian. For centuries this area had been under the sway of the Sasanid Dynasty and by the time the Muslims arrived most of its people were either Buddhist or Manichaean despite the fact the Prophet Zoroaster lived and died in this region a thousand years earlier. Transoxians also had a long and sometimes bloody relationship with a nomadic people known as the Turks. Though at times the peoples

of the towns and cities would often find themselves at war with these roaming tribes, there was a certain level of harmonious mixing between the two. Transoxiana was a region that enjoyed great prosperity. Although its climate was dry, it was well watered by two mighty rivers, the Amu Darya (Oxus) and the Syr Darya. This permitted the development of extensive agriculture.

It was trade, however, that brought real wealth to Transoxiana. A vital stop on the Silk Road (the great trade route to China), magnificent cities like Samarqand and Bukhara thrived on the overland commerce between East and West. As we shall read in later lessons, the Silk Road would continue to play an important role in Transoxiana long after the region became predominantly Muslim. The economic importance of Central Asia gave it great importance in the world and the empires and states that bordered the region understood this. They constantly vied with one another to gain complete control over it; for whoever controlled Transoxiana would control its massive earnings from trade.

Since the Mu`awiya's reign, Muslim armies were active on the borders of Central Asia. In 674 CE, they crossed the Syr Darya and clashed with roaming Turkish tribesmen. Although these early incursions did not amount to much, the cities and towns of Khorasan started to expand as they became bases for Muslim warriors (both Arab and *Mawali*) and their families. Shortly after al-Walid succeeded his father, new energy was focused on seizing Transoxiana before any other state could. The collapse of Sasanid authority left a power vacuum in Central Asia that the Chinese, Turks and Tibetans all tried to fill in some way or another. On the advice of Hajjaj, al-Walid put an effective leader by the name of Qutaiba ibn Muslim in charge of taking the lands between the Amu Darya and Syr Darya rivers.

In 706 CE, Qutaiba assailed the important city of Bukhara. After a long and ferocious siege, he seized the city and installed a king who was amiable to the Muslims. But the people of Bukhara did not respond as favorably to Arab domination. Throughout the next decade they

rebelled several times trying to reestablish their independence. Qutaiba finally decided that the only way to remedy these uprisings was to settle large numbers of Arabs into the city. The settlement of these Arabs not only provided security they acted as a means by which Islam was transferred to the native population.

Over the next five years, Qutaiba subdued nearly all of the major cities of Transoxiana. Places such as Farghana, Khawarizm and Tirmidh were all forced to come to terms with the expanding Muslim power. With the control of these cities secured, considerable wealth began to flow into Umayyad treasuries. Qutaiba was so animated by his successes he continued with his conquests. His exploits eventually brought the Muslim world into its first recorded contact with China. In 713 CE

Despite threats of internal instability, the military conquests of the Umayyads continued with rapid success.

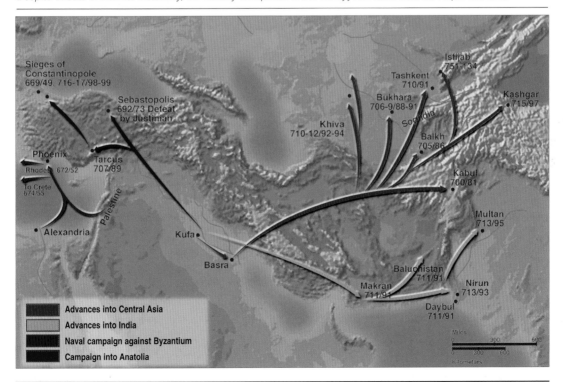

The Peoples of North Africa on the Arrival of Islam

The Arab Muslims moving west from Egypt in 642 CE encountered a landscape very similar to the Arabian Peninsula. North Africa has a very arid climate, with a belt of fertile land along the Mediterranean coast. Towns and cities had existed here since ancient times. South of the Atlas Mountains and the coast, lay the Sahara, the world's largest desert, stretching across the entire bulge of Africa from the Atlantic to the Red Sea. There is archaeological and historical evidence that it was not always so dry, and that North and Sub-Saharan Africa had been more closely linked in the ancient past. By the seventh century, however, the Sahara was like a vast ocean which could be crossed only by groups who had the skills and resources (like the camel) to endure its brutal climate.

North Africa, like Southwest Asia, was a crossroads of civilizations and peoples. It is believed that the first known races to inhabit the region were Berbers and the Libyans. They established both pastoral and settled ways of life and maintained links across the Saharan region. These people spoke languages that belonged to the Hamitic family, which is distantly connected to the Semitic branch. Around 1,000 BCE, Phoenicians from the coast of Lebanon began to arrive along the coast of North Africa. They established important ports that engaged in trade throughout the Mediterranean. The greatest of these port cities was Carthage (in modern-day Tunisia). In 146 BCE, the Romans, had conquered North Africa and destroyed Carthage.

The Roman Empire ruled North Africa for almost five centuries. During that time, North Africans adopted many aspects of Roman culture, but they preserved their own local languages. Many accepted Christianity, and Christian churches appeared throughout North Africa by the 2nd century CE. North African Christians split into various groups that rejected Roman and Greek religious influences, using their own languages in formal worship.

Two hundred years before the rise of Islam a group of Germanic invaders known as the Vandals added to this cultural and racial mix. In 429 CE, the Vandal king sailed with some 80,000 of his tribe for modern-day Tunisia. There they established a Germanic state that lasted for nearly a century until it was destroyed by the Byzantines. The Vandals (like other Germanic peoples) were noted for the fact that they followed Arianism, a sect of Christianity that did not believe in the divinity of Jesus. The Church in Rome considered them heretics, or unbelievers.

During the sixth century CE, North Africa was added to the Byzantine Empire. But the Byzantines could spare few military units to defend against invaders and to enforce Byzantine policies. The Independent traditions among North African cultures kept them apart from their new Greek-speaking masters. Their detachment became more severe when the Byzantines tried to enforce religious uniformity. The Arabs, with their similar tribal ways of life and cultural values, were not completely alien to the Berbers. On the eve of the Arab invasion, these conditions may have made North Africa particularly receptive to the Arab advances.

Qutaiba's scouts reached the city of Kashgar and held it briefly. This city was an important stop on the Silk Road and was considered part of the most western fringe of Chinese Empire. The capture of Kashgar certainly did not make a good first impression on the Chinese and China began to become troubled by the growing Muslim domination of the Silk Road. In an effort to weaken this domination it entered into an alliance with several powerful Turkish tribes. This new relationship between China and the Turks encouraged the Umayyad rulers to establish ties with the Buddhist kingdom of Tibet, a state that played a significant role in the politics of the area. Tibet and China had long been rivals in the region and the Umayyads hoped to use their alliance with Tibet to counter Chinese moves in Central Asia.

North Africa

As we read in Unit 3, Egypt was conquered in 642 CE, and an important military garrison known as Fustat was founded. Like the provinces in the east, Egypt became the home to a large number of Arab warriors and their families who came and settled there. From this post in Fustat, the Umayyad army quickly rolled down the North African coast. In 670 CE, during the reign of Mu`awiya, Muslim forces reached as far as modern-day Tunisia. In keeping with the practice of establishing garrison settlements, the Arabs set up a new one named Qairawan. From here expeditions continued further west into the highlands of Algeria and Morocco. In 683 CE (nearly sixty years after the *Hijrah*), one Muslim commander, `Uqbah ibn Nafi`, managed to reach the shores of the Atlantic Ocean after having cut across northern Morocco. Having reached the shore he was reported, as he drove his horse into the waves, to have said, "O Allah!

Were it not for this ocean I would push on for the sake of Your Glory."

In North Africa the Arabs were initially successful defeating any organized opposition. The Byzantine-controlled towns along the Mediterranean coast opened their gates without much resistance and imperial authority quickly collapsed. However the people of the interior were much more difficult to subdue. Away from the heavily Romanized coast a people known as Berbers dominated the hills and mountains. Many Berber tribes welcomed the Arab armies and enthusiastically entered into Islam. But there was fierce resistance from others and Umayyad forces initially used great brutality in dealing with those who would not submit peacefully. Coercion proved to cause nothing but further resentment and even those tribes that had embraced Islam left it to join their kinsmen in their fight against the Arabs.

As the Umayyads battled the 'Counter-Khalifah' 'Abdullah ibn Zubair, the Berbers in North Africa rose up to rid themselves of foreign rule and they quickly rallied around a powerful and charismatic woman named Dihya. Commonly known as the *Kahina* or "Witch" in Arabic writings, Dihya was commonly believed to have been of Jewish or Christian faith. She led her warriors to victory after victory over the Muslim garrisons scattered throughout modern-day Algeria and Tunisia. These setbacks were so alarming that the Umayyad commander in North Africa ordered a withdrawal of all forces back to Libya in order to fend off complete annihilation.

In 697 CE, with 'Abd al-Malik in firm control over the Umayyad state, Muslim forces in North Africa received reinforcements from Egypt. A counterattack against the Berbers was launched and the coastal areas of Tunisia and Algeria were recaptured. Muslim forces (including a number of Berbers, who on seeing the counterattack, returned to Islam) swept up into the Atlas Mountains and inflicted a series of stunning defeats over the *Kahina*. She was eventually cornered in a valley called Tarfa, where she and her followers were wiped out. It is said that in her final hours she realized that defeat was inevitable. To save her people from complete ruin, she sent her three sons to the Arab camp and told them to embrace Islam and make common cause with the Arabs. Ultimately, these very men went on to participate in the invasion of al-Andalus, Spain.

The Arabs learned their lesson from the Berber rebellion. They put off any retribution and exonerated all those who participated in the rebellion. As a result of this new policy of reconciliation, there was a whole-scale conversion of the Berber tribes throughout the Atlas Mountains. The Berbers were the only non-Arab people so far to have converted almost as a whole.

Lesson Review

1. What do you understand by the word "empire"? Why was the rule of al-Walid called the "Age of Empire"?

2. Give reasons why the control of Transoxiana (Central Asia) has been the goal of many empires throughout history.

3. Provide a brief description of the conquest of North Africa and the difficulties that Muslims faced in subduing the region.

Lesson Two

"Behind you the sea, before you the enemy!"

Looking Ahead

As you read, recognize the factors that led to Muslim incursions into the Iberian Peninsula.

Preview Vocabulary

al-Maghrib
Iberian Peninsula
Visigoths

The famous words above were uttered in 711 CE by the Berber commander Tariq ibn Ziyad as he landed his troops on the shores of southern Spain, marking the first full-scale Muslim incursion into the Iberian Peninsula. This part of Europe today is made up of the countries of Spain and Portugal. But in Tariq's day, most of Iberia was under the control of a rapidly collapsing Visigoth kingdom. Its king, Roderick, faced intrigues from the nobles of his realm, each of whom had an eye on the throne and as a result Roderick had to constantly fight to keep his power. When the plots to topple Roderick failed, the nobles called on outside support to aid in ridding themselves of their king. Across the Straits of Gibraltar in Morocco (a land known to the Arabs as *al-Maghrib*) they found help in the form of Muslim troops. In 709 CE the Umayyad governor of North Africa sent scouts across the straits and they found Iberia in such a state of turmoil and lawlessness that it could be taken with some effort.

The Iberian Melding Pot

Like most of the lands that surrounded the Mediterranean Sea, the Iberian Peninsula was a crossroads of many and often conflicting races and cultures. The earliest known people to live in Spain and Portugal were called Iberians. Very little is known

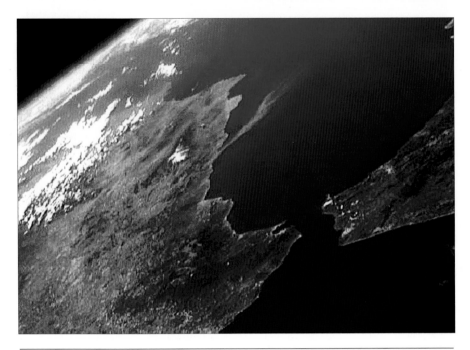

A modern satellite photo of the narrow straits that separate Spain (the land mass on the left) from North Africa (the land mass on the right). Note: East is to the top of the photo.

about these them but their culture came under the influence of later colonizers, namely the Celts, Greeks and that remarkable Semitic seafaring people, the Phoenicians. The Greeks and Phoenicians established towns and cities up and down the Mediterranean coast and a thriving system of trade grew. Many of these trading centers were found in southern Spain.

In 218 BCE, the Romans expanded their rule to the Iberian Peninsula. Within a century they would come to control all of it, from the Pyrenees Mountains to Portugal. For the next seven hundred years, the Romans brought order and stability to the land they named *Hispania* (from where the word Spain originates). One of the greatest imports that the Romans brought to Iberia was their language: Latin. Within a span of 200 years (by the 1st century before Christ) the old languages of Iberia were dying out and

nearly all those who lived in towns and cities spoke some form of Latin. This language spoken in Iberia would later come under the influence of Arabic (and to a lesser extent Berber). Over time the old Roman language spoken in the Iberian Peninsula would evolve in to what we now know as Spanish and Portuguese.

As Roman control over Europe collapsed, waves of Germanic tribes crossed over the Pyrenees Mountains into the Iberian Peninsula. Without an imperial army to stop them, these tribes soon established dominion over the entire peninsula. The first of these invading tribes were the Vandals, yet they quickly moved on to North Africa. But it is from them that the Iberia took the name "Vandalusia" which the Arabs in turn would call *al-Andalus*. After the Vandals came the Visigoth tribe in the middle of the 5th century. Unlike the Vandals, the Visigoths were able to

The Visigothic Code: (Forum Judicum) regarding the Jews

Between 649 and 652 the Kings of Visigoth Spain had their laws codified into the *Forum Judicum*. The deep animosity between Christian and Jew is visible in the many regulations found within the text.

"For while the virtue of God, by the sword of his Word, destroyed all other heresies, root and branch, we lament that the soil of our kingdom is still defiled by the wickedness of the Jews..."

Law V. Jews shall not celebrate Passover according to their faith.
Law VI. Jews shall not marry according to their faith.
Law VII. Jews shall not perform the rite of circumcision.
Law VIII. Jews shall not follow their dietary laws.
Law IX. No Jew shall subject a Christian to torture.
Law X. No Jew shall testify against a Christian in court.
Law XI. No Jew shall circumcise a Christian slave.
Law XIV. Under no circumstances shall Christian Slaves become Jews.
Law XV. All Christians are Forbidden to defend or protect a Jew.

(*The Visigothic Code*, trans. S.P. Scott)

establish some measure of stability over their newly conquered lands by keeping the old Roman system of government intact.

For the most part the Visigoths kept aloof from their Latin-speaking subjects. But the number of invaders was small. At the height of their power it is estimated that only 200,000 Visigoths ruled over a native population of about eight million. The old Roman ruling class was deprived of much of its power and nearly two-thirds of the land was handed over to Visigoth nobles. The Germanic king held absolute power and his princes could often do as they pleased. Laws were designed to keep the native population under strict control and Visigoth custom forbade intermarriage between the ethnic groups.

In addition to language and culture, one huge dividing line between the Latin-speaking natives and the Germanic Visigoths was religion. Christianity had been brought to the Iberian Peninsula as early as the 1st century CE, replacing ancient paganism. Because of its close connections with Rome, the Catholic Church reigned supreme and all other interpretations of the faith were outlawed. However the Visigoths were ardent upholders of the Arian sect of Christianity, which was viewed as threatening heresy by Catholics. Religious differences created a degree of resentment in the Catholic-majority population, so much so that when the Byzantines (who were not Catholics but Orthodox Christians who nevertheless shared common beliefs about the trinity) occupied the

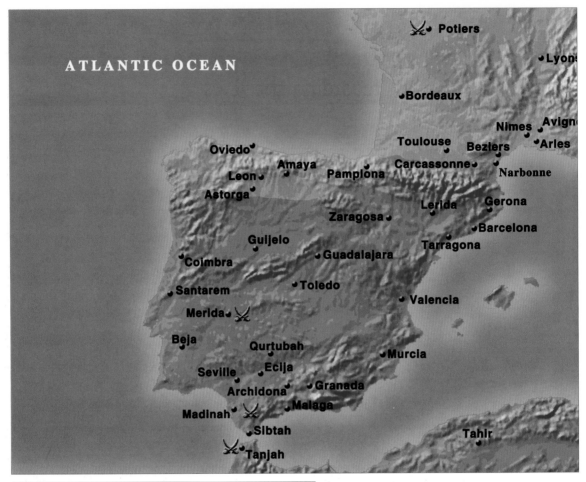

Muslim presence in the Iberian Peninsula, 712 CE -745 CE.

eastern coast of Spain in the 520's, the natives welcomed them as liberators.

Religious pressures finally reached its height in 570 CE when the Visigoth king Leovigild tried to force Arian Christianity on all his subjects. The effort failed and eventually backfired; for the king's own son and successor, Recared, converted to the Roman Catholic faith. When Recared took the throne he loosened many of the restrictive social laws that separated German Visigoth from Latin Iberian. He also outlawed Arianism thereby unifying the peninsula religiously.

Attached to this clash of cultures and faiths in Iberia were the Jews. The Jews had been living in the peninsula since the earliest days of Roman rule. They formed sizable communities that were more often located in large cities. As urban dwellers the Jews played an important role in Iberian trade. The Jews were tolerated under Roman rule at least until Christianity began to spread throughout the Iberian Peninsula. Many Christians despised the Jews as rejectors of Jesus and they blamed the Jews for Christ's Crucifixion and as a result the Jews of Iberia began to suffer oppressive discrimination and occasional outbreaks of violence.

The Visigoths however recognized that the Jews played an important role in the economy of the region and were thus a productive part of society. This thinking changed when the Ricared proclaimed Catholicism as the official religion. Harsh laws were set up against the Jews, often with the blessing of the Church. Jewish property could be capriciously confiscated by landlords and the nobility. On more than one occasion Church leaders called for the baptism of every Jewish child in the kingdom. If parents refused, the children were to be removed from Jewish homes and brought up in Christian ones. By the end of the seventh century CE, the Jews of the Iberian Peninsula had taken enough abuse from their Christian overlords. As the Kingdom of the

An Arab account of the invasion of the Iberian Peninsula

"The administrator of the area between North Africa and al-Andalus was a foreigner called Julius, Lord of Ceuta. He was also the governor of a town called Algeciras [al-Jazirah al-Khadra], situated on the side of al-Andalus. Julius was a subject of Roderick, the Lord of al-Andalus [king of Spain], who used to live in Toledo. Tariq put himself in negotiations with Julius, and treated him politely, until they made peace with each other. Julius had sent one of his daughters to Roderick, the Lord of al-Andalus, for her betterment and education; but she became pregnant with a child by the king. Julius having heard this news of this, said, "I see for him no other punishment or recompense, than that I should bring the Arabs against him." He sent word to Tariq saying, "I will provide transport for you to al-Andalus."

Tariq was at that time in Tilimsan and Musa ibn Nusair in Qairawan. Tariq replied to Julius, "I can't trust you until you send me a guarantee." So Julius sent his two daughters, having no sons. Tariq allowed them to remain in Tilimsan, protecting them. After that Tariq traveled to Julius, who was in Ceuta on the straits. The latter cheering at his coming said, "I will bring you to al-Andalus!"

But there was a huge peak now called the Mountain of Tariq [Jabal al-Tariq; Gibraltar] between Ceuta and al-Andalus. When the sunset came, Julius brought Tariq the boats, in which he made him set sail for that landing-place, where he camouflaged himself during the day, and in the evening sent back the boats to bring over the rest of his army. So they set sail for the landing-place, none of them being left behind. The inhabitants of al-Andalus did not pay attention to these boats, thinking that the vessels crossing and re-crossing were only trading vessels that were traveling back and forth.

Tariq was in the last batch of men that went across. He continued to his army. Julius with the Jewish merchants that were with him were left behind in Algeciras in order that they might encourage the Andalusians to rise up against Roderick. The news of Tariq and his army, as well as of the place where they were, soon reached the people of al-Andalus. Tariq, going along with his comrades, marched over a ridge of mountains to a town called Cartagena."

History of the Conquest of Spain by Ibn 'Abd al-Hakim (d. 870 CE)

The lands that the Muslim armies encountered in southern Spain bore a remarkable resemblance to the terrain of Southwest Asia.

Visigoths slid into anarchy, the Jews began to arm themselves. Additionally they began to send emissaries across the Strait of Gibraltar, seeking aid from the new power that was establishing itself there - the Muslims.

Tariq ibn Ziyad Lands

In 710 CE the Visigoth king Witiza died leaving the throne to his young son, Achila. However many of the noblemen disregarded this son and elected one of their own (a noble named Roderick) to be king. Achila and his supporters fled to the capital city of Toledo in the mountains. From his hideout he laid plans to

eventually get back the throne. Like the Jews, those who supported Achila looked to the Muslims as a possible source of support.

With much of the Iberian Peninsula in turmoil due to both Roderick's snatching of the throne and the Jews' rebellion, the Umayyad governor of North Africa (a man named Musa ibn Nusair) began to plan for the possibility of taking these lands for Islam. In 710 CE he sent a small detachment of soldiers across the Strait of Gibraltar to probe Visigoth defenses. When they returned with word that resistance would be minimal at best, Musa ordered a much larger force of 7,000 men (nearly all recent Berber converts) readied to make a full-scale invasion. Command of this force was handed to Tariq ibn Ziyad, one of Musa's lieutenants.

With the assistance of dissident Visigoth nobles, Tariq's men were ferried across the 30 miles of sea that separated Spain from North Africa. The Muslim army landed near mountainous rock that was forever named the "Mountain of Tariq" (*Jabal al-Tariq*) or as it is more commonly known: Gibraltar. After landing on the Spanish beaches, Tariq ordered all the boats burned in order to prevent even the thought of retreat from entering his men's minds.

For several weeks the Muslim army roamed the countryside of southern Spain until as word of the invasion reached the Visigoth king. From the royal city of Toledo King Roderick set out with a large army hoping to easily defeat the modest numbers of the invading force and he caught Tariq's men near the mouth of the Barbate River on the 19th of July, 711 CE. Despite its impressive size, the army of Roderick was no match for the skill and determination of the Muslim Berbers. The Visigoth army was annihilated and the fate of Roderick unknown, although it was believed he drowned in the river. With the army of Visigoth Iberia destroyed, all of Spain was Tariq's for the taking. He moved on to storm the royal city of Toledo but the city opened its gates without a fight.

Hoping to exploit this great opening, Musa ibn Nusair left the North African garrison town of Qairawan with 18,000 Arab and Berber warriors and headed for the Iberian Peninsula.

> "Whatever you have been given is merely a passing comfort for the life of the world, and that which is with Allah is better and more lasting for those who believe and put their trust in their Lord."
>
> *the Qur'an 42:36*

Arriving in southern Spain early in 712 CE, Musa quickly subdued the region around the city of Seville and then headed north to Toledo to join up with Tariq. By the winter of 713 CE, all of the peninsula (with the exception of the mountainous far north) was under some form of Muslim control.

Motivated by the ease in which Iberia fell, Musa ibn Nusair pressed onward. Four years after the fall of Toledo, Muslim soldiers crossed the Pyrenees Mountains into the lands of southern France. But resistance in this region was much stiffer than it had been in the Spain. Here the local Frankish noblemen proved to be much more determined to oppose the Muslims than the Visigoths had been. Forced to withdraw, raids by Muslim warriors into France (and by the Franks into Spain) continued into the coming decades.

The Province of al-Andalus

The Umayyad ruler al-Walid was delighted with the news that a prize such as Iberia fell into his hands through relatively little bloodshed. Nevertheless he became concerned with the enthusiasm shown by Musa to continue into France. One message came to Damascus stating that Musa was planing to come to Syria by marching through France, Italy, the Balkans and finally Anatolia! Al-Walid found such a plan absurd, knowing full well that such an act would only bring destruction. There was no way that Umayyad forces in Iberia, already stretch too thin, could perform such a feat. The *Amir al-Mu'minin* had Musa and his colleague Tariq called to Damascus. Before leaving Iberia, Musa appointed his son 'Abd al-'Aziz to govern the newly created province of al-Andalus. The administrative seat of al-Andalus was the southern Spanish city of Seville.

Musa and Tariq reached Damascus in 715 CE and with them they brought indescribable riches. However, by the time they arrived in the capital of the Umayyad State, al-Walid had died and his brother Sulaiman had ascended to the throne. Instead of rewarding these two brilliant commanders, he unexplainably had them stripped of their commands. It is believed that the inter-tribal rivalries that constantly influenced the Umayyad palace played a role in this shocking treatment. Regardless the two men went on to live out their lives in utter poverty.

Damascus quickly exerted its control over these newly-captured lands. A year after the dismissal of Musa ibn Nusair the governor of al-Andalus, 'Abd al-`Aziz, was assassinated. It had seemed that his becoming too much like a Visigoth lord (including his taking a Christian princess to wife) aggravated many around him. The Umayyads then sent one of their men from Damascus to rule over al-Andalus. He restored authority over the Muslim armies and began to send raiding parties again into southern France. But squabbling between different tribes of Arabs and between Arabs and Berbers soon broke out, the cause primarily being over the distribution of the newly conquered lands. Because of the spread of disunity, all Muslim military expansion in the region ground to a halt.

Lesson Review

1. What were the two branches of Christianity the people of the Iberian Peninsula followed in the 6th century CE? Contrast their differing interpretations of Christianity.

2. How do you think the phrase "burning of the boats" applies to Tariq ibn Ziyad's victory in Spain?

3. How did the Umayyad ruler Sulaiman treat the brilliant commanders Tariq ibn Ziyad and Musa ibn Nusair? Explain the possible reasons for this treatment. Remember how previous Umayyad rulers treated talented military commanders.

Lesson Three

Taking Islam to the Indus

Looking Ahead

Ponder over the characteristics of the people of Afghanistan that made it difficult to govern for foreign invaders.

Preview Vocabulary

Zabulistan
Muhammad ibn Qasim
Sindh
Mahalla

The rapid territorial expansion that took place during the ten-year rule of al-Walid (from 705-715 CE) brought Muslims into significant contact with the Indian subcontinent for the first time. This area of the world included modern-day Afghanistan, Pakistan and India. In the decades before Umayyad armies had been expanding the borders of Islam eastward into Central Asia and the highlands of Afghanistan. Although these eastern provinces had become difficult for the Umayyads to effectively govern, they were a source of great potential.

Before the coming of Islam the area that is now Afghanistan was a patchwork of small kingdoms and was comprised of many different ethnic groups. The major languages spoken there were Indo-European in origin and distantly related to Persian. Afghanistan was a meeting place of ideas coming west from the Middle East and east out of India. Buddhism (a faith that originated in India) was very widespread in the region and a great Buddhist center was found in the city of Balkh. In fact the Buddhist monasteries in Balkh continued to operate far into the Islamic period. Communities of Zoroastrians, Manichaeans as well as Christians were also found throughout the region. Moreover these foreign faiths often blended with the ancient pagan customs of the people that had existed since time immemorial.

This map shows the regions of South Asia that came into contact with Muslims early on..

The high, often impassable mountains and harsh deserts that made up the geography of much of Afghanistan presented great challenges for those who sought to conquer this land. Despite these challenges, Afghanistan had been part of several empires in the past, each of which left a clearly visible mark on its culture. In the distant past the Persians ruled over its provinces, then the armies of Alexander the Great marched through bringing with it Greek culture. The Sasanids likewise tried their best to exert their will over the people of Afghanistan. These empires, nevertheless, were never fully able to subdue these rugged people for very long.

The first place that the Arabs moved into after taking the eastern Sasanid province of Khorasan was a region known as Zabulistan, which was found in central Afghanistan. The Muslim contact with Zabulistan was as early as the time of 'Uthman, when in 647 CE some 6,000 Arab warriors penetrated the passes of the Hindu Kush mountains and looked down upon the Indus River plain. This raid proved inconclusive and no further attempts to subdue the rugged mountain folk were made until the rule of the Umayyad king al-Walid.

Muhammad ibn Qasim

With Zabulistan resolutely blocking direct routes to the east, the Umayyad governor in Khorasan began to look for a way to bypass this troublesome region. North of Zabulistan rose the towering Hindu Kush mountain range, whose very name 'the Killer of Indians' inspired fear and trepidation in all who dared cross its dizzying heights. A southern route around Zabulistan was likewise extremely difficult. Here lay an exceedingly harsh and dry desert called the Makran. Naturally given the experience gathered from their own desert-based culture the Arabs chose to bypass Zabulistan by marching through the desert of Makran.

To the east of the rugged land of Afghanistan lay the rich and fertile valley of the Indus River. Further beyond that the great plains of northern India stretch out in seemingly endless direction. And the value of India was not unknown to the Arabs. The sea routes between the Persian Gulf, Oman, Yemen and western India had been sailed since ancient times. Arab merchant vessels transported luxury goods like spices, silks and jewelry from Indian ports to markets in Southwest Asia. The expansion of the Islam in the Arabian Peninsula and the Persian Gulf region did not interrupt this flow of commerce with India. Arab Muslim tradesman continued to sail their ships into the bustling ports along the coasts of western India. This sea trade was to

inevitably bring Muslim armies into a region of the subcontinent called the Sindh.

During the *khilafah* of 'Umar ibn al-Khattab, Indian pirates (often with the support of local rulers) began to harass shipping lanes, plundering ships and terrorizing merchants. In retaliation Muslim sailors based in Oman and Bahrain launched raids on the Indian coast from the mouth of the Indus River down to Bombay. These early military contacts were soon stopped, however, because of 'Umar's reluctance to send his men out into the open sea to fight. It would not be until Mu`awiya's reign that Muslim warships resumed activities against these pirates.

At the end of al-Walid's rule, the center of Indian pirate activity was found in Debal, a now abandoned city found near modern-day Karachi. Towards the end of the year 710 CE, Hajjaj ibn Yusuf sent an army of 6,000 warriors from Syria under the command of his seventeen-year-old nephew, Muhammad ibn Qasim, with orders to force Debal into submission. The young commander led his men through the brutal deserts of Makran and out on to the Indus

The great Indus River is the lifeblood of the region. Despite its great width, it has not been an effective barrier against invasions from the west. Here people prepare to ferry camels across the river in boat styles that have been used for centuries.

plains. Despite his young age, Muhammad ibn Qasim proved to be brilliant military strategist. He took great care in organizing his forces. To keep his army well stocked with food and water he kept his men close to the coast of the Arabia Sea and then had supplies shipped in by boat. Muhammad ibn Qasim also kept his army under tight discipline and sent weekly progress reports back to Hajjaj who was at this time in Iraq.

After many weeks of hard marching Muhammad ibn Qasim reached the walls of Debal in the spring of 711 CE. His army had almost doubled in size thanks to reinforcements from Syria as well as a large number of native volunteers he picked up along the way. After a fierce assault the city was stormed. According to several accounts Hajjaj ordered Muhammad ibn Qasim to harshly punish not only the city's king but its population for the previous torture and execution of Muslim merchants captured by their pirates. But Muhammad ibn Qasim was of quite a different temperament than his uncle Hajjaj. He showed leniency to the citizens of Debal and refused to mete out retribution. As a result large numbers of them adopted Islam.

Having removed the pirate menace that arose from the Sindh, Muhammad ibn Qasim led his army northward away from the coast up the Indus River. Fortunately for him all but a few of the towns and cities along the way had received word about the proficiency of the Muslim army. Wishing to avoid any bloodshed the cities threw open their gates and hoped for clemency from Muhammad ibn Qasim. In return for their acquiescence the people living along the Indus River were granted concessions, which included exemption from paying taxes.

With many of the Sindh's cities now under Muslim control the only thing that stood in the way of complete conquest of the region was the powerful King Dahir. Learning that the Muslim army had seized many of his cities, the Dahir ordered an enormous force gathered to counter this threat. Muhammad ibn Qasim hesitated to engage Dahir's army because of the overwhelming numbers it could field. Regardless of his own opinions, Hajjaj sent instructions for Muhammad not to worry about numbers and to press forward with the attack.

Evidently King Dahir was greatly despised by much of his population and many Sindhis began to openly aid the Muslim army. Even before it could move out against Muhammad ibn Qasim, Dahir's forces began to melt away through desertion. These developments encouraged Muhammad ibn Qasim to move forward with his uncle's orders to engage the enemy. In the June heat of 712 CE (some 93 years after the *Hijrah*) Ibn Qasim met what was left of Dahir's army and crushed it. The youthful Muhammad ibn Qasim was now in complete mastery of the Sindh. Yet he did not rest on his triumphs. He continued to push to extend the lands under Muslim rule. In a single campaign he swept away the petty kingdoms in the Punjab, a large fertile region that lay to the north of Sindh. The wealth produced by this expansion was staggering. It was reported that Muhammad ibn Qasim sent 120 million dirhams in *ghanima* to the Umayyad capital of Damascus. Amazingly this was more money than Iraq gathered in taxes for a whole year!

Instead of creating garrison towns like in those in Iraq, Egypt and North Africa, Muhammad ibn Qasim had his soldiers live within the recently conquered cities. The Arab soldiers were settled in separate *mahallas*, or neighborhoods. Because most of these men did not (or could not) bring their families with them, they began to intermarry with the local population. This greatly accelerated the spread of Islam in the region. With the intermarriage between Arabs and Sindhis a new culture would gradually emerge.

With the death of the Umayyad ruler al-Walid in 715 CE, this period of astonishing expansion into India came to an abrupt halt. The new ruler Sulaiman had Muhammad ibn Qasim relieved of his command and recalled to Damascus. It appears that the new Umayyad ruler Sulaiman detested Hajjaj and waited for the day he could rid the court of his influence. But Hajjaj died in the months before Sulaiman came to power forcing him to unleash his repugnance on Hajjaj's friends and relatives. Muhammad ibn Qasim had the misfortune of being a relative. As soon as he arrived at the Umayyad palace, the young Ibn Qasim was thrown into chains, tortured and then take out beheaded. What certainly would have been a brilliant and successful career had been cruelly snuffed out.

Lesson Review

1). The Arabs were known to be excellent sailors, travellers and traders. How do you think this aspects helped the spread of Islam in the Indian Subcontinent?

2) What role did the physical geography of Afghanistan play in the difficulties which that countless invading armies have to face?

3) Who was Muhammad ibn Qasim and what was his role in the conquest of Sindh?

The End of a Dynasty

Looking Ahead

Think about the role that disunity, greed and ambition play in the downfall of any institution or community.

Preview Vocabulary

'Umar ibn 'Abd al-'Aziz
Khazars
Battle of Tours
Battle of the Zab River

Setbacks on the Frontier

The rule of Sulaiman did not last very long; less than three short years. But these years were spent taking revenge against Hajjaj by punishing his associates and undoing his policies. Sulaiman's first move was to remove all governors and military leaders previously appointed by Hajjaj. This often involved the dismissal of men who had talented abilities. Relatives of Hajjaj received treatment much harsher than forced retirement; they had their jobs taken away, their estates confiscated and were often executed.

These dismissals had serious consequences on the military campaigns that were broadening the boundaries of the Umayyad State. The disposal of capable and popular commanders like Musa ibn Nusair, Tariq ibn Ziad and Muhammad ibn Qasim effected the morale and enthusiasm of troops. In Central Asia, Hajjaj's governor Qutaibah ibn Muslim refused to submit to Sulaiman's will. He attempted to take a stand but his own soldiers refused to support him because of the harsh discipline he often enforced over them. They threw him into chains and handed him over to Sulaiman's agents.

In addition to disgracing and executing governors and military leaders, the only notable event that occurred during the reign of

Sulaiman was the unsuccessful attempt in 716 CE to capture Constantinople, the capital of the Byzantine Empire. This assault was undertaken both by land and sea. The Muslims however were routed and what was left of the force retreated back to Syria with the Byzantine army on its heels. But in spite of his senseless decisions as *Amir al-Mu'minin*, Sulaiman did manage to do one valuable deed; he appointed his cousin, 'Umar ibn 'Abd ul-'Aziz to succeed him.

The "Fifth" Righteous Khalifah

When it came to publicity, the Umayyads had a arduous time maintaining any level of popular acceptance. Even today their memory does not typically bring about a positive response from most Muslims. Their harsh treatment of the Prophet's descendants, overt discrimination against non-Arab converts to Islam, the brutal crackdowns of Hajjaj and their brazen materialism blemished the spectacular territorial expansion that took place under their rule. But from the often irreverent clan of Umayyah would come, unexpectedly, a man who would come to be called the fifth of the *Khulafa' ar-Rashidun*.

`Umar ibn `Abd al-`Aziz (known as `Umar II) was a nephew of the distinguished Umayyad ruler, 'Abd al-Malik ibn Marwan. 'Umar spent most of childhood enveloped the same privileged lifestyle as other princes of his rank. In 706 CE, he was appointed governor of the Hijaz, the region that contains the cities of Makkah and Madinah. As governor he developed a deep sense of piety that led him to long for a return to the days when nothing but faith motivated a ruler's judgements. 'Umar was effective in smoothing out the resentment many people in the Hijaz held for the Umayyads as the war with 'Abdullah ibn Zubair ended less than a decade earlier.

In Madinah 'Umar surrounded himself with advisers from the city's leading religious sages, many of whom were the sons of notable *Sahabah*. He told them, "I do not want to decide on any matter except after hearing your opinion. If you see or hear that a representative of mine is unjust, then by Allah I forbid anyone to inform anyone other than me of it." But his devotion to Islam and his quest to guarantee justice for all those under his protection would eventually cost him his life.

'Umar was relieved from his post as governor in 712 CE. During the short rule of his cousin Sulaiman, he lived in Damascus and acted as an advisor to the ruler. This brought him the confidence of the Sulaiman, who was deeply impressed with 'Umar's piety. Sulaiman trusted 'Umar and felt that he would do a better job in continuing his own reckless policies than any of his own brothers. But Sulaiman couldn't have been more mistaken. 'Umar ibn 'Abd al-`Aziz was a man of unmatched virtue.

When 'Umar ascended to the throne in 717 CE one of first acts he implemented was the removal the various restrictions placed on the *Mawali* (non-Arab Muslims). He then ordered a halt to all military operations. This was greatly needed in the wake of the disastrous assault on Constantinople the year earlier. This defeat had left the borders of Syria dangerously open to a Byzantine counterattack. 'Umar realized that the entire army needed time to regroup and reorganize.

Once this problem was dealt with, 'Umar embarked on the task of reforming Umayyad administration. He abolished the extravagant spending that rulers before him had enjoyed as well as the privileges enjoyed by Umayyad clan members. It was said that he once asked his wife to choose between staying with him or keeping

The Memory of 'Umar bin 'Abd ul-'Aziz by his Wife

Abu Yusuf (d. 182 AH / 798 AD)
Taken from the *Book of Land Tax*

When 'Umar ibn Abd al 'Aziz died, learned men came to his wife to express sympathy and say how great a calamity had struck the people of Islam by his death. And they said to her, 'Tell us about him - for the one who knows best about a man is his wife'.

And she said: "He never prayed or fasted more than the rest of you, but I never saw a servant of God who feared Him more than 'Umar. He devoted his body and his soul to the people. All day he would sit tending to their affairs, and when night came he would sit up while business remained. One evening when he had finished everything, he called for his lamp - from which he used to buy the oil from his own money - and prayed two Rak'ats. Then he sat back on his legs, with his chin in his hands, and the tears ran down from his cheeks, and this didn't stop until dawn, when he rose for a day of fasting.

I said to him, 'O Amir al-Mu'minin, is there something bothering you tonight?' And he said, 'Yes, I saw how I was occupied while governing the affairs of the community, all its black sheep and its white sheep, and I remembered the stranger and the poor and the needy, and the prisoners of war, and all like them in the far places of the earth, and I realized that God most high will ask me about all of them, and the Messenger of Allah s will testify about them, and I feared that I should find no excuse when I was with God, and no defense with the Prophet s.'

And even when 'Umar was with me in bed, where a man usually find some pleasure with his wife, if he remembered some affair of God's (people), he would be upset as a bird that had fallen into the water. Then his weeping would rise until I would throw off the blankets in kindness to him. 'By God' he would say, 'How I wish that there was between me and this office the distance of the East from the West!'

the wealth her father gave her. She chose to stay with him, and took all of her jewelry to be deposited into the state treasury.

'Umar ibn 'Abd al-'Aziz's most far-reaching attempt at social justice was the issuing of legislation that made non-Arab Muslim converts equal to Arab Muslims. Up until this time non-Arab converts had to endure many restrictions that often hindered social and economic advancement. They had to pay (with few exceptions) extra taxes in addition to the *zakat*. They were also usually excluded from positions of real authority in the government (although the military still offered chance for advancement). 'Umar wanted to implement the Islamic ideal that taught equality between all who believed. In regions where the non-Arab Muslim presence was considerable (as in North Africa and Spain), 'Umar's edicts did much to mute complaints of mistreatment that were often made by *Mawali*. An additional result of these decrees was that they encouraged more people to convert to Islam, since they would no longer be discriminated against for doing so.

'Umar's popularity among the *Mawali* grew like no other Umayyad ruler before him. 'Umar once wrote to the governor of Khorasan ordering him to invite its non-Muslim population to Islam. The *Khalifah* said, "If they become Muslim, their Islam is to be accepted by you and they are to be relieved from paying *jizya*. They will have what Muslims have and owe what Muslims owe." However one of the Arab chiefs from Khorasan realized that mass conversion would cut into the income provided from the *jizya*. They promptly wrote back to the Damascus, "By Allah, these people are too eager to accept Islam. We must test their sincerity by insisting on their circumcision." Annoyed by this side-stepping 'Umar responded to their request. "Was the Messenger of Allah sent only to circumcise?" he replied, "If they become Muslim and are good Muslims, then they will quickly move into purity."

In addition to encouraging conversion to Islam by removing any social restrictions, 'Umar also made moves to address the grievances that the Prophet's descendants held against the Bani Umayyah from the very beginning. He returned the estate of Fadak back to the hands of the *Ahl al-Bait*. He also put a final end to the ritual cursing of 'Ali from the pulpits of many government *masjids*. Such moves gained for him the sympathies of the Shi'ah, who continue to speak well of him to this day. By allotting them monetary allowances 'Umar also tried to ease the hard feelings of many of those individuals who were arbitrarily dismissed by his predecessor Sulaiman.

The long-term results of such sweeping social changes would never be realized and the idealistic goals of 'Umar ibn 'Abd al-'Aziz were cut short. Apparently his reforms (along with the anger of Sulaiman's younger brothers who were all passed over in the succession) irritated many among the Umayyad ruling class. In 720 CE, at the age of 39, 'Umar ibn 'Abd al-`Aziz fell dead after having eaten a soup laced with poison. Despite his untimely death he was to remain a man whose memory would flow on throughout the generations of coming Muslims.

Impending Breakdown

On his death bed, 'Umar appointed his cousin Yazid ibn 'Abd al-Malik as his successor. But during the short reign of this individual, nearly all of the well-intended reforms of his predecessor were dismantled and undone. The old restrictions against the *Mawali* were reimposed and those men who had been harassed and castigated during the purges of Sulaiman made their voices heard again. A major revolt broke out in Iraq lead by one of these individuals that was put down only with great brutality. The Berbers commenced to complain of discriminatory treatment and threatened once again to overthrow Umayyad control in North Africa if their grievances were not addressed.

However Yazid's death after a brief four years of rule silenced anti-Umayyad sentiments for the time being. His younger brother Hisham became *Amir al-Mu'minin* and proved to be a more capable leader than many of his immediate predecessors. Hisham brought with him the first signs of stability that Umayyad rule had seen in nearly a decade. But despite his rule of nearly two decades and initial successes, Hisham's reign would rapidly unwind towards its end causing such widespread chaos that would lead to the eventual downfall of his dynasty's hold over the Muslim world.

One of Hisham's first acts as ruler was to resume the expansion of the borders of the state. He embarked on a military campaigns against Byzantine forces in Anatolia and then tried to reorganize the government in al-Andalus where political stability had been crippled by ethnic and tribal feuds. Hisham installed a new governor in al-Andalus, a man by the name of 'Abd ar-Rahman ibn 'Abd Allah al-Ghafiqi. His orders were to restart the offensive against the Christian princes on the other side of the Pyrenees in France. In October of 732 CE al-Ghafiqi set out at the head of a large army, whose goal was to strike deep into the enemy's lands.

Within weeks the Muslim army (composed almost entirely of cavalry) reached far into north-central France. It appeared that they would easily

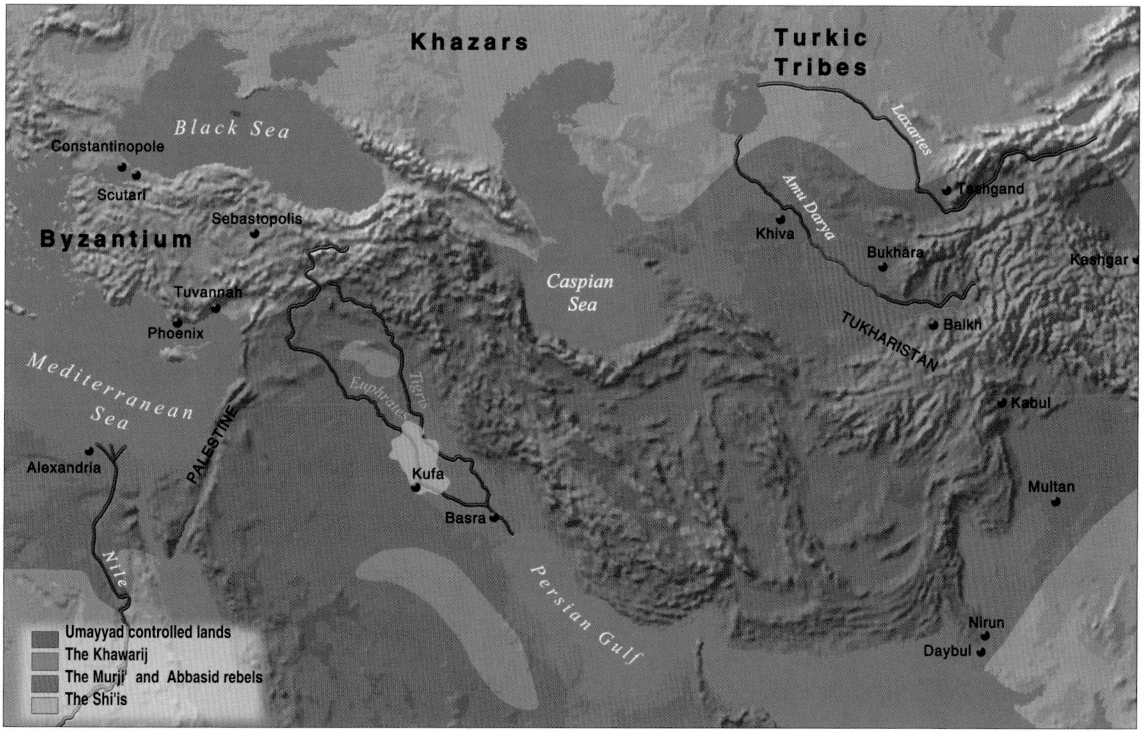
Khazars
Turkic Tribes
Black Sea
Constantinople
Scutari
Byzantium
Sebastopolis
Tuvannah
Phoenix
Mediterranean Sea
Alexandria
PALESTINE
Nile
Euphrates
Tigris
Kufa
Basra
Caspian Sea
Persian Gulf
Laxartes
Amu Darya
Khiva
Bukhara
Tashgand
Kashgar
TUKHARISTAN
Balkh
Kabul
Multan
Nirun
Daybul
Umayyad controlled lands
The Khawarij
The Murji' and Abbasid rebels
The Shi'is

The end of the Umayyads.

reach the English Channel. However a local Frankish chief, Charles Martel, mobilized his warriors and intercepted the Muslim army near a small town called Tours (Potiers). There the solid determination of the Frankish army won out and the Muslim army was routed. 'Abd ar-Rahman al-Ghafiqi was killed in the battle and what was left of his force quickly made its way back over the Pyrenees Mountains. Although Muslims continued to hold several French towns along the Mediterranean coast, internal feuding stoped any further expansion into Western Europe.

The Battle of Tours was just one of many military setbacks that occurred during the closing years of Hisham's reign. In India Muslims started to lose control of the Sindh and the Punjab to native rebels. In the Caucasus Mountains the Khazars (a Turkic people who converted to Judaism) came down out of the steppes and took the city of Ardabil from Muslim hands, the first time such an event had happened.

In Central Asia the calamities were equally as threatening. The pagan Turks united their tribes and assaulted the major city of Samarqand. The Umayyad governor quickly mustered all able-bodied Muslim men in the region and marched to break the siege. The Turks became aware of this move and they were able to ambush and wipe out the Muslim army in a narrow mountain pass. What would have been total disaster was only averted as reinforcements from Syria, Iraq and Khorasan began to pour into Central Asia saving it from being completely overrun by the Turks.

Hisham desperately tried to recuperate from this string of military catastrophes. He appointed

Too Bad We're Not Speaking Arabic

European historians have traditionally look at the Battle of Tours as one of the decisive clashes of history, where Charles Martel managed to save Europe from Muslim invasion, thus preserving both Christianity and Western civilization. The great 18th century English historian noted that if the Christian Franks would have lost at Tours "perhaps the interpretation of the Koran would now be taught in the schools of Oxford, and her pulpits might demonstrate to a circumcised people the sanctity and truth of the revelation of Mohammed." Modern historian Jack Stesney argues more would have happened had 'Abd ar-Rahman gained victory over Charles Martel.

Now, suppose the Arabs had been successful and continued to advance into Europe, bringing knowledge and culture with them? For one thing, today's world would probably contain more mosques and fewer churches and this article would probably be written in Arabic script rather than Latin letters. Maybe that's not terribly significant, but if Arab knowledge were transferred to Europe beginning in the '700s it might have proved momentous. Would the Renaissance have begun 200 years earlier? Since gifted people seem to inhabit all time periods, it is reasonable to assume that science and its attendant technology would have proceeded to develop at the same pace regardless of when it started, making modern society significantly more advanced. "The Internet, if we still had one, would now be over 200 years old. . ."

Today, Western culture and technology are the dominant force in the world, while the Arabs—except those who happen to be sitting on a lot of oil—are people with a relatively small influence. So it's fair to ask why the Arab's did not continue their scientific advances. After all, they had this technology before the Europeans but still managed to lose the race to the future. Why? One answer is that ...they became more interested in analyzing and interpreting the past rather than striking out in new directions in order to change the future. Further, since they had a well-organized scheme of government, once they decided on a course of action, they could impose that decision from one end of the empire to the other.

Suppose then that the Arabs had been successful in their conquest plans. How likely is it that this anti-innovation tendency would have taken root in Europe and instead of a great leap forward we had a great stagnation? This sort of result is possible but not very probable. History shows that even though the Arabs occupied Spain for hundreds of years, they were never able to suppress the underlying Spanish culture and to some degree even supported it. It seems reasonable to conclude that if the Arab conquest extended to Northern Europe, the same situation would have prevailed, especially since this culture emphasized individualism. After all, it was these same Northern Europeans who, after shaking off the effects of their homegrown Christian religious conformity and being exposed to Arab learning, were able to develop that combination of individuality and curiosity that fostered the rise of modern science.

(from *IT'S HAMMERTIME: THE FAILURE OF THE MILLENNIUMS* by Jack Stesney
http://www.failuremag.com/arch_history_millenniums.html)

one of his cousins to take over, a man of exceptional military talent named Marwan ibn Muhammad. Marwan first planned to deal with the biggest threat: the Khazars. From their positions in the Caucasus Mountains, the Khazars could easily strike into the rich lowlands of Iraq and Syria. In 735 CE Marwan launched a massive campaign to regain control of the Caucasus, a region that had been under Muslim control since the time of 'Umar ibn al-Khattab. Within three years Marwan had not only pushed the Khazars out of the Caucasus but he advanced far to the north destroying their capital city near the banks of the great Volga River.

As the Umayyads tried to take back territory lost to the Turks, a serious insurrection broke out among the people of Khorasan. Both Muslims and non-Muslims were angered over the increased taxes they needed to pay to supposedly cover the costs of the war against the Turks. It can be said that Hisham's greatest shortcoming was his appetite for wealth and luxury. The empire was to him a realm to be manipulated for personal material gain. He constantly pushed his governors to squeeze whatever money they could from his subjects. Enormous amounts of money were collected to pay for the needed military expeditions and when this was done, collectors had to squeeze more taxes out of the people to pay for Hisham's lifestyle. This capricious policy eventually caused indignation and frustration throughout Umayyad domains. In the eastern provinces it made the work of anti-Umayyad agents and operatives that much easier. It is no surprise that a few years later the great anti-Umayyad revolution led by the clan of Bani 'Abbas would find its strength from Khorasan .

Hisham's death in 742 CE, left the Umayyad State in the most wretched of conditions.

Hisham was succeeded by his weak-willed nephew al-Walid II, an individual completely unfit to rule. Because his uncle initially had no intention of naming him as successor, al-Walid spent his youth far from the royal palace in a mansion situated in the remote wilderness of Jordan. But when al-Walid arrived in Damascus to take his uncle's throne, he was greeted with jubilance by a population who hoped the new *Amir al-Mu'minin* would lighten the oppressive taxation of his predecessor. Al-Walid quickly proved a disappointment. After the coronation he retired back to his desert mansion where he devoted himself to a life of pleasure.

Al-Walid eventually ended up alienating not only his subjects but also many of his closest relatives. In April of 743 CE the army stormed the mansion of the pleasure-loving al-Walid and had him killed. In his place the army put one of his nephews, Yazid III, a figure who would prove to be an equally incompetent ruler. Yazid III's appointment did nothing to silence discontent within the leadership of the *Ummah*. It was no surprise then that both he *and* the brother who succeeded him were quickly toppled by the army.

After having held the leadership of the Umayyad Dynasty for nearly four decades the sons of 'Abd al-Malik were forced out of power by the general Marwan ibn Muhammad. He was a popular figure who led the Muslims to victory over the Khazars. Marwan grew tired of the incompetence of his ruling cousins and refused to recognize Yazid's younger brother Ibrahim as *Amir al-Mu'minin*. He moved into Syria with several crack units and took Damascus without opposition. Ibrahim was speedily removed. In December of 743 CE, Marwan proclaimed himself *Amir al-Mu'minin* as well as leader of the clan of Bani Umayyah. The aged but experienced leader did not stay long in the Damascus. He rapidly moved his government to Harran, a town over 200 miles to the north and the headquarters of his army.

On the basis of his long military experience Marwan set about to reorganize the army. The age-old system of paying warriors out of the revenues secured from *ghanima* could no longer withstand the strain of the lengthy campaigns needed to keep the empire's enemies at bay. The army would have to be paid through a central government treasury. Marwan also replaced the tribe-based organization of the army by creating regional regiments led by professional soldiers. These regiments were smaller, much more mobile than their predecessors.

Despite Marwan's efforts to stave off collapse, the power of the Umayyad Dynasty was in unstoppable decline. The Muslim state was still finding great difficulty in recovering from the military disasters that took place during Hisham's rule less than a decade earlier. But the most dangerous threats to Umayyad rule started to arise from the ranks of the Muslims themselves. Emboldened by the feebleness of Marwan's predecessors, the Shi'ah and Khawarij began to incite revolution. And they did not have to try hard to find support from the common people. In Iraq, Egypt and Yemen the population was fed up with the continued financial exploitation through over-taxation. Shi'i preachers called on believers to bring down their Umayyad overlords; men who deprived the Family of the Prophet of its legitimate right to rule. The descendants of the Prophet's uncle 'Abbas threw their weight behind the Shi'i cause, albeit for far different motives. In actuality members of the Bani 'Abbas sought the throne themselves and they used their blood-relationship to the *Ahl al-Bait* to garner support.

Rebellion and unrest soon found its way east to the province of Khorasan. The agents and spies of 'Abbasids were busy among the large Arab population that had settled there over the decades. Their propaganda was designed to appeal to the widest possible support base. To the disgruntled Arab soldiers who were clamoring for more pay they promised rewards. To the Shi`ah they emphasized the familial relationship between their own forefather 'Abbas and 'Ali ('Abbas was 'Ali's paternal uncle). The 'Abbasids also played on the social and political frustrations of the *Mawali* promising a return to Islamic ideals of equality and justice. They organized their supporters into secret cells, each awaiting the signal to rise up against the Umayyads.

The most outstanding of these agents was a man named Abu Muslim. Born into a family of Persian converts from the lowest rungs of the social ladder Abu Muslim displayed great skill at mobilizing diverse elements into a single group. While in Khorasan Abu Muslim finally gave the signal to begin the uprising in 747 CE. Men near and far rallied to Abu Muslim placing their swords and spears at his service all under the unfurled black flag of the Bani 'Abbas.

Over the next two years the 'Abbasid army and its revolution spread from Khorasan to western Iran and on into the farms and cities of Iraq. Marwan tried to regain control of the east but to no avail, as the Umayyad governors there either conveniently switched sides or were killed. In desperation he gathered the army of Syria and marched to meet the 'Abbasids who were now moving west through Iraq. The two forces met in 750 CE on the banks of the Greater Zab river, a tributary of the Tigris river and Marwan's army was smashed to pieces. Marwan fled the battlefield and attempted to raise a new army in Palestine along with taxes to pay for it. This only provoked more uprisings with which he could not afford to deal. He fled further west to Egypt only to be captured by 'Abbasid sympathizers. He was turned over to the new authorities and beheaded.

The 'Abbasids moved against the members of the fallen dynasty with unheard of savagery. Throughout Syria Umayyad princes were hunted down like wild animals. Only one young man (a grandson of Hisham) barely escaped the clutches of the 'Abbasids and certain death. Over the next seven years 'Abd ar-Rahman ibn Mu`wiya made his way through North Africa to Spain. There he was able to rely on the loyalty of the Syrian tribes who settled there during the nearly five decades of Muslim rule. Far out of reach of his 'Abbasid enemies 'Abd ar-Rahman announced the continuation of Umayyad rule over al-Andalus.

Lesson Review

1. Think about the treatment shown to Hajjaj's relatives by the ruler Sulaiman. What was the motive behind this treatment?

2. Why did 'Umar ibn 'Abd al-`Aziz receive the title of "the Fifth Righteous Khalifah"?

3. Give a brief description of the events that led to the downfall of the Umayyad Dynasty after the death of 'Umar ibn `Abd al-`Aziz.

4). On the following scale of 1-5, how would you rate the three-year rule of Sulaiman as *Amir al-Mu'minin*?

1= Ideal, 2= Good, 3= Fair, 4= Poor, 5= disastrous

Chapter Review

1. Many travelers throughout the ages have described the rugged landscape of Afghanistan as severe and unforgiving. Think about how the land of Afghanistan is described in your text. You may want to find books that show pictures of Afghanistan's physical features. Then write a poem of the physical setting of Afghanistan.

2. How was the Islamic state during the lifetime of the Prophet different from the Umayyad regime? How was it similar?

3. The Umayyad period saw rapid and expansive territorial conquest. How did this effect both the economy and the society of the Muslim *Ummah*?

Chapter Three

A Turbulent Growth

Lesson One

The Formation of the Shi`ah

Looking Ahead

Read, think and conceptualize the origins of the Shi'i and their interpretations of Islam

Preview Vocabulary

Interpretation
Mahdi
Wasi
Imam
Twelvers
Isma`ili
Zaidi
Ghulat

Like other religious communities, diverse ways of interpreting faith evolved among Muslims. We have already explained that differing opinions about who should rule the *Ummah* were already developing from the moment of the Prophet's death. Unlike the formation of sects and denominations in other religious traditions, these early divisions within the Muslim community had little to do with disagreements over the interpretation of the Qur'an or religious ritual. Rather they were primarily over the question of the right to leadership, a leadership that nonetheless did have definite authority over spiritual matters.

As we look back to this period in the early history of the Muslim community it is essential that our own modern concepts of what it means to be either a Sunni and Shi'i be set aside. This was a time when ideas of what it meant to be such were, for the most part, quite different than they are today. It has to be remembered that how we think of these two groups now is the result of a process of growth and evolution that has developed over fourteen centuries.

The Partisans of 'Ali

The defining element of Shi'ism is an unwavering attachment to 'Ali ibn Abi Talib, who was both cousin and son-in-law to the

Prophet Muhammad. This devotion centered on 'Ali's claim to have been clearly designated as the successor of the Prophet and the subsequent Shi'i movement accepted this claim wholeheartedly.

As we read in the last unit, when Abu Bakr was chosen for this position by the notables of Madinah, 'Ali along with members of his family and clan (the Bani Hashim) hesitated in giving their *bay'at*. The reasons for this are unclear and Muslim historians often presented conflicting accounts regarding the issue. Nevertheless 'Ali eventually did give his hand to Abu Bakr, and during the rule of 'Umar and 'Uthman we do not hear anything more from 'Ali regarding his thoughts on the issue. He did, however, have around him a small band of *Sahabah* who supported his claim. These people can be considered the first *Shi'at 'Ali* (Shi'is, or Partisans of 'Ali).

When 'Ali finally did manage to become the *Amir al-Mu'minin* nearly a quarter of a century after the Prophet's death, he found himself in an hazardous predicament. Surrounded by two powerful factions that refused to acknowledge his new authority (one led by 'A'isha and another by Mu'awiya), 'Ali had little time to implement real changes in the government. He was forced to move his base of power away from Madinah, where the people were of uncertain loyalty, to Iraq, where dissatisfaction with 'Uthman and his policies ran deep. But large numbers of 'Ali's Iraqi supporters were far from being completely devoted to his cause themselves. During the war with Mu'awiya, a considerable segment of 'Ali's army melted away, either by defecting to the enemy or joining the ranks of the extremist Khawarij.

Before 'Ali succumbed to the wounds caused by a Khawarij dagger, he appointed his eldest son Hasan as his successor. Hasan managed to rule for less than a year before he realized that further resistance to the growing might of Mu'awiya would be futile. Determined to see the bloodshed come to an end Hasan signed away his authority as *Amir al-Mu'minin* to Mu'awiya following extended negotiations. Abandoned by all but a handful of his father's faithful, Hasan left Iraq and returned to Madinah. There he and his younger brother Husain lived quietly, avoiding any involvement in politics.

This changed on Mu'awiya's death when it was announced that his will put his son Yazid on the throne. Because Hasan died before Mu'awiya it was assumed that the *khilafah* would be returned and given to Husain. In response to this affront Husain, among many others, refused to give *bay'at* to Yazid. The people of Kufa began to show signs of support for Husain. He left for the city only to be abandoned by the Kufans and left to be massacred by the Umayyads at Karbala'.

In the months following the death of Husain the people of Kufa began to develop a sense of deep regret for the abandonment of a man they called to lead them. They began to realize that it would have been far better to have perished with Husain than to go through what they now faced under the Umayyads. Four years after the Battle of Karbala, the Shi'ah of Kufa rose up in revolt. They formed themselves into bands of warriors known as the *Tawwabun*, 'the repenters'. The *Tawwabun* unfurled the banner of Husain and sought to avenge his blood. But they were no match for the experienced Umayyad army which quickly destroyed their rebellion. Driven underground by the suppression, the Shi'ah of Iraq hid their cause and nurtured in secret both their devotion to the *Ahl al-Bait* and their burning desire for vengeance.

Shortly after the failure of the *Tawwabun*, a man by the name of Mukhtar al-Thaqafi appeared in Iraq and began to reorganize armed resistance among the Shi'i. Mukhtar claimed to be acting on behalf of 'Ali's children but it appears that he did not have the total support of the Shi'ah. The only male survivor from Husain was his young son 'Ali, who was more commonly known as Zain al-`Abidin. Mukhtar had initially beseeched Zain al-`Abidin to lead a rebellion, but he declined, wanting to have nothing to do with the violence it would entail. Mukhtar then turned to another of 'Ali's sons, Muhammad ibn Hanafiyyah (who was from another of 'Ali's wives). Although the details of Ibn Hanafiyyah's involvement with Mukhtar remain ambiguous, it appears that he gave at least tacit support to the plans for restaging an armed revolt against the Umayyads.

This was all Mukhtar needed to initiate his rejuvenation of the Shi'ah. In addition to giving the call to arms he also began preaching that Muhammad ibn Hanafiyyah was the *Mahdi*, the end-of-time figure who's coming was foretold by the Prophet; a man, divinely guided, who would fill the world with justice and restore a legitimate government.

Mukhtar and his supporters took control of Kufa in 685 CE, and then began to hunt down and kill the leading figures involved in the massacre of Karbala. The Umayyad governor of Iraq sent his military to crush the Shi'i but was defeated. With this defeat, along with the threat from 'Abdullah ibn Zubair, it seemed as if the Shi'i cause would reach its desired goal.

> "Say Muhammad, 'I do not ask of you any reward except love of my relatives.' Whoever earns a good deed, We shall increase its good for him. Indeed Allah is All-Forgiving, Appreciative."
>
> *the Qur'an 42:23*

But after having staved off an Umayyad attack a bigger problem arose for Mukhtar from those living in Kufa who did not sympathize with his cause. Some of these individuals fled Kufa and went to Basra, a city then under the control of the 'Counter Khalifah' Abdullah ibn Zubair. He was a man who had little sympathy for Shi'i convictions, understandably so since both he and his father had opposed 'Ali. In 687 CE Abdullah ibn Zubair decided to consolidate his hold over Iraq and ordered a sizeable army to take Kufa from Mukhtar. In the subsequent contest Mukhtar and some 6,000 of his followers were said to have been killed and Shi'i rule of Kufa was brought to an effective end.

Despite its failure, the revolt of Mukhtar al-Thaqafi brought out the first religious doctrines that can be recognized as being exclusively Shi'i. He propagated a belief that Muhammad ibn Hanafiyyah was the rightful *Imam* despite the fact that he was not a son of Fatimah, but rather from another of 'Ali's wives. This meant he was not a grandson of the Prophet. Nevertheless most of the Shi'ah of Iraq rallied around him and after his death his devotees consider his son as their *Imam*. Mukhtar was the first to make heartfelt appeals to the *Mawali* hoping for their support. Until then Shi'ism had been totally an Arab movement that had little attraction for non-Arabs.

Historians later termed the remnants of Mukhtar's movement as the Kaisaniyya. For most of the Umayyad period the ranks of the Kaisaniyya contained a majority of those Shi'is who took up arms to restore the rule of the *Ahl al-Bait*.

But because of their unrelenting advocacy of the use of violence to overthrow the Umayyads, their numbers were decimated by constant armed confrontation. By the early 'Abbasid era the Kaisaniyya were all but wiped out.

Despite the fact that Zain al-'Abidin and his eldest son al-Baqir succeeded in staying out of the grab for political power, the Shi'ah in Iraq were far from being so restained. For them the defeat of Mukhtar's rebellion had only proven to be a momentary setback. Zain al-'Abidin's younger son Zaid was not so content with the pacifist attitude of his father and elder brother. Hoping to find supporters who would be ready to take up the sword once again, he left his home in Madinah for Kufa in 740 CE. When he arrived in Iraq the Shi'ah seemed ready to rise once more against the Umayyads. In the five decades since the failed revolt of Mukhtar, they had chaffed under the often brutal rule of Umayyad governors and endured the suffocating taxes imposed on the citizens of the Muslim state.

Zaid faced no problems rallying the disaffected to his call. He soon gathered a force strong enough to challenge the governor of Iraq. With Umayyad forces busily engaged with the Byzantines, Franks, and Khazars chances for success ran high. However, no sooner than it was ready to strike, conflict broke out in the ranks of the rebels. According to several accounts Zaid espoused views that were more accommodating to non-Shi'i understandings of leadership than many of his follower could tolerate. By that time many Shi'is in Kufa had developed adverse views of the first three *Khulafa' ar-Rashidah*. They regarded these men as having knowingly denied 'Ali the right to rule, a view that non-Shi'i Muslims found not only distasteful but unacceptable. Zaid's views were that Abu Bakr and 'Umar were good men at heart although they made an error in passing over 'Ali. But, Zaid declared, they had only acted in what they thought at the time was in the best interests of the *Ummah*. In addition to his views on past events, Zaid also claimed that the position of *Imam* could be claimed by any male descendant of 'Ali (either through Hasan or Husain) who was ready to rise up and fight for it. This doctrine differed from

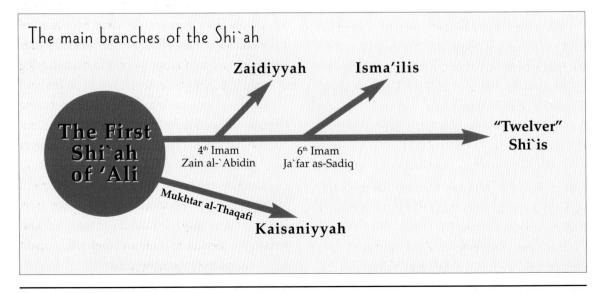

The main branches of the Shi`ah

The First Shi`ah of 'Ali

Mukhtar al-Thaqafi

Kaisaniyyah

4th Imam Zain al-'Abidin

Zaidiyyah

6th Imam Ja`far as-Sadiq

Isma'ilis

"Twelver" Shi`is

many Shi'is who held that the *Imam* could only come from the line of Husain.

The beliefs that Zaid brought with him to Iraq alienated many of the Kufan Shi'is, who were in no frame of mind to compromise their long-held dedication to the *Ahl al-Bait*. They gradually deserted Zaid leaving only his most devoted followers in the face of a huge Umayyad army that was moving into Iraq. Zaid launched several attempts to slow down the advance of the enemy but to no avail. Months after his rising in Iraq, Zaid along with those Shi'i who remained loyal to him were wiped out.

But the movement Zaid initiated was determined to survive. His son Yahya fled east into Khorasan where he continued to champion the cause of the *Ahl al-Bait*. Yahya found a ready audience among many of the Muslims of Khorasan who were fed up with the Umayyads and were looking for any pretext to hoist the flag of revolt. Although he was hunted down and killed, his death gave further stimulus to the coming 'Abbasid revolution that would burst out of Khorasan in the coming years. The followers of Zaid and Yahya scattered to remote areas of the empire and regrouped. Their movement, known as the Zaidiyyah, continued to play a role in openly opposing both Umayyad and 'Abbasid rule in the decades to come and faithfully upheld the views of their founding *Imam*.

The Shi'i Cause

The beliefs of the early Shi'ah focused on the belief that the Prophet Muhammad had clearly chosen 'Ali to be his successor (*wasi*). This succession was not merely a matter of temporal leadership, but of the spiritual realm as well. Many Shi'is saw the *Ahl al-Bait* as having an unrivaled status in the continuation of the prophetic mission. They explained their position by stating that God would never leave human beings without the guidance of a Messenger (*rasul*), Prophet (*nabi*) or their successors, the *Imams*. The community had no choice in the matter of who was to be *Imam*. He was appointed by God *via* decree of the Prophet. The *Imam* therefore had authority to appoint a successor who would in turn inherit the same lofty rank.

The *Imamate*, which evolved into a clear doctrine in the second century after the *Hijrah*, is the most distinct and universal of the Shi'i beliefs. The status of the *Imam* was one of the chief differences that Shi'is had with other Muslims. Most early Shi'ah groups (with the exception of the Zaidiyyah) believed that because of his spiritual rank, the *Imam* was infallible and sinless. His decrees were given equal importance to those of the Prophet, since the *Imam* was seen as the highest living interpreter of the Qur'an and *Sunnah*. Therefore the Shi'ah acknowledged religious and political guidance exclusively from their *Imams*.

There were, however, different opinions among the Shi'is regarding exactly who the rightful *Imam* was. The first *Imam* is considered by all Shi'i groups to be 'Ali, the second his son Hasan, followed by the third, Husain. After Karbala a split came: the bulk of the Shi'i lined up behind Mukhtar and his claims while a small number followed Zain al-`Abidin, Husain's only surviving son. Those few who devoted themselves to Zain al-`Abidin and his son Muhammad al-Baqir (who both lived in Madinah) believed that an individual could only attain the rank of *Imam* by appointment of the preceding *Imam*. And unlike most of the Shi'ah of this period, they asserted that the true *Imams* could only be of the lineage of Husain.

After the death of Zain al-`Abidin the movement split further between those who supported Zain's eldest son, Muhammad al-Baqir and the majority of Shi'ah (who were found primarily in Iraq) fell in behind Zaid. After Zaid's death the Shi'ah of Iraq further splintered. Since many believed that the *Imam* had gone into hiding, they were left virtually leaderless. Some supported Zaid's son and those of the *Ahl al-Bait* who espoused Zaid's less rigid position on the requirements of the *Imam*. Other individuals began to put forward extreme and fantastic views that the *Imams* were nothing short of God Himself! Those who followed such views were called the *ghulat*, the extremists, and were quickly denounced by more conservative Shi'is.

Because of their pacifist stance the Shi'i who followed Muhammad al-Baqir managed to avoid open clashes with the authorities. Although they were continually watched and often harassed by Umayyad (and later 'Abbasid) agents, the *Imams* from this lineage continued uninterrupted down to a twelfth *Imam*, who was believed to be the *Mahdi*. The twelfth Imam mysteriously disappeared from the world in 941 CE and would one day return again at the due time. The Shi'ah who accepted this line of *Imams* are often referred to as "Twelvers". This branch of Shi'ism, though a small minority at this time, would eventually grow and expand into the dominant school within Shi'ism. "Twelvers" make up more than 85% of Shi'is living in the world today.

After the disappearance of the 12th Imam, the "Twelvers" developed a strong tradition of religious scholarship. Without the physical presence of an *Imam*, these religious leaders (known as *Mujtahids* or *Ayatullahs*) were looked to for guidance by the community.

But this line of *Imams* was not itself devoid of splits. Following the death of the sixth *Imam* Ja`far as-Sadiq the community divided into two rival groups. The majority upheld Ja`far's nomination of his young son Musa al-Kazim as his successor. But others challenged this claim. They held that Ja'far's eldest son, Isma'il, was the authentic choice. While it was widely believed that Isma'il would indeed succeed his father, a crisis arose when Isma'il died several years before his father. Ja`far was therefore obliged to appoint a new successor. Those who sided with Isma`il and his descendants became known as the Isma'ilis. They stated that since an *Imam* was infallible his initial choice for *Imam* had to have been correct. Those who sided with Ja'far's younger son contested this claim and presented alternate versions of the events.

Both groups, however, began to develop separate communities and cloaked their activities in secrecy to avoid persecution. And while the followers of Musa al-Kazim quietly continued to teach and pray, the Isma`ilis would burst onto the stage of history in the decades to come.

Lesson Review

1. In a few paragraphs trace the origins of the Shi'ah movement in your own words.

2. Who is the Mahdi?

3. List the main differences between Sunnis and Shi'ahs.

4. Make a chart showing the major divisions within the Shi`is. Describe what you feel to be the main cause for splits within the ranks of the Shi`is.

Lesson Two

Calling to the World

Looking Ahead

As you read this lesson understand the reasons why mass conversion to Islam was not encouraged by Umayyad authorities.

Preview Vocabulary

Mawali
Jizya
Murji'i
Disassociate
Abu Hanifa
Qadari
Ahl al-Hadith
Ahl al-Sunnah wa al-Jama'
Jahm ibn Safwan

Converting to Islam

It would not be erroneous to state that Muslim Arabs sought to establish rule over the lands that came under their control in the name of Islam. But this is not to say that Islam was imposed upon those subjected to their rule. Despite the claims of many that Islam spread by the sword, it fell far outside of the goals of the Umayyad state to convert non-Muslims through the compulsion. In fact it often seemed as if conversion to Islam was hindered. Many among the Umayyad ruling class wanted to ensure the continuation of tribe-based Arab domination over the conquered lands. They believed that any mass conversion of non-Arabs would encourage demands for equal treatment and in the end threaten Arab rule. There were also motives for deterring conversion that were clearly materialistic. Non-Muslims living under Muslim rule were required to pay the yearly tax known as the *jizya*. Naturally with a huge non-Muslim population the *jizya* provided huge financial intake. This income logically declined as the Muslim population of any given province increased.

Despite the lack of initiative on the government's part to propagate the Islamic faith, non-Muslims did convert through one means or another. Through daily interaction Arabs often encouraged those Muslim with whom they had close personal

The spread of Islam's universal message does not appear to have been a priority for most of the Umayyad rulers.

contact to accept Islam. Slaves, servants, retainers and even merchants were no doubt often under some form of pressure to convert, though not legally obliged. A class of individuals who completely focused on piety and religious scholarship (who would in later generations come to be known as the *Ahl al-Hadith*) readily understood Islam's universal message. Having studied at the feet of the the *Tabi'in* (the generation after the *Sahabah*) the pious class promoted the egalitarian and often anti-tribal values of Islam. These scholars in turn established their own schools in Madinah, Iraq and Syria. In spite of the initial variations in legal rulings that existed between these circles of Islamic learning, they formed the foundation for what would later be the *Ahl al-Sunnah wa al-Jama'*, the Sunni branch of Islam.

Although there were scattered incidents where people were persuaded to embrace Islam by less than peaceful persuasion (most occurring during the revolt of the population in Transoxiana),

forced conversion remain throughout the Umayyad period a very rare occurrence. Often enough it was simply the Muslims' character and tolerance that won over hearts. Local Christian leaders often complained that their people so readily gave up the faith of their fathers' without pressure. Around 770 CE an anonymous Aramaic-speaking writer from northern Syria noted of his fellow Christians that, "The gates were opened to them to Islam...Without blows or tortures they slipped towards apostasy in great numbers; they formed groups of ten or twenty or thirty or a hundred or two hundred or three hundred without any sort of compulsion...going down to the town Harran and becoming Moslems in the presence of their officials."

Where it did occur, conversion to Islam during the Umayyad Period almost certainly meant Arabization, at least in Southwest Asia. New converts adopted Arabic names and learned Arabic, the language of the Qur'an and Islamic worship. They were then attached as

Mawali, adopted ones, to an Arab chief or to a tribe. The term *Mawali* soon came to be used to describe all non-Arab Muslims. The rank of *Mawali* gave new Muslims a place in Arab society, virtually at the bottom. Despite Islamic injunctions against it, the *Mawali* in several regions were required to pay the *Jizya*. *Mawali* soldiers were rarely given their fair share of *ghanima* after a military campaign. In Spain unequal distribution of land and wealth caused bitter feuding between the ruling Arabs and Berber warriors that would last for generations.

Conversions in the Umayyad Period most commonly took place in the vicinity of the Arab settlements and the large Arab garrison towns. The *Mawali* did not hesitate to perform their duties to their newly adopted faith. In the province of Khorasan, Persian-speaking *Mawali* are mentioned as serving in the Muslim army shortly after its conquest. The role of newly converted Berber tribes in the spread of Muslim rule over North Africa and Spain has already been in previous lessons.

Expounding the Faith

The study of the Qur'an and the need to teaching it gave rise to that most characteristically Muslim literary activity - the science of *Hadith*. In the late Umayyad period two important names stand out: Hasan al-Basri (died in 728 CE) and Ibn Shihab al-Zuhri (died in 742 CE). Hasan al-Basri was highly regarded as a transmitter of *Hadith*, and he was believed to have known personally seventy of the *Sahabah* who took part in the Battle of Badr. Most of the religious movements within

Islam trace their origin back to al-Basri. The Sufis (a mystical movement that will be discussed in the following volume) felt throughout the ages the lasting influence of his piety, the Sunnis never tired of quoting his sayings and even the Mu'tazila considered him as one of themselves.

The Muslim scholars centered on the Iraqi city of Kufa made important contributions to Arabic philology and Muslim learning. 'Amir ibn Sharahil al-Sha'bi (died in 728 CE) and his famous pupil Abu Hanifah flourished during this period. And we have it on the authority of al-Sha'bi that he himself was sent by the Umayyad ruler 'Abd al-Malik on an important mission to the Byzantine emperor in Constantinople.

Muslim scholars began to record their history at the time of the Umayyads in the form of *Hadith*. It was therefore one of the earliest disciplines cultivated by the Arab Muslims. The desire of the Umayyad rulers to note the proceedings of kings and emperors before their time, the interest of the believers in collecting the old stories about the Prophet and his *Sahabah*, and the necessity of knowing the genealogical relationship of each Muslim Arab for the purpose of determining the amount of stipend, all encouraged for historical research. 'Abid ibn Sharyah is reported to have gone to Damascus from southern Arabia on the invitation of Mu'awiya to inform the ruler about "the early kings of Arabia and their tribes." Ibn Sharyah wrote a number of works, one of which , *Kitab al-Muluk wa-Akhbar al-Mada'in*, is reported to have been in wide circulation by the 10th century CE.

> "It was by the mercy of Allah that you (Muhammad) were lenient with them. Had you been stern and hard-hearted, they would have dispersed from around you."
>
> *the Qur'an 3:159*

The Umayyad period also saw the beginnings of many of religio-philosophical movements which would become much more significant in the centuries to come. In the first half of the eighth century there lived in the southern Iraqi city of Basra a certain Wasil ibn 'Ata'. He has widely been credited with founding of the famous school of rationalism known later as the Mu'tazila. The heart of Wasil's teachings was that any Muslim who commits a great sin can no longer be called a believer yet (unlike the Khawarij position) the sinner is not an unbeliever either. Interestingly Wasil was a pupil of Hasan al-Basri, although Wasil later split with his teacher after several heated disagreements. The Mu'tazila would achieve their greatest popularity and prominence in the 'Abbasid era, when for a while it was upheld as the official government doctrine.

In addition to the Mu'tazila a group known as the Qadaris were the earliest school of philosophy in Islam. The Qadaris achieved a fair degree of popularity and it is said that two of the Umayyad caliphs, Mu'awiyah II and Yazid III, attached themselves to their doctrine. They took their name from the word *Qadar* which means God's power of all events, including the actions of people. The Qadaris asserted that *Qadar* belongs to man, and man himself chooses his acts, good or evil and not his Creator. Later Sunnis considered Qadari movement to be groundless and a heresy, but in Umayyad period the issue of free will was not so rigidly defined as it would become in the coming generations.

Taking a Middle Ground

Most pious Arab Muslims were seriously distressed with the second-class treatment of

Murji'i: A Term with Loaded Connotations

The term 'Murji'i' originates from an Arabic word meaning 'to postpone' or 'to defer'. It was originally used to signify someone who believed that judgement regarding the faith of Muslims should be left to the next life and basically anyone who claimed to be a Muslim was to be taken as so. The history of Murji'ism is complex because later Sunni scholars counted it as a heresy. This raises one important question: so how could a respectable man as Abu Hanifa be counted among them? For example, al-Ash'ari, the great Sunni theologian, condemned Abu Hanifa as a Murji'i because he was a member of a rival legal school at a time when the various schools of thought (*Madhhabs*) had not yet coalesced into a single Sunni entity. Later scholars such as al-Baghdadi (d. 1037) and Shahrastani (d. 1153) could no longer regard the founder of the Hanafi *Madhhab* as a sectarian. But they continued to list the Murji'i as heretics in order to round out the list of 72 sects foretold by the Prophet.

Abu Hanifa: Early Islam's Man of Learning

Nu`man ibn Thabit al-Taimi, al-Imam Abu Hanifa (d. 150), called "*the* Imam" by Abu Dawud, and "one of those who have reached the sky" by Ibn Hajar. He is known in the Islamic World as "The Greatest Imam" and his school has the largest number of followers among the four Sunni schools of thought. He is the first of the four *Mujtahids* and the only Successor (*Tabi`i*) among them, having seen the Companions Anas ibn Malik, `Abd Allah ibn Abi Awfa, Sahl ibn Sa`d al-Sa`idi, Abu al-Tufail, and `Amir ibn Wathila.

Abu Hanifa was the first scholar to organize the writing of *Fiqh* under sub-headings embracing the whole of the Law, beginning with purity (*Tahara*) followed by prayer (*Salat*), an order which was retained by all subsequent scholars such as Malik, Shafi`i, Abu Dawud, Bukhari, Muslim, Tirmidhi, and others. All these and their followers are indebted to him and give him a share of their reward because he was the first to open that road for them, according to the saying of the Prophet, "He who starts something good in Islam has its reward and the reward of those who practice it until the Day of Judgement, without lessening in the least the reward of those who practice it. The one who starts something bad in Islam will incur its punishment and the punishment of all those who practice it until the Day of Judgement without lessening their punishment in the least." Al-Shafi`i referred to this when he said, "People are all the children of Abu Hanifa in *Fiqh*."

Al-Khatib narrated from one of Abu Hanifa's students, "Muslims should make *Du`a* to Allah on behalf of Abu Hanifa in their prayers, because the *Sunnah* and the *Fiqh* were preserved for them through him." Al-Dhahabi wrote one volume on the life of each of the other three great *Imams* and said, "The account of Abu Hanifa's life requires two volumes!"

Abu Hanifa was painstakingly pious and refused Ibn Hubaira's offer of a judgeship and was beaten for the refusal. Like al-Bukhari and al-Shafi`i, he used to make 60 complete recitations of Qur'an every Ramadan: one in the day, one in the night. Al-Marwazi said, "Four are the Imams that recited the entire Qur'an in a single prayer: `Uthman ibn `Affan, Tamim al-Dari, Sa`id ibn Jubair, and Abu Hanifa." Ibn al-Mubarak said, "Abu Hanifa would often pray all five prayers with a single ablution."

Al-Suyuti related that a certain visitor came to observe Abu Hanifa and saw him all day long in the *Masjid*, teaching relentlessly, answering every question from both the scholars and the common people, not stopping except to pray. Then he stood at home in prayer when people were asleep, hardly ever eating or sleeping, and yet he was the most handsome and gracious of people, always alert and never tired, day after day for a long time, so that in the end the visitor said, "I became convinced that this was not an ordinary matter, but Friendship with Allah."

Sufian al-Thawri praised Abu Hanifa when he said, "We are in front of Abu Hanifa like small birds in front of the falcon," and Sufian stood up for him when Abu Hanifa visited him after his brother's death, and he said, "This man holds a high rank in knowledge, and if I did not stand up for his knowledge I would stand up for his age, and if not for his age then for his piety, and if not for his piety then for his opinions."

----*(excerpt from the writings of Shaikh G.F. Haddad)*

non-Arab converts that persistantly took place in the Muslim state. They regarded such policies as a flagrant breach of Islam's condemnation of any form of racism, tribalism or ethnocentricity. For them Islam was a message that had to be presented to the world, not just kept as the private property of the Arabs. Soon the cause of many of new converts was taken up by in many vocal religious circles.

These movements began to form shortly after the collapse of the great Shi'i revolt led by Mukhtar. Known as the Murji'i movement it called for a return to unity of the Muslim community, the like of which existed in the days of the Prophet. To do this Murji'ites avoided all discussing any of the controversies surrounding the *Khulafa' ar-Rashidah*. Their basic contention view that Abu Bakr and `Umar, under whom unity had prevailed among the *Ummah*, deserved praise while what happened to 'Uthman and 'Ali should be left to the judgement of Allah and to Allah alone. By taking such a position the Murji'a distanced themselves from not only the Shi'ah (of whom most disassociated themselves from the figures that preceded 'Ali), but the Khawarij (who condemned not only 'Ali but 'Uthman as well) and the Umayyads (who loathed 'Ali) as well.

The Murji'ites were at first mainly concentrated in Iraq where the rate of conversion was quite pronounced. Unlike other movements of the time they did not oppose Umayyad rule and, in principle, they taught that a Muslim should never shed the blood of a fellow Muslims except in self-defense. For the Murji'ites no Muslim should be denied his status as a Muslim because of wrongdoing or sin. This position clearly went against the Khawarij who believed that any Muslim who committed even the slightest infraction of Divine Law became an unbeliever. Despite the fact that it may have seemed that the Murj'ites avoided involvement in politics they strongly advocated the duty of every Muslim to speak out against social injustice.

The involvement of Murji'ites in the struggle for the rights of the *Mawali* and in the large scale conversions in Central Asia were first mentioned during the rule of 'Umar II. As an individual deeply committed to Islam, 'Umar II wholeheartedly supported conversion and was sympathetic to the cause of the Murji'ites. In 719 CE one convert complained before the the *Amir al-Mu'minin* that nearly 20,000 *Mawali* served in military campaigns in Central Asia without pay and that many of these new converts were even forced to pay *jizya*. 'Umar II ordered his governor in Khorasan to stop taking *Jizya* from "all those praying in the direction of the Ka'bah." With this restrictive policy lifted thousands hurried to accept Islam.

But 'Umar's policies encouraging conversion did outlive his death. In 729 CE the governor of Khorasan asked his advisers to find him a virtuous man whom he could send throughout Central Asia to summon the native people to Islam. They suggested that the best man for the job was one Abu Saida. In keeping with the precepts of Islamic Law he declared that whoever embraced Islam would be exempted from paying the *jizya*. Because of this the people of the lands around Samarqand hurried in massive numbers to join Islam.

Soon government officials began to complain to Damascus that the income from taxes was heading into a sharp decline. The governor of Khorasan sent a letter to the mayor of Samarqand stating that, "The financial power of the our state rests on the *jizya*. I have now learned that the people of your area have not become Muslims out of a desire for faith but rather only to avoid the *jizya*. From now on only those who have been circumcised, perform the obligations of Islam and who is able to recite one *surah* of the Qur'an, only they shall be exempt from the *jizya*." Consequently many of those who had recently embraced Islam were once again forced to pay *jizya*.

Abu Saida protested the taking of *jizya* from all converts and stated that the people had become true Muslims and had even built their own *masjids*. But the governor refused to listen and the *jizya* was enforced over the Muslim converts once again. In protest 7,000 of them assembled outside of the city of Samarqand demanding the rights given them by the Qur'an and the *Sunnah*. Abu Saida joined them there along with an Arab poet named Thabit Qutna, a well-known upholder of the Murji'ite position. The Umayyad mayor of Samarqand had Abu Saida and Thabit Qutna imprisoned and the *jizya* was squeezed out of the people with great ruthlessness. This harsh reaction to the protests caused many to abandon Islam and ally with the pagan Turks, who were then mounting a challeng to Muslim rule in Central Asia. Others, however, stuck with their new faith but took up the sword against the Umayyad rule.

In 734 CE, a great revolt of the *Mawali* in Central Asia erupted under the leadership of the Arab Murji'ite Harith ibn Suraij. That this uprising dragged on for more than a decade clearly displays the depth of resentment felt among the Murji'is and their *Mawali* allies. Several years into the rebellion Harith and his men were later pushed out of Umayyad-controlled lands and he began to forge alliances with several pagan Turkic tribes. Forming ties with pagans to fight fellow Muslims caused speedy reproach from religious circles throughout Muslim lands. This risky political move cost Harith the backing of most moderate Murji'ites not only in Central Asi but throughout the Muslim lands.

During this time of the rebellion an individual named Jahm ibn Safwan became the religious spokesman of Murji'ite opposition. What had begun as a protest against social injustice was now turning to a sectarian religious struggle. Jahm was condemned by pious Muslim circles in Iraq, Syria and Madinah on account of his religious interpretations. Jahm upheld the Murji'ite position that one only needed to have faith in the heart and a verbal declaration not a prerequisite. Yet Jahm also was alleged to have taught an extreme doctrine regarding the issue of *qadar* by stating that Allah's power compels human action and therefore individuals are not truely responsible for any of their actions. Jahm's views were upheld by Harith ibn Suraij and his followers in Central Asia although they were rejected by Murji'ite circles in other Muslim regions.

While rebellion raged in Central Asia and discontent with Umayyad rule grew in virtually every segment of the population, the Murji'ite movement in Iraq was taking a direction that was radically different from that of Harith ibn Suraij and Jahm ibn Safwan. In Iraq a young man named Nu`man ibn Thabit began to take interest in matters of religion and faith. Abu Hanifa, as Nu'man was popularly known, would later rise to such prominence in the world of Islamic scholarship that an entire school of thought (*madhhab*) would be based on his convictions and legal rulings.

Abu Hanifa was associated with apolitical Murji'ites though he strongly supported the

Qur'anic injunction to "enjoin the good and forbid the evil" when it came to standing against social injustice. He had even shown sympathy for and gave financial support to the doomed revolt of Zaid ibn 'Ali. Yet Abu Hanifa spoke out against many of the radical religious opinions of Jahm ibn Safwan. Because of his popularity and his ability to avoid serious censure from government authorities Abu Hanifa quickly became a focus of popularity. He attracted many students as well as critics from other scholarly circles.

By 747 CE Abu Hanifa's reputation as a religious scholar had achieved such notoriety that the Umayyad governor of Iraq tried to force Abu Hanifa to accept a position as chief *faqih* of the province. Given Abu Hanifa's disdain for the often un-Islamic policies of the Umayyads he rejected the offer and was given the lash for his noncompliance. He subsequently fled to Makkah and only managed to returned to Iraq years later after the 'Abbasid revolution had lifted Umayyad rule from his home province.

Lesson Review

1). What is the *jizya*? Who is required to pay it? What are the services a Muslim government had to provide for those who payed the *jizya*?

2) Who were the Muji'is? Briefly discuss there position regarding the *Khulafa' ar-Rashidah*.

3). Who was Abu Hanifa? Write about his contribution to Islamic learning.

Lesson Three

Building a Society

Looking Ahead

As you read this lesson, see how society in the Umayyad period differed from that of the pre-Islamic and early Islamic periods.

Preview Vocabulary

Decree
Clerk
Currency
Karavansarai
Hajib
Katib
The Dome of the Rock

A Coming together of Cultures

The advent of Muslim rule over the whole of Southwest Asia that finally occurred during the Umayyad period brought stability that was not seen since the time of the Roman Empire. And even in Roman times the continual tension between the empire and Parthians (and later Sasanid) which prevented total tranquility. In many ways the Muslims succeeded in unifying a large and important part of the world as it had never been before. From the Indus River in the Indian Subcontinent to the Tagus River in the Iberian Peninsula trade routes grew as security and cultural interaction began on a massive scale. But for most of the Umayyad period these openings were still in the formation stage. It would not be well into the 'Abbasid period that full fruition would take place.

Clearly the Arabs were the dominant ethnic and cultural component of the Muslim State during the period between Prophet's death and the fall of the Umayyad Dynasty. Despite being numerically a very small minority in lands such as Persia, North Africa and India, Arabs nonetheless held the reigns of political and military power. The Arabian Peninsula historically had limited contact with the world beyond and the common Arab could never have imagined the great variety of peoples that existed in neighboring lands.

As Arab rule was consolidated over Southwest Asia and North Africa a Muslim social structure that was largely based on tribe and, to some extent ethnicity, took hold. Arab tribal solidarity was still ran strong throughout most of the Umayyad period and antiquated tribal and clannish identities often overrode religious differences. Many tribes living in the Arabian Peninsula possessed intimate ties with Arab Christians living on the fringe of Iraq and Syria that dated back to pre-Islamic times. After the Muslims had taken over those areas these alliances and bonds remained in many instances kept intact. Although tribes of Christian Arabs did convert to Islam *en masse*, many others did not.

Conversion to Islam was not imperative for being granted a position in the Umayyad administration and many non-Muslims held key posts in the secretariat and the treasury. Conversely non-Arab Muslims were given little opportunity to exercise influence in both the government and the military. This was a reality that greatly disturbed many Arabs who frequented religious circles.

As we have read in previous lessons the social inequality between the Arabs and the ever increasing numbers of non-Arab Muslims started to grow into a serious source of friction. Some historians have asserted that it even played a major part in the downfall of the Umayyad dynasty and the subsequent rise of the Abbasids. The de facto overthrow of the ancient tribe-based way of life by the 'Abbasid revolution brought drastic changes not only to the government but also to the social structure of most of the Muslim world as well. The power exhibited by the *Mawali* during the revolution was a clear indication of their growing influence.

But such changes would come generations ahead of the time in question. During the high point of Umayyad power local cultures (those of the Berber, Coptic, Greek, Persian and Aramaic-speaking populations) continued to flourish, and the Arabic element of the population was at first just another element among many. The strong tribal customs and the spectacular military and economic successes were strong incentives for the Arabs to maintain the old ways in new surroundings. There was also an awareness of cultural supremacy that came with being members of a ruling class which was often linked with the strong sense that they, the Arabs,

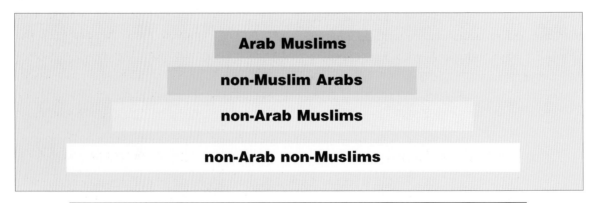

Arab Muslims

non-Muslim Arabs

non-Arab Muslims

non-Arab non-Muslims

For the most part, Umayyad society was still based on the old pre-Islamic system of tribes. Arab non-Muslims were still given precedence over non-Arab converts.

An actual silver dinar from the time of the ruler Hashim. Umayyad coins have been found as far away as England and Russia.

were the couriers of the Prophet's message.

During the Umayyad period the Arabic language was spoken as a mother tongue by only one ethnic group among many, but its diffusion and spread would be one of the unifying factors of the developing Muslim community. Encouragement for adopting Arabic was an unplanned part of later Umayyad policies as it became required for use in all government and administrative documents.

During the time of the *Khulafa' ar-Rashidah* and the first decades of Umayyad rule the situation was quite different. Muslim governors relied on local administrators, who more often than not had no acquaintance with Arabic but who did have intimacy with the complex governmental layouts of both Byzantium and Sasanid Persia, something that the Arabs lacked. As a result the majority of managerial records in these early years were kept in language of the local people, be it Persian, Greek or Aramaic.

The Umayyad ruler `Abd al-Malik embarked on massive reforms in the administration of his state. He ordered the removal of the non-Muslims from critical government positions and appointed in their place Muslims who could both speak and write Arabic. In addition to this managerial measure, the Arabic language was introduced in all government offices as the only language to be used for official business.

In some areas of Southwest Asia, North Africa and Spain the use of the Arabic language would eventually become so widespread that it displaced native tongues. Non-Arab peoples began to adopt the Arabic language to such an extent that their own languages gradually fell into disuse over the centuries.

But social evolution effected the Arabs as well. In time they ceased to be occupiers and a people with little interest in the lives of those they had dominion over. They settled down on the land and adopted many of the customs of the non-Arab population. By the very end of the Umayyad period (which was almost five generations removed from the death of the Prophet) ethnic divisions between the various Muslim peoples became more and more blurred. Intermarriage, the Arabization of local peoples and the spread of Islamic knowledge contributed to the formation of an identity based primarily on religious confession and not on race, ethnicity or language. A blending of traditions took place and the foundations of a truly new civilization were established.

The grand Umayyad Masjid in Damascus was originally a Byzantine church. As the population of Damascus gradually converted to Islam, the number of Christians began to shrink and churches fell into disuse. Many of these were later turned into masjids.

The Ahl al-Dhimma

As Muslim rule spread beyond the borders of Arabia, various legal documents created the basis for dealing with conquered people. The People of the Book, *the Ahl al-Kitab* - Jews, Christians and small mysterious sect known as the Sabians- were accepted in the Qur'an as co-believers in one God. Both they and their places of worship were to be treated with respect and left alone. All told this divine dictate was followed to the letter and the *Ahl al-Kitab* lived under great tolerance. One telling letter testifies to what most Christians living under Umayyad rule enjoyed: "As for the Arabs, to whom God has at this time given rule over the world," wrote the Patriarch Ishoyahb III to a fellow Aramaic-speaking Christian around

the year 650 CE, "you know well how they act toward us. Not only do they not oppose our faith, but they praise it, honor the priests and saints of our Lord, and give aid to our churches and monasteries." There is a general misconception that despite this toleration shown towards Jews and Christians, the followers of non-monotheistic faiths were given only the choice of conversion or death. In reality there is little evidence to support this belief. Zoroastrians were given the status of one of the *Ahl al-Kitab* even thought they are not mentioned as such in the Qur'an. Buddhists communities in the Sindh and Afghanistan were allowed to continue to freely practice their faiths and we have read in previous lessons how the Afghan city of Balkh remained a center of Buddhist learning well into the 'Abbasid period.

However it would be incorrect to suppose that incidents of coercion (though rare) never occurred. In order to keep the freshly converted people of Bukhara from backsliding into their former Zoroastrian faith, the Umayyad governor Qutaiba, ordered all the fire-temples of the city demolished and replaced with *masjids*. He then offered to pay all those who came to the Friday prayer 2 *dirhams* as encouragement to observe Islamic ritual. But such pressure was infrequent and scattered and in the neighboring city of Merv one Christian priest complained that his people had, "turned aside like idiots from the true faith [Christianity] and rushed headlong

The Nature of the Jizya

The *jizya* or "poll tax" was a tax levied on all non-Muslims living in an Islamic State. In many ways it resembles the *zakat* which was levied on all capable Muslim citizens. Ideally the *jizya* was utilized for the general welfare of the state, and in return, non-Muslims were given rights as citizens of the state, including military protection as well as financial assistance in times of need. Accordingly the *jizya* was not to be collected from the poor. The great general (and *Sahabah*) Khalid ibn al-Walid announced on his conquest of Iraq, "The old, the crippled and the poor are to be freed from the paying the *jizya*." In his chapter on taxation the great Sunni jurist of the 8th century CE, Abu Yusuf, stated that, "No *jizya* is due from single women or young children."

When the *jizya* was paid the non-Muslims were to be granted freedom of religion and treated fairness. They are called *Ahl al-Dhimma*, the "Protected People", because their rights were guaranteed by Allah and the Prophet. In his book *Futuh Al-Buldan*, the historian Al-Baladhuri commented, "When Khalid Ibn Al-Walid, on entering Damascus, he gave a guarantee of security to its citizens, their properties and churches. It was the decree of Allah, he said, and of the *khalifah* and all believers to keep them safe and secure on condition they paid the dues of the *jizya*." The above-mentioned Abu Yusuf listed the following report, "After obtaining terms from the people of Syria and collecting the *jizya* and a land-tax, news reached Abu 'Ubaida ibn al-Jarrah that a Byzantine army was massing to attack. The general messages to the rulers of cities with whose citizens he had made peace, and asked them to return the *jizya* and the land-tax, with this message: 'We hereby return to you the money you paid us because we can no longer guarantee your safety. If God grants us victory we will keep the treaty between us.' When this was delivered to the *Ahl al-Dhimma* and their money returned to them, they told the Muslims, 'May God give you victory over them!'"

Many have looked on the payment of the *jizya* as proof that non-Muslims were discriminated against in an Islamic state. But if one takes into account the fact that Muslim citizens had to pay *zakat* (which was not required of non-Muslims) in addition to the *kharj* (a land-tax required from all citizens), then the case for discrimination generally falls apart. There were even cases in the Umayyad period where Muslims themselves were ordered to pay the *jizya*.

into the pit of faithlessness [Islam]...Out of the thousands who were Christian, not a single victim was made holy unto God through the shedding of his blood for the true faith."

On a political level non-Muslims differed from their Muslim neighbors: they were required, with few exceptions, to pay a tax known as the *jizya*. This tax was intended to be used to support the continued maintenance of the Muslim state. As non-Muslims were not usually required to join the Muslim army though they were nonetheless to be defended by it. The payment of the *jizya* was in lieu of this military service. Although they were allowed to continue with their centuries-old customs and faiths, non-Muslims (with the exception of Christian Arabs in the early Umayyad period) were in many ways politically and socially second-class citizens. There were certain legal and social restrictions placed over the *Ahl al-Dhimma*, especially when it came to relations with the Muslim population. It was, for instance, prohibited for non-Muslims to openly propagate their faith among Muslims and legal rulings often put non-Muslims at a disadvantage in litigation involving a Muslim party.

Yet Muslim tolerance for other faiths (something absolutely nonexistent in Christian lands of the time) and the care in following the Qur'an-based code of warfare which prohibited wanton destruction and terror, left deep impressions on the inhabitants of the old empires, people who were long accustomed to religious intolerance, bigotry and social injustice. Many found in Islam a superior way of life. Slowly over the generations Islam grew into the predominant faith of Southwest Asia. But that would be far off into the future and at the close of the Umayyad period, Muslims, both Arab and non-Arab, were a small minority in a sea of other faiths.

The Rule of Law

It was no secret that the Umayyad rulers led lives far removed from the simple lifestyles of the *Khulafa' al-Rashidah*. They did nonetheless keep up the most of the central religious duties expected from the leader of the *Ummah*. He was, for example, to publicly perform the five daily prayers and he also had to preach the Friday sermon, or *khutbah*, in the capital's main *masjid*. In those masjids far away from the capital, the *khutbah* was read in his name. This was a primary duty every ruler had to perform without fail, and it remained so until the last sultan of the Ottomans was deposed in 1925.

The *amir al-mu'minin* also had to grant audiences to any of his subjects who so desired one, be they Arab or non-Arab, Muslim, Christian or Jew. These royal audiences took place in a great hall, or *majlis*, that was attached to the palace. These audiences were an attempt at maintaining an age-old Arab egalitarian custom. However it now resonated with all the protocol of an imperial court. In center of the hall sat the *amir al-mu'minin* on his dais, a lavishly decorated raised platform. To his right would stand any of his relatives who held positions of authority. His brothers and sons would also be present, and further behind the courtiers were grouped with the dignitaries (who could be anyone from Christian bishops to tribal chieftains), then the poets, and finally the people waiting to have their complaints addressed. Poets would often appear on the scene and recite verses in praise of the *amir al-mu'minin*, expecting a big tip!

A regal lifestyle cost money; and lots of it. In addition to paying armies, administrators had to be salaried. To cover these expenses the population had to be taxed. During the time of the *Khulafa ar-Rashidah* the collection of taxes was overseen by the military leaders who also exercised the highest functions of the government in the lands his troops controlled. From the very beginning of Umayyad rule a policy of complete decentralization prevailed in regards to finances. The first Umayyad ruler Mu`awiya separated the finances of the state from political administration. He appointed in each province a governor for political, military and social administration and then placed responsibility for the collection of taxes in the charge of another individual who was to act independently from the governor.

The taxes of a province then would flow into the treasury of the governor or the officer entrusted with the collection of taxes. These taxes were to cover the cost of administration as well as pay for soldiers, veterans and their relations. It was only then that the remaining balance, if any, was sent to the treasury in Damascus.

Another measure of equal importance that occurred during the Umayyad period was the introduction of new coins and the removal of foreign coinage (mostly Byzantine and Persian) from circulation. The care and precision with which the first Muslim-minted gold coins were struck is amazing. Every coin was to weigh exactly 4.25 grams and judging from the ones that survived to the modern period most met the decree. Notwithstanding this exactness, 'Abd al-Malik's currency reform still was based upon a fusion of Byzantine and Persian standards since the tradition of currency was hardly known among the Arabs in the days prior to the great expansion.

`Abd al-Malik also considerably improved the system of communications. Relays of riders were provided on the main roads that connected the most important towns of the realm, and carried with remarkable speed government dispatches between the provinces and Damascus. To fully appreciate this feat one should keep in mind the great distances involved in sending messages throughout the Muslim state. From Damascus to Cordova in Spain a messenger had to cover over 3,000 miles, which meant roughly two months by horse. To reach the Indus River from Syria an individual would have to travel nearly the same distance but often through much less hospitable terrain.

In addition to the reforms of 'Abd al-Malik, the short reign of `Umar II marked another turning point in the development of Muslim government. Immediately after he took the throne, 'Umar II enforced the general redistribution of taxes, ordering all governors to pay back to the central treasury any money obtained through less than legal means. Those who refused or delayed in their repayment were removed or imprisoned. This decree helped to bring about his eventual death but with the money obtained from this new source 'Umar II ordered the construction of *karavansaries*, or traveler's hotels, at fixed distances along trade routes as far away as Khorasan.

Imperial Robes

The Umayyads embraced many of the administrative and social practices of the Byzantines, particularly the pomp and ceremony of court life. The most notable governmental positions created during this were the *wazir*, the minister of a given department responsible directly to the ruler; the *hajib*, palace bodyguard; and the *katib*, the royal secretary. In time the office of *wazir* became so important that any weak-willed ruler might turn all power over to him. The *hajib* became powerful too, as he was in charge of the palace guard and had daily personal contact with the *amir al-mu'minin*. He had control over the doors and gates. In practice the *hajib* had power over who received royal audience or not. The ruler 'Abd al-Malik once told his *hajib*, "I have made you in charge of my door. Only three persons may enter without your permission: the one who calls for prayer, since he is the representative of Allah; the mailman, by virtue of what he carries; and the waiter who brings my food." Everyone else was forced to meet the approval of the *hajib*. The old Arab ideal, so stressed by 'Umar ibn al-Khattab, of the chief being accessible to all his people at any time and any place, had forever disappeared.

The *katib* was also an individual who had immediate access to the *amir al-mu'minin*. The Prophet Muhammad himself had a number of secretaries who wrote down both Qur'anic revelation as well as official correspondence. As the Umayyad state grew in size, so did the need for its own official correspondence. The role of the *katibs* increased in importance correspondingly. These were men who were very well educated and who might become well-known for abilities with the Arabic language, or for the quality of their calligraphy. And because of their access to sensitive information (they did have to write it down!) the *katibs* had to be men of undivided loyalty.

Evenings for the Umayyad rulers were normally set apart for entertainment. Mu'awiya was known for being particularly fond of listening to historical narratives and anecdotes. Such gatherings were often refreshed with the favorite drink of the palace and the ruling elite: rose-flavored sherbet, celebrated in song and still enjoyed in Damascus. Mu`awiya's son Yazid, however, was said to have been fond of much harder drink. He was the first ruler of the dynasty to enjoy the pleasures of wine drinking.

Among the more fashionable pastimes that engaged the interest of the ruling class were hunting and horse-racing. Polo, which became a wide-spread sport under the 'Abbasids, was probably introduced from Persia towards the end of the Umayyad period. The hunt was a sport well known in Arab tradition, where the saluki breed of dog had been used since time immemorial.

Horse-racing was extremely popular during the Umayyad period . Al-Walid, son of 'Abd-al-Malik, was the first ruler to institute and patronize public horse-races. His brother and successor, Sulaiman, had just completed arrangements for a state-wide competition in horse-racing when death overtook him. In one of the races organized by their brother Hisham, the number of racers from the royal and other stables reached 4,000!

Architectural Achievements

Among the outstanding achievements of the Umayyads were the many architectural monuments that were erected during their rule, few of which have survived to the present day. In 691 CE 'Abd al-Malik ordered built in Jerusalem the magnificent Dome of the Rock (*Qubbat al-Sakhrah*). Over a century later the structure underwent restoration by the 'Abbasid ruler Ma'mun. Near the dome 'Abd al-Malik erected another *masjid*, possibly on the ruins of a church that was destroyed by the Sasanids. Local usage designated this place as the *Masjid al-Aqsa*, but the term is also used in a more general sense to include the whole collection of sacred buildings on that site. This *masjid* is considered the third most sacred shrine in Islam after the Ka'bah and the Prophet's tomb.

Perhaps the greatest Umayyad patron of architecture was al-Walid, the son of 'Abd al-

Malik, whose rule was one of relative peace and prosperity. So great was his eagerness for building that during his reign it was said that whenever people in Damascus chatted, fine buildings were the main topic of conversation. Al-Walid enlarged and beautified the great *masjid* of Makkah, rebuilt the one in al-Madinah, erected in Syria a number of schools and places of worship. He also sponsored institutions for lepers, the lame and the blind. He was the first ruler in early medieval times to build hospitals for individuals with chronic diseases, and those that later developed in the Christian Europe followed this precedent. But al-Walid's greatest architectural achievement came to completion in 714 CE. Damascus was home to a splendid church known as Cathedral of St. John the Baptist, which was built on the site of an earlier pagan temple. When the Arabs took the city from the Byzantines in 636 CE, the Muslims entered into an agreement with the Christians to share the structure for their respective religious rites. But in the nearly eighty years prior to al-Walid's rule, the Muslim population of Damascus had grown so large that the church could no longer contain it. To rectify this problem he added a great masjid on to the already existing structure.Through the employment of local craftsmen this building became a stunning example of early Islamic architecture.

Lesson Review

1. Give reasons for the spread of the Arabic language during the Umayyad period.

2 Discuss the services of social welfare instituted during the rule of `Umar ibn `Abd al-`Aziz.

3. Compare the developing bureaucracy during the Umayyad period with the simplicity of the government during the rule of the *Khulafa' ar-Rashidah*. Discuss your conclusions.

Chapter Review

1. Give reasons for the spread of the Islam faith during the Umayyad period. What religious movements do you think appealed the most to new Muslims?

2 Write a letter to your school newspaper giving your opinions on the following statements: "Islam is a religion to be shared with all people" and "Islam is a faith for Arabs alone". Support your opinions with evidence from the Qur'an, Hadiths and other information.

3. Imagine you are one of the Ahl al-Dhimma living in the Umayyad State. Despite certain social restrictions, what benifits would you enjoy living under Muslim rule?

Glossary

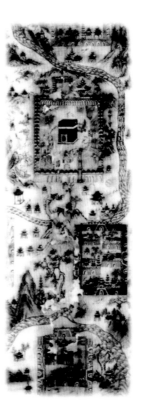

Abdullah ibn Zubair: the son of the Prophet Muhammad's companion Zubair; attempted to dislodge the Umayyad Khalifah Yazid by an open revolt.

Abu Dharr: one of the close companions of the Prophet Muhammad. During the rule of 'Uthman, he was exiled due to his open opposition to the corruption within the Islamic government, most notably against Mu'awiya, the governor of Syria.

Abu Hanifa: a scholar of Islamic jurisprudence (fiqh) and great piety during the Umayyad period; the Hanafi school of thought (madhhab) of the Sunni branch was founded by him.

Abu Sufyan: one of the leading members of the Makkan populace, as well as a leading enemy of the Muslims during the time of the Prophet Muhammad.

Abu Talib: the uncle turned guardian of the Prophet Muhammad; became the Prophet Muhammad's guardian when Muhammad was seven years old.

Adhan: the Muslim call to prayer.

Adobe: bricks formed by a straw and sun-dried clay conglomerate.

Ahl al-Bayt: the direct family of the Prophet Muhammad, notably his cousin and son-in-law 'Ali, his daughter Fatima, and his grandson's Hasan and Husain, the sons of 'Ali and Fatima; Arabic for "The House of the Prophet".

Ahl al-Hadith: a class of individuals whose main focus centered on piety and religious scholarship during the time of Umayyad rule.

Ahl al-Sunnah wa al-Jama': a term applied to the majority of the Sunni branch; began as religious scholars during the Umayyad epoch interpreted and defined the Qur'an and the Hadith into a system and way of thought, developing also the Shari'ah.

Ahura Mazda: in the Zoroastrian tradition, the Supreme God and the impetus of good.

Ajnadain: an area west of the city of Jerusalem where Muslim armies, under the leadership of Khalid ibn Walid, Amr ibn al-'As, and Yazid ibn Abi Sufian, fought the Byzantine army, exactly on April 24th, 634 CE.

Al-Amin: a title given to the Prophet Muhammad when he was of early adulthood, due to his reputation of being trustworthy; Arabic for "the Trustworthy One."

al-Faruk: an Arabic word meaning "The Just". A cognomen given to Umar ibn al-Khattab, a close companion of the Prophet Muhammad and the second leader of the Muslim community.

al-Fustat: a garrison town established by 'Amr ibn al-'As along the east bank of the Nile River; Arabic for "The Pavillion".

Al-Khutbah al-Wada': Arabic for "The Farewell Sermon"; the last sermon delivered by the Prophet Muhammad on the plain of Arafat, located several miles from Makkah.

Al-Maghrib: the Arabic term equated to Morocco.

Al-Sadiq: a title given to the Prophet Muhammad when he was of early adulthood, due to his reputation of being truthful; Arabic for "the Truthful One."

Amesha Spenta: the seven characteristics surrounding Ahura Mazda, aiding in the fight against evil.

Amiable: of pleasant and friendly disposition.

Amir: a leadership position chosen by the Khalifah, who is to preside over an area and administer policies and generally oversee the affairs of the community, sharing the same responsibilities as the Khalifah.

Angra Manyu: in the Zoroastrian tradition, the originator of evil; the embodiment of all evil characteristics; the antigod.

Ansar: the natives of the city of Medinah who hosted the Prophet Muhammad and his fellow companions from Makkah.

Arabia Felix: a name applied by the Romans specifically to the land of Yemen due to its production of sweet scents and other luxuries.

Armed Conflict: a battle, war, etc., between two or more sides, using armaments for offensive and defensive purposes.

Arsacids: an Iranian dynasty founded in the 2nd century BCE by an Iranian people known as the Parthians.

Artisans: a class of manual workers skilled in construction. Often they are tied to professional groups called guilds to protect their particular craft.

Assassination: the act of murdering an individual, especially a political or religious figure, under political or religious motives.

Autonomy: the right of a people to govern itself; the right of self-government.

Avesta: various sacred texts, from the Gatha to other scriptures, ranging from different time periods of the Zoroastrian tradition, collated to form the sacred text of Zoroastrianism.

Aws: one of the tribes that inhabited Yathrib (Madinah) during the time of the Prophet Muhammad.

Ayat: an Arabic term applied to verses of the Qur'an; Arabic for "a sign".

Banu Ghassan: an Arab Christian tribe located in Northern Arabia; after killing a Muslim postman trying to send a message to Byzantine Emperor Heraclius, a Muslim force led by Zaid, adopted son of the Prophet Muhammad, fought them and Byzantine reinforcement troops in the eighth year of Hijrah.

Banu Lakhm: an Arab tribe that occupied southern Iraq and of Nestorian Christian backround. They were under the rule of the Sasanid Empire during the rule of Abu Bakr.

Banu Quraizah: the last remaining Jewish tribe in Madinah by the time of the Battle of the Trench in 627 CE.

Battle of Badr: the first of a series of battles between the Muslims and the Quraish of Makkah, taking place about eighty miles southwest of Madinah, at the Wells of Badr, in 624 CE, second year of the Hijrah.

Battle of the Camel: The battle taken place outside of Basra between the forces of 'Ali and the forces of 'A'isha, Talha and Zubair in 656 CE.

Battle of the Ditch: the third battle between the Madinan Muslims and the Quraish, taking place in 627 CE, where the Muslims dug a trench around Madinah as a defense tactic at the suggestion of Salman al-Farsi, one of the close companions of the Prophet Muhammad.

Battle of Hunain: a barren valley ten miles outside of Makkah and the site of a battle between the Muslims and the pagan tribes of the Banu Hawazin and the Banu Thaqif, taking place shortly after the Muslims captured the city of Makkah.

Battle of Siffin: a city located in Syria and the site of a battle between the army of 'Ali and the army of Mu'awiya in 657 CE.

Battle or Tours: a battle between the Umayyad army under 'Abd ar-Rahman ibn 'Abd Allah al-Ghafiqi against Frankish Lord Charles Martel and his warriors at the city of Tours in northern central France in 732 CE.

Battle of the Zab River: a battle between the Umayyad army under Marwan II and the Abbasid insurgency army, taken place at the Zab River, a tributary of the Tigris River, in 750 CE.

Basra: a city in Iraq from where 'A'isha, Talha and Zubair organized an army to battle 'Ali in the famed Battle of the Camel. It was also a stronghold of 'Uthman's supporters.

Bay'at: a pledge of allegiance given to an individual, usually given to a leader.

Bedouins: a term describing nomadic Arabs, often residing in Arab or North African lands.

Berber: an indigenous people residing in North Africa.

Bogomil: a neo-Gnostic group with dualistic tendencies, predominantly residing within the Balkans.

Boycott: to economically ostracize a group of people by not buying or selling with them, often done to show disapproval of and to put pressure on them to change their habits.

Canonical: something held as authoritative or accepted, usually ascribed to divine scriptures.

Celibacy: abstention from sexual relations and from marriage, especially for religious reasons.

Central Government: a type of government characterized by all power and governmental initiatives centralized within an executive officer or a particular group in office.

Clerk: someone employed by a court, bank, etc., to keep records, accounts, etc.

Colosseum: an ancient Roman amphitheater built for public spectacles and where early Christian dissidents to the Roman Empire were sent to be executed for their beliefs.

Commerce: the exchange of buying and selling of goods involving transport to different areas.

Communication system: a way of coordination to effectively transmit information from one place to another place.

Consolidate: to make something solid or to reinforce something to make it strong.

Constantinople: the former name of the city in Istanbul in Turkey and the center of the former Byzantine Empire.

Coptic: an Afro-Asiatic language spoken in ancient Egypt and used liturgically in the Coptic Church.

Co-religionists: those who are of the same religion or hold the same beliefs.

Counter-Khalifah: an opposition leader to the established Khalifah, claiming to be the legitimate Khalifah. This was the case between Abdullah ibn Zubair, the opposition Khalifah, against the Umayyad dynasty.

Cuneiform: wedge-shaped writing, impressed upon clay in ancient Babylonia, also used throughout the ancient Middle East.

Currency: a medium of exchange usually taking place within the sphere of buying and selling, holding monetary value.

Decree: an official mandate issued by a legal authority, becoming law of the land.

Demiurge: in Gnosticism, a god subordinate to the Supreme God, aimed at the corruption of the Supreme God.

Demure: of shy, composed, and reserved temperament; coy.

Detachment: a separate unit in an army, etc., used for specific purposes.

Diligence: persistent yet careful attentiveness in effort.

Disassociate: to disconnect oneself from a group, movement, etc.

Dissention: disagreements giving rise to contention among factions.

Distressed: to be in a state of strain that affects the body or the mind.

The Dome of the Rock: site of the Prophet Muhammad's ascent to Heaven during the Isra' wal-Miraj. Masjid al-Aqsa was built next to the site by Umayyad Khalifah Abd al-Malik

Dualism: a term describing the belief in two equal yet opposing forces of good and evil.

Dynastic rule: the dominance of office in government by a single family or clan.

Dynasty: a succession of rulers of a particular empire that are of the same line of descent.

Edict of Milan: the proclamation made by Emperor Constantine in 313 CE that ended the oppression against Christians.

Empire: a state composed of groups of land and people ruled under a single supreme authority, especially an emperor.

En masse: all together or in a mass.

Essene: a member of an ancient Jewish sect marked by their asceticism and communal living.

Excommunication: to officially exclude a person from partaking in the sacraments or from formal communion with the church.

Explicit: expressed in detail, leaving nothing ambiguous.

Fertile Crescent: the fertile region that extends in a crescent shape from the Eastern Mediterranean in Egypt and Syria, to the Persian Gulf in Iraq.

Feud: a prolonged state of hostility between two or more families, clans, groups, etc., marked by violent attacks of revenge.

Fiqh: religious guidelines on judgments and practices; Islamic jurisprudence.

Fitnah: dissention and civil strife within a community leading to feuds, causing serious divisiveness.

Forfeit: to surrender in battle, often accompanied with a penalty or fine by the defeated side.

Frankincense: a gum resin from the Burseraceae tree mainly found in East African and Arabian areas; used in making incense.

Gatha: the sacred text of the Zoroastrian religion, containing the original words of Zoroaster. These words put forth the precepts by which every Zoroastrian is to abide by to attain salvation in the next life.

Ghanima: the Arabic term for booty, the spoils collected after a battle.

Ghulat: a sect of Shi'is that believe the Imams were God incarnate.

Gnostic: a member of Gnosticism, coming from the Greek word gnostikos meaning "one who knows."

Gospel: the teachings and revelations of Jesus Christ, recorded in the first four books of the New Testament.

Hajib: the palace bodyguard of the Umayyad court.

Hajjaj ibn Yusuf: initially head of the Shurta, or, military police, he was placed as head of the Umayyad army by Abd al-Malik in 691 CE to reestablish Umayyad dominance in Muslim lands.

Hallowed: something sanctified, consecrated, etc.

Hanifs: a term describing the few individuals in Arabia that believed in Allah as one God and is free of any partners, especially from the other Arab deities.

Hellenism: a term applied to ancient Greek culture, specifically from the time period of the death of Alexander the Great to the time of Augustus.

Heretic: one who holds an unorthodox view opposed to an accepted view.

Hilm: an Arabic term collating different virtues equated with leadership, such as self-restraint and judiciousness.

Hira: the mountain where the Prophet Muhammad would seclude himself and meditate.

Husain: the son of the companion 'Ali ibn Abu Talib, and grandson of the Prophet Muhammad. He was martyred in the city of Karbala alongside his family by an army of the then Khalifah Yazid.

'Ibadah: the Arabic term for "worship." Worship in Islam consists in the Five Pillars that all Muslims must carry out.

Iberian Peninsula: the area comprising Spain and Portugal.

Icon: Christian sacred imagery, often depicting Jesus Christ, the Virgin Mary, and Christian saints, painted on wooden panels, and is a center of veneration for the Eastern Christian tradition.

Iconography: traditional or conventional images or symbols that correlate to a subject, specifically to religious figures.

Infanticide: the killing of an infant.

Imam: a title given to an individual in a leadership position; title given to the leaders of the early Shi'i community and some current Shi'i branches.

Infallible: to be in a state of purity from error; unable to err.

Initiation: a ceremony involving the admittance of a person into society, office, etc.

Initiative: to originate an idea, action, etc. or take the lead in an action, judgment, etc.

Injil: the term referred to in the Qur'an as the lost teachings of Jesus Christ.

Interpretation: to explain or understand something, an idea, belief, etc., in a specific way.

Inviolable: something that has not been violated or is not profane; sacred.

Irreproachable: to be of exemplary character and integrity.

Isma'ili: a sect of the Shi'i branch upholding the belief in Isma'il being the rightful successor to Ja'far as-Sadiq, the sixth Imam, the Imamate continuing in an unbroken chain from Isma'il to the present.

Jahm ibn Safwan: one of the spokesperson for the Murji'i cause during the Umayyad period.

Jibril: the Arabic name of the Archangel Gabriel, who would bring sacred verses from God to the Prophet Muhammad throughout Muhammad's prophetic career.

Jizya: an annual tax non-Muslims paid living under Muslim rule.

Jum'ah: weekly communal prayers held every Friday for Muslims.

Justinian Code: a work of civil law enacted by Byzantine Emperor Justinian that created civil order in the empire. These laws were drawn from interpretations of Roman codes and reworked to fit the customs of the times; officially termed the Corpus Juris Civilis (Body of Civil Law).

Kahina: a name in Arabic texts referring to a woman named Dihya, who lead Berber revolts in North Africa against the Umayyads; Arabic for "witch".

Karbala: a city in modern day Iraq and the site of the martyrdom of Husain, grandson of the Prophet, and his family members by an army of the second Umayyad Khalifah Yazid.

Karavansarai: traveler's hotels established along major trade routes between major cities; erected by the order of Umar II, Umayyad Khalifah.

Katib: the royal secretary in the Umayyad court.

Khadijah: the Prophet Muhammad's first wife; she was a widow and prominent business woman when they married.

Khan: a term of Turkic origin, designated to people of societal rank, most often attributed to a king of a empire or a tribal chieftain.

Khawarij: a group that initially splintered away from 'Ali's forces, forming a new faction in the desert of Nahrawan in Arabia. They claimed that both 'Ali and Mu'awiya were unbelievers due to using their own judgments on certain matters instead of solely relying on the Qur'an.

Khazaj: one of the tribes that inhabited Yathrib (Madinah) during the time of the Prophet Muhammad.

Khazars: a Turkic people who converted to Judaism residing in the Caucasus Mountains at the time of the Umayyad Khalifah Hisham.

Kufa: an Iraqi garrison town located in Iraq where 'Ali found support and raised an army to battle 'A'isha, Talha and Zubair and their army in the Battle of the Camel.

Leniency: merciful and patient in temperament in face of difficulty or in exacting judgment.

Luminous: emitting a glowing, steady light.

Madinat an-Nabi: the title given to the city of Yathrib, meaning "The City of the Prophet." It effectively changed the city's name from 'Yathrib' to 'Madinah' for short.

Magu: members of a priestly caste in ancient Persia.

Mahalla: an Arabic term meaning districts, neighborhoods, etc.

Mahdi: explained in eschatological Islamic traditions as a figure to come at the end of time and establish peace and justice in a then morally corrupt world. His entrance onto the world stage is believed by Muslims to be one of the signs of the Day of Judgment. This figure would be the direct descendant of the Prophet Muhammad; Arabic for "he who is rightly guided".

Mawali: a term applied to non-Arab Muslims during the Umayyad period; after conversion, the convert would attach himself or herself to an Arab tribe to be recognized.

Mala'ikah: the Arabic term for angels. Angels in Islam are believed to be purely good and perfectly obedient to God.

Mani: the founder of Manichaeism.

Masjid: a place for Muslims to worship; Arabic for "place of making prostration."

Mazdayasna: meaning "worship of God, Ahura Mazda," the term implies walking the righteous path, and is what Zoroastrians entitle their religion.

Meditation: an act of intense reflection and contemplation, often clearing the mind, the fruition being increased wisdom and insight into matters of this world or spiritual ones.

Mobad: a priest of the Zoroastrian tradition.

Monophysite: a sect of Christianity residing in Egypt, believing only in Jesus' Godly nature, in loggerheads with the Roman Catholic and Greek Orthodox Nicene Doctrine of Jesus' dual nature, as both God and human.

Monotheism: the belief or worship of only one God.

Monsoon winds: strong torrential winds that occur periodically in the year in India and adjacent southwest Asian countries.

Morale: the mental bearing of an individual, group, etc., especially in regards to confidence, discipline, etc.

Muhajirun: those people who emigrated with the Prophet Muhammad from the city of Makkah to Medinah.

Muhammad ibn Qasim: young military commander of the Umayyad period who conquered most of what is now Pakistan, adding these lands under Muslim rule.

Mukhtar al-Thaqafi: a sympathizer of the Shi'is and sought to reorganize them in Iraq in 686 CE.

Munafiqun: members of the populace of Madinah who openly professed Islam as their religion yet in reality held enmity toward the Prophet Muhammad and the Muslims; Arabic for "hypocrites."

Muqawqas: the Arabic name applied to Cyrus the Caucasian, the bishop of Egypt presiding over Christian affairs in Egypt appointed by Heraclius the Byzantine Emperor.

Murji'i: a term applied to an individual who believed that an Muslim is not deprived his or her right to be a Muslim due to sin.

Musailimah: the chief of the Bani Hanifa tribe in the area of the Najd who proclaimed himself a prophet during the time of the Prophet Muhammad.

Mushaf: the printed text of God's speech, equated to the Qur'an.

Mut'ah: an area in Southern Syria where the Muslims fought the Banu Ghassan and Byzantine forces in the eighth year of Hijrah.

Mystery religions: the different beliefs prevalent in the Roman Empire that held secret religious rite that were exclusive to its members only.

Nagasi: a term applied to the kings of Aksum, a city in Ethiopia.

Nahj al-Balagha: the speeches and letters of 'Ali, collated into book form; Arabic for the "Peak of Eloquence".

Najd: a region in central Arabia with its capital being the city of Riyadh.

Naphtha: an ignitable oil derived from dry distillation of organic substances such as coal.

Nazarene: a member of the earliest Christian sect.

Negotiations: to confer with others, especially between two or more opposing sides, to reach a compromise or agreement on a certain issue

Nicene Creed: the formal statement of Christian belief adopted from the Council of Nicaea in 325 CE.

Original Sin: a transgression all of humankind is born with in consequence to the Fall of Adam.

Overrun: to overwhelm and conquer an area.

Pantheon: the deities of a group of people.

Pastoral: expressing the roaming life of herdsman, usually a life depended upon livestock.

Patriarch: the title of a chief bishop in the Greek Orthodox Church.

Peasant: historically a class of individuals in society depended upon subsistence farming for survival; of the lowest echelon in society.

Persecution: to tyrannize a person, group, etc., especially on grounds of holding a certain political or religious belief.

Pharisee: a member of the ancient Jewish sect marked by their strict observance of the traditional and written law.

The Plain of 'Arafat: located several miles outside of Makkah and site of the Prophet Muhammad's final sermon to the Muslim community before his passing.

Plague: a deadly disease spreading rapidly over a wide area.

Polytheism: the belief or worship of more than one god.

Pope: a Latin term meaning "Father," and is recognized as head of the Roman Catholic Church.

Preach: to urge acceptance or abandonment of a specific action, idea, belief, etc., often done within a religious or spiritual context.

Precedent: a previous decision taken as an example to guide subsequent decisions.

Proselytize: to convert a person or people from one belief to another belief.

Prosperous: marked by success or especially economic well-being.

Qadar: the Islamic belief in God's control and knowledge of all events.

Qadari: a school of philosophy during the Umayyad period believing that man had free will, ruling out predestination as a plausible explanation to why events take place in this life.

Qadisiyyah: a plain in Iraq that ran along the Euphrates River and the battle site between Muslim armies under the leadership of Sa'd ibn Abi Waqqas and the Sasanid army under Rustam, supreme general of Yazdigird III, in 637 CE.

Qairawan: a garrison settlement located in modern day Tunisia established by the Arabs.

Quarantine: to isolate individuals within a confined area in order to halt the spread of a disease amongst a given population.

Qunya: a pseudonym or nickname by which someone is popularly known as.

Rabbi: a Jewish scholar or teacher of the Jewish faith, especially the law.

Relic: an object accorded veneration due to its association with a religious or sacred figure, such as a saint or prophet.

Renounce: to repudiate a former claim; to withdraw from an idea, action, etc.

Riddah: an Arabic term meaning "apostasy" or, leaving the faith, in this case, Islam.

Rigid: to be unwavering, strict, etc. in action or temperament.

Sadducee: a member of the ancient Jewish sect marked by its strict adherence of the Scriptures, denying belief in the Day of Judgment and resurrection of the dead, for there are no references to these beliefs in the Scriptures.

Sahabah: those companions of the Prophet Muhammad who have seen him and, further more, took an active interest in helping Prophet Muhammad establish the message of Islam.

Sanskrit: ancient Indic language; the classical language of India and used in Hindu sacred texts.

Saqifah: an Arabic term applied to a hall in which meetings take place.

Schism: divisions within a group or community, leading into varying fractions or parties.

Sedentary: describing people, such as townsfolk or farmers, permanently settled in a area.

Semitic: the languages of the Arabian Peninsula, especially those of Arabic and Hebrew.

Shah: a title given to the kings of Iran; a sovereign of Iran.

Shahadah: Arabic for "to bear witness"; an expression of the testimonial phrase that one must say to become a Muslim.

Shaman: a priest who uses magic for curing the sick, predicting the future, and/or deals with the supernatural.

Shari'ah: the divine law derived from the sacred texts of the Qur'an and the Sunnah of the Prophet Muhammad, collated and interpreted by Islamic scholars over the centuries of Islam's existence.

Shi'at 'Ali: the title given to those who followed 'Ali and held the same positions as he had, including in believing that he should have been the rightful successor to the Prophet Muhammad; Arabic for "Party of 'Ali".

Shura: individuals of moral conviction and intelligence relied upon by a leader of a Muslim community to give advice to the leader where needed.

Shurta: the military police of the Umayyad dynasty.

Siege: a military tactic in which the attacking force seeks to compel a fortified force, city, etc., to surrender by cutting off its supplies, etc.

Silk Road: an ancient trade route extending from China to the Mediterranean Sea, a large portion lying in Muslim lands, which served as a major trade route for merchants in Asia.

Sindh: the historical region of now modern day southern Pakistan running along the Indus River.

Sirah: a history of the Prophet Muhammad's life.

Steppes: level grassy unforested plains especially in southeastern Europe and Siberia.

Stipulation: to specify or demand something in a pact or agreement.

Strife: conflict and discord among fractions of a community.

Synagogue: a place of worship for a Jewish congregation to meet for religious observance.

Tabi'in: the generation following the Companions of the Prophet Muhammad; Arabic for the "followers".

Tabuk: a city near the southern borders of Syria and the site of an expecting battle between the Muslims of Arabia and the Byzantine army. However, the Byzantines never arrived and the battle never occurred.

Ta'if: a city in Arabia to which Muhammad looked towards for help during the boycott of the Muslims. Instead he and his followers were chased out by the city's inhabitants with children hurling stones at them.

Talmud: the Jewish text comprised of Jewish civil and ceremonial teachings and legends taught by the rabbis.

Tawwabun: an armed force of Shi'is in Kufa who were distraught in abandoning Husain at Kerbala and, seeking redemption, sought to dislodge the Umayyads from power; Arabic for "those who repent."

Tashkil: vowel sounds designated by characters that marked different letters in Arabic texts, especially designed for the Qur'an, making it easier for non-Arabs to read the Qur'anic text appropiately.

Transoxiana: a classical Greek term meaning "lands over the Oxus River", applies to the lands of Central Asia.

Tribal: of or relating to tribe; characteristics of a tribe.

Trinity: the three persons of the Christian Godhead, that of the Father, Son, and the Holy Ghost.

Turks: an indigenous people residing in the Central Asian region.

Twelvers: a term applied to the main sect of the Shi'i branch, characterized by their belief in Muhammad al-Baqir being the true successor to the fourth Imam, Zain al-'Abidin, and Musa al-Kazim being the successor to the sixth Imam, Ja'far al-Sadiq, and the Imamate continuing in an unbroken chain down to the twelfth Imam, al-Mahdi, who went into hiding in 941 CE, and is believed to return at the end of time.

Tyrant: one who rules harshly, using excessive force, and wields power arbitrarily.

Uhud: a mountain ten miles from the city of Madinah and the site of the second battle between the Madinan Muslims and the Quraish in 625 CE, the third year of Hijrah.

Umar ibn 'Abd al-'Aziz: the Umayyad khalifah who ruled from 717 CE to 720 CE. Despite his short stint of rule, he procured sweeping policy changes for the Malawi (non-Arab) Muslims, putting them on an equal footing with Arab Muslims, as well as offering support to the Ahl al-Bayt and the Shi'i; known as the Fifth Righteous Khalifah, alongside the Khulafa ar-Rashidun.

Ummah: a term applied to the whole Muslim community, whether in a specific region, or universally.

Ummuhat ul-Mu'minin: a term applied to the wives of the Prophet Muhammad; Arabic for "Mothers of the Believers".

`Umrah: a supererogatory pilgrimage to the Ka'bah; known as the lesser Hajj (pilgrimage).

Universalize: to belong to or done by all persons in the world or in the class concerned; applicable to all things.

Untenable: something that cannot be sustainable; baseless, or unsupportable.

Usamah ibn Zaid: one of the companions of the Prophet Muhammad; near the death of the Prophet Muhammad, he was placed as leader of the military campaign against the Byzantines despite only being eighteen years old.

Veracity: honesty; an accurate statement, proof, etc.

Visigoths: a Germanic tribe that established rule over the Iberian Peninsula from the middle of the 5th century CE to 711 CE, when they were dislodged by Arab Muslim forces.

War of Fijar: a tribal feud between the Quraish and the Qais in Arabia that escalated into a war.

Wasi: the Arabic term for successor, in terms of leadership.

Yarmuk: a river located in a shallow valley in northern Palestine and the battle site between Muslim armies under Khalid ibn al-Walid and the Byzantine army under Armenian general Vahan during the reign of Byzantine Emperor Heraclius, in 636 CE.

Yazata: other characteristics, other than the Amesha Spenta, that aid in the fight against evil.

Year of the Elephant: the year named after when Abraha and his forces attacked Makkah and tried to destroy the Ka'bah with a cavalry of elephants.

Year of Sorrow: the year in which Muhammad's guardian, Abu Talib, and Muhammad's wife, Khadijah, both passed away due to the strains of the boycott placed on the Muslims by Muhammad's opponents.

Zabulistan: an area in central Afghanistan that the Umayyad king al-Walid first entered after conquering Khorasan.

Zaidi: a sect of the Shi'i branch supporting the political cause of Zaid, the younger son of Zain al-Abidin, against the Umayyad oppression of the Shi'is.

Zaid ibn Thabit: a notable companion of the Prophet Muhammad responsible for compiling all verses divinely revealed to the Prophet Muhammad into a book.

Zamzam: the famous water source in Makkah where by traditional sources sprung miraculously from the ground for the parched Isma'il and his mother Hagar, son and wife of the Prophet Abraham.

Zealot: a member of the ancient Jewish sect marked by their militancy and their aim for a world Jewish theocracy.

Ziggurat: a rectangular stepped tower in ancient Mesopotamia crowned by a temple.

Appendices

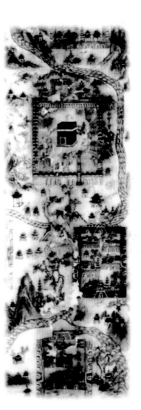

The Bani Hashim

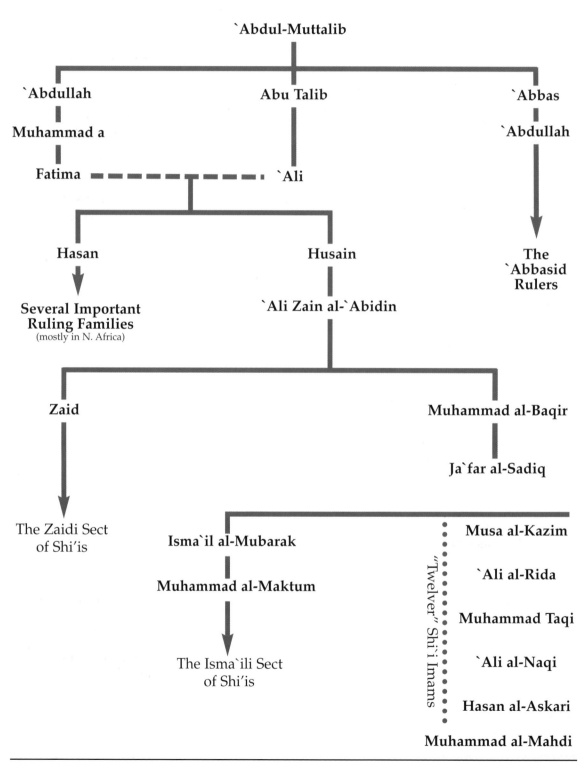

`Abdul-Muttalib

`Abdullah — Abu Talib — `Abbas

Muhammad a

`Abdullah

Fatima ---- `Ali

The `Abbasid Rulers

Hasan

Husain

Several Important Ruling Families
(mostly in N. Africa)

`Ali Zain al-`Abidin

Zaid

Muhammad al-Baqir

Ja`far al-Sadiq

The Zaidi Sect of Shi'is

Isma`il al-Mubarak

Muhammad al-Maktum

The Isma`ili Sect of Shi'is

"Twelver" Shi`i Imams

Musa al-Kazim

`Ali al-Rida

Muhammad Taqi

`Ali al-Naqi

Hasan al-Askari

Muhammad al-Mahdi

The Isma`ili Imams

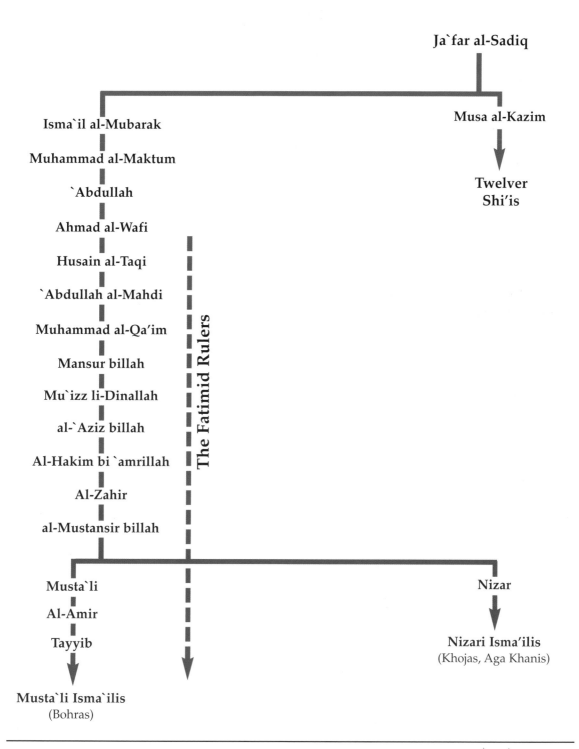

Ja`far al-Sadiq

Isma`il al-Mubarak

Muhammad al-Maktum

`Abdullah

Ahmad al-Wafi

Husain al-Taqi

`Abdullah al-Mahdi

Muhammad al-Qa'im

Mansur billah

Mu`izz li-Dinallah

al-`Aziz billah

Al-Hakim bi `amrillah

Al-Zahir

al-Mustansir billah

The Fatimid Rulers

Musa al-Kazim

Twelver
Shi'is

Musta`li

Al-Amir

Tayyib

Nizar

Musta`li Isma`ilis
(Bohras)

Nizari Isma'ilis
(Khojas, Aga Khanis)

The Umayyad Dynasty
661 CE to 750 CE

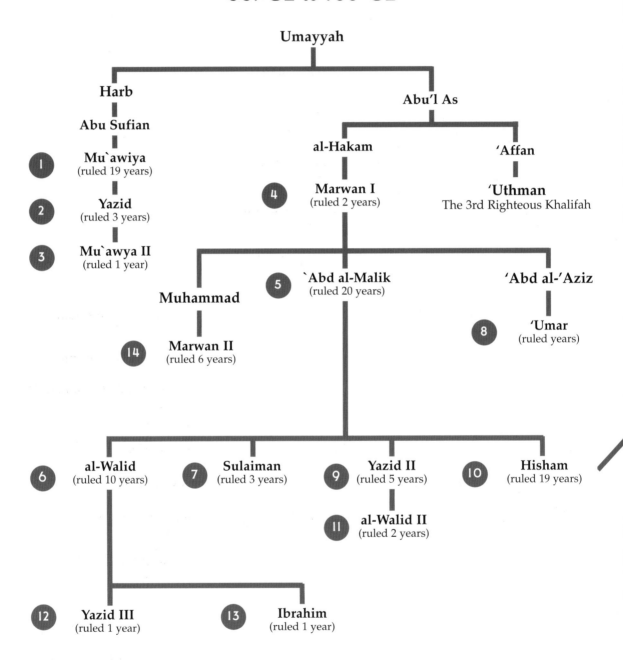

This diagram shows the relationship between the rulers of the Umayyad Dynasty. The numbers in parenthesis signify the individual's ascension to the throne. Make a list showing these rulers in chronological order.

The Umayyad Dynasty in al-Andalus
756 CE to 1031 CE

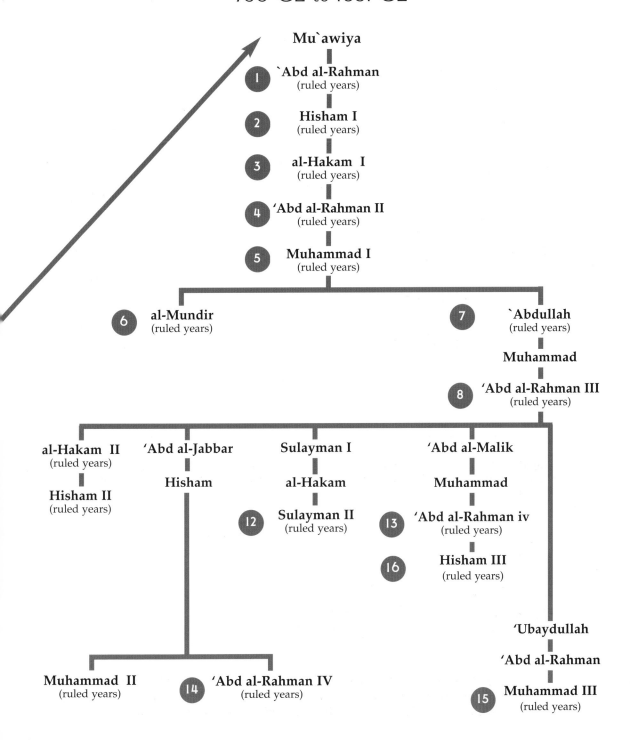

Mu`awiya

1 `Abd al-Rahman
(ruled years)

2 Hisham I
(ruled years)

3 al-Hakam I
(ruled years)

4 'Abd al-Rahman II
(ruled years)

5 Muhammad I
(ruled years)

6 al-Mundir
(ruled years)

7 `Abdullah
(ruled years)

Muhammad

8 'Abd al-Rahman III
(ruled years)

al-Hakam II
(ruled years)

Hisham II
(ruled years)

'Abd al-Jabbar

Hisham

Sulayman I

al-Hakam

12 Sulayman II
(ruled years)

'Abd al-Malik

Muhammad

13 'Abd al-Rahman iv
(ruled years)

16 Hisham III
(ruled years)

Muhammad II
(ruled years)

14 'Abd al-Rahman IV
(ruled years)

'Ubaydullah

'Abd al-Rahman

15 Muhammad III
(ruled years)

Timeline

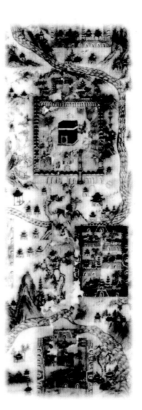

The Life of the Prophet Muhammad

545: Birth of Abdullah, the Prophet's father.

571: Birth of the Prophet; Year of the Elephant; invasion of Makkah by King Abraha.

577: Muhammad a visits Madinah with his mother, Aminah; death of his mother.

580: Death of Abd al-Muttalib, the grandfather of the Prophet.

583: Muhammad's journey to Syria in the company of his uncle Abu Talib; his meeting with the monk Bahira at Bisra (Syria) who foretells of his future greatness.

586: Muhammad participates in the War of Fijar.

591: Muhammad becomes an active member of *Hilf al-Fudul*, a league for the relief of the distressed.

594: Muhammad becomes the manager of the business of Khadijah and leads her trade caravan to Syria and back.

595: Muhammad marries Khadijah.

605: Muhammad arbitrates a dispute among the Quraish about the placing of the Black Stone in the Ka`bah.

610: The first revelation in the cave at Mt. Hira. Muhammad is commissioned as the Messenger of God.

613: Declaration on the Hill of Safa inviting the people of Makkah to Islam.

614: Invitation to the Banu Hashim to accept Islam.

615: Persecution of the Muslims by the chiefs of the Quraish. A party of Muslims leaves for Ethiopia.

616: A second Hijrah to Ethiopia.

617: Social boycott of Banu Hashim and the Prophet by the Quraish. Banu Hashim are shut up in a valley outside of Makkah.

619: Lifting of the boycott; deaths of Abu Talib and Khadijah; this is the "Year of Sorrow".

620: Journey to Ta'if. Ascension to the heavens (Isra` and Mi`raj).

621: First bay`ah (pledge) at Aqaba.

622: Second bay`ah at Aqaba. The Prophet and the Muslims migrate to Yathrib (Madinah); this is the **HIJRA**.

623: The Nakhla expedition.

624: Battle of Badr; the treason and expulsion of the Banu Qainuqa from Madinah.

625: Battle of Uhud; treachery and expulsion of Banu Nadir from Madinah.

626: Expedition of Banu Mustaliq.

627: Battle of the Trench; treason and punishment of Banu Quraizah in Madinah.

628: Truce of Hudaibiyah; expedition to Khaibar; the Prophet a addresses letters to various heads of states.

629: The Prophet performs the pilgrimage at Makkah; expedition to Muta`.

630: Conquest of Makkah; the Battle of Hunain and the siege of Ta`if.

631: Expedition to Tabuk; the "Year of Deputations".

632: Farewell pilgrimage at Makkah.

632: The passing of the Prophet from this world.

The Era of the Khulafa' ar-Rashidah and the estabishment of Umayyad Rule

632:    Farewell pilgrimage at Makkah.

632:    Death of the Holy Prophet. Selection of Abu Bakr to be Khalifah. The Riddah Wars begin.

633:    Raids begin into Sasanid Iraq. The Battle of Daumatul Jandal .

634:    The death of Abu Bakr.'Umar ibn al-Khattab becomes Khalifah.

635:    Battle of Bridge in Iraq and the conquest of Damascus. .

636:    The battles of Yarmuk and Qadisiyya. Mada'in, the capitol city of the Sasanid state, falls.

637:    Capture of Jerusalem.

639:    The Muslims advance into Egypt.

641:    Conquest of Alexandria.

642:    The Muslim armies push deep into Persia.

643:    Conquest of Azarbaijan

644:    The death of 'Umar. 'Uthman ibn 'Affan is selected as the next Khalifah.

647:    Campaigns into North Africa. Muslim forces land on the island of Cypus.

648:    Campaigns against the Byzantines.

652:    Disaffection with the rule of 'Uthman arises.

656:    'Uthman is assassinated. 'Ali ibn Abi Talib becomes Khalifah. Battle of the Camel.

657:    'Ali moves the capital from Madinah to Kufa. Battle of Siffin.

658:    Battle of Nahrawan.

659:    Conquest of Egypt by Mu'awiyah.

661:    Assasination of 'Ali. Mu'awiyah forces Hasan to abdicate in his favor. Mu`awiya becomes Amir al-Mu'minin. This move signals the start of the Umayyad Dynasty.

670:    `Uqba ibn Nafi'i founds Qairawan in Tunisia. Conquest of Kabul.

674:    Muslim armies cross the Amu Darya.

677:    The first siege of Constantinople.

680:    Death of Mu`awiya. Yazid becomes Amir al-Mu'minin. The Battle of Karbala.

682:    Muslim armies reach the Atlantic

683:    Death of Yazid. His young son Mu'awiya II succeeds him and dies shortly thereafter.

684:    Abdullah ibn Zubair declares himself Khalifah in Makkah. Marwan I becomes leader of the Umayyads.

685:    Death of Marwan I. His son 'Abd a-Malik becomes the Amir.

686:    Mukhtar al-Thaqafi rises in Kufa.

687:    Abdullah ibn Zubair crushes Mukhtar's Shi'i rebellion.

691:    Iraq falls to the Umayyads.

692:    The fall of Makkah and the death of Abdullah ibn Zubair.

695:	Khawarij revolts in Jazira and Ahwaz. Campaigns against Berber rebels in North Africa.
700:	Campaigns against the Berbers in North Africa.
705:	Death of 'Abd al-Malik. Accession of Walid I .
711:	Conquest of Spain, the Sindh and Transoxiana.
713:	Conquest of much of the Punjab.
715:	Death of Walid I. Accession of Sulaiman.
716:	Second attack on Constantinople.
717:	Death of Sulaiman. Accession of 'Umar II ibn 'Abd al-`Aziz.
720:	Death of 'Umar II ibn 'Abd al-`Aziz. Accession of Yazid II.
724:	Death of Yazid II. Accession of Hisham.
732:	The Battle of Tours in France.
740:	Shi`i rebellion led by Zaid ibn 'Ali. Berber revolt in North Africa.
743:	Death of Hisham. Accession of Walid II.
744:	Overthrow of Walid II. Accession of Yazid III followed quickly by Ibrahim and his over throw. Accession of Marwan II.
745:	Kufa and Mosul occupied by the Khawarij.
746:	Kufa and Mosul retaken by Marwan II.
747:	Revolt of Abu Muslim in Khurasan.
749:	Capture of Kufa by the Abbasids. 'Abdullah as-Saffah proclaims himself Khalifah in Kufa.
750:	Battle of Zab. Fall of Damascus. End of the Umayyads.

Further Reading

The Code of Hammurabi [18th Century BCE]

Of the several law codes surviving from the ancient Middle East, the most famous after the Hebrew Torah is the Code of Hammurabi, sixth king of the Amorite Dynasty of Old Babylon. It is best known from a beautifully engraved diorite stela now in the Louvre Museum which also depicts the king receiving the law from Shamash, the god of justice. This copy was made long after Hammurabi's time, and it is clear that his was a long-lasting contribution to Mesopotamian civil ization. It encodes many laws which had probably evolved over a long period of time, but is interesting to the general reader because of what it tells us about the attitudes and daily lives of the ancient Babylonians. In the following selection, most of the long prologue praising Hammurabi's power and wisdom is omitted. What do these laws tell us about attitudes toward slavery? What indication is there that some Babylonian women engaged in business? Clearly men had more rights than women in this society; but what laws can you identify that seem aimed at protecting certain rights of women? Which laws deviate from the egalitarian standard of "an eye for an eye and a tooth for a tooth?" What qualities does this text say a ruler should have to enable him to write new laws?

. . . Anu and Bel called by name me, Hammurabi, the exalted prince, who feared the Creator, to bring about the rule of righteousness in the land, to destroy the wicked and the evil-doers; so that the strong should not harm the weak; so that I should rule over the black-headed people like Shamash, and enlighten the land, to further the well-being of mankind. . . .

-If any one take a male or female slave of the court, or a male or female slave of a freed man, outside the city gates [to escape], he shall be put to death.

- If any one receive into his house a runaway male or female slave of the court, or of a freedman, and does not bring it out at the public proclamation of the [police], the master of the house shall be put to death.

-If any one be too lazy to keep his dam in proper condition, and does not so keep it; if then the dam break and all the fields be flooded, then shall he in whose dam the break occurred be sold for money, and the money shall replace the [grain] which he has caused to be ruined.

-If he be not able to replace the [grain], then he and his possessions shall be divided among the farmers whose corn he has flooded.

-If a [woman wine-seller] does not accept [grain] according to gross weight in payment of drink, but takes money, and the price of the drink is less than that of the corn, she shall be convicted and thrown into the water.

-If conspirators meet in the house of a [woman wine-seller], and these conspirators are not captured and delivered to the court, the [wine-seller] shall be put to death.

-If a "sister of a god"[nun] open a tavern, or enter a tavern to drink, then shall this woman be burned to death.

-If a man's wife be surprised [having intercourse] with another man, both shall be tied and thrown into the water, but the husband may pardon his wife and the king his slaves.

-If a man violate the wife (betrothed or child-wife) of another man, who has never known a man, and still lives in her father's house, and sleep with her and be surprised [caught], this man shall be put to death, but the wife is blameless.

-If a man bring a charge against [his] wife, but she is not surprised with another man, she must take an oath and then may return to her house.

-If the "finger is pointed" at a man's wife about another man, but she is not caught sleeping with the other man, she shall jump into the river for [the sake of her] husband. (2)

-If a man wishes to separate from his wife who has borne him no children, he shall give her the amount of her purchase money and the dowry which she brought from her father's house, and let her go.

-If a man's wife, who lives in his house, wishes to leave it, plunges into debt [to go into business], tries to ruin her house, neglects her husband, and is judicially convicted: if her husband offer her release, she may go on her way, and he gives her nothing as a gift of release. If her husband does not wish to release her, and if he take another wife, she shall remain as servant in her husband's house.

-If a woman quarrel with her husband, and say: "You are not congenial to me," the reasons for her prejudice must be presented. If she is guiltless, and there is no fault on her part, but he leaves and neglects her, then no guilt attaches to this woman, she shall take her dowry and go back to her father's house.

-If she is not innocent, but leaves her husband, and ruins her house, neglecting her husband, this woman shall be cast into the water.

-If a son strike his father, his hands shall be [cut] off.

-If a [noble-]man put out the eye of another [noble-]man, his eye shall be put out.

-If he break another [noble-]man's bone, his bone shall be broken.

-If he put out the eye of a [commoner], or break the bone of a [commoner], he shall pay one [silver] mina.

-If he put out the eye of a man's slave, or break the bone of a man's slave, he shall pay one-half of its value.

-If a man knock out the teeth of his equal, his teeth shall be knocked out.

-If he knock out the teeth of a [commoner], he shall pay one-third of a [silver] mina.

In future time, through all coming generations, let the king, who may be in the land, observe the words of righteousness which I have written on my monument; let him not alter the law of the land which I have given, the edicts which I have enacted; my monument let him not mar. If such a ruler have wisdom, and be able to keep his land in order, he shall observe the words which I have written in this inscription; the rule, statute, and law of the land which I have given; the decisions which I have made will this inscription show him; let him rule his subjects accordingly, speak justice to them, give right decisions, root out the miscreants and criminals from this land, and grant prosperity to his subjects.

Hammurabi, the king of righteousness, on whom Shamash has conferred right (or law) am I. My words are well considered; my deeds are not equaled; to bring low those that were high; to humble the proud, to expel insolence.

[Adapted from a translated by L. W. King (1915), and edited by Paul Brians]

The Mystery Religions

The cult of the Egyptian goddess Isis was one of the most important of the Mystery Religions in the later Roman Empire. Below is a selection from a novel written by Lucius Apuleius entitled The Golden Ass. *In this passage the goddess Isis appears to Lucius and claims to be an embodiment of all the deities. In this passage we can notice the blending of many religious traditions and myths. Lucius's experience is followed by a piece written by a fellow Roman named Prudentius, who was a devout Christian. Unlike Lucius, Prudentius presents us with a less than moving account of an initiation ceremony into the cult of the goddess Cybele, a Mystery Religion popular in Asia Minor.*

Isis, Queen of Heaven
When I had ended this prayer, and made known my needs to the Goddess, I fell asleep, and by and by appeared unto me a divine and venerable face, worshipped even by the Gods themselves. Then by little

and little I seemed to see the whole figure of her body, mounting out of the sea and standing before me, and so I shall describe her divine appearance, if the poverty of my human speech will allow me, or her divine power give me eloquence to do so.

First she had a great abundance of hair, dispersed and scattered about her neck, on the crown of her head she wore many garlands interlaced with flowers, just above her brow was a disk in the form of a mirror, or resembling the light of the Moon, in one of her hands she bore serpents, in the other, blades of corn, her robe was of fine silk shimmering in divers colors, sometime yellow, sometime rose, sometime flamy, and sometimes (which sore troubled my spirit) dark and obscure, covered with a black robe in manner of a shield, and pleated in most subtle fashion at the skirts of her garments, the welts appeared comely, whereas here and there the stars peaked out, and in the middle of them was placed the Moon, which shone like a flame of fire, round about the robe was a coronet or garland made with flowers and fruits. In her right hand she had a timbrel of brass, which gave a pleasant sound, in her left hand she bore a cup of gold, out of the mouth whereof the serpent Aspis lifted up his head, with a swelling throat, her sweet feet were covered with shoes interlaced and wrought with victorious palm.

Thus the divine shape breathing out the pleasant spice of fertile Arabia, disdained not with her divine voice to utter these words unto me, "Behold Lucius I am come, thy weeping and prayers has moved me to succor thee. I am she that is the natural mother of all things, mistress and governess of all the elements, the initial progeny of worlds, chief of powers divine, Queen of heaven, the principal of the Gods celestial, the light of the goddesses: at my will the planets of the air, the wholesome winds of the Seas, and the silences of hell be disposed; my name, my divinity is adored throughout all the world in divers manners, in variable customs and in many names, for the Phrygians call me Pessinuntica, the mother of the Gods: the Athenians call me Cecropian Artemis: the Cyprians, Paphian Aphrodite: the Candians, Dictyanna: the Sicilians , Stygian Proserpine: and the Eleusians call me Mother of the Corn. Some call me Juno, others Bellona of the Battles, and still others Hecate. Principally the Ethiopians which dwell in the Orient, and the Egyptians which are excellent in all kind of ancient doctrine, and by their proper ceremonies accustomed to worship me, do call me Queen Isis. Behold I am come to take pity of thy fortune and tribulation, behold I am present to favor and aid thee. Leave off thy weeping and lamentation, put away thy sorrow, for behold the healthful day which is ordained by my providence, therefore be ready to attend to my commandment."

[Lucius Apuleius: *Metamophoses or The Golden Ass*. Book 11, Chap 47. Adapted by Paul Halsall from the translation by Adlington 1566 in comparison with Robert Graves translation of 1951]

Initiation into the Cult of Cybele

The high priest who is to be consecrated is brought down under ground in a pit dug deep, marvellously adorned with a flowers...his hair combed back under a golden crown, and wearing a silken toga caught up with Gabine girding. Over this they make a wooden floor with wide spaces, woven of planks with an open mesh. They then divide or bore the area and repeatedly pierce the wood with a pointed tool until it is full of small holes. Then a huge bull, fierce and shaggy in appearance, is led, adorned with flowery garlands, and with its horns sheathed. The forehead of the bull sparkles with gold, and the glitter of metal plates adorns its hide. As is ordained, the beast sacrificed, and its chest is pierced with a sacred spear. The wound emits a gusher of blood, and the river flows into the woven structure beneath it ...Then through the thousand openings in the lattice the falling shower rains down a foul dew, which the priest buried within catches, putting his shameful head under all the drops, defiled both in his clothing and in all his body. He throws back his face, he puts his cheeks in the way of the blood, he puts under it his ears and lips, and in his nostrils. He washes his eyes with the fluid, nor does he even spare his throat but moistens his tongue, until he actually drinks the dark gore. Afterwards, the men drag the corpse, stiffening now that the blood has gone forth, off the lattice, and the priest, horrible in appearance, comes out, and shows his wet head, his beard heavy with blood, his dripping fillets and sodden garments. This man, dirtied with such blood and foul with the gore of the recent sacrifice, all hail and worship at a distance, because profane blood and a dead ox have washed him while concealed in a filthy cave.

[Prudentius, *Peristephanon*, X, 101 1-50]

The Edict of Milan

The Edict of Milan was the edict of Constantine granting religious freedom to Christians. It was proclaimed the following year after the Battle of Milvan Bridge, in 313, by which Christianity raised to the status of a state religion and accorded full freedom of worship. Restitution was ordered of all the sacred buildings and other property seized by the government during the late persecution.

When I, Constantine Augustus, as well as I Licinius Augustus did fortunately met near Mediolanum (Milan), and were considering everything that pertained to the public welfare and security, we thought -, among other things which we saw would be for the good of many, those regulations pertaining to the reverence of the Divinity ought certainly to be made first, so that we might grant to the Christians and others full authority to observe that religion which each preferred; whence any Divinity whatsoever in the seat of the heavens may be propitious and kindly disposed to us and all who are placed under our rule And thus by this wholesome counsel and most upright provision we thought to arrange that no one whatsoever should be denied the opportunity to give his heart to the observance of the Christian religion, of that religion which he should think best for himself, so that the Supreme Deity, to whose worship we freely yield our hearts) may show in all things His usual favor and benevolence. Therefore, your Worship should know that it has pleased us to remove all conditions whatsoever, which were in the rescripts formerly given to you officially, concerning the Christians and now any one of these who wishes to observe Christian religion may do so freely and openly, without molestation. We thought it fit to commend these things most fully to your care that you may know that we have given to those Christians free and unrestricted opportunity of religious worship. When you see that this has been granted to them by us, your Worship will know that we have also conceded to other religions the right of open and free observance of their worship for the sake of the peace of our times, that each one may have the free opportunity to worship as he pleases ; this regulation is made we that we may not seem to detract from any dignity or any religion.

Moreover, in the case of the Christians especially we esteemed it best to order that if it happens anyone heretofore has bought from our treasury from anyone whatsoever, those places where they were previously accustomed to assemble, concerning which a certain decree had been made and a letter sent to you officially, the same shall be restored to the Christians without payment or any claim of recompense and without any kind of fraud or deception, Those, moreover, who have obtained the same by gift, are likewise to return them at once to the Christians. Besides, both those who have purchased and those who have secured them by gift, are to appeal to the vicar if they seek any recompense from our bounty, that they may be cared for through our clemency,. All this property ought to be delivered at once to the community of the Christians through your intercession, and without delay. And since these Christians are known to have possessed not only those places in which they were accustomed to assemble, but also other property, namely the churches, belonging to them as a corporation and not as individuals, all these things which we have included under the above law, you will order to be restored, without any hesitation or controversy at all, to these Christians, that is to say to the corporations and their conventicles: providing, of course, that the above arrangements be followed so that those who return the same without payment, as we have said, may hope for an indemnity from our bounty. In all these circumstances you ought to tender your most efficacious intervention to the community of the Christians, that our command may be carried into effect as quickly as possible, whereby, moreover, through our clemency, public order may be secured. Let this be done so that, as we have said above, Divine favor towards us, which, under the most important circumstances we have already experienced, may, for all time, preserve and prosper our successes together with the good of the state. Moreover, in order that the statement of this decree of our good will may come to the notice of all, this rescript, published by your decree, shall be announced everywhere and brought to the knowledge of all, so that the decree of this, our benevolence, cannot be concealed.

Translated in University of Pennsylvania. Dept. of History: Translations and Reprints from the Original Sources of European history, (Philadelphia, University of Pennsylvania Press), Vol 4:, 1, pp. 28-30.

The Roman Destruction of Jerusalem

In the Spring of 66 CE, the Jews of Roman Judea had had enough of Roman rule. Without any apparently plan or organized leadership, Rebels seized control of Jerusalem and then finally massacred the sole cohort of Roman infantry. The Emperor Nero sent 60,00 men to crush the rebellion. In September 70 CE, after a seven month seige. The temple and much of the city was leveled, captives were shipped off to the gladiatorial games or the mines. One of the most detailed accounts of the Jewish revolt existing was made by theRoman historian Flavus Josephus (37 CE-100 CE) who was himself of Jewish origin.

So the Romans being now become masters of the wars, they both placed their ensigns upon the towers, and made joyful acclamations for the victory they had gained, as having found the end of this war much lighter than its beginning; for when they had gotten upon the last was, without any bloodshed, they could hardly believe what they found to be true; but seeing nobody to oppose them, they stood in doubt what such an unusual solitude could mean. But when they went in numbers into the lanes of the city, with their swords drawn, they slew those whom they overtook, without mercy, and set fire to the houses wither the Jews were fled, and burnt every soul in them, and laid waste a great many of the rest; and when they were come to the houses to plunder them, they found in them entire families of dead men, and the upper rooms full of dead corpses, that is of such as died by the famine; they then stood in a horror at this sight, and went out without touching anything. But although they had this commiseration for such as were destroyed in that manner, yet had they not the same for those that were still alive, but they ran every one through whom they met with, and obstructed the very lanes with their dead bodies, and made the whole city run down with blood, to such a degree indeed that the fire of many of the houses was quenched with these men's blood. And truly so it happened, that though the slayers left off at the evening, yet did the fire greatly prevail in the night, and as all was burning, came that eighth day of the month Gorpieus upon Jerusalem; a city that had been liable to so many miseries during the siege, that, had it always enjoyed as much happiness from its first foundation, it would certainly have been the envy of the world. Nor did it on any other account so much deserve these sore misfortunes, as by producing such a generation of men as were the occasions of this its overthrow.

Now, when Titus was come into this city, he admired not only some other places of strength in it, but particularly those strong towers which the tyrants, in their mad conduct, had relinquished; for when he saw their solid altitude, and the largeness of their several stones. and the exactness of their joints, as also how great was their breadth, and how extensive their length, he expressed himself after the manner following: "We have certainly had God for our assistant in this war, and it was no other than God who ejected the Jews out of these fortifications; for what could the hands of men, or any machines, do towards overthrowing these towers!" At which time he had many such discourses to his friends; he also let such go free as had been bound by the tyrants, and were left in the prisons. To conclude, when he entirely demolished the rest of the city, and overthrew its wars, he left these towers as a monument of his good fortune, which had proved his auxiliaries, and enabled him to take what could not otherwise have been taken by him.

And now, since his soldiers were already quite tired with killing men, and yet there appeared to be a vast multitude still remaining alive, Caesar gave orders that they should kill none but those that were in arms, and opposed them, but should take the rest alive. But, together with those whom they had orders to slay, they slew the aged and the infirm; but for those that were in their flourishing age, and who might be useful to them, they drove them together into the temple, and shut them up within the walls of the court of the women; over which Caesar set one of his freed men, as also Fronto, one of his own friends; which last was to determine every one's fate, according to his merits. So this Fronto slew all those that had been seditious and robbers, who were impeached one by another; but of the young men he chose out the tallest and most beautiful, and reserved them for the triumph; and as for the rest of the multitude that were above seventeen years old, he put them into bonds, and sent them to the Egyptian mines. Titus also sent a great number into the provinces, as a present to them, that they might be destroyed upon their theaters, by the sword and by the wild beasts; but those that were under seventeen years of age were sold for slaves. Now during the days wherein Fronto was distinguishing these men, there perished, for want of food, eleven thousand; some of whom did not taste any food, through the hatred their guards bore to them; and others would not take in any when it was given them. The multitude also was so very great, that they were in want even of corn for their sustenance.

Now the number of those that were carried captive during this whole war was collected to be ninety-seven thousand, as was the number of those that perished during the whole siege eleven hundred thousand, the greater part of whom were indeed of the same nation, but not belonging to the city itself; for they were come up from all the country to the feast of unleavened bread, and were on a sudden shut up by an army, which, at the very first, occasioned so great a traitness among them that there came a pestilential destruction upon them, and soon afterward such a famine, as destroyed them more suddenly.

From *The Works of Josephus*, translated by William Whiston Hendrickson Publishers, 1987

The Character of the Prophet

Muhammad was of a little above average in height. He was sturdy of build with long muscular limbs and tapering fingers. The hair of his head was long and thick with some waves in it. His forehead was wide, his eyelashes were long and thick, his nose was aquiline, his mouth was moderately large and his teeth were well set. His cheeks were shallow and he had a warm smile. His eyes were large and black with a speckling of brown. His beard was ample and at the time of his death, there were seventeen gray hairs in it. He had a thin line of fine hair over his neck and chest. His gait was firm and he walked so fast that others found it arduous to keep up with him. His face was cheerful, but at times, when he was deep in thought, there were long periods of stillness, yet he always kept himself busy with something. He did not speak unnecessarily and what he said was always to the point. At times he would make his meaning clear by repeating what he had said. His laugh was mostly nothing more than a smile. He kept his emotions under firm control - when harassed, he would turn aside or keep silent, and when pleased he would lower his eyes. (from the Shama`il Tirmidhi)

The Prophet dress usually consisted of a shirt, trousers, a sheet thrown round the shoulders and a turban. On rare occasions, he would put on costly robes presented to him by foreign emissaries in the later part of his life (from Ahmad)

The Prophet wanted people to put on simple but clean clothes. Once he saw a person putting on dirty clothes and remarked, "Why can't this man wash them." (from Abu Dawud)

The Prophet's house was but a hut with walls made of unbaked clay and a thatched roof of palm leaves covered by camel skin. He had separate lodgings for his wives, a small room for each made of similar material. His own apartment contained a rope cot, a pillow stuffed with palm leaves, an animal skin spread on the floor and a water-bag of leather and a few weapons. These were all his earthly belongings, besides a camel, a horse, and some land that he had acquired in the later part of his life.
(from the works of Bukhari, Muslim, Abu Dawud).

When he died there was nothing in his house except a few seeds of barley left from a mound of the grain bought from a Jewish man through pawning his armor. (from Bukhari)

The Prophet would not deny courtesy even to the wicked. It is stated that a person came to his house and asked permission to enter. The Prophet remarked that he was from the ranks of the enemy but might be admitted. When he came in and while he remained in the house, he was given courtesy. When the man left 'A'isha said, "You did not think well of this man, but you treated him courteously." The Prophet replied, "He is indeed an inferior man who does not behave courteously and people shun his company because of his bad manners." (from Bukhari)

The Prophet disliked people to stand for him, such was his humility. However he himself would stand up when any dignitary came to him. He avoided sitting in a noticeable place in a gathering, so much so that people coming in had difficulty in spotting him and they would have to ask which man was the Prophet. Quite frequently uncouth Bedouins addressed him in their own brusque and rude manner but he never took offence. (from Bukhari)

There was no type of labor too low or too undignified for him. 'A'isha stated, "He always joined in house work and would mend his clothes, repair his shoes and sweep the floor. He would milk, tether, and feed the animals and do the shopping." (from Qadi Iyad)

He was especially fond of children and used to get into the spirit of childhood while in their company. He would have fun with those children who had come back from Ethiopia and he tried to speak in Amharic with them. It was his practice to give rides on his camel to children when he returned from journeys. (from Bukhari)

The Sahabah 'Abdullah ibn Sahal was assigned to collect rent from the Jews of Khaibar. His cousin Mahisa escorted him but, on reaching Khaibar, they were separated. 'Abdullah was waylaid and killed. Mahisa reported this murder to the Prophet and it was suspect that it was a gang of Jews that committed the crime. But as there were no eyewitnesses to identify the guilty, the Prophet did not allow any penalty imposed on the Jews of Khaibar and instead paid the blood money out of the Bait al-Mal. (from Bukhari)

On another occasion he was travelling on his camel over hilly terrain with a ' Uqba ibn Amir. After going some distance, he asked 'Uqba to ride the camel, but 'Uqba thought this would be showing too much disrespect. But the Prophet insisted and 'Uqba complied. The Prophet himself walked on foot as he did not want to put too much load on the animal with two riders. (from Nasa'i)

During a stop on a journey, the Sahabah distribute work among themselves in preparing the dinner. The Prophet took it upon himself to collect firewood. The Sahabah pleaded that they would do it and that he need not take the trouble, but he replied, "I do not like to ascribe any distinction to myself. Allah does not like the man who considers himself superior to his friends." (from Darqani)

If he saw any animal over-loaded or ill-fed he would pull up the owner and say, "Fear Allah in your treatment of animals." (from Abu Dawud)

A Madinan was once starving. He entered an orchard and picked some fruit. The owner of the orchard gave him a sound thrashing and stripped off his clothes. The poor man ran to the Prophet who said to the owner, "This man was unaware and you should have dispelled his ignorance; he was hungry, you should have fed him." His clothes were reinstate to the Madinan and some grain was given to him. (from Abu Dawud)

The Prophet's love for the poor was so deep that he used to pray, "O Allah, keep me poor in my life and at my death and raise me at Resurrection among those who are poor." (from Nasa'i)

...From The Message of Mohammad by Athar Husain

On The Selection Of a Successor To The Prophet

'Umar ibn al-Khattab once said: I am about to say to you something that Allah has willed that I should say. He who understands and considers it, let him take it with him wherever he goes. I have heard that someone said, "If 'Umar were dead, I would hail So-and-so." Let no man deceive himself by saying that the acceptance of Abu Bakr was an unplanned affair that was then approved. Admittedly it was, but Allah turned away the evil of it. There is none among you to whom people would devote themselves as they did to Abu Bakr. He who accepts a man as ruler without consulting the Muslims, such acceptance has no validity for either of them...What happened was that when Allah took away His apostle the Ansar opposed us and gathered with their chiefs in the hall of the Banu Sa'ida; and 'Ali and Zubair and their associates withdrew from while the Muhajirun gathered to Abu Bakr.

I then told Abu Bakr that we should go to our brothers the Ansar in the hall of Banu Sa'ida. In the middle of them was their leader Sa'd ibn 'Ubada who was feverish. Their speaker then continued: "We are Allah's helpers and the advanced guard of Islam. You, O Muhajirun, are a family of ours and a company of your people come to settle." And so they were trying to cut us off from our dignity and take authority from us. I wanted to speak, but Abu Bakr said, "Gently, 'Umar!" I did not like to anger him and so he spoke in his unequaled manner better than I could have done. He said, "All the good that you have said about yourselves is certainly justified. But the Arabs will recognize authority only in this tribe of Quraish, they being the best of the Arabs in lineage and rank. I offer you one of these two men; receive which one you please." Thus saying he took hold of my hand and that of Abu 'Ubaida ibn al-Jarrah who had come with us. Nothing he said rankled me more than that. By Allah, I would rather have come forward and have had my head struck off -if that were no sin - than rule a people of whom Abu Bakr was one. One of the Ansar said, "Let us have one ruler and you another, O Quraishis." Argument increased and voices were raised until when a complete rupture was to be feared I said, "Stretch out your hand, Abu Bakr!" He did so and I gave him my allegiance. The Muhajirun followed and then the Ansar.

----from The Way of the Prophet by Ibn Ishaq (d. ca. 768 CE)

Abu Bakr's Injunctions On The Jihad

Abu Bakr went out to the army and he was walking, while Usama rode. 'Abd al-Rabman ibn 'Awf was leading Abu Bakr's horse. Then Usama said to him, "O Khalifah you will either mount, or I shall dismount." He replied, "By Allah you shall not dismount, and I will not mount. I must get my feet a little dusty in the path of Allah, for warrior with every step he takes has 700 merits credited to him and he is raised 700 degrees in rank, while 700 sins are forgiven him!" When he had walked enough, he said to Usama, "If you see fit to let 'Umar stay in Madinah to help me, please do so." And Usama gave 'Umar leave to stay behind. Then Abu Bakr said. "O warriors! Listen while I give you words of advice, and learn them from me. Do not act deceitful; do not act disloyally; do not act neglectfully. Do not mutilate the dead; do not kill little children or the old, or women; do not cut down the palm-trees or burn them; do not cut down the fruit trees; do not slaughter animals except for food. You will pass by Christian monks who have devoted their lives in seclusion; leave them and their prayers alone. You find people who bring you platters in which are all sorts of food; if you eat any of it, be sure to mention the name of Allah over it. You will meet men who have laid bare the tops of their heads, and left something like strips of cloth around it: smite them a good one with your swords. Arise now in the name of Allah, and may He give you death by a wound or an epidemic, because surely there is martyrdom in these two!"

----from History of Prophets and Kings by al-Tabari

The Conquest of Syria

When Abu Bakr was done with the incident of those who apostatized, he saw fit to direct his troops against Syria. He wrote to the people of Makkah, Ta'if, Yemen, and all the Arabs in the Najd and the Hijaz calling them for jihad and stirring their desire for it and as well as the ghanima from the Byzantines. Consequently, men began to flock to Madinah, including those propelled only by greed as well as those looking only for divine compensation.

It is reported through the authority of al-Waqidi that Abu Bakr appointed 'Amr ibn al-'As to Palestine, Shurabil and Yazid ibn Abi Sufian to Damascus saying to them all, "When you fight together, your commander is the one in whose region you are fighting." It is also reported that Abu Bakr gave to 'Amr verbal instructions to lead the prayers in case the armies were united, and to have each commander lead the prayer in his own army when the armies were separate. In the beginning each commander had 3,000 men under his leadership, but Abu Bakr kept sending reinforcements until the total of all three was increased to 24,000.

On his arrival in the province of Palestine, 'Amr sent a message to Abu Bakr informing him of the great number of the enemy that had gathered there. Abu Bakr immediately wrote to Khalid ibn al-Walid - who was at that time fighting the Persians in Iraq - commanding him to proceed to Syria.

When Khalid received Abu Bakr's letter at Hira, he set out at the head of 800 men in the month of Rabi' al-Thani in the year 13 AH [634 CE]. He made an assault on a place called Quraqir which was a spring belonging to the Bani Kalb. From there he crossed the desert to Suwa, a spring held conjointly by the Bani Kalb and some men of the Bahra. When Khalid wanted to cross the desert, he gave the camels all they could drink and muzzled them lest they should get thirsty again. The quantity of water he carried along, was depleted on the way. So Khalid had to slay the camels one after the other and drink with his men the water contained in their bellies. He came to Marj Rahit and led a raid against the Bani Ghassan on Easter day - they being Christians. He took some captives and killed others. Khalid arrived at Thaniat in edge of Damascus, and encamped at the eastern gate.

The Muslims conquered all the region of Hawran and restrained it. Then the battle of Ajnadain unfolded. About 100,000 Byzantines took part. Heraclius was in the city of Hama. Against this army, the Muslims fought a furious battle, and Khalid distinguished himself. At last, by Allah's help, the enemies of Islam were routed and smashed to pieces. Those Muslims who suffered martyrdom on this day included many notable people. When the news of defeat came to Heraclius, his heart was filled with panic and he was perplexed. Accordingly, he took to flight to the town of Antioch from Hama. The battle of Ajnadain took place on Monday twelve days before the end of Jumada al-'Awwal, year 13 AH [634 CE].

The Greeks met in great numbers and were hardened by Heraclius. The Muslims encountered them at Marj as-Suffar on their way to Damascus on the first day of the year 14 AH. The clash that ensued was so furious that blood flowed along with water and turned the wheels of the flourmill. Of the Muslims about 4,000 were wounded. At last the unbelievers took flight and were scattered, ignoring everything until they came to either Damascus or Jerusalem. On that day Ibn Sa'id fell a martyr. The evening before he was married to Umm Hakim, daughter of Harith al-Makhzumi. Hearing the news of his death, Umm Hakim pulled out a wooden post of her tent and fought with it. On that day, according to a report, she killed seven Byzantines, and her face was still covered with the henna used on her wedding night.

When the Muslims were done at Marj, they resolved to deal with Damascus. This took place fourteen days before the end of Muharram, year 14 AH. The oasis and its churches the Muslims took by force. The inhabitants of Damascus closed the gates of the city. Khalid and some 5,000 men camped outside the East gate.

The Christian bishop who hàd furnished Khalid with food at the beginning of the siege was used to stand on the wall. Once Khalid called him, and when he came, Khalid greeted him and talked with him. The bishop said, "Your case is prospering and you have a promise to fulfill for me; let us make terms of surrender for this city." At which point Khalid wrote, "In the name of Allah, the Compassionate, the Merciful. This is what Khalid will grant to the inhabitants of Damascus: he promises to give them security for their lives, property and churches. Their city wall shall not be demolished; neither shall any Muslim be lodged in their houses. We give them the pact of Allah and the protection of His Prophet and the believers. So long as they pay the jizya, nothing but good shall happen to them."

One night a friend of the bishop came to Khalid and told him that it was a feast for the inhabitants and that they had only blocked the gate with stones and left it unguarded. Occupants of the convent, by which Khalid's army camped, brought him two ladders. The gate was guarded only by one or two men. The Muslims cooperated and opened the door. The conquest was concluded in the month of Rajab, year 14 AH.

Heraclius mobilized a large number of Greeks, Syrians, Mesopotamians and Armenians numbering about 200,000 under the command of one of his choice men. He sent as a vanguard the Ghassanid chief

Jabala at the head of the Arabs of Syria resolving to fight the Muslims. By Allah's help, some 70,000 of the enemy were killed, and their remnants routed. When Heraclius received the news of this defeat he fled from Antioch to Constantinople, and as he passed by ad-Darb he said, "Peace unto you, O land of Syria, and what an excellent country this is for the enemy!"- referring to the numerous green pastures in Syria.

Heraclius then massed his troops against the Muslims, and the Muslims heard that they were coming to meet them, they refunded to the inhabitants of the city of Hims the jizya they had taken from them, saying, "We are too busy to support and protect you. Take care of yourselves." But the people of Hims replied, "We desire your rule and justice far better than the oppression and tyranny under which we lived before. We shall indeed, with your (governor's) help, repulse the army of Heraclius from our city." The Jews of the town also rose up and said, "We pledge by our Holy Torah, no army of Heraclius shall enter Hims unless we are first crushed and expended." Saying this, they closed the gates of the city and guarded them. The inhabitants of the other cities - Christian and Jew - that had capitulated to the Muslims did the same. When, through Allah's help, the unbelievers were defeated and the Muslims victorious, the Christians and Jews opened the gates of their cities, went out with the singers and music-players and paid the jizya to the Muslims.

----from The Conquest of the Lands by Ahmad ibn Yahya al-Baladhuri (d. ca 892 CE)

On 'Umar Carrying The Lash and his Instituting The Ledgers

'Umar was the first to carry a lash and beat with it, and he was the first in Islam to draw up ledgers and write down in them the stipends given out to the tribes…'Umar ibn al-Khattab, may Allah be pleased with him, consulted with the Muslims concerning the keeping of ledgers, and 'Ali ibn Abi Talib said to him, "Hand out every year whatever property has accumulated and do not keep anything." 'Uthman ibn 'Affan said, "I see a lot property which will suffice for all the people and which cannot be counted until one can distinguish between those who have taken and those who have not. I do not like things to be in disarray." Al-Walid ibn Hisham said to him, "0 Commander of the Faithful, I have been to Syria and seen their rulers, when they form any military regiment they write everything down in a ledger. You should keep these to organize things." 'Umar adopted his advice and called 'Aqil ibn Abi Talib and Makhrama ibn Nawfal and Jubair ibn Mut'im, who were the best genealogists of the Bani Quraish, and he said to them, "Make a list of the people according to their standing!"

And they wrote, beginning with the clan of Bani Hashim, following them with Abu Bakr and his kin and then 'Umar and his kin, that is, following the order of the Khilafah. When 'Umar looked into the ledger he said, "I wish to Allah it were as you have written, but begin with the kin of the Prophet of Allah, may Allah bless and save him, then continue in order of nearness until you put 'Umar where Allah has put him."

'Usama ibn Zaid ibn Aslam (on the authority of his father, on the authority of his grandfather) who said: "I saw 'Umar ibn al-Khattab, may Allah be pleased with him, when the writing was shown to him, with the Banu Taim after the Banu Hashim and the Banu 'Adi after the Banu Taim. And I heard him say, 'Put 'Umar in his proper place. Begin with the kin of the Prophet of Allah in order of nearness." And the Banu 'Adi came to 'Umar and said, "You are the representative of the Prophet of Allah." And he answered, "Yes, the representative of Abu Bakr, and Abu Bakr was the deputy of the Prophet of Allah." And they said, "Why do you not put yourself where these individuals have put you?" 'Umar responded sharply, "Well done, O Banu

'Adi! Do you want to eat off my back? Do you want me to sacrifice my honor to you? By Allah, not until your turn comes, even if the register closes on you and you be written last among the people. I have two masters who followed a specific path, and if I abandon them, I shall be destitute. Whatever abundance we have gained in this world, whatever reward for our deeds we hope from Allah in the next world, is through the hand Muhammad alone. He is our honor, and his kinfolk are the noblest of the Arabs, and then the rest, in order of nearness of relation to him. Indeed, the Arabs are exalted only by the Prophet of Allah, and perhaps some of them have many ancestors in common with him. As for us, it is clear that our pedigrees match, and right back to Adam there are but few ancestors that we do not have in common. But despite this, by Allah, if the non-Arabs come with deeds and we come without them, they shall be nearer to Muhammad than we on the Day of Judgment. Let no man look to his family tree but rather let him do Allah's work, and if any man's deeds fall short, his ancestry will not help him."

═══════════════════════════

Two Accounts Of The Conquest Of Egypt

1. A CHRISTIAN ACCOUNT OF THE FALL OF BYZANTINE EGYPT

And in those days Heraclius had a dream in which it was said to him, "Truly there shall come against you a circumcised people, and they shall defeat you and take possession of the land." So Heraclius thought that this people would be the Jews, and so he gave orders that the Jews in all the regions under his rule should be baptized into Christianity. But after a few days there appeared a man of the Arabs in Makkah whose name was Muhammad. He brought the knowledge of the One God back to polytheists, and told them declare that he was the Messenger of the One God. His people were circumcised in the Hesh, not by the law, and prayed towards the South, turning towards a place that they called the Ka'bah. Muhammad secured Damascus and Syria, and crossed the River Jordan, and dammed it up. And the Lord abandoned the army of the Romans, as a punishment for their corrupted faith, and because of the abominations uttered against them, on account of the Council of Chalcedon, by our ancient Church fathers.

So when ten years of the rule of Heraclius had passed together with the Colchian, who sought for the patriarch Benjamin, while he was fleeing from him from place to place, hiding himself in the fortified churches, the prince of the Muslims sent an army to Egypt, under one of Muhammad's trusty companions, named 'Amr ibn al-'As, in the year 357 of Diocletian, the slayer of the martyrs. And this army of Islam came down into Egypt with great force, on the twelfth day of the month Baunah, which is the sixth of June, according to the months of the Romans.

'Amr destroyed the fortress, and burnt the boats with fire, and defeated the Romans, and took possession of portion of the country. For he first arrived by the desert and the cavalry took a road through the hills, until they arrived at a fortress built of stone, between Upper Egypt and the Delta, called Babylon. So they pitched their tents there, until they were prepared to fight the Byzantines, and make war against them; and afterwards they named that place, I mean the fortress, in their language, Bablun al-Fustat; and that is its name to the present day.

After fighting three battles with the Byzantines, the Muslims defeated them. So when the captains of the city saw these things, they went to 'Amr, and received a treaty of security for the city, that it might not be plundered. This was a kind of treaty that Muhammad, the chief of the Arabs, taught them in what they called the Law. He said with regard to it. "As for the province of Egypt and any city that agrees with its inhabitants to pay the land-tax to you and to submit to your authority, make a settlement with them, and do them no harm. But plunder and take as prisoners those that will not consent to this or resist you." For this reason the Muslims kept their hands off the people and their properties, but destroyed the nation of the Byzantines, whose general who was named Marianus. Those of the Byzantines who escaped fled to the city of Alexandria, and shut its gates upon the Arabs, and fortified themselves within the city.

And in the year 360 of Diocletian, in the month of December, three years after 'Amr had taken possession of the city of Memphis, the Muslims captured Alexandria, destroyed its walls, and burnt many churches with fire. They burnt the church of Saint Mark, which was built by the sea, where his blessed body was laid and this was the place to which the father and patriarch, Peter the Martyr, went before his martyrdom, and blessed Saint Mark, and committed to him his reasonable flock, as he had received it. They [the Arabs] burnt this place and the monasteries around it.

When 'Amr took full possession of the city of Alexandria, and settled its affairs, that schismatic, the Byzantine governor of the city feared that 'Amr would kill him. Therefore he took poison and died on the spot. But Sanutius, a true Christian duke, made known to 'Amr the state of affairs of the righteous bishop Benjamin, and how he was a fugitive from the Byzantines because of his fear of them. 'Amr, son of al-'Asi, wrote to the provinces of Egypt a letter, in which he stated, "There is to be protection and security for Benjamin, the patriarch of the Coptic Christians, and peace from God. Therefore let him come out of hiding and administer the affairs of his Church, and the government of his community." Therefore when the blessed Benjamin heard of this message, he returned to Alexandria with great joy, clothed with the crown of patience through the conflict which had befallen the pious Coptic people through their persecution by the heretic Byzantines, … When Benjamin appeared, the people and the whole city celebrated, and made his arrival known to Sanutius, the duke who believed in Christ, who had settled with the commander 'Amr that the patriarch should return, and had received a safe-conduct for him. Immediately Sanutius went to the commander and announced that the patriarch had arrived, and 'Amr gave orders that Benjamin should be brought before him with honor, reverence and affection. 'Amr, when he saw the patriarch, received him with respect, and said to his companions and private friends, "Verily in all the lands of which we have conquered I have never seen a man of God like this man." For the Father Benjamin was radiant in appearance, fluent in speech, converse with calmness and dignity.

Then 'Amr turned to him and said to him, "Resume the government of all your churches and of your people, and administer their affairs. And if pray for me that I go to the lands of the West and take possession of them, as I have done with Egypt, and then return to you in safety, I will do for you all that you ask of me." Then the holy Benjamin prayed for 'Amr, and uttered an eloquent sermon, which made 'Amr and those present with him marvel, and which contained words of counsel and much profit for those that heard him; and he revealed certain matters to 'Amr, and departed from his presence honored and revered. And all that the blessed father said to the commander 'Amr, son of al-'As, he found true, and not a letter of it was unfulfilled.

-----*From Sawirus ibn al-Muqaffa, History of the Patriarchs of the Coptic Church of Alexandria, (trans. Basil Evetts, Paris: Firmin-Didot, 1904)*

2. THE OPENING OF EGYPT

'Amr kept on his way until he arrived at Alexandria whose inhabitants he found ready to resist him, though the Coptic population in it preferred peace. The Muqawqas communicated with 'Amr and asked him for peace and a truce but 'Amr reject this. The Muqawqas then ordered women to stand on the wall with their faces turned towards the city, and for men stand armed, with their faces towards the Muslims, hoping to scare them in to thinking that a large army was on the ramparts. 'Amr sent word, saying, "We see what you have done. It was not by numbers that we conquered those we have conquered. We have met your emperor Heraclius, and there happened to him what has happened." Hearing this, the Muqawqas said to his people, "These Arabs are telling the truth. They have chased our emperor from his lands as far as Constantinople. It is better that we surrender." His followers, however, spoke rudely to him and insisted on resisting. As a result the Muslims fought fiercely against the Byzantine Greeks and assailed them for three months. At last, 'Amr overpowered the city by the sword and pillaged all that was in it, but sparing its inhabitants of whom none was killed or taken captive. He reduced them to the position of dhimmis like the people of Alyunah. He sent news of the victory to 'Umar ibn al-Khattab through Ibn-Hudaij al-Kindi (later as-Sakuni) and sent with him one-fifth of the ghanima.

The Byzantines wrote to Constantine, son of Heraclius, who was their emperor at that time, telling him how few the Muslims in Alexandria were, and how their condition was, and how they had to pay the jizya. Constantine sent one of his men, named Manuel, with 300 ships full of soldiers. Manuel then entered Alexandria and killed all the Muslim guards that were in it, with the exception of a few who by the use of crafty means took to flight and escaped. This took place in the year 25 after the Hijrah. Hearing the news, 'Amr set out at the head of 15,000 men and found the Byzantine Greeks committing depravities in the Egyptian villages near to Alexandria. The Muslims met them and for one hour subjected them to a shower of arrows, during which they were covered by their shields. The Muslims then advanced courageously and battle raged with great ferocity until the polytheists were routed. Nothing could now divert or stop the Muslims before they reached Alexandria. Here they fortified themselves and set up catapults. 'Amr made a heavy assault, set the ballistae, and destroyed the walls of the city. He pressed the fight so hard until he entered the city by assault, killed the soldiers and carried away their children as captives. Some of its Greek inhabitants left to join the Greeks somewhere else and the enemy of Allah, Manuel, was slain. 'Amr and the Muslims destroyed the walls of Alexandria in fulfillment of a covenant that 'Amr had made to that effect, in case he had to reduce the city…'Amr ibn al-'As conquered Alexandria, and some Muslims took up their abode in it as a garrison. ---From Baladhuri, The Book of Conquests

---

'Uthman's Murder
(from at-Tabari)

Al-Sari wrote to me what he had hard from Shu'aib, from Saif, from Abu Haritha and Abi 'Uthman and Muhammad and Talha, who said, "The siege lasted for forty days and their stay was seventy days. Eighteen days after it had begun, two groups of riders came and told the besiegers that the people on the border were marshalling against them- Habib from Syria, and Mu'awiya from Egypt, and al-Qa'qa' from Kufa, and Mujashi` from Basra. Then they isolated 'Uthman from his people and denied him everything, even water. 'Ali sometimes supplied some of his need. They sought to provoke a fight them, but they were given no excuse to. One night they threw stones at the house so that they would be stoned in return and could say, 'We have been attacked.' But he beseeched them, 'Do you not fear Allah? Do you not know that there are others in the house besides me?' They answered, 'By Allah we did not throw at you.' He asked, 'Who threw then?' They said, 'Allah did.' He replied, 'You are lying. If Allah had thrown stones at us He would not have missed us, as you did.'

Once 'Uthman appeared before the Bani Hazm, who were his neighbors, and sent one of the sons of 'Amr to tell 'Ali that they had refused him water and to send some water if he could. He likewise sent messages to Talha and to Zubair, and to 'A'ishah, and to the other wives of the Prophet. The first to answer 'Uthman's call were 'Ali and Umm-Habiba [the Prophet's widow]. 'Ali came as the night was ending and harangued the people, 'What you are doing is done neither by the faithful nor by the unbelievers. Do not withhold water from this man. When the Romans and the Persians take prisoners of war they give them food and water to drink. This man did not even attack you. How then can you justify assaulting and murdering him?' They replied, 'No, by Allah we shall not even allow him to set his eyes upon food and water.' 'Ali then hurled his turban to the floor to show all that he had done what 'Uthman had asked him to do, and he left.

Then Umm Habiba came on her mule, and on it there was a woman's saddle with a water skin. Someone said, 'Look! There is the Mother of the Faithful, Umm Habiba.' And they hot the forehead of her mule. She said, 'Why do you assail me? The wills of the Bani Umayya are in the trust of 'Uthman. I only wish to see him to ask about them so that the property of orphans and widows will not be lost!' They shouted, 'You lie!' And they cut the rope of her mule with a sword, and the mule became frightened and ran off unrestrained with Umm Habiba. Some people ran to grab the mule as its saddle fell to one side, and they grasped Umm-Habiba. She was ready to die and they took her to her house.

'A'isha saw how they treated Umm Habiba and she prepared to escape Madinah by going on a pilgrimage to Makkah. She asked her brother Muhammad [a leader of the rebels] to go with her, but he repudiated her. She said, 'By Allah if I were able, with the help of Allah, to prevent them from doing this to 'Uthman I would have done so.'"

Hanzala al-Katib came to this same Muhammad ibn Abu Bakr and said, 'Muhammad, the mother of the Faithful, 'A'isha, has asked you to accompany her. How can you refuse while the wolves among the Arabs call you to something that is criminal and you follow them?' He answered, 'What is this matter to you?' Hanzala replied, 'O Ibn al-Khath'amiyya, this matter is a matter of discord. It is up to the clan of 'Abd al-Manaf to judge it.' And he departed, reciting the following verses:

'I wonder at the conceitedness into which men fall
When they seek the passing of the Caliphate;
For if it passes, Allah's blessing also goes,
And, like the Jews and the Christians,
All will lose their way.'

So Hanzala went to Kufa, while 'A'isha left to Makkah filled with anger against the Rebels. Marwan ibn al-Hakam came to her saying, 'Mother of the Faithful! If you remain they will been more disposed to pay respect to this 'Uthman.' She retorted, 'Do you want them to do to me what they did to Umm Habiba, and I will find no one to defend me? No, by Allah, I will not be so disgraced! I do not know how to avoid the depravity of those men!'

When the news of what had happened to 'Ali and Umm Habiba reached Talha and Zubair, they stayed near their houses. 'Uthman continued to drink the water that the Bani Hazm brought when the guards were not watching. Once 'Uthman appeared before his people and called to 'Abdullah ibn 'Abbas, who was among those who were defending the door to his house. When he was brought to him, 'Uthman said, 'Go from here. You are the leader of the pilgrimage this season.' Ibn 'Abbas said, 'But I would rather fight against these rebels than lead the pilgrimage.' But 'Uthman implored him in the name of Allah to go. So finally Ibn 'Abbas left and led the pilgrimage that season. Then 'Uthman charged Zubair to prepare his last will, and Zubayr... 'Uthman then said, 'O my people, let not the separating from me encourage you so that there comes to pass what befell the people of Noah! O Allah, arbitrate between these groups and what they eagerly desire. As was done with their allies of former times.'

Laila, the daughter of 'Umais, sent for Muhammad ibn Abi Bakr and Muhammad ibn Ja`far and told them, 'The wick of the candle burns itself while giving light. Do not commit an offense whose punishment may fall upon others who did not sin with you. For what you are trying to do today will be laid upon the laps others tomorrow. Shun a deed today that may distress you later.' But the two men refused to drop their plan and they went away annoyed, saying, 'We shall not forget what 'Uthman did to us.' And Laila said, 'Indeed he has done nothing but keep you close to Allah.' As they were leaving Sa`id ibn al-'As met them. There were already bad feelings between Sa`id ibn al-'As and Muhammad ibn Abu Bakr, and they ignored each other when they met. Muhammad then spoke this verse as a proverb:

Hold dear your affection for your friend,
Do not be a headstrong, backbiting deserter.

And Sa`id replied:
You will have a hard struggle with one
Who is far from sin, and free of it.

News came that a relief army was coming to Madinah to save 'Uthman. Soon Satan took hold of rebels and they said, 'The only thing that can save us is the death of this man. For the people will be occupied with that and thereby will be diverted from us.' The only way in which they hoped to be saved was by killing him. They tried to gain entry into 'Uthman's house through the door but they were held off by Hasan ibn 'Ali and 'Abdullah ibn al-Zubair and Muhammad ibn Talha, Marwan ibn al-Hakam, Sa`id ibn al-'As and their backers among the sons of the Sahabah. And they fought the rebels with swords. 'Uthman called to them, 'Fear Allah, fear Allah! Don't fight! You are all freed from your obligation to defend me.' But they refused to desert him. So he opened the door and went out with a shield and sword to keep them off, and when the Egyptians saw him they disengaged. The supporters of 'Uthman pursued them but he held them back and they withdrew. Both parties were anxious. 'Uthman appealed to the Sahabah to go but they refused, and entered into his house. He then closed the door on the Egyptians.'

Mughira ibn al-Akhnas, who was among those who had gone on the pilgrimage, hurried back to Madinah and he reached 'Uthman before his murder. He saw the battle and was among those who entered the house, and sat by the door. He asked 'Uthman, 'What excuse would we have before Allah if we left you by yourself, when we can prevent them from killing you while we still have breath?'

'Uthman took to the Qur'an as he had promised, praying and the keeping the Book close to him. And when he became tired of praying he sat and read in it, for people regarded the reading of the Qur'an as a form of worship. And his supporters, whom he had held back, were between him and the door. When there was no one left to keep the Egyptians from reaching the door, and they still could not get in, they brought fire and set fire to the door and the corridor. It burned so fiercely that when the wood burned the corridor fell on the door. The people inside were furious, and while 'Uthman was praying, they prevented people from entering. The first to go out against them was Mughira ibn al- Akhnas, who recited the following verses:

The fair one with the necklace and the jewels,
Knows I am swift and sure with the sword,
And that I defend my trusted friend
With a smooth even-edged blade.

And Hasan ibn 'Ali went out, saying:
Their religion is not mine, and I am not of them,
Even though I journey to the heights of Shamam.

And Muhammad ibn Talha went out, saying:
It is I who defended him in the battle of Uhud,
And turned away his enemies in spite of Ma'add.
And Sa`id ibn al-'As went out, saying:
On the Day of the House we waited as death drew near,
Baiting with our swords to protect Ibn 'Arwa
Exchanging blows face to face,
While death lay all around.

The last to leave was 'Abdullah ibn Zubair, whom 'Uthman had ordered to go to his father with his will. He also asked him to go to the people in his house and ask them to go home. 'Abd-Allah ibn Zubair was the last one to leave. And he never ceased to demand that 'Uthman's will be carried out, and to tell the people about the last moments of 'Uthman's life.

...From Tarikh at - Tabari

Al-Mukhtar and Ibn Hanafiyyah

The Shi'ah gathered to Mukhtar and they made themselves the authority in Kufa. Mukhtar then wrote 'Ali, son of Husain, asking him to accept the bay'ah and claim the rank Imam, but 'Ali declined to accept and went on to denounced him. When Mukhtar gave up trying to convince 'Ali ibn Husain, he wrote to 'Ali's paternal uncle Muhammad ibn al-Hanafiyyah who then went to his cousin Ibn 'Abbas and told him the story. Ibn 'Abbas advised him, "Sit quiet, for you do not know what 'Abdullah ibn Zubair may do to you." So Ibn Hanafiyyah followed this advice, and kept quiet about Mukhtar's faults.

The forces of Mukhtar grew stronger in Kufa, and people flocked to him. He made his claims equal to their rank and their spiritual and intellectual background. To some he exhorted the Imamate of Muhammad ibn al-Hanafiyyah; to others he rejected that and announced that an angel came to him with revelations and gave him knowledge of the unseen. He chased down the murderers of Husain, and killed them.

'Abdullah ibn Zubair grew enraged with those of the Bani Hashim who were in Makkah, and he restricted them in a cramped back street, with a great quantity of wood, such that if a spark landed in it, not one of them would escape the inferno. Among the detained was Muhammad ibn al-Hanafiyyah and Mukhtar sent a force from Kufa to liberate them. They told him, "Permit us to set upon Ibn al-Zubair," but Ibn al-Hanafiyyah refused, and left them for Ubulla [a town in southern Iraq], where he lived for some years until Ibn al-Zubair was slain. Those who came to the rescue of Muhammad ibn al-Hanafiyyah are the Kaisani Shi'is, who believe that he was the Imam, but after that they differed: some are stop with his death, and some assert that he did not die, and is living in the mountains. This sect too is divided into sects. They are only called "Kaisani" because they followed Mukhtar, whose surname was Kaisan.

Some claimed that Ibn al-Hanafiyyah entered the valley of Ra'wa with a band of his followers, and that nothing more is known of them to this day. Many suppliers of stories mention that the famous poet Kuthair was a Kaisani who held that Ibn al-Hanafiyyah was the Mahdi who will fill the earth with justice as it is filled with oppression and tyranny. He wrote in verses, where he mentions Ibn al-Hanafiyyah:
The Imams from Quraish, the friends of Truth are four equals:

'Ali and three of his sons, they sons guaranteed.
The heir to his faith and pious devotion,
The son who disappeared at Karbala,
The son unseen 'til he leads the horsemen lead by banners,
Veiled from sight for a time
In Ra'wa with honey and water.
Also on this, Sayyid al-Himyari, who was a Kaisani says:
Oh, tell the Vicegerent My life be your ransom!
Long in that mountain now grows your stay.
And they oppress the band of your friends,
All of us who call you Imam and Inheritor.
The peoples of Earth count seventy years since you left us,
But the son of al-Hanafiyyah has not tasted death,
And the earth has not covered his bones.'
Deep in the valley of Ra'wa he stays,
and angels answer his speaking.

-----from Meadows of Gold and Mines of Gems by Abu'l Hasan 'Ali al-Mas'udi

Kharjii Khutba

Abu Hamza the Khariji entered Madinah. He was one of active Khariji sermonizers. He ascended the pulpit leaning on his bow. Malik ibn Anas said, "Then Abu Hamza preached us a sermon which would have thrown hesitancy into the most sharp-witted and refuted any hard opponent."

The Khariji said, "I admonish you to fear Allah and obey Him, to act according to His Book and the Sunnah of His Prophet- blessing and peace be on him-and to respect the ties of kinship, and praise the truth of Allah which oppressors have forsaken, and to forsake the lies they have praised. I warn you to put to death the injustice they have brought forth, and to bring back to life the just laws they have let disappear. I tell you to obey Allah for those who obey Allah surely disobey others in obedience to Him, for there is no submitting to a creature which disobeys its Creator. We call you to the Book of Allah and the Sunnah of His Prophet, and to equal sharing, and to justice for the Mawali, and to putting the portions of the ghanima in the places Allah established from them.

As for us, we have not taken up arms thoughtlessly or frivolously, for fun or entertainment, or to make a change of government in which we somehow hope to immerse ourselves, or for revenge that was taken from us. Rather we did it when we saw that the earth had grown corrupt, and evidence of oppression had appeared, and espousers of religion increased, but still men did as they pleased, and laws of Islam were disregarded and the virtuous were put to death, and speakers of truth handled brutally. We heard a harbinger calling us to Truth and the Straight Path, so we answered the summoner of Allah... and by His favor we became brethren.

O People of Madinah! Your outset was the best beginnings but your end will be the lowest endings, for you have lent your ears to your reciters of Qur'an and your legalists, and they cut you off from the Book which contains no falsehood, but rather they brought you to the explanations of the illiterate and the pretexts of foolhardy, so that you strayed from the Truth, and became indifferent and cold-blooded.

O People of Madinah! Offspring of the Muhajirun and the Ansar! How loyal were your foundations, and how fetid are your branches! Your fathers were men of certitude and religious knowledge but you are a people of falsity and foolishness...For Allah opened the door of Islam for you, yet you allowed it become blocked with garbage. He padlocked the doorway of this world for you, yet you forced it open again. You are chasers of temptation and stragglers in the way of the Prophet; blind to the proof of Truth and deaf to real knowledge, captives to avarice and partners of adversity! How excellent was the legacy your fathers left, if only you had you preserved it, and how miserable will be that of your children if you hold on to that! Them He guided to Truth but you He deserts to your error. Your ancestors were few and pious, and you are many and vicious. The preachers of the Qur'an cry out to you, yet you are not humbled? They warn you, do not you ponder?

O people! Praise be to Allah! And peace be on our Prophet, who never postponed or rush except by Allah's command. Allah sent down to him a Book in which He showed him what was to come and was to be feared. Surely there is no doubt about His religion, and no double meaning to His commands.

Then Allah took our Messenger, when he had taught the Muslims the principles of religion, and Abu Bakr led the Ummah in their prayers. The Muslims entrusted Abu Bakr with the matters of this world, since Allah's messenger had deposited with him the matter of his religion. Abu Bakr fought the people of apostasy, and acted in accord with the Book and the Sunnah, and then he passed away, may Allah have mercy on him! Then ruled 'Umar ibn al-Khattab, may Allah's mercy be on him, and he went in the way of Abu Bakr and acted in accord with the Book and the Sunnah. He gathered the jizya and distributed the shares. He gave 80 lashes for drinking wine, and then passed away, may Allah have mercy on him! Then came 'Uthman ibn 'Affan. For six years he walked in the path of his two predecessors, but he was a man less than they. And in his last six years he brought about nothing like what he had done in the first six years, and then he passed his way. Then 'Ali ibn Abi Talib ruled, and he did not attain truth, and no lamp was given to him for guidance, and he passed away. Then ruled Mu`awiya son of Abu Sufyan, loathsome to Allah's messenger, and son of one damned. He made slaves of Allah's servants and possessions of Allah's property, and a briar patch of Allah's religion, so anathematize him with Allah's curse! Then came Yazid the son of Mu`awiya, the Yazid of wine, the Yazid of the pet monkeys and hunting panthers! Yazid of lustful loins and the effeminate rear end! May Allah and His angels damn him!"

And one by one the Khariji preacher related the doings of rulers until he reached 'Umar the Pious, son of 'Abd al-'Aziz, and he passed over without mentioning him.

"Then came Yazid ibn 'Abd al-Malik," continued he. "A debauchee and unscrupulous in behavior, in whom was never discerned right guidance. Allah has said about the wealth of orphans, 'If you perceive in them right guidance, deliver them their property' (Qur'an 4:6), and the matter this Ummah is more than any property! He ate prohibited food, and drink wine. He wore a robe worth a 1,000 dinars,. through which one could see his private parts so that the shrouds of modesty were ripped apart. And Hababa, his singing-girl on his right, and Salama, his singing-girl on his left, both singing and if you would had taken his booze away from him, he would have torn off his clothes! And he would turn to one of his girls and say, 'Shall I fly? Shall I fly?' Yea, he flew. Flew straight to Allah's damnation, and the burning Inferno, and an agonizing torture!

Certainly the offspring of Umayya are a band of reprobates, and their strength is the strength of oppressors. They take their imagination for their guide. They judge as they please, and put men to death by their anger and not by justice. They govern by fantasy, and take the law out of context, and distribute our public moneys to those not entitled to them for Allah has shown us those who are entitled, and they are eight classes of people. He says, 'The freewill offerings are for the poor and the needy, those who work is to collect them, those whose hearts are to be reconciled, and slaves and debtors, and those in the Way of Allah, and travelers.' (Qur'an 9:60) And they dare to make themselves the ninth! Such are those who rule by what Allah has not sent down.

As for the Shi'ah of 'Ali, they are an assemblage which discarded the Book of Allah in order to disseminate lies about Him. They have not reproached the Ummah because of some insight into religion as we have done, or because of some deep knowledge of the Qur'an. Rather they punish those who commit crimes and yet they commit themselves the very same crimes when given the chance. They are a people of chaos and know of no way out of it. Crude indeed is their understanding of the Qur'an, following nothing but fortune-tellers and magicians, teaching people about the Afterlife and then anticipating the return of their dead imams to this world. May Allah ruin them! How wicked they are!"

===================

Religious Tolerance In Persia

In 671 CE the Umayyad governor of Basra sent one 'Ubaidullah to the region of Sistan, now located in southeastern Iran. His initial assignment was to lay waist to all the land's Zoroastrian fire temples and kill the chief magu, Shahpur. However the local Muslim garrison protested this order citing its inconsistency with the Prophetic example of religious tolerance.

Before his departure, Ziad ibn Abihi gave him ['Ubaidullah] the following order: "When you go to Sistan, kill Shahpur, the chief of their priests and extinguish their sacred fires." So 'Ubaidullah proceeded to Sistan to carry out this assignment. In due course, the Zoroastrian landlords and their people resolved that they would rebel because of this order. Whereupon the Muslim soldiers in Sistan said, "If our Prophet (may Allah's peace and blessings be upon him) or our first four Khulafa' had done such a thing to a people who made peace with them, then we shall carry out this order; but if this was not the case, then we must not act in a manner contrary to Islamic law or our peace treaty." So they wrote a letter to Damascus in protest and the reply came saying, "You must not harm the Zoroastrians because they have made a treaty of friendship with us and those places of worship are theirs. The Persians say, 'We worship Allah and we have our fire temples and our sun. But it is not the fire or the sun we pray to; on the contrary, they are symbols in the same way the mihrabs and the Ka'bah are to you.' In much as this is true, you should not level their houses of worship since they have fire temples in the same way the Jews have synagogues and the Christians churches. Since they are all People of the Book, what difference does the place of worship make, since we all worship Allah?...Furthermore they are vexed by the destruction of any object or building of ancient standing. If our Prophet (may Allah's peace and blessings be upon him) had so desired he would have permitted none of these places to exist, and would have destroyed all the nonbelievers and all creeds other than Islam. However, he did not do so, and did not abolish them, but rather he made peace with them on the basis of the payment of jizya..." Thus 'Ubaidullah did not carry out the initial order of Ziad ibn Abihi.

-----from Tarikh-i Sistan

On 'Umar Ibn 'Abd al-'Aziz

When 'Umar ibn 'Abd al-'Aziz became Khalifah, he wrote to Hasan al-Basri asking him to write a description of how a just ruler should behave, and Hasan wrote back, "Know, Commander of Believers, that Allah has made the just ruler the support of every leaner, the straightener of every deviator, the reformer of the corrupt, the strength of all weak, the justice of all oppressed, and the refuge of all who are pitied. The just ruler, O Commander of Believers, is like a herdsman, worried for the camels he tends, desiring the sweetest pasture for them, driving them away from any dangerous grazing place, safeguarding them from beasts of prey, and shielding them from the harms of heat and cold.

"And the just ruler, O Commander of Believers, is the guardian of the orphan, and the treasury of the poor, fostering the little ones, and providing for the old ones. The just ruler, O Commander of Believers, is as the heart is to the members of the body: all are sound when it is sound, and all corrupt when it is corrupted. The just ruler, O Commander of Believers, stands as an intermediary between Allah and His servants; listening to Allah's Word, and making them to listen; looking to Allah, and making them to look; obedient to Allah, and making them obedient.

"Therefore, O Commander of Believers, act not in what Allah the Mighty and Glorious has given you like a slave whose master has trusted him and given into his care his wealth and his children, who then wastes his master's wealth and drives his children away, and reduces the family to poverty and scatters their fortune.

"And know, O Commander of Believers, that Allah has sent down the legal punishments to keep people away from wickedness and immorality. How shall it be, if he who dispenses them, deserves them? And He sent down the law of retaliation to give life to His servants. How will it be if the man who gives them retaliation puts them to death?

"Remember, O Commander of Believers, death and what comes after it, and how few supporters you will have there. Therefore make preparation for death, and against the greater terror which follows it.

"And know, O Commander of the Believers, that there is a place for you other than the place where you now are. Your stay there will be long, and your friends will be separated from you. You will be commended to its depths as a completely solitary individual. Therefore, make provision of what you may take with you-"On the Day when a man shall flee from his brother, his mother, his father, his consort, his sons" (80:36), and remember, Commander of the Believers, "When that which is within the tombs shall be cast out, and that which is in the breasts be exposed" (100:9), when secrets are made manifest, and "The Record leaves nothing, great or small, without numbering it." (18:49)

"And now, Commander of Believers, you are in leisure, before the dissolution of death and the severing of hope. Therefore Commander of Believers, do not give judgement among the servants of Allah according to the usages of the pre-Islamic period (bi-1.zukm al-jahilin), and do not travel the way of transgressors with them, and do not put the arrogant in power over the humble, for such will not watch over any believer or the protected religious groups (dhimma), so that you will have to acknowledge your own faults and the faults of others, and bear your own burdens and other burdens too. Do not be deceived by those who would lead a pleasant life by causing damage to you, and eat the good things of this world by causing the good things of your afterlife to disappear. And do not regard your power in this world, but look toward what will be your power when you are a captive in the bonds of death, and forced to stand before Allah Most High in the company of the angels and prophets and apostles, and faces are turned to the Living and Self-subsisting One.

"And I, a Commander of the Believers, though I have not attained by my rigors what prudent men attained before me, yet have I not desisted from offering you solicitude and advice, sending you my letter as a doctor causes a beloved friend to drink disagreeable medicine, because he hopes thus to offer him health and soundness. And peace be upon thee, O Commander of the Believers, and the mercy of Allah, and His blessing's.

-----from The Necklace, by Ibn 'Abd ar-Rabbihi (d 940 CE)

On Allah's Empowering Man

From 'Abd al-Malik ibn Marwan to Hasan ibn Abu'l-Hasan al-Basri: Peace be with you, and I glorify Allah, beside whom there is no other. As for what follows, there has come to the Amir al-Mu'minin about you that concerning the description of qadr the likes of which have never come to him from any in the past. The Amir al-Mu'minin cannot remember any of the Sahabah saying what it has come to him that you have said. He has always known good things of you in your ways; your excellence in religion and knowledge of fiqh and your search and your eagerness for knowledge. But the Amir al-Mu'minin found repugnant this doctrine ascribed to you. Therefore write to him about the position you take; whether it is a tradition from one of the Sahabah or only a theory of yours. For truly, we have heard no one discuss this matter prior to you. Present your opinion to the Amir al-Mu'minin and clarify it. Peace be with you, and the mercy of Allah and His blessings.

From Hasan al-Basri to Allah's servant 'Abd al-Malik: Peace be with you, O Amir al-Mu'minin! I glorify Allah, beside whom there is no other. As for what follows, may Allah bless the Amir al-Mu'minin. May He place him among His friends who do works of devotion and desire His good pleasure and hasten to follow what He has commanded.

Those among the Sahabah who carried out Allah's command and related His wisdom and followed the tradition of His Messenger, on whom be peace and Allah's blessing, never denied a truth or vindicated a wrong or affiliated with the Lord anything He did not affiliate with Himself. Allah has said, "I have not created the jinn and mankind except to serve Me." (51:56-57). Allah would not create them for something and then come between them and it for He is not a tyrant over his creation. None of those who went before disagreed with that, or even disputed it, because they were in agreement about it. We ourselves only began to talk about it when people began to repudiate it following their dubious motives and committing grave sins. What Allah forbade is not from Him, because He is not pleased with what He is angry about, and not angry at what He is pleased about, and if unbelief (kufr) were by Allah's edict and ordaining, then it would please Him from whomever it came. It is unthinkable that He would decree something and then be unhappy with His own decree. Allah would not prohibit His servants something, and then secretly decree it for them, as some foolish and uninformed men now say. Were that the case, Allah would not have said, "Let him who so desires believe and him who so desires disbelieve." (74:4). That is because Allah has placed in them power (qudra) so that the actor of good may merit Paradise and the actor of evil may merit hellfire. If the matter were as foolish have perceived it, it would not be in people to progress spiritually or fall into error, and there would be no praise for the doers of good or censure for the doers of evil. According to what they say, power does not come from individuals and should not be credited to them, rather, it is a thing that works by means of them. They follow the obscure verses in the Qur'an, seeking discord. They argue that Allah, be He exalted, has said, "Allah leads astray whomsoever He will, and guides to Him all those who repent" (13:27), and they do not look at what comes before it and after it.

Know, Amir al-Mu'minin, that those who differ from Allah's orders are those who overstep the bounds of their religion, and in their ignorance assign responsibility to predestination (qadr). If you tell any of them a matter concerning religion, he says, "The Pen has been lifted, and it is written on our foreheads whether we shall be happy or miserable." But if you said to one of them, "Do not tire yourself seeking the world, or go out in the morning in the heat and cold, and jeopardize your life on a journey, for your nourishment has been decreed," then he would argue with you about that.

Their idea is that Allah has charged His servants to take what they have no power to take, and to leave what they have no power to leave, but Allah, be He exalted, gives them the lie with His Word: "Allah burdens on no soul beyond its ability" (2:286). Surely Allah has known that kufr will come from people as it happens, by their own choice.

Know, Amir al-Mu'minin, that Allah did not predestine matters for His servants, but He said, "If you do such and such, I will do with you such and such, and if you do so and so, I will do with you so and so."

Speak to yourself, Amir al-Mu'minin. Do not say, "Allah has predestined for His servants what He prohibited for them, and came between them and what He ordered them to do, and then sent the prophets to call them to opposite of what He has commanded for them, as to torment them everlastingly if they did not do what He did not let them do." Allah is exalted far above what reprobates allege! This is the response to what you asked me about. I have explained it and clarified it. Please reflect on it, for it is a cure for what is in the heart.

– from a letter to an Umayyad caliph by Hasan of Basra (d. 728 CE)

The Fall of The Umayyads

One day a group of people gathered in the presence of 'Abbasid ruler al-Mansur, and they spoke of the Umayyads, their way of life, their conduct and the causes that led to their loss of power. Al-Mansur said, "'Abd al-Malik was an oppressor who took no thought of what he did. Sulaiman cared only for his belly and his private parts. 'Umar ibn 'Abd al-'Aziz was like a one-eyed man among the blind. The best man of that clan was Hisham. The Umayyads kept a firm hold on the power that had been arranged for them, retaining it, bolstering it, and sheltering what Allah had given them, while keeping to the highest and rejecting the lowest of things.

This continued until their power passed to their spoiled sons, whose only care was the pursuit of desire and the quest for pleasure in those things which are prohibited by Almighty Allah, unaware of the coming Allah's vengeance. So they forsook the safekeeping of the Khilafah, made light of the rights of Allah and the duties of ruler, and became too impotent to govern. Then Allah deprived them of power, covered them with shame, and withdrew His grace from them."

Salih ibn 'Ali said, "0 Commander of the Believers, when 'Abdallah ibn Marwan fled to the land of the Nubians with his entourage, the king of the Nubians asked about their position and condition, about what had happened to them and about how they behaved. When he had learned all this, he rode to meet 'Abdullah and asked him several questions about the affairs of his clan and the cause of their downfall. He then said to him some words that I do not recall, but after the conversation the king expelled them from his country. If the Commander of the Faithful cares to call for 'Abdullah, he could tell the account himself."

Al-Mansur therefore had him brought 'Abdullah the Umayyad out of prison, and when he was in his presence he said to him, "'Abdullah, tell me the story of your encounter with the king of the Nubians." 'Abdullah replied, "0 Commander of the Faithful, I arrived in Nubia and I had been there for three days before the king came to me. He sat on the ground, although a valuable carpet had been spread in front of him, and when I asked him what prevented him from sitting on my carpet he replied, 'Because I am a king, and it is a king's duty to humble himself before the might of Allah Who gave him authority.' Then he asked me, 'Why do you drink wine, when it is forbidden to you in your Book?' I answered, 'Our slaves and associates did so out of ignorance.' The king asked, 'Why do you wear embroidery and silk and gold when all these are forbidden to you in your Book and in your religion?' I replied, 'We have lost our kingdom, and we have sought the assistance of non-Arabs who entered our religion and wear these kinds of clothes in spite of us.' The king bowed his head, sometimes turning his hand and sometimes tapping the ground. Then he raised his head and said, 'It is not as you have said, but you are people who have made lawful what Allah has restricted and have done what you were forbidden to do and abused where you have ruled. Accordingly, Allah took away your power and clothed you in humiliation on account of your sins. Allah's retribution against you has not reached its end, and I fear that His punishment may come down on you while you are in my country and that it may touch me together with you. According to custom hospitality is to be given for three days. Therefore take whatever provisions you need and depart from my realm.' And so I did."

Al-Mansur was dumbfounded and sat for a while in silence. Then he took pity on 'Abdullah and thought of setting him free, but one 'Isa ibn 'Ali reminded him that this was man who had received the oath of allegiance as heir-apparent, so he sent him back to the dungeon.

-----from Meadows of Gold and Mines of Gems by Abu'l Hasan 'Ali al-Mas'udi

Index

Aa

Abd al-Malik 219, 256, 259, 260, 263, 267, 284, 286, 289, 303, 311, 315, 316, 317

Abd al-Muttalib 94, 99, 100, 101, 103, 105, 154

Abdullah ibn Zubair 249, 250, 252, 253, 255, 256, 259, 267, 284, 295

Abraham 17, 23, 25, 32, 79, 84, 89, 95, 99, 100, 106, 148, 153

Abu Bakr 72, 110, 115, 121, 155, 163, 164, 165, 166, **167**, 169, 171, 174, 178, 180, 183, 184, 185, 187, 188, 189, 190, 193, 194, 195, 200, 211, 213, 218, 219, 223, 228, 244, 294, 306

Abu Hanifa 301, 304, **305**, 307, 308

Abu Jahl 115, 131

Abu Lahab 110, 115

Abu Muslim 290

Abu Sufian 129, 130, 131, 139, 147, 166, 205, 243, 244

Achaemanid 20, 53

Adam 128, 159

Afghanistan 21, 52, 57, 58, 59, 70, 82, 214, 260, **277**, 278, 279, 291, 312

Africa 15, 22, 28, 43, 47, 58, 63, 76, 77, 78, 83, 89, 92, 104, 214, 267

Ahl al-Bait 165, 227, 257, 286, 290, 294, 295, 296, 297, 298

Ahl al-Dhimma **312**, 313, 314, 317

Ahl al-Hadith 301, **302**

Ahura Mazda 28, 51, **52**, 53

A'isha 155, 189, 229, **231**, 232, 233, 253, 294

Akkadians 17

Aksum 77, 78, 83, 84, 101

Al-Walid 133, 141, 147, 172, 180, 185, 195, 196, 203, 263, 268, 275, 277, 279, 289, 313, 316

Alexander the Great 21, 23, 32, 54, 69, 76, 278

Ali ibn Abi Talib 210, 219, 224, 230, 238, 293

America 3, 4, 65

Anatolia 15, 18, 20, 28, 64, 195, 214, 246, 265, 275, 286

Ansar 120, 123, 124, 125, 129, 133, 163, 164, 165, 166, 188, 257, 309, 315

Arabian Peninsula 15, 17, 18, 19, 20, 35, 79, 81, 84, 87, 89, 92, 96, 99, 113, 141, 145, 147, 151, 173, 177, 183, 185, 187, 199, 217, 256, 266, 279, 309, 310

Arabization 311

Arabs 35, 59, 69, 79, 82, 90, 91, 94, 95, 96, 100, 111, 115, 129, 137, 140, 146, 148, 164, 168, 173, 178, 181, 184, 186, 191, 197, 199, 200, 204, 215, 246, 259, 265, 266, 267, 270, 273, 279, 288, 301, 304, 309, 310, 312, 317

Aramaic 17, 18, 38, 45, 302, 310, 312

Arius 45, 47

Arsacids 69

Aryans 20

Asia 13, 15, 17, 18, 19, 20, 25, 27, 43, 51, 57, 63, 70, 75, 76, 80, 180, 246, 263, 266, 277, 283, 306, 307, 310, 314

Assyrians 17, 19, 20

Augustus 22, 59

Avars 71, 72

Bb

Babylon 17, 18, 19, 20, 22, 31

Balkan Peninsula 20

Balkh 59, 277, 312

Bani 'Abbas 289, 290

Bani Ghatafan 136

Bani Hashim 103, 116, 166, 257, 294

Bani Hawazin 149, 150

Bani Lakhm 177, 178

Bani Nadir 135, 136, 137

Bani Qainuqa 132

Bani Quraizah 136, 137, 139, 140

Bani Thaqif 149, 150, 259

Bani Umayyah 213, 229, 236, 243, 244, 249, 250, 253, 256, 259, 286, 289

Battle of Ajnadain 186, 189, 195

Battle of Badr 129, 131, 132, 135, 303

Battle of Mu'tah 151

Battle of Qadisiyyah 195, 197, 200, 214

Battle of Siffin 235, 236

Battle of the Camel 231, 233, 253

Battle of the Ditch 135

Battle of the Zab 283, 290

Battle of Tours 283, 287, 288

Battle of Uhud 133, 135, 145

Battle of Yarmuk **195**, 214, 253

Bedouin 82, 86, 88, 90, 181, 190, 256

Berbers 266, 267, 268, 275, 286

Bible 27, 33, 54, 76

Bilal ibn Rabah 115

Bilqis 80

Britain 22

Buddhism 51, **59**, 157, 277

Byzantium 56, 63, 64, 65, 66, 69, 70, 71, 72, 78, 83, 84, 141, 146, 151, 154, 171, 177, 178, 179, **183**, 195, 211, 246, 265, 311

Cc

Charles Martel 287, 288

Chatal Huyuk 9, 11, 12

China 13, 18, 58, 59, 65, 70, 82, 180, 216, 247, 264, 265, 267

Christianity 25, 28, 35, 37, 38, 40, 42, 44, 46, 47, 51, 55, 57, 67, 68, 76, 77, 83, 84, 95, 100, 157, 158, 177, 178, 196, 266, 271, 272, 288, 313

Christians 7, 22, 26, 28, 29, 38, 39, 41, 42, 43, 44, 45, 46, 48, 55, 57, 68, 73, 77, 78, 83, 92, 95, 158, 179, 180, 184, 196, 203, 204, 266, 271, 272, 302, 310, 312, 317

Confederates 92, **135**, 137, 139, 140

Constantine 44, 45, 46, 64

Constantinople 46, 47, 64, 65, 66, 71, 77, 178, 185, 204, 243, 246, 284, 303

Coptic 48, 75, 77, 310

Council of Nicea 45, 46, 47, 48, 77

Cstesiphon 72, 178, 197, 200

Dd

Damascus 39

David 20, 32, 34, 104

Debal 279, 280

Dhu-Nuwas 78, 83, 84

Dualism 51, 53

Dustur al-Madinah 123, 125, 132, 135